Understanding Employee Relations

Understanding Employee Relations

A Behavioural Approach

DEREK ROLLINSON
University of Huddersfield

ADDISON-WESLEY PUBLISHING COMPANY

Wokingham, England • Reading, Massachusetts • Menlo Park, California • New York
Don Mills, Ontario • Amsterdam • Bonn • Sydney • Singapore
Tokyo • Madrid • San Juan • Milan • Paris • Mexico City • Seoul • Taipei

Cover designed by Chris Eley
and printed by The Riverside Printing Co. (Reading) Ltd.
Typeset by Columns Design & Production Services Ltd, Reading
Text font is 10/12 point Century Schoolbook.
Printed in Great Britain at William Clowes, Beccles, Suffolk

First printed 1993

ISBN 0-201-56892-6

British Library Cataloguing in Publication Data
A catalogue record for this book is available from the British Library

Library of Congress Cataloging in Publication Data applied for.

Acknowledgement

The publishers wish to thank the following for permission to reproduce material: Atkinson J. (1982). Flexible manning: the way ahead. *Institute of Manpower Studies*, Report No. 88; Kelly J. and Nicholson N. (1980). The causation of strikes: a review of theoretical approaches and the potential contribution of social psychology. *Human Relations,* **33**(12), p.871, © Plenum Publishing Corporation; Crouch C. (1982). *Trade Unions: The Logic of Collective Action.* London: Fontana, © HarperCollins Ltd; Purcell J. (1989). Mapping management styles in employee relations. *Journal of Management Studies,* **24**(5), pp.533–48, © Basil Blackwell Ltd; HMSO 'Industrial Relations Code of Practice', 'The Role of Management in Industrial Relations', and 'Commission on Trade Unions and Employer Associations'. Crown copyright. Reproduced with the permission of the Controller of Her Majesty's Stationery Office

Brief Contents

Contents

Chapter 1
An introduction to employee relations   1

Chapter 2
The individual and workgroups   29

Chapter 3
Collective organizations of employees   55

Chapter 4
Management in employee relations   **81**

Chapter 7
Communications in employee relations   **163**

Chapter 8
Involvement and participation   **185**

Chapter 9
Collective bargaining **203**

List of figures and tables

Tables

Introduction

About this book

This book is about employee relations in Great Britain. It has been written to make it suitable for students and lecturers of industrial relations, personnel management and human resource management. However, it is specifically directed at final year undergraduate students or postgraduate students taking these subjects as part of a degree or diploma in management or business studies, and also at those taking the professional examinations of the Institute of Personnel Management.

The relationship between an organization and its employees has been of interest to both practitioners and academics for a long time. Whilst there have been many different approaches to this matter, there are two perspectives which can be singled out as particularly influential: the subjects of industrial relations and organizational behaviour. Both of these have yielded a great deal of useful information, but they approach the study of the relationship between an organization and its employees from somewhat different perspectives.

Industrial relations is almost exclusively concerned with the ways that the interests of employers and employees conflict, and the patterns of industrial behaviour that result from this. In addition the 1970s and 1980s saw a pronounced trend for scholarship in the area concerned with tracing links between the nature of wider society and the conduct of issues within firms. Examples of this are Fox's radical approach (Fox, 1985) and the Marxist perspectives of Wood and Elliot (1977), Hyman (1975) and Hyman and Brough (1975). The second subject, organizational behaviour, has a very different approach. It focuses on the behaviour of people in organizations, and to some extent the behaviour of organizations themselves. It also differs from industrial relations in terms of scale. Usually it focuses on matters at individual or small-group level.

Nevertheless it is an important source of information on factors at work which can influence the nature of the relationship between an organization and its employees, some of which are rarely considered by industrial relations. Two examples are the way that organizational structures can influence the actions of employees (Child, 1984), and the huge volume of work on the internal dynamics of workgroups, for example Homans (1950). Having said this, there are justifiable criticisms of the way that organizational behaviour deals with some important issues. To start with, it often sidesteps fundamental differences of interest that can exist between the two parties to the relationship. In addition, although it recognizes that there is conflict in organizations, its treatment of the topic is less than satisfactory. The vast majority of work in the area concerns conflict at interpersonal or inter-group levels, and so it ignores patterns of organized collective action. Indeed, if their existence is acknowledged at all, trade unions at best get a passing mention. Thus whilst either subject is a fertile source of information about some aspects of the organization–employee relationship, a more complete picture can be obtained by drawing on both.

This is not really a new idea. A number of scholars have pointed out that industrial relations and organizational behaviour have a great deal to contribute to each other. Indeed there have been periodic calls for concerted attempts to be made to integrate the two bodies of knowledge (Margerison, 1969; Williams and Guest, 1969; Shimmin and Singh, 1972). Despite this they have largely stayed apart, and if the reader will permit the injection of a personal note, the need for both to be taken into consideration became abundantly clear to the author in over ten years of handling industrial relations matters at organizational level. For this reason the book purposely sets out to draw on and integrate material from the two subject areas.

However, it is important to note that whilst it draws heavily on literature from both industrial relations and organizational behaviour, it departs from the traditional approach of either one. So far as industrial relations is concerned, although the book acknowledges that employers and employees often have fundamentally different interests, these differences are not its primary focus. Rather there is an underlying assumption that the relationship between employer and employees has similarities to any other continuing relationship between two parties. That is, as well as differences in interests, there are also interests in common; otherwise there would be no incentive for the parties to continue their relationship. Thus whilst the way that conflicting interests can affect the relationship is explored, this is considered to be just one factor amongst many that can influence its nature. The second departure from a traditional industrial-relations approach is in the matter of factors external to the firm. There is no attempt to deny that these are important, and throughout the book the reader is reminded that they can have a huge impact on employee relations in an organization. However, as the name implies, employee relations is mainly concerned with matters inside a firm. Thus its major focus is on the relationship between employer and employees, together with the dynamics of the interaction between the two parties. For this reason, external factors are not really of interest in their own right, but more as variables which constrain the behaviour of one or more of the parties.

There is also a difference in approach to organizational behaviour. To some extent this has had to be adopted because of the aim of integrating material from the subject with that from industrial relations. In many ways this has been a daunting task. The perspectives of scholars in the two subjects are often so divergent that they can be somewhat hard to reconcile. Moreover, both subjects have such a huge volume of material to draw from that it is difficult to decide what to include and what to leave out. Fortunately the decision is made a little easier with both subject areas by focusing the book almost exclusively on matters at the level of the firm. Thus it mainly contains material that deals with the industrial relations of the workplace. This in turn enables very pragmatic criteria to be used to select material from organizational behaviour, where for the most part the only material used is that which either enriches the discussion of industrial relations or is of practical utility in understanding other matters in the employee–organization relationship.

It is largely from this general approach that the title of the book, and more particularly its subtitle, is derived. That is, it reflects the author's concern to deal with the relationship in a way that draws on a somewhat wider range of subject matter than would be the case if a traditional industrial-relations perspective were adopted. It must be admitted, however, that there is another reason for using the term 'employee relations' rather than the more traditional one of industrial relations. In current terminology, employee (rather than industrial) relations is increasingly used in industry to describe the activity of managing the relationship between an organization and its employees. Indeed the Institute of Personnel Management (IPM) now refers to the subject in this way.

The structure of the book

Although the book is not subdivided in any other way than into chapters, the chapters themselves fall fairly naturally into four sections. Chapter 1 deals with the contexts of employee relations. It introduces the subject on the assumption that the reader has not been exposed to it before, and examines the factors which shape the general nature of employee relations in an industrialized society. It also establishes that British employee relations has somewhat unique characteristics in comparison to other countries, and goes on to describe some of the emerging responses of firms to their increasingly problematic environments.

The next four chapters (2 to 5) deal with the parties and institutions in employee relations, and each chapter takes a progressively wider focus. Chapter 2 deals with individuals and workgroups, and this leads fairly naturally into Chapter 3, which covers collective associations of employees. The topic of Chapter 4 is management as a player in employee relations, and Chapter 5 deals with the State and its influence on matters in organizations.

The gradual progression from individual level to a wider focus is repeated in the following six chapters, which cover important processes in employee relations. Chapter 6 deals with the individual issues of discipline and grievance, and in Chapters 7 and 8, which cover the processes of communication and participation, the focus is slightly wider. Chapters 9 and 10 then deal with the organizational-level processes of collective bargaining and negotiation, whilst Chapter 11 explores a topic which has wider social as well as organizational aspects, that of industrial action.

In the final two chapters of the book, a return is made to the management of employee relations. Chapter 12 examines a number of management-initiated processes, all of which have become associated with a more recent approach to employee relations: that of human resource management (HRM). Finally Chapter 13 considers the important topic of policy and strategy.

Whilst the main focus of the book is on employee relations at enterprise level in Great Britain, there is a sense in which it also has something of an international flavour. For example, the first chapter includes a brief comparison of the UK and other countries, so that the reader can more easily appreciate the rather unique nature of British employee relations. At various points throughout the text, attention is also drawn to other international aspects, for example the idea that employee-relations practices are being imported into the UK from elsewhere, and that increased foreign investment and EC membership could influence the nature of things in Great Britain.

How to use the book

Each of the chapters in the book deals with a separate topic, and can, if so desired, be used in this way for teaching purposes. Here much depends on the degree of importance (and therefore depth of coverage) that is attached to each topic by an individual lecturer. The text has purposely been written in a manner that leaves sufficient scope for it to be supplemented with journal articles or exercises. However, at the end of each chapter, specific suggestions are made for additional reading. In addition, the literature cited in the text is listed so that students can, if they wish (or are so directed), read more deeply into the topic. One feature of the book is that it makes extensive use of diagrams or models to supplement the text. These can often make understanding of a complex topic much easier, and thus save a considerable amount of time in teaching or revision. A second feature is a short overview or preview section at the end of each chapter. This highlights some of the major conclusions that can be drawn, and also directs attention to the other chapters in the book where there is a strong connection with the material that has been covered. The aim is that the reader shall never lose sight of the fact that in employee relations, the topics are not discrete parcels of knowledge, but are all connected to each other.

From Chapter 2 onwards, each one also contains a number of progress questions or small case-studies. Most of these are drawn from real-life situations: some are from the author's own experience of handling employee-relations issues within an organizational context, and others are issues and cases where the author collected material directly whilst conducting research. In addition there are some that were reported to the author by students or colleagues, and which were subsequently written up into cases. These are designed to test students' understanding, and to provide material that can be used in tutorial sessions to supplement lectures. Whatever method of instruction is used, it is strongly recommended that students are encouraged to answer these questions. If necessary this can be done by using them as discussion topics for class work, or for course-work assignments. As befits its subject matter, the final chapter is the only one containing an extended case-study. This has been included because it is felt that it would be difficult for students to appreciate the complexity of strategy and policy without an exposure to the multitude of problems that can all arise together.

1

An introduction to employee relations

Introduction

This book is about employee relations. In this opening chapter the subject is defined, and to avoid confusion it is distinguished from the closely allied area of industrial relations. Whilst the book deals mainly with employee relations within firms and businesses, it is noted that this is heavily influenced by a number of factors in their environments, and to explain the effects of these factors two models are given. The first shows that there are important general contextual factors which can influence virtually all organizations within a national environment. The model is then used to give a brief comparison of four countries which illustrates the unique nature of employee relations in Great Britain. The second model deals with the more immediate contexts of a single firm, and is used to point out that with most organizations in the UK the environment is currently a huge source of uncertainty. As a prelude to topics covered later in the book the chapter then describes some of the emerging responses of firms to their increasingly turbulent and uncertain environments, and the effects that these could have on employee relations.

Employee relations defined

To some people the term 'industrial relations' is probably a more familiar one than 'employee relations'. Indeed, for many there can be an assumption that both expressions mean the same thing. However, although they are closely allied subjects, there are some important differences, and thus it is important to distinguish between them.

One difference is in terms of the subject's general focus. Whilst industrial relations is composed of several different schools of thought and each one has its own particular concerns, the focus of the mainstream approach to the subject in Great Britain is to look upon it as 'the study of the rules governing employment, and the ways in which the rules are changed, interpreted and administered' (Bain and Clegg, 1974). Since rules are made by people, of necessity this embraces the study of organizations such as trade unions, management and employers' associations, and government and its agencies, all of which take part in the rule-making process (Clegg, 1979). It follows, therefore, that the primary focus of industrial relations tends to be on the institutions that take part in rule making, the processes of interaction between the parties, and the rules that result.

Employee relations also has a strong interest in institutions and rules. However, these are not its primary focus. The first and foremost concern is with the nature of the relationship between an organization and its employees in a wider sense. Although the parties themselves, the rules that they construct, and the processes that they use for rule making and administration are clearly all of interest, they tend to be viewed more as features which characterize a relationship. Therefore, at the risk of oversimplifying matters, this difference between the two subjects can perhaps most easily be grasped by contrasting their positions on the rules that regulate the employment relationship. In employee relations both formal and informal rules tend to be regarded as things which emerge from the relationship itself. That is, the rules that arise are generally seen to be a reflection of the type of relationship that exists. Conversely, in industrial relations there is a far stronger tendency to see the relationship as an outcome of the rules, that is, it is what it is because of the rules which have been constructed. However, whilst this contrast is a fairly accurate reflection of the two perspectives, a note of caution should be sounded. Neither one sees matters in quite such a simple way, and both acknowledge that rules and relationships interact. That is, rules can affect relationships and vice versa.

A second distinguishing feature is the level at which the two subjects focus. A great deal of traditional industrial relations is concerned with the way in which wider social factors such as class, property ownership, political ideologies and economic variables all become part and parcel of events within an organization. Indeed, with some schools of thought in the subject, notably those which adopt a Marxist or Radical frame of reference, these are the most important factors at work. Although employee relations in no way underrates the importance of these matters, they are usually given far less prominence. As will be seen throughout the book, it is firmly acknowledged that factors outside an organization do have a bearing on the nature of the relationship between an organization and its employees. However, these are not factors which are under the control of either employers or employees in conducting their relationship. For this reason the subject tends to view them less as an integral part of employee relations within a firm, but more as constraints which limit the nature of the relationship between the two parties.

Another important difference is that employee relations has a somewhat stronger focus on management as an influential player in the relationship. Whilst traditional industrial relations has always acknowledged that management's role is an important one, until comparatively recently trade unions received the lion's share of attention in the subject. Since the primary focus of employee relations is on the relationship between an organization and its employees, and managers have a huge influence on this matter, it is natural that management should receive a great deal of attention. This does not mean, as is asserted by some writers such as Marchington and Parker (1990), that the subject has 'a focus on management alone'. Indeed employee relations is equally interested in any party that is influential in shaping the relationship.

A final distinguishing feature, and one that has some connection with the previous one, is the way that the interests of organizations and their employees are treated. Traditional industrial relations contains an assumption that there are inherent and fundamental differences in the interests of the two parties. Hence the high prominence it gives to rules as a method of regulating these potential conflicts, which in turn implies that in organizations, industrial relations is a matter of conflict management. Historically the role of personnel managers has been to find a fit between the sometimes conflicting needs of organizations and their employees. Thus industrial relations as an activity and personnel management as an occupation have largely come to be seen as synonymous.

Whilst employee relations acknowledges the existence of these fundamental differences of interest, it does not focus anywhere near as much on their conflictual implications. Neither does it regard the relationship between an organization and its employees as something which is necessarily shaped solely, or even mainly, by personnel professionals. It is perhaps for this reason that employee relations has (wrongly) become associated with what is now fashionably called the human resource management (HRM) or new industrial relations approach. Some of the practices associated with this approach will be covered later in the book, and so an extensive discussion would be out of place here. However, it is important to note that HRM is highly oriented to the needs of management. Unlike personnel management which is aimed at gaining the compliance of employees, theoretically it goes well beyond this by emphasizing the need to gain their commitment and involvement. As such HRM has a concern with the relationship between an organization and its employees, and therefore has one point in common with employee relations. However, one point in common does not mean that they are completely the same thing. To start with, as a set of practices (but not however as an area of academic research) HRM contains an assumption that the interests of managers and employees can be co-aligned sufficiently for any differences to become negligible, or at least to be glossed over. Employee relations contains no such assumption. HRM is also highly prescriptive, and somewhat one-sided in favour of managers about what it considers to be the desirable terms of a relationship. Employee relations is much more wary of prescriptions about relationships. Instead it studies their nature, and acknowledges that a wide variety of relationships are possible, some of which are more inherently conflictual than others.

With these points in mind, the broad working definition of employee relations adopted for this book is:

> The study of the relationship between an organization and its employees. This covers the full range of interactions and communications between employers and employees, and also the processes by which they adjust to the needs and wants of each other.

In accordance with this definition, the book will largely concentrate on understanding matters within organizations. Nevertheless it is important to note that employee relations and its processes do not exist in a vacuum. They are affected by a host of contextual factors, and the remainder of this chapter is mainly devoted to describing them. There are two main reasons for doing this. First, some of these external factors have such significant effects that it will be necessary to refer to them throughout the book. Thus they need to be noted and understood early on. Second, some of them give employee relations in Great Britain a rather unique flavour, and make it different from elsewhere in the world. This is important because British managers currently have a tendency to attempt to import employee-relations techniques from overseas. However, it has been argued that the successful use of some of these practices could depend acutely on an appropriate match with national contextual circumstances, and for this reason it is still an open question whether they can be used as successfully here.

The contexts of employee relations and an international comparison

To explain how factors outside an organization influence matters inside can be a difficult and complex task. This is particularly true in employee relations, where some of the factors can be rather unspecific in terms of their effects. Some act in combination, or have indirect effects which are hard to identify, and so any description or explanation is open to criticism, either as being too simple, or because it is incomplete. An example which still generates controversy is the first model of this type to appear: John Dunlop's (1958) 'Industrial Relations Systems Model'. Here a much simpler scheme will be used, and although it has some things in common with Dunlop's model, it has the much more modest aim of drawing the reader's attention to the importance of some external factors and highlighting their potential effects on employee relations within firms. To do this the model will be applied to four countries, and those chosen for comparison – Great Britain, the USA, West Germany and Japan – have purposely been selected with two aims in mind. First, it is much easier to satisfy the aim of illustrating the effects of contextual factors by contrasting situations where the form that they take is very different. Second, the particular countries are of some interest because either there is a tendency to import their employee-relations practices into the UK, or there could be some importation in the future. For example, the human resource management approach originates in the USA, and British managers are currently engaged in a highly passionate love affair with Japanese working practices. Germany has now been unified as one nation, and so the term West Germany is something of a misnomer. Nevertheless, employee-relations practices in the former communist bloc part of the country are virtually certain to come into line with those prevailing in what was West Germany. Since this will take some time to happen, the term West Germany is retained to describe the more developed situation. Here it can be noted that West Germany has a well-developed system of employee participation, some elements of which could well be on the agenda for the UK if social legislation proposed by the EC is adopted.

Before making this international comparison, however, it is first necessary to give the model which is to be used. This is shown in Figure 1.1. Since it is the

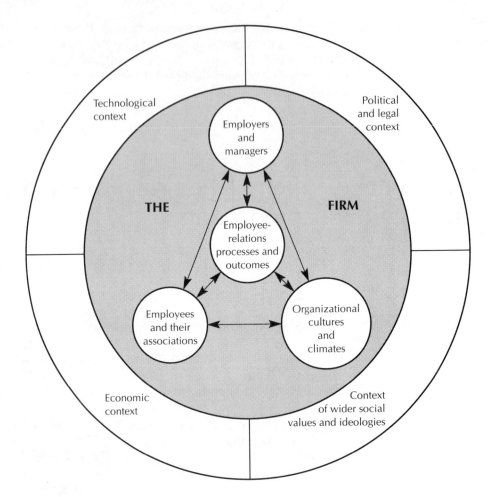

Figure. 1.1   The contexts of employee relations.

first diagram or model in the book, and from now on they are used extensively, a general cautionary note about the way they should be interpreted is in order. Models are only simplified representations of reality. Therefore, the reader is asked to remember that whilst they can aid understanding, they are of necessity incomplete, and can never fully capture the richness and complexity of the real-world situation.

Starting at the centre of the model, the term *employee-relations processes and outcomes* refers to two things. First, the general characteristics of the relationship between organizations and their employees. For example, whether the two parties tend to have an adversarial or cooperative relationship. Second, the processes used to arrive at or modify these relationships. Here the most important feature is whether this tends to be done through a formalized constitution of rules, or alternatively to be handled more flexibly. Both processes and outcomes are shown as being influenced by three major factors within firms.

Employees and their associations describes two crucial features: first, whether it is common for employees to collectivize in order to be able to influence the nature of the relationship between themselves and their employing organizations; second, the general nature of the collective institutions that are formed. *Employers and managers* is used to represent the general characteristics of these actors; for example, the way that they view their roles in organizations, their general approach to the management of human resources in firms, and the techniques they use to go about this. *Organizational cultures and climates* is used to describe the general mood or ethos that tends to exist within firms. This influences how employees and managers view each other, and whether relationships tend to be close or distant, and low or high in trust. These factors within firms are shown as being affected by an environment consisting of four major contexts.

The *economic context* is used to denote certain key characteristics of a country's economy, such as whether or not it is a buoyant, prosperous one. The *technological context* refers to the choices made by firms and businesses about the technology that they use in their activities. This can have very far-reaching effects on employee relations, and the word is used here to denote *how* tasks are performed, rather than the tasks themselves, that is, *what* is performed. However, it should be noted that there is clearly some connection between task and technology. Technological innovation can make some tasks unnecessary, or even create new ones. For this reason it can have a huge impact on the numbers of people employed, and the nature of the jobs that they do. Since the four countries compared all have very similar technological contexts, matters will only be described for the UK, and the reader should assume much the same context elsewhere.

The *political and legal context* deals with the extent to which the State plays a role in employee relations. This can occur in one of two ways. Where direct intervention takes place, the government or one of its agencies plays an active and ongoing role in determining relationships between organizations and their employees. Indirect intervention is rather different. It occurs when the State passes a law that constrains one or other of the parties in terms of the details of the relationships that they can enter into, or the way that they are allowed to behave when the relationship has been formed. The *context of wider social values and ideologies* is used to describe the behavioural norms which are influential in shaping the nature of the relationship between firms and their employees. Three important values are whether work and non-work are seen as two distinctly different compartments of people's lives, whether deference to authority is a natural part of their behaviour, and whether hard work and diligence are seen as desirable personal traits.

In what follows, countries will be compared and contrasted by starting at the outside of the model. Some of the influences that these contexts can exert on the three factors within the firms will then be traced, together with the resulting general characteristics of employee-relations processes and outcomes. Because the current characteristics of employee relations can be influenced by past events, it is sometimes necessary to include a brief history.

The wider contexts

Economic

This has long been a crucial influence on British employee relations. Following World War II, full employment resulted in rising affluence and aspirations in the working population. However, there were certain fundamental weaknesses in the British economy, notably declining competitiveness compared to other industrialized nations. By the 1970s decline had firmly set in, and manufacturing industry was particularly hard hit. Although many European countries had similar problems, the position in Great Britain was far worse than elsewhere. For example, of the 5.5 million manufacturing jobs lost throughout Europe in the 1970s, 2.5 million were in the UK alone. In the main this was due to Britain's poor productivity record, and the situation was made worse by the emergence of newly industrialized countries in the Far East, such as Taiwan, where labour costs were much lower. This trend continued well into the 1980s, and although by the middle of the decade government economic policies had lowered inflation, this was at the price of higher interest rates, a sharp rise in unemployment, and a vastly contracted manufacturing sector, all of which gave Great Britain its worst slump ever (Taylor, 1982).

Although for many years it had a relatively low rate of inflation and modest but consistent economic growth, the USA has also had its economic problems. Whilst it is heavily engaged in international trade, it is relatively independent of exports for its prosperity. However, in the last decade, its domestic markets have faced increasingly stiff competition from imported goods, especially from Japan. This has resulted in strong recessionary pressures, rising unemployment, and a great deal of change in firms attempting to regain a competitive edge.

In contrast the economic situation in the remaining two countries has been much more favourable. In West Germany sustained growth and low price inflation since the Second World War have given a situation that has been dubbed an economic miracle. Only since the mid 1970s has there been a rise in unemployment, and even then to nowhere near as high a level as either America or the UK. Japan's economy is second in size only to that of the USA, and for several decades it has enjoyed extremely low price inflation and has had economic growth rates over three times the level of most Western countries. Thus compared to the other three nations, it has a very buoyant economy with relatively low unemployment, although of late this has tended to increase slightly, particularly amongst older workers (Kuwahara, 1987).

Technological

Technological innovation can have two major effects. First, new *products or services* can appear, and this affects the demand for those that already exist. Second, there can be dramatic effects on the *process* of providing goods or services. *Product* innovations have had a huge impact on the demand for the outputs of traditional British industries such as steelmaking, shipbuilding and textiles. Whilst this has been offset to some extent by the rise of newer industries, they tend to use quite different techniques of manufacture, and in terms of employment opportunities, they do not fully compensate for the losses in traditional ones. Product innovations have also had effects on the composition of the workforce, notably the dramatic growth of non-manual work, which now accounts for over 50 % of the employed labour force. Whilst some of this is associated with changes in manufacturing techniques, a great deal is due to the growth in service industries such as retailing and financial services. These make extensive use of new technology, and a large proportion of the jobs are performed by women, many of whom work part-time. Indeed, part-time working has grown at an astonishing rate and, for example, from 1951 to 1985, 2.3 million full-time jobs disappeared (1.9 million male and 0.4 million female), with an increase in part-time jobs of 3.7 million (0.7 male and 3.0 million female). The net result of these changes is a reduction in the national manpower requirements in manufacturing, and a workforce with a greatly changed composition, where an estimated 25 % work only part-time (Robinson, 1985).

From the early 1970s onwards, *process* innovations based on new technology have become an increasingly attractive way for firms to try to survive. This accounts for some of the job losses in manufacturing industry described above, but just as important has been the changed nature of jobs for those who remain. One of the most significant changes is the increased use of information technology, the full results of which have perhaps yet to be realized. This has a potential to replace a great deal of the mental effort which characterizes skilled manual, white-collar and managerial work, particularly in the service industries. In financial services, for example, cash dispensing machines can replace people, and in retailing the bar-coding of goods greatly simplifies stocking processes. Process innovations have also resulted in changed occupational structures. The recession has given employers in manufacturing increased bargaining strength, and this has often been used to erode traditional skill boundaries. Thus flexible, multi-skilled workforces are now far more common (Hakim, 1987), as is temporary, part-time and subcontracted work (Rajan and Pearson, 1986).

Whilst the USA has experienced similar effects to Great Britain, matters in Japan and West Germany have not been so severe. Both are more prosperous economically and therefore new technology has been used more to boost output than to reduce the labour force.

Political and legal

In Great Britain, the law is regarded as independent of Parliament, and the government officially abstains from any direct involvement in employee or industrial relations. Nevertheless the State has been increasingly active in passing laws that influence the relationship between organizations and their employees, and it is more convenient to regard political and legal contexts as one. Since 1979 when the Conservative Party took power, there has been a great deal of legislation which has placed the balance of power firmly in the hands of employers. This has weakened trade unions in order to 'free the market' and the government has attempted to introduce what it calls a 'new economic realism' into wage bargaining. Moreover, legislation has been enacted which enables employers to use legal remedies against industrial action. There have also been a number of moves to promote a more individualistic focus in the employment relationship, in some cases through employee-relations legislation, but also in other ways which verge on an attempt to change the national value system; these are described under social ideologies.

In the USA the national government has minimal direct involvement in employee relations. However, prior legislation has a strong influence on the employer–employee relationship. The Wagner Act of 1935 gives employees the right to organize collectively, and requires employers to bargain in 'good faith'. Indeed, providing a properly supervised ballot of employees is conducted and won, a firm cannot refuse to recognize a trade union for bargaining purposes. In addition each state has its own labour laws specifying minimum wages and limitations on working hours (Banks, 1974). In non-unionized firms, although labour law has to be observed, a very different state of affairs applies. This however is more appropriately dealt with when discussing management.

In West Germany there is a complete abstention from any direct intervention by the government. As in the USA, there is a clear legal framework within which the parties must operate, and in addition there are federal laws that regulate labour standards, hours of work, sick pay, dismissal protection, discrimination and health and safety. In all firms employing five or more people, employees have a right to seats on a works council which deals with a large number of matters that affect their relationship with the organization. Since 1978 they have also had a right to a number of seats on the supervisory board of a firm. Here it should be explained that German firms have a two-tier system of boards of directors. The higher (supervisory) board meets about four times each year, and in turn appoints (but cannot interfere with the workings of) the executive board, which is responsible for policy making and the day-to-day running of the enterprise. In Japan neither employees, employers nor the State itself see a necessity for anything more than the very minimum of intervention. However, there is some labour legislation; for example, to protect the autonomy of 'enterprise unions' from employer interference (Kuwahara, 1987). In addition, there are central and local labour-relations commissions, which are state agencies that provide conciliation and mediation services in the very rare event of disputes which cannot be resolved by the parties involved.

Wider social ideologies and values

In broad terms Great Britain is a capitalist democracy with a deeply ingrained social tenet that property rights are sacrosanct. From this springs the idea that accepting employment carries with it the obligation of obedient service (Fox, 1985), which means that stratification at work mirrors stratification in wider society. Just as the social classes see themselves as distinct, so the relationship between employer and employee is often one of detachment. Work values are underpinned by the Protestant work ethic, which promotes the idea that those who are diligent and conscientious are morally superior (Tawney, 1961). However, there is a strong division between work and non-work as two distinct parts of people's lives, all of which means that there is little to promote an ethos in which all members of an organization feel that they are bonded into a work community. Postwar full employment, the welfare state and the growth of trade-union membership largely saw the demise of a deferential society, and also produced rising aspirations of security, affluence and basic living standards. However, since the 1980s, the economic influences described earlier have negated many of the social developments of earlier decades and increased the gap between the 'haves' and 'have-nots'. Legislation has also reduced the power of organized labour, and this has been accompanied by a rhetoric designed to create the impression that the natural order of things has been restored. Much employment legislation has been designed to de-emphasize collectivism and promote individualism, an orientation which to some extent had probably been strengthening in the British working population for some years (Phelps Brown, 1990). In addition there have been a number of social and economic messages from government designed to promote the virtues of individualism and 'every man for himself'. Examples of these are the mass sale of council housing, which create a push towards individual materialism, the privatization of the nationalized industries which exhorted people to become entrepreneurs and make a fast killing out of shares, and the fostering of a spirit of opportunism and self-interest by government funding for the set-up and development of small businesses: the so-called enterprise culture.

Perhaps the most outstanding feature of American social values is that it is the most fiercely capitalist country in the world. Individualism is a strongly held social value (Hofstede, 1980), and Americans have a passionate belief that their society is and should remain a meritocracy. Although it is nowhere near as much a class-based society as Great Britain, it is perhaps the most strongly achievement-oriented society in the world (McClelland, 1961).

Germans have a strong sense of national identity, which gives a correspondingly strong sense of community (Fox, 1974). Moreover, since Germany epitomizes a thorough absorption of the Protestant work ethic (Weber, 1976), competence, diligence and hard work are all highly valued attributes.

Japan only emerged from being a feudal society a little over a century ago, and industrialization, which took place hastily in the 1880s, was virtually grafted onto feudalism. One legacy of feudalism is that Japan is what is technically called a gerontocracy. Age is revered and respected, and regarded as synonymous with wisdom. A characteristic of the Japanese value system is its fairly low degree of individualism (Hofstede, 1980), and another is the extent to which being similar to, and interdependent with, others is positively valued. Personal identity is far less derived from being an individual than from being Japanese, and this gives a highly collective spirit. Hand in hand with this goes a fairly pronounced tendency towards uncertainty avoidance (Hofstede, 1980). People feel threatened by ambiguous situations, risk taking is discouraged, and uncertainty and its associated stress are combated by hard work, career stability and intolerance of deviancy.

In contrasting these wider contexts it is important to note that Japan and Germany both have sound, buoyant economies. This gives a backdrop of confidence and security to employers and employees, and makes it less likely that any changes necessitated by environmental conditions are perceived as threatening. Social values in these two countries also support a great deal of harmony in organizations. Conversely (although it has been for different reasons), British and American economies have been highly turbulent in the past decade, and firms in both countries have had to make stringent and sometimes drastic changes in order to try to regain their competitiveness. Thus in both countries economic conditions have put power into the hands of managers. In America, however, the law protects the role of trade unions and the contracts they have negotiated on behalf of their members, whilst in Great Britain the changed legal framework has resulted in hamstrung trade unions.

The organizations

Employees and their associations

In the UK the workforce is relatively strongly unionized. British trade unions are the oldest in the world, and there are still over 300 of them, which gives rise to complex patterns of representation. In the private sector, workplace trade union organization is relatively highly developed, particularly in manufacturing industry (Boraston *et al.*, 1975), and the public sector has for a long time been heavily unionized. Most British trade unions are affiliated to the Labour Party and have some say in shaping its policies. Indeed, since the party was formed by them in 1906 as a means of pursuing the interests of the working class by constitutional parliamentary means, they usually avoid direct political action.

In America only 20 % of employees belong to trade unions, and there are sharp differences between unionized and non-unionized firms. Where they are recognized, trade unions are almost exclusively concerned with bread-and-butter issues, and have few, if any, wider social or political objectives. Indeed, the Taft Hartley Act of 1947 explicitly forbids the expenditure of union funds on political activities. The vast size and wide diversity of the USA makes it virtually impossible for national bargaining to take place for whole industries, and union organization rests on a very well-developed system of 'locals', who bargain with employers. Agreements are very detailed and legally enforceable, and trade union organization at the workplace is largely devoted to policing the agreements to see that they are scrupulously observed.

German trade unions are very large, and have stable, highly bureaucratized patterns of centralized authority. They were reconstructed under the occupying powers shortly after the end of the Second World War, and in order to avoid what were seen as the worst features of trade unions elsewhere, industrial unions which represent all workers in a given industry or group of industries were formed. There are only 17 trade unions, and bargaining about basic terms and conditions takes place with employers' federations, either nationally or regionally. Since trade unions are essentially national bodies, they concern themselves with a wide range of matters beyond simple bread-and-butter issues such as pay, and act as pressure groups on government. Much of the labour law mentioned above was prompted by trade union initiatives, and governments of all persuasions usually consult with them regularly about most aspects of social and economic policy. At workplace level, although there is a trade-union presence which includes shop stewards, strictly speaking it has no official place in representing employees. This is the role of works councils, which consist of managers and elected employees. Although shop stewards may be elected as works councillors, and in that role they represent constituencies of employees, they do not do so as officials of the trade union.

In Japan, although a trade union is usually affiliated to an industry federation, it is essentially part of the firm: an 'enterprise union' which identifies strongly with the employing organization. All permanent employees from the very top to the bottom are members of the same union, and the Japanese believe that this way of doing things is far more able to deal with situations that are specific to the firm than is external unionism. Since only permanent employees become union members, a relatively small proportion of the Japanese workforce is unionized. For example, small firms, which employ about 88 % of all Japanese workers (Kuwahara, 1987), seldom have permanent employees.

Employers and managers

In Britain employers and managers vary widely in their approach to employee relations. Some regard employees purely as a commodity to be acquired when needed and dispensed with at will, and there are others who see employees more as a valuable asset, to be nurtured and developed into a high-performing resource (Purcell, 1987). The most common management style in unionized organizations has traditionally been that of restrained opportunism, in which concessions are granted when employees hold the balance of power and are then wrested back when it shifts more in management's favour (Purcell and Sisson, 1983). The idea of managerial rights or prerogatives still runs very strong in Britain, and to some extent this is rooted in social values. Nowadays, however, there is perhaps a greater tendency to adopt a more sophisticated approach, which is directed more at encouraging involvement and commitment to the organization and less at simply obtaining employee compliance.

In much of the USA managers have a great deal of outright hostility to trade unions (Wheeler, 1987). Many of them prefer to deal directly with employees in order to avoid the incursion of trade unions (Barbash, 1988), and in un-unionized firms, although management generally determines the terms of the relationship, this does not necessarily mean that they are harsh or exploitative. For example, to lower the incentive to collectivize, management often employs a strategy of making things just that little bit better than in unionized firms (Wheeler, 1987; Kochan and McKersie, 1983; Fiorito *et al.*, 1987), and a whole range of positive personnel policies, human resource management techniques and behavioral science methods are used to promote worker motivation and job satisfaction.

German managers tend to be standard bearers of some of the national values and ideologies. The factory system which developed in Germany in the late 19th century has left a strong legacy of paternalism, and managers tend to see sharing influence in works councils as a way of achieving their ideal of a community of interests (Clegg, 1976). In Japan employers are strongly paternalistic which, to some extent, is a legacy of the feudal origins of industry. From this has sprung some of the stronger features of the Japanese employment system. For example, low status distinctions between managers and their subordinates are seen as an essential part of their way of managing.

Cultures and climates

In Britain, because managers can have widely different approaches, organizational cultures and climates vary widely. Where the increased power placed into the hands of managers by the economic, political and legal events of recent years has been used in a repressive way, the 'us and them syndrome' with latent conflict just beneath the surface is probably quite common. Where management has perhaps been more benign, cultures and climates can be far more cooperative. The same variable state of affairs almost certainly exists in the USA. However, since American trade unions are almost as fiercely devoted to the free enterprise system as employers, they have a business unionism philosophy of 'what is good for the company is good for its employees' (Banks, 1974). American managers are also much more willing to use a wide range of applied behavioral science techniques to try to improve cultures and climates, a feature stimulated by claims in the 1970s of widespread discontent and alienation among American workers (Lawler, 1975) from which sprang what has become known as the 'quality of working life' (QWL) movement. Perhaps because of their different educational backgrounds, American managers are also far less hidebound than their British counterparts about maintaining traditional work relationships and methods (Dubin, 1970; Steele, 1977). Thus they tend to make far more use of such techniques as job enrichment, job enlargement and participative decision making to try to promote cooperative climates.

In Germany the sense of community derived from wider social values and ideologies has its effects within organizations. Managers and employees usually have a very positive approach to each other, and in works councils there is a great deal of cooperation, which extends to discussing matters of mutual interest which are well beyond those normally covered in collective bargaining (Clegg, 1976). Wider social values also have their effects in Japan, notably in the larger firms where there is a strong sense of everyone being a member of the same big family, or 'community of fate'. Generally speaking, managers and employees have a 'high trust' relationship (Fox, 1974), in which they both share ownership of problems and strive together to overcome them (Thurley, 1983). Indeed, since the desirable Japanese state of affairs is where everybody sees the firm as a family, the endemic conflict, confrontation and adversarial relationships found in some Western organizations are largely absent (Dore, 1973).

Employee-relations processes and outcomes

In Britain the major structural changes in industry have resulted in fewer employment opportunities, and recessionary pressures coupled with changes in the composition of the labour force have resulted in a situation where prior aspirations of job security and upward mobility are not now so easily met. This in turn has probably given some shift in the attitudes of employees, and these feelings are likely to have been reinforced by the strategies adopted by firms to seek flexibility in the use of labour in order to meet increased competitive pressures.

To give managers more freedom of action, there has been some tendency to reduce the influence of trade unions, usually by moving towards consulting employees rather than negotiating with them. That is, management informs employees about its proposals and listens, but still reserves the right to implement. More rarely, stronger steps have been taken, for example by withdrawing from recognition of trade unions altogether. Some employers have also sought to deal with what they have traditionally seen as a problem caused by the structure of British trade unions: multi-unionism. This can sometimes make it very hard for managers to be able to reach an agreement that applies to all of the workforce and, for this reason, there is an increasing interest in 'single-union' deals. Some organizations have also taken positive steps to pull away from earlier conflictual relationships. This has been attempted by a stronger focus on individualism, and an increasing use of 'positive personnel policies' aimed at achieving employee commitment to the enterprise. To some extent, other changes at enterprise level have facilitated this by breaking down prior patterns of collectivism and promoting a more individualistic ethos. For example, individual merit as a basis of payment (Towers, 1987) and multi-skilling (Brown, 1986) have both become more widespread. The use of either could have some effect in weakening the traditional basis of collective solidarity which is rooted in occupational groupings.

In unionized firms in the USA negotiations normally take in a whole range of fringe benefits such as medical insurance, pensions and so on, as well as pay and conditions. This is one reason why American unions have little need to pursue these things on a political front, for example by seeking social legislation. Agreements tend to be complex and highly detailed, and most run for between one and four years. They are legally enforceable and are assumed to contain a no-strike clause. That is, unless it can be demonstrated that the agreement has not been honoured, strictly speaking industrial action is illegal. Bargaining relationships are often very professional, if somewhat competitive in nature. Moreover, the 'business unionism' approach has resulted in American trade unions being prepared to give up some of the benefits obtained in earlier, more prosperous times in order to save the firms from going out of existence in the recessionary 1980s (Dworkin *et al.,* 1988). In non-union firms management is generally more proactive in determining the employee–organization relationship and, as noted above, often in a way that gives conditions which are as good as elsewhere. In both unionized and non-unionized organizations the use of applied behavioral science to influence the organization–employee relationship is probably far more common than in the UK. Whilst this seldom extends to full-blown worker participation in decision making, it often results in a strong focus on personnel and human resource policies aimed at making the relationship a cooperative one. Although techniques such as these are unlikely to bring a complete end to adversarial relationships, they could well be a way of breaking down low-trust relationships (Katz *et al.,* 1983), and there have been some promising results in this direction (Katz *et al.,* 1985).

In summary, in America and Great Britain cultures and climates are found which are somewhat less than supportive of harmony, and so processes and outcomes are often far from cooperative. However, whilst employers and managers in both have an equally strong belief in their right to command, there is a difference in the way that they have sought to bring about changes prompted by wider contextual factors. American industry is not so heavily unionized as in the UK, and business unionism perhaps results in a more pragmatic approach to handling the economic crises faced by organizations. Because the law protects trade unions, partly by inclination and perhaps partly to stay within the law, managers in unionized firms have tended to adopt a far more sophisticated approach. Human resource management strategies have been more widely used, and to some extent these have been successful in wooing employees away from union influence (Kochan *et al.,* 1984; Barbash, 1988).

In Great Britain, although there is some tendency to follow the American example, managements have largely been able to get their own way in forcing through changes by using the increased power put into their hands by the twin weapons of economic recession and the legal emasculation of trade unions. As such, although it is by no means universal, an adversarial note is still more prevalent than in the USA.

In Germany processes and outcomes are very much a product of the twin principles of shared influence and the idea of the enterprise as a community of interests. Employee representation at board level and on works councils not only ensures effective communications between managers and employees, but also gives employees an active role in determining a great many of the features of the organization–employee relationship. Works councils determine such things as plant rules, disciplinary policy, piece-work rates, introduction of new work methods and new payment systems, and they tend to be seen by both employees and managers as a highly effective method of working out or modifying the terms of the relationship. Therefore, unlike many other countries where new technology is seen as a threat or destroyer of jobs, in Germany it is not. Rather it tends to be viewed as a potential benefit, the impact of which depends less on what it is, and more on how it is introduced (Feurstenberg, 1987).

Japanese personnel and employee relations practices are also a personification of the national culture and traditions (Abegglen, 1958; Hanami, 1979). Most large Japanese companies recruit permanent employees direct from school or university, and they are expected to remain there with guaranteed employment for the rest of their working lives. Training is within the firm, for the firm, and includes a measure of normative instruction to promote the proper attitudes and values. This encourages identifying with the organization, and to some extent the families of employees are looked upon as peripheral members of the firm (Dore, 1973). If, on some occasions, the interests of the family and firm do not coincide, the firm is expected to come first. Differences in wages and fringe benefits between managers and workers are usually quite modest compared to Western standards. Moreover, pay is related more to seniority and length of service than to specific roles. Japanese companies tend to look upon themselves as employing the whole man, not just paying the market price for a job that needs to be done, and for this reason, permanent employees are seen as a valuable resource worthy of a training investment. The assumption is that the longer a person has been with the firm, the greater is their range of skills, and this is reflected in their pay. Paternalism still runs strong, and responsibility for the personal welfare of subordinates is seen to be very much part of a supervisor's role. There is a strong alignment between employer and trade union about almost everything, especially those things that affect the firm's competitive advantage. Work conditions and security are seen to be strongly linked with company success, and thus enterprise unions cooperate strongly with management about technical change, which is seen as inevitable. Indeed, the union philosophy is generally 'no new technology – no further growth' (Kuwahara, 1987). In order not to damage the spirit of community and to subdue any tensions that they give rise to, when grievances arise they are much more likely to be settled informally rather than through a formal procedure. Work rules and union–management agreements are very comprehensive and specific, and tend to be framed so that the rights and obligations of employee and employer are permanently fixed in order to avoid future ambiguity and misunderstandings.

Therefore, in both Japan and Germany processes are cooperative, which to a large extent stems from their correspondingly cooperative climates and cultures. Social values in both countries support a paternalistic outlook towards employees on the part of employers and managers. Importantly, although it manifests itself in a rather different way, in each one managers and employees both have a strong sense of common identity. In Germany, social values promote the idea of the firm as rather like a society in miniature, or a community of interest, whilst in Japan there is more of a sense of the firm as a family. This gives some clue as to why cooperative processes in each country take a somewhat different form. As well as the obvious differences in size between a community and a family, there are important differences in the way that each one tends to regulate the conduct of its members. Communities usually evolve formal rules, whilst families tend to operate much more informally. In Germany the State has provided a legislative framework that is highly formalized, and which facilitates the sharing of decisions in a way that suits the German national character. Japan has its own methods of shared decision making, and again these fit comfortably with its social values of teamwork, togetherness and belonging.

The major features in terms of contexts and outcomes for each country are summarized in Table 1.1. As can be seen, although the foregoing descriptions are only in outline form, each country's contextual circumstances can have a strong impact on relationships within firms, and each nation has its own unique brand of employee relations.

Table 1.1 Major contextual circumstances and outcomes: Great Britain, USA, West Germany and Japan.

	Great Britain	*USA*	*West Germany*	*Japan*
Employee-relations processes & outcomes	Adversarial but constitutional	Where unions are recognized, constitutional and competitive	Constitutional & cooperative	Flexible and highly cooperative
Cultures & climates	Highly variable from hostile to benign	Highly variable from hostile to benign	The firm as a community of interests	The firm as a family
Employers & managers	Emphasis on rights of management. Some use of more sophisticated personnel methods	Wide hostility to unions, and greater sophistication in personnel methods	Paternalistic	Paternalistic
Employee assocations	Trade unions independent of firms	Business unionism	Trade unions have no official role in firms	Enterprise unions
Context of social values and ideologies	High individualism. Work and non-work separate. High emphasis on property rights	As Great Britain	Medium individualism, cohesive	Low individualism, cohesive
Political/legal context	No direct intervention, but law framed to restrict trade union activities	No direct intervention, and law framed to protect collective bargaining and trade unions	No direct intervention, but law framed to promote co-determination in firms	Non-interventionist
Economic context	Tendency to instability	More stable than Great Britain	Buoyant and stable	Buoyant and stable

The firm in a developed economy: problems and current responses

Environment and task environment

Because the aim was to highlight differences in employee relations between countries, so far the effects of environment have been considered in a very general way. For a single firm, however, environment is not simply 'everything out there'. Some parts are of far greater significance than others, and to distinguish between them and the remainder, the terms *task environment* and *wider*

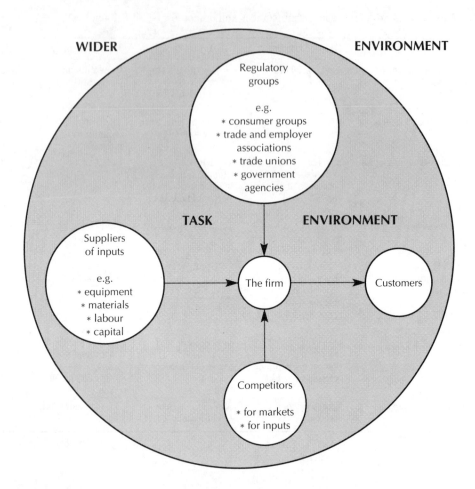

Figure 1.2   The task environment of a firm (after W.R. Dill, 1958).

environment will be used. The easiest way to think of task environment is as that part of the wider environment which is most relevant (or potentially relevant) to an organization in terms of achieving its goals or objectives. Its impact on firms is experienced as immediate, pressing and direct, and is therefore where they usually have to concentrate most of their attention. Using the ideas of William Dill (1958) who first coined the term, task environment can be divided up into four major segments for the purpose of analysis. This is shown in Figure 1.2. Each of the four segments of task environment can be a source of disturbance and uncertainty for firms.

Customers

Clearly the level of demand for a firm's products can have an obvious and dramatic effect on its chances of survival. The more volatile are its markets, the lower is the stability of employment in the firm, and this is a factor which has been associated with the industrial-relations problems experienced by the Ford motor company in the 1960s (Beynon, 1973). In a mature economy the tastes of consumers can change and certain product attributes become more important, which can force firms to make dramatic adjustments. For these reasons it is impossible to ignore the idea that market factors could have discernible effects on employee relations within a firm. As yet, however, it is not possible to say what market characteristics are associated with specific employee-relations practices. Although the connection has long been acknowledged at a theoretical level (Thurley and Wood, 1983; Thomason, 1984; Kochan *et al.,* 1984), it is only fairly recently that a concerted attempt has been made to identify these links (Schuler and Jackson, 1987; Marchington, 1990; Marchington and Parker, 1990).

Suppliers of inputs

On the input side of an organization there are a number of elements that can be equally important as markets. After all, there is little point in identifying a superb marketing opportunity if it is not possible to acquire the resources to provide what the market wants. *Suppliers of capital* such as shareholders and banks can be crucial to a firm because they usually have expectations about its level of profits. In today's depressed or volatile markets, managers can come to feel that the only way to meet these expectations is to reduce costs through greater internal efficiency, which can result in radical alterations to working arrangements and possibly the use of new technologies. Indirectly, *suppliers of materials* are also suppliers of capital to a firm. If a firm takes longer to pay suppliers than it does to collect debts from customers, the nearer it gets to using the capital of other organizations to finance its own operations. Doing this, however, greatly depends upon the willingness of suppliers to give extended credit. The reliability and stability of suppliers can also be crucial to a firm. Certain industries such as vehicle manufacturing rely heavily on bought-in components; for example, electrical equipment and tyres. If its suppliers go out of business, or have problems that affect their output, this can have an immediate impact on a firm.

Suppliers of labour, which largely means the firm's employees, are also a vital consideration. To serve their markets firms have to acquire the appropriate quantity of human resources of the right quality, and at the right time. This often requires complex, long-term strategies. For example, because of low birthrates in the 1970s, the number of young people entering the labour market in the 1990s has been much reduced; the so-called demographic time-bomb effect (NEDO, 1988, 1989). Therefore, some firms are paying increasing attention to developing employment policies designed to attract groups such as married women back into the labour market (Glascock, 1990; Shipley, 1991). *Suppliers of equipment* are another important group on the input side. The past decade has been one of fairly rapid technological change. Therefore in a developed economy, a vital item of equipment is knowledge, and acquiring new equipment and techniques, together with the knowledge to use them, has become a vital weapon in the battle for survival.

Competitors

Very few goods and services have no substitutes, and the very fact that there are competitors for markets puts very severe limitations on a firm's room for manoeuvre. Similarly, competition for resources such as capital, equipment, materials and labour can prompt internal changes, which have knock-on effects on a firm's relationship with its employees.

Regulatory groups

Although not involved in the input–output chain in a direct way, this segment of task environment contains sources of disturbance which can affect inputs, outputs, or internal processes.

Consumer groups come in a variety of forms. For example, public utilities such as telecommunications, gas, electricity and water are all subject to scrutiny and regulation of the prices which they can charge. Somewhat less powerful in formal terms, but highly influential in terms of media publicity, are bodies such as the Consumers' Association. Almost every industrialized country has an increasingly influential environmental lobby, and anti-pollution legislation is beginning to appear, which could force radical changes in production methods and processes. Thus all of these groups can exert very powerful pressures on a firm's markets and/or internal processes. In certain industries *trade and employer associations* can have a huge impact on a firm's conduct, and in some instances have a direct influence on its employee relations, for example associations that negotiate on behalf of employers with trade unions. Some associations can also play a part in regulating competition between their members, which clearly has market-related effects. *Trade unions* are the most prominent regulatory group so far as employee relations is concerned. Indeed, the basic purposes of a trade union is to limit management's freedom of action *vis-à-vis* the employees it represents. Finally *government* can influence the firm in many ways. Some of its activities concern commercial matters such as exporting, which has an effect on the size of a firm's markets. Others such as employment legislation can have a more direct impact on employee relations.

The implications of task environment and some current responses

In practice, although all the parts of a firm's task environment are at work together, different segments can be more problematic at certain times, and give contingent circumstances to which the firm has to try to adjust. Environments which give changes of some magnitude, and even those where there is a host of smaller changes that occur at high frequency, are said to be turbulent (Emery and Trist, 1963). The more turbulent is a firm's task environment, the greater the level of uncertainty that it faces, the basic effect of which is that it becomes difficult to plan ahead and fine-tune activities so that they can be conducted in an effective and efficient way.

In the past fifteen years the task environments of firms in the UK have become increasingly turbulent. This has been most visible on the output (market) side, where a variety of factors such as heightened competition in both home and overseas markets has given widely fluctuating conditions. Importantly this has occurred in circumstances where there has been a great deal of turbulence on the input side as well; for example, fluctuations in interest and foreign exchange rates. This has prompted many firms who traditionally had costs associated with holding inventories of raw materials and finished goods to try to adopt 'just-in-time' methods imported from Japan. That is, input stocks are kept to near zero levels, and deliveries are received virtually daily and used almost as soon as they arrive. There are, however, considerable doubts about how well British firms have been able to introduce these measures (Sayer, 1986; McKenna, 1988; Oliver and Wilkinson, 1989). In addition, to release much-needed financial assets and to obtain economies of scale, many firms have centralized their operations. Some have had to contract the scale of their operations as well as undertake a fair measure of re-equipping with the use of new technologies. For example, there has been a huge increase in the use of computer technology, much of which has been directed at automating the production of goods and services.

However, even after (or perhaps as part of) these changes, firms have still found themselves faced with difficulties in coping with the high degree of environmental fluctuation that exists. Thus their greatest need has been to adopt radically new structural forms that give much more internal flexibility. This has strong implications for the relationship between an organization and its employees, and perhaps the easiest way to describe matters is by using what has become known as the 'flexible firm' or 'core–periphery' model (Atkinson 1984a, 1984b; Atkinson and Meager, 1986), which is shown in Figure 1.3.

The flexible-firm concept is an 'ideal type' model that describes what would happen if all the characteristics were present together. It is most applicable to large manufacturing organizations, and the key idea is that the firm becomes

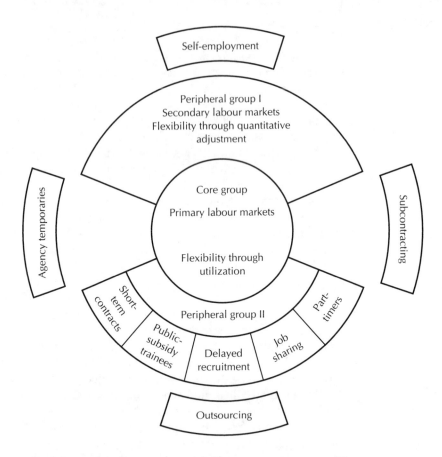

Figure 1.3 The flexible firm. Source: IMS, 1984.

much more responsive to changes in its product markets if the workforce is structured into two main groups. The first consists of a permanent core workforce of highly skilled and to some extent multi-skilled workers. This gives the firm a high degree of *functional flexibility* which permits it to adapt its products and production processes rapidly. To ensure that this core group has the skills to deliver the needed flexibility, the firm has a vested interest in providing training and retraining as necessary. Therefore, because the skills of the workforce are akin to an investment, the firm seeks to retain this group of employees with an attractive package of rewards.

To obtain *numerical flexibility,* so that it can adjust its levels of output, the firm has two peripheral subgroups of workers. The first consists of employees with skills that are important to the firm. However, they are skills that are general and easily imported at short notice. There are also permanent employees, such as typists and word-processor operators, where jobs are often occupied by people who exit and re-enter the labour market. This gives a fairly high level of natural turnover, which can be used to adjust numbers. The subgroup also consists of employees such as part-time workers whose hours can quickly be adjusted upwards if need be, and people on government-sponsored training schemes who are employed by the firm in an even less permanent way. The second subgroup consists of workers who are never employed by the firm itself, but who enter it from time to time to give an additional degree of numerical flexibility. These are shown as the four blocks on the edge of the model.

The model is of course essentially a conceptual one, and was never designed to present a picture of what is taking place in a wholesale way throughout the UK. Neither does it offer a universal prescription for success. Rather it is simply a theoretical framework that explains steps taken by some firms to achieve higher degrees of labour flexibility. Having said this, since flexibility has become something of a watchword in British industry, the model is an important one. Flexibility in the use of human resources is widely seen as an essential ingredient of a firm's ability to weather market conditions (OECD, 1986). Perhaps more significantly, the flexible use of labour is seen by many managers as one of the key characteristics that explains the success of Japanese companies (Piore, 1986). The core–periphery concept clearly has some similarities to the Japanese employment system of permanent and temporary workers that was described earlier in the chapter, and the just-in-time technique also originates in Japan. Thus it gives rise to two important questions. To what extent has the flexible-firm model been widely adopted in Great Britain, and is the search for increased flexibility in the use of human resources a reflection of the adoption of Japanese methods of management, or to phrase it slightly differently, the 'Japanization' of British industry?

With respect to the first question, there is a small amount of case-study research which supports the real-world utility of the core–periphery model (IMS, 1984, 1985; IOD, 1985; Atkinson, 1984a, 1984b). Throughout the 1980s, there was a general tendency for firms to try to achieve labour flexibility through restructuring (ACAS, 1985), and a more recent survey of over 500 firms (ACAS, 1988) revealed in a more specific way how flexibility has been sought. A large number had aimed to increase numerical flexibility by the use of part-time and temporary workers, fixed-term contracts, homeworking and contractors. An equally large number had pursued functional flexibility by moving in the direction of multi-skilling and reduced demarcation between jobs. Perhaps most significant of all, most of the firms surveyed were planning to increase the use of these techniques in the future. For the most part, therefore, firms' intentions involve specific alterations to working arrangements, mainly in the direction of a multi-skilled workforce and the removal of traditional craft boundaries (Cross, 1985; IDS, 1986; IRS, 1986). Most of the changes have been introduced through negotiation rather than being imposed by management, and since employees usually receive substantial pay increases for their implementation (Marsden and

Thompson, 1990), there is some evidence of a trend towards one aspect of the core–periphery model: a more functionally flexible, multi-skilled core workforce.

Nevertheless, the evidence suggests that a complete core–periphery design is comparatively rare, and is confined to about 10 % of British firms. The majority, although having a manpower strategy of some sort, tend to use only selected elements from the core–periphery menu; for example, by using more part-timers, temporaries and subcontractors as an expedient reaction to an unexpectedly full order book (Hakim, 1990). Thus the techniques which have become associated with the core–periphery design could be little more than an explicit statement of isolated practices that have been used for some time. In the long term, however, if the design is widely adopted it could have very far-reaching effects, and bring about a restructuring of firms that produces a radical change to traditional patterns of work organization in Great Britain.

Turning now to the second issue of 'Japanization', in many ways this is a question to which there is no definitive answer. There are several features of Japanese industry, such as quality circles, enhanced employee communications and the single-status workforce, which have been adopted in some British firms. However, in Japanese firms all these things tend to be found together, and are part of an integrated set of human resource and production practices. An example is the use of just-in-time techniques to reduce inventories. These result in a production process having a lower tolerance to errors, and thus a rigorous and continuous total control of quality is also vital. This in turn requires that inspection cannot be left to the end of the production process, but each stage has to be monitored so that defective work does not cause a hold-up later on. In Japan this inspection is done by production workers themselves, and depends acutely upon everyone seeing themselves as working towards a common goal and giving a great deal of feedback to earlier stages. Without this spirit of cooperation, techniques such as task flexibility, workforce involvement, just-in-time and total quality management are unlikely to work in a satisfactory way (Sayer, 1986). Japanese firms not only have national cultures which are compatible with this way of working, they also have human resource or employee relations strategies designed to reinforce the necessary attitudes in employees.

In British firms, whilst there is evidence that some Japanese employee relations and production techniques have been adopted, this has rarely been part of a coordinated strategy. Usually one or two production techniques such as just-in-time or total quality management are used. Similarly, attempts to adopt employee-relations practices such as quality circles have been made. However, each practice tends to be used in isolation to try to solve a specific problem (McKenna, 1988), and seldom, if ever, is there a thorough integration of both human resource and production techniques (Turnbull, 1986; Oliver and Wilkinson, 1989). For this reason it cannot be said that Japanization in the strict sense of the word has occurred in British industry in any widespread way.

Overview and preview

This chapter has described the environmental circumstances surrounding firms and how these can affect employee relations. Throughout the description, a constant theme has been that organizations are not sealed off from the rest of the world, but are in constant interaction with their environments. Thus what happens in firms takes place against a backdrop of external events that can often have a strong influence on what happens inside.

The remainder of the book will largely be concerned with employee relations within organizations. Nevertheless, in many of the topics covered it will be impossible to ignore factors external to the firm. In the next four chapters for example, when discussing the parties in employee relations, the actions of employees and managers will be seen to be partly a product of the external cultural and ideological influences that have been described in this chapter. Similarly the State, which is discussed in Chapter 5, is a powerful external influence that has a strong impact on employee relations. Many of the internal processes discussed in Chapters 6 to 11 are also subject to external influences, although not always in an obvious way. All of them, for example, have a legal aspect which exists because of the actions of the State, and with some, notably those dealt with in Chapters 7 to 11, the influence of practices common in other parts of the world can also be detected. Thus although the remainder of the book focuses mainly on people and events within organizations, the reader is asked to remember that all of this concerns the behaviour of humans. People inevitably bring some of the outside world to work with them, and when they arrive, their actions are further influenced by additional outside forces.

Further reading

Dunlop J.T. (1958). *Industrial Relations Systems*. New York: Holt

The first, and many would say only, attempt to construct a general theory of industrial relations. Gives a very comprehensive description of how contextual and internal factors interact to give distinctive patterns of industrial relations.

Clegg H. A. (1976). *Trade Unions Under Collective Bargaining: A Theory Based on Comparisons of Six Countries*. Oxford: Blackwell.

> A very scholarly work, which on the basis of an international comparison argues that the nature of trade unions is heavily influenced by the bargaining relationships of which they are a part.

Bamber G. J. and Lansbury R. D., eds. (1987). *International and Comparative Industrial Relations*. London: Allen and Unwin

> An excellent introduction to the international perspective, which describes the parties and the processes in nine different countries.

Curson C., ed. (1986). *Flexible Patterns of Work*. London: Institute of Personnel Management.

> A book of readings which covers most of the major techniques now becoming common amongst employers to achieve workforce flexibility.

2

The individual and workgroups

Introduction

Employees are one of the two parties directly involved in the employment relationship and, in this chapter, they are examined as individuals. It starts by examining some of the ways in which they can differ, together with the implications that these differences have for employee relations. Still at individual level, the subject then turns to the legal relationship between an organization and its employees: the contract of employment. Whilst the contract is acknowledged to be important, it largely treats the relationship as a matter of economic exchange, and for this reason the strict legal perspective has limitations. Therefore, an alternative way of viewing the relationship that is more adequate in expressing its richness and complexity is examined: the social exchange perspective.

People seldom exist in isolation in organizations. They are brought together into workgroups and departments, and this can influence their behaviour. Therefore, as a prelude to the next chapter, the final topic in this one is groups and their potential importance in employee relations.

Individuals and their differences

To some extent all individuals are unique. Thus a fitting start to this chapter is a brief look at some of the ways in which people can differ, and the implications that this has for employee relations. To many people, the most obvious and fundamental difference between individuals is in what we call **personality.** In psychology there are technical definitions of what this word means, but for simplicity it will be used here to denote the characteristic pattern of behaviour and dispositions of a person. Whilst it is generally accepted that personality plays a leading part in the way that an individual adjusts to his or her surroundings (including to other people), opinion is divided in psychology about the permanence of a person's personality characteristics. The position taken here is a middle one. That is, behavioral traits and dispositions are taken to be relatively permanent, but it is also acknowledged that over time they can change according to the situations in which an individual is located for long periods (Mischel, 1968).

Since certain of a person's aptitudes and abilities are partly a function of personality, it can be an important factor that influences their suitability for different organizational roles. However, when it comes to assessing personality in a selection and placement context, there can be problems. Although there are a number of well-developed tests to do this, their capability to predict future job behaviour is not usually very high (Epstein, 1980; Monson *et al.*, 1982). This does not necessarily mean that there is no connection between personality and behaviour. It may just be the case that in predictive terms, the tests used are somewhat crude. An even bigger problem is that most personality judgements made about individuals do not even benefit from these tests.

Individuals are often categorized in a purely subjective way which, as will be seen in later chapters, can have some very significant employee-relations implications.

Intelligence is another way in which individuals can be differentiated. A significant problem, however, is that the word itself tends to provoke controversy and emotive reactions. In psychology there is some disagreement about the actual meaning of the word (Miles, 1957); also whether intelligence can be measured, and if so, how. Nevertheless, the idea that intelligence is an important mental attribute is as old as civilization itself, and is part of the everyday vocabulary of organizations. Thus the psychological debate will be put aside, and for the purpose of discussion intelligence will be taken to mean 'an innate, general cognitive ability' (Burt, 1955).

In organizations, the practical importance of individual differences in general cognitive abilities is similar to that of personality, that is, it is likely to make people more suitable for some roles than others. It is perhaps for this reason that the idea of intelligence being innate generates emotive reactions. However, whilst it is generally accepted that it has a hereditary component, this does not mean that intelligence is totally inherited. Indeed, it is more usual to regard it as something which results from an interaction between hereditary factors and the experiences to which people have been exposed as they develop. Moreover, in most organizations there are usually attempts to avoid purely subjective evaluations of intelligence by using more objective criteria. For example, educational qualifications or even IQ tests can be used. Problematically, in their own way these measures can be just as controversial as subjective judgements. Education is an experience to which a person has been exposed. A person's exposure to educational experience is frequently more a matter of social origins than anything else, and to some extent a facility with IQ test questions can be developed with practice. Thus using these criteria as indicators can be a poor basis on which to compare people in terms of their intellectual potential.

Another important individual difference is **social background**. An individual enters this world with an extremely wide range of potential behaviours. However, in the process of childhood socialization they are induced to accept the sentiments, emotions, beliefs and behavioural patterns which are acceptable to the group in which they spend their early formative years. Thus a person usually has a somewhat narrower range of actual behaviour than the total range of which he or she is potentially capable. It does not, however, mean that a person's entire repertoire of behaviour is fixed irrevocably for all time. To some extent people are resocialized by the new groups that they come to belong to. Nevertheless, early social experiences can have an enormous influence on subsequent orientations to work. For example, the work of the American social psychologist McClelland (1961) shows that 'the need to achieve' can be traced back to child-rearing and socialization practices. In other words it is a 'socially induced' personality trait. Since it is much more strongly developed in some individuals than others, and has effects on their work motivation, it can be very important to organizations. Of more direct significance in employee relations is the point that social background and origins can be an important factor in shaping industrial attitudes and behaviour. For example, someone with a middle-class upbringing and education is perhaps more likely to look only for professional or white-collar work. In addition social background has been used to explain why trade unions of manual workers have traditionally been more willing to take industrial action than those representing salaried staffs (Routh, 1966). The expectations that social background gives rise to has also been used to explain why white-collar workers, who for a long time remained relatively un-unionized, eventually joined trade unions in large numbers. That is, they were no longer able to rely on the prospects for individual advancement that their backgrounds had led them to expect, and chose the collective path instead (Bain 1970; Roberts *et al.,* 1972).

Another important way in which individuals can differ is in terms of their **perceptions**. Few of us are actually able to see reality, but rather we infer the reality of a situation in a rather selective way. This is particularly true in highly dynamic situations; for example, when interacting with another person. Not only are we confronted with a host of different sources of information at the same time, but the information keeps changing. This becomes far too much for us to assimilate and integrate, and so we select certain pieces of information and attend to them. Thus what a person perceives is seldom a faithful reproduction of what is there, but rather a partial reproduction (Krech *et al.,* 1962). Perception, however, is not just something that happens. It is an active mental process, and in a given situation any two people will pay attention to different features, sometimes dramatically so. What they take to be reality is generally influenced by the situation itself, characteristics of the object perceived, and importantly, the personal characteristics of the beholder (Levine and Shefner, 1981). Indeed the latter can be highly important. Mood, disposition, attitudes and personality can all affect perceptions, and so perceptual processes can be strongly influenced by some of the individual differences already discussed. Moreover, social background can also play a crucial part. It teaches people how to interpret events, and can thus shape perceptions.

The employee-relations implications of these individual differences are all too clear. To start with, since people are equipped differently, they have different aptitudes which makes them more suitable for some types of work and less suitable for others. This does not mean that their different roles have to be looked upon as inferior or superior.

However, organizations have to be directed and controlled, which inevitably results in a hierarchy of authority. Because of differences between individuals it is all too common for those that have authority to assert that it is not only derived from their formal positions in the hierarchy, but also from a personal superiority which makes them best fitted to command the actions of others. Clearly those with less formal authority can sometimes dispute these claims, which has fairly obvious employee-relations consequences.

Secondly, because the way that someone perceives a situation tends to have more influence on their behaviour than the realities of the situation itself, there are a number of outcomes of perception that have significance for the employment relationship. One of these is the phenomenon of **projection**, in which a person can see their own qualities or attributes in other people. For example, someone who is power conscious can see others in the same light; so much so that they are interpreted as a threat to the perceiver's power aspirations. People can also **stereotype** others. That is, they put people into categories, associate certain characteristics with membership of a category, and assume that someone in a category will have all of these characteristics. A similar phenomenon is the

halo effect, in which a generalization is made about all of a person's characteristics from the presence of just one. Both stereotyping and halo effects have been shown to be prevalent in situations where managers have to make important decisions about other people, notably in job interviews (Dipboye, 1982) and performance appraisals (Feldman, 1981). For example, all women can be perceived as less fit for responsible jobs than men, all managers are viewed as the enemy, or even all manual workers are seen as only being motivated by money.

Thirdly, these differences can result in people and groups perceiving or experiencing the same set of organizational circumstances in different ways. Like-minded individuals have a tendency to gyrate towards one another, and to form groups. As will be seen later, groups can take on a life of their own, and their members become highly cohesive in terms of shared perspectives, aims and objectives. For this reason, most organizations consist of different groups that have somewhat different aims, and this can mean that there is a potential for them to be at loggerheads with each other. Therefore, messages transmitted throughout the organization will not always be interpreted in the same way by every group. This effect can be particularly strong with information transmitted downward from the managerial group, which can sometimes be interpreted quite differently by recipients and senders.

CASE-STUDY 2.1

Individual differences and opinions of others

Consider the following situation.

Fred Smith joined Precision Products Ltd one year ago direct from university with a degree in production engineering. He is about to have his first annual performance review interview with his manager Mr Brown. Fred is keen, energetic and quite innovative. Across the past year he has made a number of suggestions to Mr Brown about improvements that could be made to production methods, if only more modern manufacturing techniques were used. However, he has heard nothing about these suggestions, and he suspects that they might still be resident in Mr Brown's in-tray. Although keen, conscientious and serious in other respects, Fred has a somewhat flamboyant taste in clothes. In a good-humoured way he has become the source of some amusement to shop-floor workers, who often make ribald remarks about his style of dress.

Mr Brown is in his mid 50s and has been with the firm since leaving school at sixteen. He started as a production worker, was promoted to chargehand, later to foreman, and after some years was made departmental manager. About five years ago he was appointed to the post of production manager. He is a very sober character, who is proud of the fact that without any qualifications he has risen to his present post by diligence, hard work and a thorough knowledge of the firm. Indeed, he is well known throughout the company for his adherence to tried and trusted ways of doing things, and for an insistence that supervisors and managers should keep their subordinates at a distance in order to command their respect.

Question

How could the differences between Fred Smith and Mr Brown affect the outcome of the interview that is shortly to take place, and how could this have an impact on employee relations at Precision Products?

The employer–employee relationship: the legal concept

Legally the relationship between employer and employee is expressed in the contract of employment, which is generally taken to be the cornerstone of British labour law (Kahn-Fruend, 1967). The contract views the relationship as an individual one, made between two parties of equal bargaining strength, and regards the essence of the relationship as a promise made by each one: a promise to work (or to be available for work) in return for which payment is promised. It also assumes that since there has been a free exchange of promises, the two parties have reciprocal, but different, rights and obligations (Kahn-Fruend, 1977a). The basic concept of the contract contains features which date from reforms which took place in master–servant legislation in the 19th century. Prior to this, the master–servant relationship had its foundations in medieval and Elizabethan law. Servants were liable to punishment for not accepting work, for not doing exactly as they were told, or for deserting their master. Their wages could be fixed by justices of the peace, which effectively meant that the poor and destitute could be directed into compulsory work on terms dictated by justices, who were themselves masters and had a vested interest in keeping wages low. Even after the first attempts at reform, the laws could be, and were, used very effectively by masters to subordinate workpeople. A recognized tactic was to have strikers arrested for breach of duty, and then to confront them with the alternative of returning to work on the employer's terms, or face three months' imprisonment. Between 1858 and 1875 it has been estimated that an average of 10 000 such prosecutions occurred each year (Simon, 1954). Repeal occurred largely because of pressures exerted by the early trade unions, and although this removed many of the impediments to genuine freedom of contract, some of the older ones which remain have a lasting impact on modern legislation. For example, the rights established by legislative reform were by no means universal, and varied according to the nature of a person's work. Thus craftsmen and labourers had different rights from servants. Whilst these differences have largely disappeared, there are still some important ways in which the idea of a master–servant relationship persists.

One example of is this is given in the Employment Protection (Consolidation) Act (1978), where a contract of employment is defined as 'a contract of service or of apprenticeship between an employer and an individual employee' (EPCA, 1978, c. 44, sc. 153).

The words 'of service' are a legal device, largely designed to distinguish the relationship between employer and employee as different from one with a sub-contractor where there is a 'contract for services'. However, the fundamental test used to make this distinction (the control test) still rests on the master's power to command the actions of the servant (Whincup, 1990). As will be seen in what follows, this has an important legacy, and effectively gives the employer a great deal of power to decide unilaterally what the terms of the contract should be (Hepple, 1983). For this reason there is a strong element of unreality in the notion that a person who accepts an offer of employment is fully conversant with all the terms and details it contains. Indeed, it has been powerfully argued that the contract is not even an agreement about terms and conditions, but simply an agreement to enter into a relationship, the terms and conditions of which have yet to emerge (Honeyball, 1989).

Terms which make up the contract

Whether or not the offer and acceptance are in writing, an employee who accepts an offer of employment has, in strict legal terms, entered into a binding contract of service. Even though nothing specific may have been said at the time, when this happens the terms and conditions under which both parties can later be deemed to have honoured the contract will have been fixed. These terms come from a variety of sources. Some of them are more readily visible than others, but for simplicity, they can be grouped under six headings, and a brief explanation is given in what follows.

Unlike some of the inclusions that are silently assumed to be part of the contract, there are usually several **expressly agreed terms**, which are the specifics of what has been agreed. Most of them are, or should be, stated in any written offer of employment that is made. In addition, Section 49 of the Employment Protection (Consolidation) Act 1978 (EPCA) requires that within thirteen weeks of taking up an appointment, employees should be given a written statement of particulars of employment, and that this should cover certain minimum details. Whilst most employees have a statutory right to receive this document, there are certain excluded categories. Those required to work for less than 16 hours per week, registered dockers, seafarers, Crown and some NHS workers, and those whose contract is totally written are all examples where the statement of particulars is not legally required. The statement should cover the following:

(1) The identities of the employer and employee.

(2) Date of commencement of employment, and whether any previous service with the employer counts as continuous.

(3) The job title, nature of work (but not necessarily a full job description), and normal location.

(4) The rate of remuneration (including overtime rates) or methods by which it is calculated.

(5) Whether paid weekly, monthly, or at some other interval.

(6) Hours of work and normal working hours.

(7) Holidays, rights to holidays, and pay on termination.

(8) Provision for sickness and injury and entitlements to pay.

(9) Pension rights.

(10) The amount of notice to be given by either party to terminate the contract.

(11) Disciplinary rules that apply.

(12) The person to whom application can be made of a dissatisfaction with any disciplinary action, or to raise any other grievance.

(13) The procedure to be followed on any such application.

(14) Whether a contracting-out certificate is in force under Social Security pensions provisions.

(15) If the contract is for a fixed period, the date of its expiry.

The intention of the legislation is that the document should reduce the scope for future ambiguity. However, it is not in itself the contract, nor is it conclusive proof of all of its terms and conditions. Rather, it is a statement of what the employer believed the major terms to be at the time the contract was made. Neither is it required that the document spell out in explicit detail the information covered in items 1–11 and 13. It can simply refer the employee to other documents which contain the details, and to which access can be gained on request.

Where trade unions negotiate terms and conditions of employment, parts of **collective agreements** can become incorporated into the contract of each individual. Usually this will be explicitly acknowledged in the statement of written particulars, by noting that pay, hours, holidays and other substantive terms are fixed and varied from time to time in negotiations between the employer and recognized trade unions. Normally, the only terms which get incorporated in this way are the substantive ones, and procedural agreements, such as those covering grievance and disciplinary handling, are not usually binding parts of the contract.

There are also a number of **terms and conditions arising in legislation** which are swept up into the contract, and become binding on almost all employers. Many of these are aimed at preventing unfair discrimination, and examples are:

Sexual discrimination	The Sex Discrimination Acts, 1975, 1986 and Employment Bill, 1989
Equal pay	Equal Pay Act, 1970 and 1983 amendment
Racial discrimination	Race Relations Act, 1976
Spent convictions	Rehabilitation of Offenders Act, 1974
Disabled persons	Disabled Persons Acts, 1944, 1958
Union membership and performance of trade-union duties	Employment Protection (Consolidation) Act, 1978
Health and safety	Health and Safety at Work Act, 1974

In certain industries, collective bargaining is relatively undeveloped, perhaps because employers and employees are too dispersed and fragmented to be able to organize themselves for negotiating. Some of these industries are covered by statutory bodies called 'wages councils', the origins and functions of which are covered more extensively in Chapter 5. Here it is sufficient to note that they set basic terms and conditions for the industries that they cover, and that failure on the part of an employer to observe the award of a council is a criminal offence. About 30 of them currently exist and since 1986, they have been restricted to setting pay and are excluded from establishing other conditions of service.

One of the most controversial inclusions in the contract can be **works or organizational rules**. Moreover, because they sometimes only exist in an informal way and can vary from place to place, it can sometimes be a difficult matter to determine whether they are part of the contract. Where they are written down, especially if they are brought to the attention of employees, perhaps by giving them a rule book or posting the rules as notices, they are likely to become contractual terms. What makes them controversial is the fact that the sole author of the rules is invariably the employer. Moreover, a prospective employee is hardly likely to be shown, or made aware of, the rules as part of the selection process. Therefore because there has been no opportunity to assent or dissent, the terms are effectively imposed in silence. Problematically, since the law usually gives employers a great deal of scope in varying these rules, this part of the contract can be somewhat open-ended (Honeyball, 1989). Thus the whole practice of including works rules tends to negate the idea that the contract is an agreement made between two equally well-informed parties.

In some situations, local or workplace **custom and practice rules** govern the conduct of the parties as much as written agreements (Brown, 1972; Terry, 1977). Bonus payment rates, notice periods, disciplinary penalties, and speed and conditions of work are all matters that can be decided by local custom, and this can become part of the contract. In general terms a custom becomes part and parcel of the contract where three conditions are met: first, where it is deemed to be reasonable, although to a large extent the courts take the employer's view about this; second, where it is universally observed so that everyone concerned knows about it; third, if employees are knowledgeable about the effects it has on them.

In addition to the foregoing, there are a number of terms **implied by common law** as part of all contracts of employment. Those affecting the employer are regarded in principle as duties that a reasonable employer owes to his employees. The major items are:

- To pay wages and salaries promptly, and to pay backdated increases that may become due; for example, after prolonged negotiations.
- Not to make unauthorized deductions from pay.
- To reimburse employees for monies they have expended on the employer's behalf.
- In certain circumstances to provide work for the employee; for example, where payment is totally by commission or for work completed.
- To provide a safe system of work which in practice can mean providing safe plant, materials and tools, adequate supervision and training to ensure safe working.
- To obey the law and not to require employees to break the law in performing their duties.
- In certain specified circumstances to allow time off from work (not necessarily with pay); for example, for trade union and certain public duties.

Those incumbent on the employee are:

- To work and cooperate, which includes turning up for work (on time) and not to be absent unless authorized.
- To obey reasonable instructions so long as they are lawful.
- To competently and proficiently perform the job for which they are employed.
- To take reasonable care in performing the job, so that the employer's property is not damaged and injury to others is avoided.
- To be trustworthy, honest and have integrity; for example, to work only for the employer in the employer's time, and to safeguard trade secrets, confidential knowledge and business interests.

Most of these implied terms have been handed down from the master–servant conception of employment. The fact that the law regards them as fundamental has been argued to result in a situation where employees are virtually forced to give a very general and diffuse degree of obedience and loyalty, which is seldom returned by the employer (Fox, 1985). One problem is that legislation is often so complex and incomprehensible to laymen that they lack knowledge of their common-law rights, which makes the rights inaccessible in a practical way. Conversely, employers usually have personnel or other specialists to advise them, and this gives them a far greater capability to assert their rights in common law (Hyman, 1975). For this reason individual labour law really needs to be seen as little more than what one prominent lawyer has described as a 'floor of rights' (Wedderburn, 1971, 1980). That is, the law is something to fall back on, if all else fails. This is the position taken by most trade unions, who tend to see the rights conferred by individual labour law as something they have already achieved (and in many cases exceeded) by collective bargaining. Or, to quote from the doyen of British labour lawyers: 'trade unions are a more effective force in redressing the imbalance of power inherent in the contract than the law is, or ever could be' (Kahn-Freund, 1977b, p 10).

An alternative view of the employer–employee relationship

Important though it is, the legal view of the relationship between organization and employee is somewhat oversimplified. Ultimately it rests on the idea that the relationship can be reduced to an economic contract, the terms of which can be exactly specified. Whilst there undeniably is a contract, for the exchange of service for rewards, the relationship between employee and organization is arguably much more complex than this. To start with, an exchange that is purely economic takes place at a point in time, and what is exchanged can be precisely specified beforehand, as, for example, in purchasing a house or a car. In the employment relationship, whilst there are some items of exchange that can be precisely specified, there are many others about which it can be notoriously difficult to be specific. In addition, the relationship is not a one-off transaction. It extends into the future, and so it can be difficult to state precisely what terms of exchange will be needed then. These features add a whole new dimension to the employment relationship and the nature of the exchange process which it involves. Fortunately, there is a framework which is capable of capturing some of the potential complexity. This is social exchange theory (Homans, 1961; Blau, 1964), which has a view of the exchange process that is much more subtle than the economic one. To explain this, a brief excursion will be made to state some of the theory's basic features.

Social exchange theory acknowledges that the basic motivation for individuals to enter into a relationship is the rewards that they expect to obtain. However, an exchange relationship not only brings benefits to the parties; they also incur costs. Indeed, it is because both parties incur costs that they feel that the other person is under some obligation to provide benefits. In addition, because people are usually realistic enough to recognize that their benefits are the other person's costs, they feel obliged to provide some benefits in return. This means that each participant has a ratio of costs to benefits. However, few people consciously work out this ratio, but more commonly evaluate things in a subjective way. Nevertheless it has an important implication. For the relationship to come into existence both parties must see their own exchange ratio as fair, the usual criterion of 'fairness' being where each one feels that the costs they incur are balanced by the benefits they receive.

This gives rise to a second important feature of the theory. Social exchange contains a host of unspecific expectations and obligations. Assume for the moment that at the start of a relationship both parties feel that the exchange is fair, and that to obtain future benefits, they wish to make the relationship an ongoing one. The major incentive for both of them to do so is the belief and expectation that their returns will continue to be commensurate with costs. However, this is seldom, if ever, specified in advance, and since evaluations of costs and benefits are largely made subjectively, it is unlikely that people even make this explicit to themselves. Therefore, each party has an unvoiced and unspecific expectation that the other one will continue to provide benefits in a 'fair' ratio to costs. In return each one will incur an equally unvoiced and unspecific obligation to do the same.

This in turn gives rise to a third important point. No individual can be completely certain that the other party will honour their obligations. Therefore trust is necessary for the relationship to work. Problematically, if we trust someone whose behaviour cannot be completely controlled then we are more vulnerable to his/her actions, and that person has a potential power advantage (Zand, 1972). Nevertheless, trust is the essential lubricant of all ongoing relationships. Trust evokes trust in return, and mistrust evokes mistrust. Thus both parties must trust each other to play fair in the future, and for this to happen, each one has to be seen as trustworthy.

The final point is that the relative power of the parties can affect the conditions of exchange, power being defined as: 'the capacity of an individual or group to modify the conduct of other individuals or groups in a manner which they desire, and without having to modify their own conduct in a manner which they do not desire' (Tawney, 1931, p. 229). Social exchange theory explicitly assumes that there is always an imbalance of power in the relationship. The source of this imbalance can very much depend upon how much each party needs what the other one has to offer, or as Blau cogently puts it: 'the greater the difference between the benefits obtained by an individual and their ability to obtain them elsewhere, the greater is the power held over them' (Blau, 1964, p. 120). For this reason, if one person is more committed to keeping the relationship in existence than is the other one, he or she has most to lose if it is severed, and is potentially at a power disadvantage.

All of these features apply to the employment relationship, and this is what makes it such a complex and sometimes problematic area. Indeed there are a number of themes and issues that keep surfacing in employee relations, and these tend to arise largely because the relationship is one of social exchange.

The first, **fairness**, tends to be defined by people in a very personal and sometimes subjective way. When a person accepts an offer of employment he or she will almost certainly weigh up their whole package of benefits, such as security, income and fringe benefits. These will be compared with the costs they will incur; for example, hours of work, working conditions and lowered degree of self-determination. Similarly, the employer will weigh up the benefits obtained against the costs of employing the person. Because neither of them is likely to draw up an explicit statement of costs and benefits, the evaluation is almost bound to contain an element of intuitive judgement. Nevertheless, assume for the moment that both parties are satisfied, albeit intuitively, and assess their respective balances of costs and benefits as fair ones. If conditions were unchanging, everything would probably be fine. However, things are almost certain to change, and some of the biggest problems in employee relations arise in change situations when conceptions of fairness are brought to the surface. Both employer and employee will have opened their relationship with expectations about the future which were never voiced at the outset. They are likely to expect that if their own costs rise, benefits will go up to keep the balance the same. If this does not happen, they can begin to feel that the relationship has become rather one-sided. For example, in a harsh recessionary climate, where profits are under pressure and there is a surplus of people looking for jobs, management might well have a very modest idea of what is a 'fair' wage rise. Employees are not likely to see things in the same way, and in the absence of a rise that compensates them for any increase in their living costs, they are likely to view management's offer as unfair, and respond accordingly.

An allied issue, and one from which evaluations of fairness often arise, is **equity**. Because there are no absolute standards for a fair exchange, the expectations of individuals and groups are usually linked to their particular circumstances. This inevitably means that 'fairness' is evaluated in comparison with some other individual or group, that is, by comparing one's own balance of costs and benefits with what is assumed to be the balance of another individual or group. Comparison groups are usually selected from those that are perceived to be broadly similar, and in close proximity; for example, from within the same firm or locality (Brown and Sisson, 1975; Gartrell, 1982; Scase, 1974; Hyman and Brough, 1975). If an individual or group perceives that it is under-rewarded in comparison to the reference group, it feels a sense of '**relative deprivation**' (Runciman, 1966), which often leads to behaviour to redress the imbalance. In the long run, of course, it can result in all the groups engaging in 'leapfrogging claims' to keep restoring the *status quo* (Mann, 1977).

As noted earlier, power occupies a central place in social exchange theory. **Authority**, which is the most usual claim to power in organizations, is simply a special way in which power can manifest itself, and is also one of the most prominent issues in employee relations. For example, it is commonplace for a trade union to claim that it has the authority of its members to act in a certain way, and for managers to dispute this. Similarly, management often claims it has the legitimate authority to make certain decisions without reference to employees, and the workforce or its union will assert in return that management is exceeding its authority.

It is important to recognize that where the matter of management's authority is concerned, there are competing and sometimes contradictory rationals at work. Management has its own rationale to legitimize its authority, and since this is considered in detail in Chapter 4, it will not be explored here. However, any legitimization of management authority by employees is a matter of social convention and norms more than anything else. Most people are socialized from an early age into accepting that employment involves a degree of direction and control, and that failure to accept the situation inevitably results in sanctions of some sort (Fox, 1971). Like most things there are boundaries to this acceptance, and where these boundaries lie often depends on how much authority management claims. For this reason the ways in which boundaries are established, and sometimes contested, is one of the most important topics in employee relations.

No ongoing relationship can exist without **trust**, and this is as true in employee relations as anywhere else. For example, trust is necessary between trade unions and management in order to be able to reach agreements; and for day-to-day activities to be completed smoothly, trust is necessary between a workgroup and their supervisor. However, whilst trust is essentially an interpersonal process, it is important to realize that there are subtle and crucial ways in which the design of an organization makes a trusting relationship more or less likely to occur. This is explained lucidly by Fox (1974), in his concept of **institutionalized trust**. The way that jobs, and the rules that regulate jobs, are designed in organizations tends to express management's degree of faith and confidence in the workforce. For example, if jobs are designed to give people very little discretion, and work rules make it clear that their behaviour will be supervised, the situation is often interpreted by the people concerned as a signal that they are not trusted to obey the rules. As was pointed out earlier, trust tends to beget trust in return, and mistrust to beget mistrust. Thus it is hardly surprising to find that where job design results in 'low discretion' work roles, the organization is often one which has a correspondingly low degree of trust in its employee relations processes.

The final issue is that of **individualism versus collectivism**. Because there have been strong moves in the UK to individualize the employment relationship and to de-emphasize its collective aspects, this is currently a very important issue in employee relations. Whether this move has been part of a concerted strategy to weaken the power of trade unions, or more a way of trying to improve productivity by a greater emphasis on individual incentives, is still a matter of some debate. However, although this emphasis is in line with the legal view that the employment relationship is an individual one, it can be argued in return that things are much more collective in nature. That is, on one side there is a collective consisting of the owners and other financial stakeholders such as banks who are represented by managers, and on the other a second collective comprising the employees of the organization.

Which of these two frames of reference (individualist or collectivist) holds sway can be extremely important for the nature of employee relations. Perhaps because our whole conception of democracy hinges on the freedom of individuals to express their feelings and thoughts in action, the idea that the individual is paramount is almost a sacred tenet of our society. However, society itself has rules and laws of conduct which it devises for the collective well-being of all of its members, and requires that individuals observe them. Thus the very idea of a 'wider society' contains a strong recognition of collective interests, and in some respects a parallel situation exists in organizations. When an individual joins an organization, it is assumed that he or she will observe its rules. However, only some of these rules apply to everyone in the organization. Other rules are designed for specific groups performing particular tasks, and are applied only to them. Therefore, although the contract of employment views the relationship between an organization and each employee to be an individual one, organizations are not designed in this way. They are structured into departments and groups. These are subject to their own rules of conduct, and this means that the organization has been divided into a number of collectivities. Thus some aspects of the employment relationship are collective matters, rather than individual issues. It is therefore hardly surprising that a group (or indeed all employees) will act collectively if it feels the need to improve its lot, or defend itself against changes which are perceived as unfair.

CASE-STUDY 2.2

The Engineering Assistant's role

Consider the following two descriptions of a job in a large organization. The first, *A*, is an outline of the formal job description for the post, and the second one, *B*, describes the post holder and his experiences in the job.

A   Job description

Job title	Engineering Assistant, Technical Service Department, Groundwell Components PLC
Salary	Grade 10
Minimum qualifications	HND Mechanical Engineering or equivalent
Position to whom incumbent reports	Ultimately to Technical Service Manager, but works under direct supervision of designated Technical Service Engineer
Positions reporting to incumbent	None

Main duties personally performed

i Provides assistance as directed to designated Technical Service Engineer on selected aspects of investigations into failures and complaints from customers, concerning the company's products.

ii Answers customers' queries, verbally or in writing (as appropriate) on technical matters concerning the application and utilization of the company's products.

iii Visits customers on their premises and carries out on-site investigations concerning failure, application and utilization of the company's products.

iv Prepares reports for circulation to appropriate personnel within the company on items 1 to 3 above.

v Provides technical assistance to the company's sales staff as directed.

Other responsibilities

Equipment	All tools, instruments and equipment in the incumbent's charge
Cash and valuables	Nil
Vehicles	Uses pool car when travelling on company business and must therefore possess current driving licence
Other	May occasionally be required to deputize for a Technical Service Engineer in the event of the latter's prolonged absence from duties
Hazards in position	Nil

B   The position and its occupant

Morris Green is an engineering assistant in the Technical Service Department of Groundwell Components PLC, a post he has occupied since he joined the company two years ago on 1st March 1990. The department is a fairly small one, consisting of a technical service manager and three technical service engineers, each of whom has two engineering assistants reporting to him. On appointment Morris was paid monthly at the bottom point of Grade 10 (£10,000 p.a.) and since then he has received two automatic annual increments, plus a total of 14 % in cost-of-living rises. The latter were negotiated by the trade union to which most engineering personnel in the company belong. On the day he joined he was given a staff handbook which he found most useful in learning about the company and the standards it expected of its employees.

Morris very quickly acclimatized himself to his new position, which he found stimulating and interesting. The man to whom he directly reports is outgoing and considerate with his subordinates, and seems to go out of his way to ensure that they have a wide variety of different jobs to do. Morris is a married man with a young child and frequently works more than the standard 37 hours, partly for the overtime, but mainly because it is normal practice in the department to adopt a flexible approach to hours if there is a tricky problem that needs solving quickly. This flexibility he regards as part of the normal give and take in the job, and in return has always found the firm to be understanding if he needed time off for some reason. For example, when his wife gave birth to their child about six months ago, she needed a great deal of practical support because she was ill for some time after the birth.

All things being considered, Morris is happy with his lot. The job is pensionable and secure, a thing that he particularly values now that he is a father, and he is more than content with the way the firm has treated him. About one year after he joined, his immediate superior underwent serious surgery and was absent for three months. In his absence Morris took over the running of the section, and without his ever asking for it, the departmental manager made sure that he was paid a monthly bonus equivalent to the difference between his salary and that of a technical service engineer.

Questions

i Imagine you are a member of the Personnel Department in the above company, and as per the requirements of the Employment Protection (Consolidation) Act 1978, you are about to write the letter of written particulars to Morris Green at the end of his first 13 weeks with the firm. Using *A* and *B* as appropriate, draft this letter.

ii Using *A* and/or *B* note those points which seem to you to go beyond the formal contract and make Morris Green's relationship with his employing organization one of social rather than purely economic exchange.

The individual as a group member

Individuals seldom exist in isolation in organizations, and because of this, work is full of social experiences. These experiences can affect individual behaviour, and an important result is that all the individuals in a group often come to behave in common about certain matters. This collective behaviour is not simply the result of being together. To a large extent it can be influenced by the contextual

Figure 2.1   A model of workgroup behaviour (after G.C. Homans, 1950)

circumstances of a group, and this has strong implications for employee relations. Some of these matters will be considered in the next chapter, which deals with collective organizations of employees. For the present, however, it is important to consider the fundamental unit of collectivism: the workgroup.

An important distinction which must be made at the outset is between formal and informal groups. Strictly speaking, a formal group can be regarded as something which is anywhere between the extremes of a large permanent department and a small temporary project team. These groups are created by the organization as part of its process of dividing up the overall task into specific and separate subtasks. Thus the group's structure, including what its actions should be and who is in charge, is laid down by the organization. Informal groups are not created in this way, but exist because the organization is a social venue as well as a workplace. Perhaps because they are like-minded, or perhaps because they share a common problem, people voluntarily associate with each other. The result is an informal group which chooses its own structure and leader, and has its own values and norms of behaviour as well.

There is a saying in psychology that only saints and psychotics try to exist completely alone. Therefore most people have an almost irresistible urge to be part of a group. Whether it is formal or informal, a group of some sort usually gives an opportunity for a great many personal needs to be satisfied, and if this sounds remarkably like social exchange again, so it is. In return for giving something of themselves to it, people receive rewards from being members of a group. Thus by far the greater part of social exchange in organizations takes place between group members, rather than between superior and subordinate. Through this process of exchange individuals learn to conform to the sentiments, values and norms of the group, and in return have an opportunity to help shape these things. There is a huge volume of evidence to show that groups can and do enforce their own standards of behaviour on their members (Roethlisberger and Dickson, 1935; Harkins *et al.*, 1980; Albanese and Van Fleet, 1985). Since the processes at work are extremely complex, it is not possible to do more than give a brief overview here. To do so, a simplified version of a very comprehensive explanation, the 'Homans Model of Workgroup Behaviour' (Homans, 1950) will be used. This is shown in Figure 2.1, and at appropriate points in the explanation, some of the employee-relations implications of the model will be highlighted.

The model portrays some of the more significant factors that account for patterns of group behaviour. At the centre are shown the organizational effects of the behaviour, and just outside this, the behaviour itself. Working from the outside, the factors which eventually culminate in the outcomes are grouped into four stages, and each stage has an influence on the next one inwards.

Stage 1: background contextual factors

These are shown on the periphery, and there are four important factors at work. To start with there is the *physical layout, technology and job design* of the group's working environment. For example, consider a group of employees doing highly routine work on an assembly line. It might be observed that the repetitive, machine-paced nature of their jobs made social interaction difficult. Therefore, if and when it can occur, for example at break times, social interaction would be a welcome relief. Another group of factors at this stage is the *organizational policies and practices* which are built into the work system. These are largely management-determined, and consist of management's behavioral style, the organizational rules it imposes, and the assumptions about people that underpin both rules and style. With the example of the production-line workers, it could perhaps be noted that the basis of payment for their work is designed to encourage maximum effort by linking output directly with pay. This tells us something of management's assumptions about what motivates employees. These are the values, expectations, social norms and attitudes that each of them brings into the workplace. All of these background factors interact with each other to influence those in the next stage of the model.

Stage 2: required and given behaviours

These consist of the behaviours which the organization requires of the group members: the *activities* they are expected to perform, the *interactions* they are required to have with each other in doing so, and the *sentiments* the organization expects them to hold with respect to performing their tasks. With the production-line group, for example, management probably considers it essential that they do exactly what the tightly specified task demands, and confine their interactions with each other to passing on an article once work has been performed on it. The sentiments expected are probably that the maximum amount of effort will be expended on the task in hand, so that there is no stoppage of the line. Again, all of these factors interact to influence those at the next stage.

Stage 3: emergent (actual) behaviours

In the example used so far, if the group were observed very closely both on and off the production line, certain *sentiments* and *behavioral norms* might be seen to be at work. The nature of the work and the rather severe style of supervision could give rise to a tacit norm that if they are to be regarded by management as only motivated by money, then they will behave that way. They could, for example, stick together and refuse to accept any change to the job unless it is guaranteed beforehand that it will not adversely affect their earnings, and preferably increase them. In addition, certain *activities* and *interactions* could emerge to reinforce this cohesive spirit. Owing to the inability to interact in work itself, they might all take meal breaks together. Moreover, they might give each other covert support in escaping the drudgery of the line for short periods. Flowing from these, the group is likely to evolve a *social structure*. Because they are unlikely to consider their manager or supervisor to be part of the group or even a friend, the group might well have an unofficial leader or spokesperson to deal with management on their behalf. If the workforce is unionized the spokesperson role would be likely to emerge as a more official one, and be called a shop steward. Perhaps most important of all, since the group has evolved a social structure as well as stable norms and patterns of behaviour, anyone who joins it as a new member will be quickly induced to conform.

This capability to bring new and existing members into line is one of the most significant features of groups. Very few people like to be the odd one out, and so groups find it quite easy to get members to change their behaviour and conform (Asch, 1955; Milgram, 1974). Indeed, matters may well go a lot deeper than people simply conforming in behaviour. A member of a group who is induced to behave in a certain way for any length of time will find it virtually impossible to do so without adopting sentiments, feelings and attitudes which are concordant with the behaviour (Festinger, 1957). For example, Zimbardo (1973) reports an experiment in which ordinary people were required to act out the roles of warders and prisoners. When placed in groups, so strongly did the participants immerse themselves in their roles that some who were playing the parts of warders confessed to feeling something akin to hate towards the prisoner subjects. Indeed, their behaviour became so violent and aggressive that the experiment had to be terminated after two days. Thus the emergent behaviour on the part of a group can have a huge impact in terms of the outcomes, which are shown in the centre of the model.

Stage 4: outcomes

In the case used here, so long as the group members earn enough to satisfy their needs, *productivity* could well be the lowest level that they can get away with without attracting management attention. *Satisfaction* is largely found in what small opportunities exist for them to interact as a group, and *personal development* as individuals is negligible, except in finding new ways to 'beat the system'. To some extent management and supervision would probably be aware of these things. The paradox is that whilst management's assumptions about work and people play a huge part in shaping the outcomes, this is unlikely to result in the assumptions being questioned. Instead the outcomes are much more likely to be viewed by management as evidence that their assumptions were correct in the first place, which would probably result in even tighter supervision and control.

Clearly the circumstances described in this example do not apply to all employees. However, they should not be dismissed as impossible. In some industries where mass-production or assembly-line techniques are used, these conditions can and do persist (Walker and Guest, 1957; Beynon, 1973). It is perhaps for this reason that there is a greater interest in methods of work organization which allow employees a degree of autonomy and decision making in their tasks.

CASE-STUDY 2.3

Customer enquiries clerks

The group of clerks described here all work in the Customer Enquiries Department of a large public utility. It has approximately 2.5 million domestic (householder) customers, and the department is a fairly large one, headed by a Customer Enquiries Manager, with about 30 teams, each of five clerks. The organization is somewhat sensitive about its image, and for this reason the department was set up some five years ago so that the many customer queries could be answered in a courteous and efficient way by specialist staff. One of the five clerks is designated team leader, and is paid a grade higher than the other four. Each group of five clerks is located at a pentagonal set of desks as shown in Figure 2.2.

The team deals with a specific geographic area of about 60 000 customers. All incoming telephone calls are routed through a central exchange, and when the customer's address has been obtained, the call is switched through to the appropriate team. The team's basic task is to answer all enquiries from domestic customers. These can be very simple matters, such as a billing query or making an appointment for a service call, but sometimes they are more complex and require technical knowledge. In the latter case the team leader usually takes the call off one of the other clerks, and if necessary makes contact with one of the organization's technical departments for specialist advice. About 80 % of all customer queries can be answered on the spot over the telephone, but some require an answer in writing. In these cases, and contrary to the normal practice throughout the rest of the organization where only departmental heads can sign external letters, the clerks are allowed to sign their own. The aim is that customers should not feel that they are dealing with a faceless bureaucracy, but will have an identifiable point of contact.

The job is a secure one and regular update training is given so that the clerks have the knowledge to answer queries. Each clerk has a visual display unit (VDU) connected to the organization's mainframe computer on which customer records are stored. Thus a customer's personal record can be very quickly accessed to answer queries. For other information such as product prices, service charges or technical information, each pentagonal work station has a rotating carousel in its centre which is shared by the team. This contains manuals that give the required information. Each work station is required to be manned by at least three clerks at all times and therefore staggered meal breaks are necessary. For refreshments at other times, there is a vending machine near at hand, and usually the team members take it in turns to fetch coffee for the whole team.

The team in question is composed of women, all of whom live in a nearby private residential area. Joyce, the team leader, is in her mid 40s and returned to work about five years ago after her only child left home. Two of the others, Pam and Jayne, are married women in their late 30s whose children are at school, but old enough to care for themselves. Another, Anne, is married but as yet has no children. The final member, Mary, is engaged and soon to be married. About once each month the

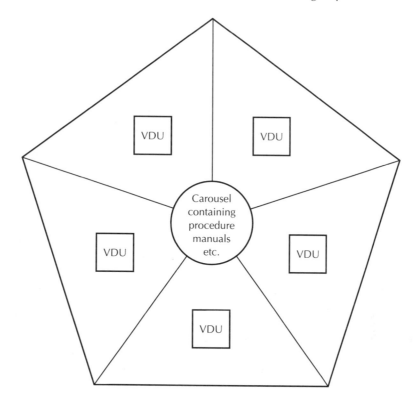

Figure 2.2 Desk layout for customer enquiries clerks (Case-study 2.3).

group meets outside work for a social night out, sometimes with their husbands, but more often just the team members.

Question

In the light of the above information, use the Homans model to analyse what you would expect the emergent behaviour, social structure and outcomes of the work group to be. Give reasons why you would expect this to be the case.

Conclusions and preview

In outline there have been several main themes in this chapter. First, because individuals are unique and differ in many respects, they all bring their own personal attributes to the work situation. Second, the legal concept of the employment relationship is that each employee has a personal contract with the employing organization. This view, however, has its shortcomings, primarily because it relegates the employment relationship to a matter of simple economic exchange. Therefore, since the relationship is much richer and more complex than this, the social exchange perspective can be a more fruitful way of portraying its nature. The final theme has been that the work situation contains very powerful forces which induce people to abandon some of their individuality. Organizational structures bring people together into groups or departments, and this inevitably means that they develop a sense of collective identity about some matters. The net result is that many of the issues in employee relations are virtually certain to be collective ones.

Some of the implications of these matters will surface again in the chapters that follow. In the next chapter, for example, collective organizations of employees are considered in greater detail, and in Chapters 9, 10 and 11 the ways in which the interests of employees are represented collectively will be considered. When these subsequent chapters are reached the reader is therefore asked to remember that whilst trade unions are a much more formal method of collectivization than the workgroup, it is the sense of collective identity that arises in workgroups which gives them their source of power and support. In Chapter 5, when some of the laws governing the conduct of employee relations are considered, the contract of employment will emerge again. Similarly in Chapter 6, which deals with the handling of discipline and grievance, a matter briefly referred to earlier in this chapter will be reconsidered. This is the way that subjective judgements are made about the reasons for an individual's behaviour. Finally, the topic of individualism will resurface in Chapter 12. Here a range of management-led initiatives are described, some of which are aimed at individualizing the employment relationship.

Further reading

Blau P. (1964). *Exchange and Power in Social Life.* New York, Wiley.
   The most comprehensive statement and description yet of social exchange theory.

Davis J. H. (1969). *Group Performance*. Reading, MA: Addison-Wesley.

A short but extremely comprehensive book which thoroughly covers most aspects of group functioning, including the effects of the group on its individual members.

Fox A. (1974). *Beyond Contract: Work Power and Trust Relations*. London: Faber and Faber.

Arguably one of the most important books written on the subject of employee relations, and one which makes wide use of social exchange theory to explain relationships.

Organ D. W. and Bateman T. S. (1991). *Organizational Behavior* 4th edn. Homewood IL: Irwin

A comprehensive textbook on the subject of organizational behaviour, which includes a sound basic coverage of individual differences and group processes.

Homans G.C. (1950). *The Human Group*. New York: Harcourt Brace and World

A very comprehensive description of the internal dynamics of workgroups and factors shaping their behaviour.

Whincup M. (1990). *Modern Employment Law: A Guide to Job Security and Safety*. Oxford: Heinemann

Basic book on employment law, which has useful and easily understood chapters on the contract of employment.

3

Collective organizations of
employees

Introduction

This chapter picks up from the previous one, and deals with collective organizations of employees. Since these can take many different forms, the three major types are contrasted to highlight some of their main characteristics. Trade unions, which are by far the most important type, are examined next, and their origins and development are traced, together with the current structure of British trade unionism. Discussion then moves to the functions that trade unions perform, the way in which a large national trade union is typically organized, and the all-important question of how useful trade unions are to different types of employees.

Since the focus of this book is on matters at the level of individual firms and enterprises, the remainder of the chapter deals with the trade unionism of the workplace. The nature of trade unions at this level is examined, to explain why they can sometimes be very different from their parent organizations. Following this the structure of workplace trade union organization is described, together with an examination of the roles and functions of shop stewards. Finally, some of the factors that can shape the characteristics of trade unionism at this level are discussed, and recent changes are noted.

Alternative forms of collective organization

It would probably be impossible to estimate how many British employees belong to collective organizations of one sort or another. The only reliable figures are for bodies which are registered either as professional associations or trade unions, and this would exclude many of the smaller, in-house associations confined to a single employer. It must also be pointed out that not all employees join collective organizations. Neither are there any watertight rules for predicting whether they are likely to do so. There are, however, some general trends. Collectivization is much more common in large organizations than small ones, and more prevalent in manufacturing than in many of the service industries. The density of collective membership (the percentage of eligible employees who are actually members) tends to be higher in the public sector. Collective organization is more prevalent amongst manual workers than salaried staffs, and also more common with men than women. Nevertheless, there are exceptions even to these trends. There are some very large organizations where there is no collective, two notable examples being Marks & Spencer and IBM.

Although there are many types of collective organizations to which employees can belong, there are three major categories. Whilst these can be poles apart in terms of their rules and articles of association, in their own distinctive ways they can all represent the collective interests of their members by playing a part in regulating terms and conditions of the employment relationship. Within each category there is inevitably bound to be a great deal of variation between individual associations. As such the reader is asked to bear in mind that 'ideal type' descriptions are given in what follows. That is, because the descriptions are designed to contrast the three types, their differences are portrayed in a somewhat exaggerated way.

Professional associations

One accepted definition of a professional association is 'any organization which directly aims at the improvement of any aspects of professional practice: for example by providing a qualification, by controlling conduct, by coordinating technical information, by pressing for better conditions of employment' (Millerson, 1964, p. 33) The official aims of most of these bodies are derived from a bygone era when their members were largely fee earners in independent practice, and the major role of an association was to coordinate their activities as a form of labour cartel (Prandy *et al.*, 1983). These days, however, many professionals are in paid employment; for example, in the public service where collective bodies such as the British Medical Association and British Dental Association are extremely active in protecting and improving the working conditions and remuneration of their members. Indeed both of these associations use many of the same methods as trade unions to do so. However, since many, but not all, professional bodies are qualifying associations as well, to some extent they can also regulate the number of new entrants to the profession. This gives them a very powerful means of keeping the market value of their members' services high, which interestingly was the very tactic used by the early unions of skilled tradesmen. Thus it is with some logic that professional associations have been dubbed 'the craft unions of a different social group' (Bain *et al.*, 1973).

Staff associations

The term 'staff association' is usually applied to in-house collective organizations that cater for employees who all work for the same employer. However, some care is needed in using the expression. In certain parts of the civil service, the term is used to describe independent trade unions that cater for particular grades of staff. Nevertheless, as the name implies, they usually represent only salaried staff, and are therefore more prevalent in organizations such as banks, building societies and insurance companies (Prandy *et al.*, 1983).

In trade-union circles the term 'staff association' is often used in a highly pejorative way. For example, it is frequently asserted that by their very nature they are under the control of the employer, and lack the independence to represent their members' interests properly. Most associations, however, would hotly deny this (Morell and Smith, 1971), and it should be noted that the evidence on the matter is mixed. In legal terms, some staff associations are registered as trade unions, and to do this they have to satisfy a government official (the Certification Officer) that they are independent of the employer. Nevertheless, it is probably fair to say that an in-house association can hardly be expected to be as independent as an externally based trade union. Thus perhaps the most penetrating observation comes from a study of white-collar unions, in which staff associations were also examined. The majority were formed at the initiative of the employer, possibly to head off the entry of trade unions, and only one was found which was genuinely independent. Most did not engage in negotiating the salaries and other service conditions of their members, but were merely consulted by management (Bain, 1970).

Trade unions

In employee relations, this is by far the most significant and important type of collective organization, and is legally defined as:

> 'an organization, whether permanent or temporary, which consists mainly of workers of one or more descriptions and is an organization whose principal purposes include the regulation of relations between workers of that description and employers or employers' association' (TULRA, 1974, Section 28)

Clearly this is a very broad definition, and because there are significant differences between many organizations, all of which can be classified as trade unions, it needs to be. For this reason, in industrial relations literature it is usual to classify trade unions into different types. One way of doing this is on the basis of the type of employee that they represent. For example, the traditional classification is into **craft unions**, which are restricted to craftsmen that have served an apprenticeship, **industrial unions**, which theoretically represent all employees of any grade or occupation in a single industry, and **general unions**, which represent any employee of any grade in any industry. Although this is appealing in its simplicity, the scheme unfortunately has a number of shortcomings.

To start with, because there are a number of unions which restrict entry to salaried staffs, for completeness a fourth type, **white-collar unions**, would need to be added. The biggest problem, however, is that in today's conditions the scheme can be extremely misleading. There have been a large number of trade-union mergers, and on top of this the technologies and industries on which union categories were based have vastly changed (Clegg, 1976). Most of the original craft unions now represent unskilled and semi-skilled workers as well, and most unions of all types have their own white-collar sections. Thus it would be virtually impossible to find any trade union in the UK that exactly matched the original specifications. For this reason other schemes such as **open unions** (those which recruit over a wide range of occupations and grades) and **closed unions** (those which restrict entry) have been suggested (Turner, 1962).

Perhaps the most significant criticism of all schemes of classification, however, is that whilst they are of interest in academic terms, to those who belong to trade unions, or to those who have to deal with them on a day-to-day basis, they probably have little practical significance. For most people, it is what trade unions do and how they go about doing it that are by far the most important considerations. In part these are a function of their origins and development, and are described next.

Trade unions in Great Britain

Origins and development

The current form of British trade unionism has emerged from a complex inter-action of social, legal and economic variables. Trade unions are largely a conse-quence of the factory system which developed in the industrial revolution. Until 1825 when the Combination Acts of 1799 and 1800 were replaced with the Combination Laws, most trade-union activities were illegal. Until then, just about all that working people were allowed to do in terms of collective action was to form mutual benefit or 'friendly societies' (Pelling, 1987). With the repeal of the Combination Acts, however, trade unions were allowed to exist, but not allowed to engage in striking, which was still illegal. Thus they were unable to pursue their objectives in a free way (Hawkins, 1981).

These early unions were very locally based, and almost exclusively con-fined to skilled craftsmen. However, in 1851 the first forerunner of a national trade union as we know things today was formed. This was the Amalgamated Society of Engineers (ASE), from which developed the present Amalgamated Engineering and Electrical Union (AEEU). Its unique feature was a structure of officials from national down to local branch level, and some of these officers were employed full-time on trade-union activities. This form of organization, known as 'New Model Unionism', spread fairly rapidly to other unions.

One of the major strengths of these unions was their control of the appren-ticeship system. As such, skilled craftsmen could regulate the number of work-ers in a particular trade, which kept their market value high and meant that they were not as vulnerable to recessionary periods as the unskilled. In the 1880s there was a very severe recession, and labourers, who had seen the advantages that craftsmen had gained from collectivizing, also banded themselves together in large numbers. The resulting organizations were the forerunners of today's large general unions; for example, the Transport and General Workers Union (TGWU), and General Municipal and Boilermakers and Allied Trade Union (GMBATU). By the late 19th century, embryonic unions of non-manual workers also began to appear. These were mainly in public-sector occupations such as school teaching and local government staff. However, private-sector occupations such as clerks and draughtsmen also eventually unionized.

From their inception, trade unions faced laws which were hostile to their very existence. Prior to the Union Act of 1871 and the Conspiracy and Protection of Property Act of 1875, trade unions could legally be regarded as criminal conspiracies, since restraining trade was a criminal act, and there was an assumption in law that two or more persons acting in contemplation or fur-therance of a trade dispute were purposely acting in restraint of trade. Even when the Acts of 1871 and 1875 were passed, and the assumption of criminal conspira-cy was removed, trade unions were still open to civil claims of conspiracy, this time for inducing their members to breach their individual contracts of employment. It was not until the passing of the Trades Disputes Act of 1906 that this restraint was completely removed; an Act which gave them immunity in this respect, and also made peaceful picketing lawful.

No account of trade-union development would be complete without some mention of the Trades Union Congress (TUC). Essentially this is an organ of trade-union coordination and cooperation, and not as is sometimes assumed a body which has automatic authority over all trade unions. Indeed, the only authority which it has in this respect is that which its member unions voluntarily cede to it. Like trade unions themselves, it has its origins in local organizations, **trades councils**, which were formed to coordinate activities in cities throughout Great Britain. In 1886 a national body to coordinate their activities was formed, and because the legal climate in the late 19th century was extremely hostile towards trade unions, from the start it became a vehicle to pursue legislative reform.

In 1871 the TUC formed its parliamentary committee, a body which subsequently became the TUC General Council in 1920. Initially, support was given to the more radical Liberal members of parliament, who were more sympathetic to trade unions. However, in 1893 the Independent Labour Party was formed. In 1906 the TUC formed a labour representation committee, and 29 parliamentary seats were won in that year's election. The committee subsequently changed its name to the Labour Party, and became a separate organization. Thus because today's Parliamentary Labour Party was created by the trade-union movement, the two still maintain very close links.

The structure of British trade unionism

In industrial-relations literature, the term 'structure' is usually applied to the trade-union movement as a whole, and covers such features as which unions represent certain groups of workers. The current structure is one of the legacies of the rather piecemeal pattern of development of trade unionism, in which at different points in time successive groups of workers recognized that they had interests in common, and collectivized to pursue them. As noted, craft unions of skilled workers came first, and had the basic aim of preserving the better conditions for themselves, which to some extent they achieved by controlling the apprenticeship system. The unskilled, who came next, had no craft lines on which to organize themselves, and had to rely more on size and industrial action for their bargaining power. Finally, white-collar unions, and in more recent times a managerial variant of these, had an imperative to collectivize in what they saw as the erosion of their position and privileges *vis-à-vis* manual workers.

Another factor which has a bearing on the current structure of trade unionism is that whilst trade unions were developing across the past 150 years, whole industries have changed. Thus new trades and skills have appeared, and others have disappeared. In addition, for reasons which will be explained later, trade unionism as a whole, and some trade unions in particular, have experienced periods of growth and decline. Both of these factors have affected membership boundaries, and there has been a process of merger and amalgamation as unions have tried to keep pace with industrial changes. A prime example is the changes that have taken place in what were originally craft unions in the engineering industry. In the 1920s increasing mechanization gave rise to an influx of semi-skilled workers. Strictly speaking, because they had not served an apprenticeship, these workers were not eligible to join craft unions. However, to protect their territory, the unions changed their rules to admit them. Later on in World War II, when much semi-skilled work was done by female labour, the unions had to change their rules again to admit women. Therefore, the historical picture is one of constant flux and change, and perhaps the simplest way to portray matters is with reference to Tables 3.1 and 3.2.

The most obvious feature that emerges from Table 3.1 is a progressive decline in the number of trade unions, largely as a result of mergers and amalgamations. This is a trend which is forecast to continue, and will clearly result in a much smaller number of large unions (Neill, 1988). Indeed, the process is already well advanced, and as can be seen by examining the dispersion of membership shown in Table 3.2, the ten largest unions already account for over sixty per cent of total union membership.

Table 3.1 Trade unions, membership and density for selected years from 1900 onwards.

Year	A Number of trade unions	B Total trade-union membership (millions)	C Working population (millions) See note	D Trade-union density (B/C) %
1900	1323	2.0	16.0	13.0
1910	1269	2.6	17.6	15.0
1920	1384	8.3	18.5	45.0
1930	1121	4.8	19.1	25.0
1940	1004	6.6	20.0	33.0
1950	732	9.3	21.1	44.0
1960	664	9.8	22.8	43.0
1970	543	11.2	23.4	48.0
1979	453	13.3	24.3	55.0
1987	330	10.5	21.9	47.9
1989	309	10.2	22.9	44.6

Note: In official statistics trade union density is calculated as total trade union members divided by 'the UK workforce in employment', which includes members of the armed forces who are not allowed to unionize, the self-employed and unemployed both of whom are unlikely to unionize, and persons on government training schemes. This can be extremely misleading, and so here density is calculated by dividing total trade-union membership by working population, i.e. employees in employment.

Table 3.2   Membership distribution of British trade unions, 1992.

Size band (thousands)	Number of trade unions in band	Membership total of all trade unions in band (thousands)	Percentage of all UK trade-union members
Over 250 000	10	6131	60.4
100 000 to 249 999	13	2032	20.0
25 000 to 99 999	31	1372	13.5
10 000 to 24 999	17	291	2.9
2500 to 9999	45	216	2.1
500 to 2499	68	95	0.9
Less than 500	125	23	0.2
Totals	309	10 160	100.0

Another point which can be seen in Table 3.1 is that there have been periods of fairly rapid union growth, and some of decline, the most recent of which occurred from 1979 onwards. Perhaps the most thorough explanation of these changing fortunes is given by Bain and Price (1983), who identify a number of variables which have affected the potential for trade-union growth. These are shown in a simplified way in Figure 3.1, where the variables are clustered into three major groups.

The first group, *contextual variables*, consists of factors such as management ideologies, workforce structures and social values. If there is a prevailing management ideology that considers trade unions to be an unwarranted intrusion, this will obviously result in opposition to them gaining entry into firms. Because manual workers in most industries have always shown a higher tendency to unionize, and white-collar workers have been somewhat less willing to join, workforce structures can be an important variable. Finally, social values are important in that the more that unions are accepted as a normal part of society, the more that joining becomes a naturally accepted act.

The second group of factors are *economic variables*. For example, as the real prices of goods rise, employees tend to unionize to protect their standards of living. When real wages rise, people tend to give the credit to trade unions, which reinforces the predisposition of people to join. Another economic factor is unemployment. If people are in work and perceive unemployment as a threat, they join trade unions for defensive reasons. However, if they work for an anti-union employer, and fear that their membership might be penalized, there can be a tendency in the reverse direction.

The final group of factors are *organizational variables*, such as increasing concentration of ownership into large organizations and the social demographics of workforce populations. Unionization is much more common in larger organizations, and with the possible exception of the public sector, unionization is usually much lower in a workforce that is predominantly female.

From their analysis, Bain and Price draw the conclusion that since the

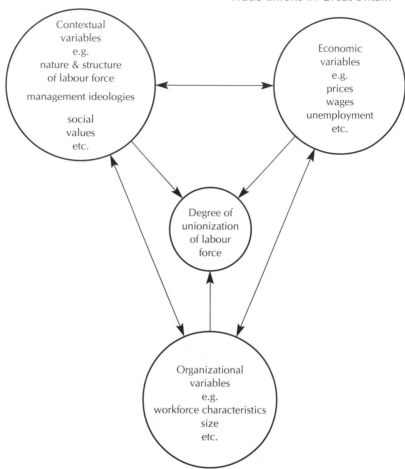

Figure 3.1   Influences on level of trade-union membership (after G.S. Bain and R. Price, 1983).

Second World War, these variables have had different effects in different sectors of the economy. In the public service and manufacturing, where trade-union growth was highest, economic factors, favourable public attitudes to trade unions and favourable employer policies all combined to give a major expansion. However, in sectors such as private services, although the first two factors were as positive as elsewhere, they were not strong enough to overcome the hostility of employers.

Whilst this analysis largely explains matters in the past, its most important implications are perhaps for the future. In the recessionary periods since 1980 the greatest job losses have been in those areas where union growth took place in earlier years. Any compensatory increase in employment has been in white-collar work and among females, and these are the very areas where trade unions found it impossible to expand, even in the earlier years when conditions favoured growth. Moreover, these are the areas in which any future employment growth will most likely occur, and so to say the least, the scope for future trade-union recovery looks bleak.

The functions of trade unions

If the rule book of any trade union is examined it will reveal a bewildering array of aims and objectives. Strictly speaking, some of these are means rather than ends, and regardless of rule books the aim of most British unions can be more simply summarized as '. . . to defend and if possible improve their members' terms and conditions of employment' (Flanders, 1970, p. 42).

There are, however, a wide variety of ways and means which can be used to pursue this aim, and the ones which are emphasized are likely to vary from time to time. One way that has been used to portray the differences between trade unions in terms of their aims and methods is in terms of their **character**. However, this can be a confusing term. In psychology, it is usually taken to denote the visible aspects of personality, and in industrial relations it is used in a rather similar way to indicate the fundamental nature of a trade union. For example, Blackburn and Prandy (1965) encapsulate character into an umbrella term 'unionateness', which is the extent to which an organization is committed to the general principles and ideology of trade unionism. This, so they assert, can be expressed along seven dimensions:

(1) Whether a given body declares itself to be a trade union;
(2) Whether it is registered as a trade union;
(3) Whether it is affiliated to the TUC;
(4) Whether it is affiliated to the Labour Party;
(5) Whether it is independent of employers for the purposes of negotiation;
(6) Whether it regards collective bargaining and the protection of members' interests as employees as a major function;
(7) Whether it is prepared to be militant, using all forms of industrial action which may be effective.

Problematically, the most frequent use of terms such as character and unionateness has been in connection with white-collar trade unions, often to assert in some way that they are not 'proper' unions in the true sense of the word. For example, for many years they remained peripheral to the movement, were extremely restrained in their activities, and tended to distance themselves from methods used by other trade unions. Indeed, in the 1960s they were described as 'an army that shows up well on the parade ground, but about whose willingness to shoot there must remain some doubt' (Routh, 1966, p. 201).

These days, however, a degree of militancy can often be found in white-collar unions, especially in the public sector. In any event the term 'character' can be problematic in other respects. It implies that there is only one set of legitimate criteria against which a trade union can be judged, and that this is something to do with the way it pursues its aims. As pointed out earlier, different unions arose at different times to represent very discrete sectional interests. As such, each one carries the legacy of its own history, and to some extent this will be reflected in its actions now. This means that each union is in some respects unique, and there can be no universally accepted criteria against which they can be judged as 'proper' or not. Therefore, it is sufficient to note that there are many ways in which even very similar aims can be pursued, and a general classification of these is given in what follows.

Economic regulation is one of the prime activities of most trade unions. That is, they will usually pursue a policy of trying to secure the highest real wages that are consistent with full or high employment of their members. To do so, however, will inevitably mean that they affect the level of profits in firms. Indeed, arguments rage about whether their pursuit of wages and protection of jobs has meant that they are also responsible for certain features of the British economy such as low productivity. Whilst it can perhaps be expected that politicians, who are always ready to identify a scapegoat, should assert that they are responsible for many of the economic ills of the UK, amongst serious economists opinion is divided on this matter. There are some who argue that this is the case (Roberts, 1987; Metcalf, 1988). Conversely, there are those who point to evidence from the USA which suggests that trade unions are associated with higher productivity in firms (Nolan and Marginson, 1988), primarily because their presence raises the calibre of management (Bemmels, 1987; Cameron, 1987).

For most of the time, and in the majority of trade unions, **job regulation** would probably be regarded as their most significant role. It can be defined as 'the making and administering of rules which regulate employment relationships, whether these are seen as formal or informal, structured or unstructured' (Bain and Clegg, 1974, p. 95). At face value this might seem to be simply bargaining over the exchange of rewards for services which was described in the previous chapter. However, job regulation can be said to serve other important functions as well. Because it gives trade-union members the opportunity to become the joint authors of rules that lay down the rights and obligations of both employers and employees, job regulation can also be seen as a vehicle of industrial democracy (Flanders, 1970).

Another way of pursuing their aims, which clearly influences their ability to use the two means specified above, is **power holding**. Indeed, a trade union's credibility and persuasiveness is ultimately underpinned by its potential capability to take retaliatory action if no attention is paid to what it says. Thus a trade union's first and foremost means to pursue its aims is to become an agency of power (Hyman, 1975).

From their earliest days trade unions realized that to protect or advance their member's interests could require that they pursue **wider social change** (Jackson, 1982). For this reason, one of their important roles has become political lobbying and pressure tactics, usually to try to persuade the government of the day to legislate in a way that benefits all employees. A prime example is the passing of the Health and Safety at Work Act 1974. Until then health and safety legislation was extremely piecemeal, and very difficult to enforce. Although responsible employers have always been conscious of the need to protect the health and safety of their employees, to do so costs money, and puts the responsible employer at a potential disadvantage to the less scrupulous. For a long time trade unions pressed for legislation that would require all employers to observe the same standards, the result of which was this Act.

Trade-union government

Whilst structure is used to denote patterns of organization in the whole trade-union movement, the term 'government' describes the internal structures, management and organization of individual trade unions.

One result of the mergers and amalgamations described earlier is large trade unions which have memberships drawn from a wide range of occupations, and which can be highly dispersed throughout the country. For this reason, all but the smallest usually have a federal system of government. There are, however, several ways in which federalism can be used. Geographical federalism gives some autonomy to districts or regions. Alternatively a union can adopt a federal system which gives a degree of autonomy to its different occupational groups. The most complex system of all is where both geographic and occupational federalism exist together. With some variations most of the larger unions follow this principle, for example GMBATU, the TGWU and NALGO (the National and Local Government Officers Association). Using the latter as an example, the government of the union is portrayed diagrammatically in Figure 3.2.

NALGO is exclusively a non-manual trade union which organizes parts of the public sector and what before privatization were the nationalized industries. It has eight major groupings of members: universities, local government, new towns (now largely disappeared), the National Health Service, electricity, gas, water and transport industries. With the exception of universities and the National Health Service, it is the dominant white-collar union wherever it has members. For reasons which are rooted in its history, the branch is its fundamental unit of organization, and in the majority of cases there is only one for each employing organization. Even where this is not the case, branch organization commonly follows management structure to cover sub-units of the employer. All branches relate to the parent union through one of NALGO's twelve regional subdivisions: District Councils. All branches within a district are entitled to seats on the District Council, and at this level a number of representatives from each service are chosen to form District Service Conditions Committees.

Within the confines of national policy, local service conditions committees can set their own objectives, policies and strategies for pursuit at district level.

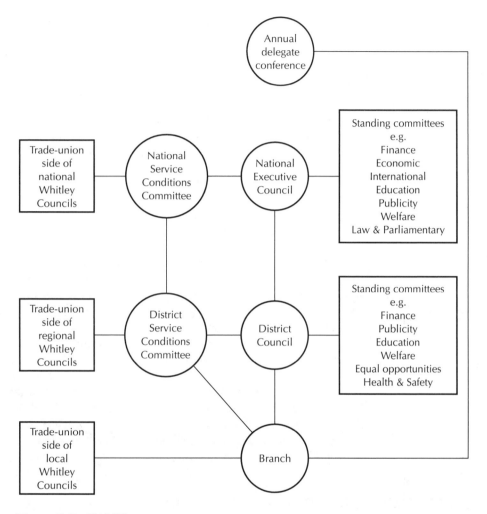

Figure 3.2 NALGO structures.

To do so a number of members of the committee are selected as the trade union side of local joint forums of employers and employees: provincial Whitley Councils. The practical importance of these local joint forums varies somewhat in different services. In local government where there is normally a single trade-union branch for each local authority, provincial Whitley Councils tend to be of less importance as a negotiating forum than the machinery within the employing organization; usually called the Joint Consultative or Local Joint Committee. In gas, electricity and water industries, the regional machinery, usually called Regional Joint Councils, is much more significant because this is the level at which the whole employing organization is represented. In the water industry national pay bargaining was abandoned some years ago, and on privatization the industry was broken up into independent companies. Thus Regional Joint

Councils are very significant bodies. In services other than water, District Service Conditions Committees also elect one of their members to a National Service Conditions Committee, from which is drawn the national negotiating team.

In addition to service conditions machinery, District Councils also maintain standing committees, that is, Finance and General Purposes, Publicity, Education and so on. The role of these is broadly to implement district policies with respect to their respective functions, and to aid branches in organizing activities beyond their scope. Each district also elects a number of its members for service on the National Executive Council of the union. At national level a structure of service and standing committees exists which, with some additions, mirrors that at district level.

The government of NALGO, although fairly complex, has a number of advantages for a trade union that represents employees in such a wide diversity of settings. In each service there is a hierarchy of organizing units which allows rank-and-file members of a particular industry to become involved in formulating and negotiating their own aims and objectives. At the same time, all the different services are part of a larger parent organization to which they can look for support. Members in diverse industries can benefit from the economies of scale available to a large organization, and this allows the union to pursue aims which are common to all services, whilst at the same time, each service can exercise self-determination on matters which affect it alone.

For example, the union employs full-time legal, publicity and education specialists, who provide much valuable advice and help to the membership. In addition the union has its own research officers who are able to do much of the detailed background work which is necessary to prepare a successful pay claim. Finally, branch officers and stewards in employing organizations are supported by front-line full-time officers who can give direct support and advice.

Democracy and representativeness

Because trade unions are often large and diverse, there is sometimes a disparity between national policies and actions and the feelings of the rank-and-file membership. The overall direction of activities is invariably in the hands of a small number of high officials who, although they are lay members, hold quite different views from the average rank-and-file member. Thus a question which is often raised about trade-union government is whether it is genuinely democratic. To some extent the whole question can be traced back to Michels' famous Iron Law of Oligarchy (Michels, 1915), which foretold of an inevitable divorce of trade-union leaders from those whom they represent, even to the point where they might pursue their own interests by siding with employers rather than the membership. It is highly unlikely that the truth of this will ever be uncovered, and in any event, because the word 'democracy' can be interpreted in a rather fluid way, the essential question often comes down to what it is taken to mean. If the criterion of democracy is whether or not rank-and-file members of trade unions have an adequate opportunity to select those who direct matters on their behalf, the answer must be an unequivocal yes. With a few notable exceptions which attract a disproportionate amount of attention from a Press which is usually hostile, most trade unions have an impeccable record in this respect (Edelstein and Warner, 1975; Donaldson and Warner, 1974). Virtually all of them have their ballots for the national leadership supervised by independent bodies, usually by the well-respected Electoral Reform Society. Even though the proportion of members voting in elections is usually abysmally low, this in no way detracts from the democratic nature of the election. Members are given the opportunity to take part in the selection process.

A more important criterion, however, is perhaps whether the rank and file have an opportunity to shape national policy in the first place. In most unions it is not the national leadership which is the supreme policy-making body, but the national delegate conference. These conferences take place every one or two years, and the national leadership merely oversees the implementation of policy between conferences. At branch meetings, rank-and-file members invariably have the opportunity to instruct their conference delegates on how to vote. Again, although attendance at these meetings is often low, the opportunity to shape policy is readily presented. Thus by either criterion, trade unions must be regarded as democratic bodies.

The usefulness of trade unions to employees

The mere availability of a collective body does not necessarily mean that employees will flock to join it. They have to see it as advantageous to do so, and even where large numbers do join, it can be dangerous to infer too much from this. It is not synonymous with wholehearted support or active participation, and to put matters another way, there is a vast difference between 'joining' and 'joining in'.

Indeed, the whole matter is considered in a very penetrating way in Olson's (1965) analysis of voluntary associations. He points out that there is a paradox with voluntary associations such as trade unions. The addition of a single member adds little to the strength of the organization, but the benefits to anyone of joining are strongly related to the number of people that are already members. Moreover, there are costs as well as benefits associated with membership. Joining means that the person has to pay subscriptions and observe the association's rules. Where a firm is already unionized, normally all employees (not just trade-union members) would be likely to reap the benefits of advances negotiated by the union. Thus the most rational course of action for any individual employee would be to become a 'free rider', that is, to take the benefits of membership, but avoid its costs by not joining. Indeed, even when they join, there is still a risk that they will seek to avoid some of the costs. They might, for example, refuse to take part in a strike; something that is made a lot easier if there are large numbers of non-members in the workplace. Therefore, even though the addition of a single individual adds little to its strength and attractiveness, a trade union has a vested interest in pulling all employees into membership. Here Olson points out that it can employ either one or the other, or indeed a combination, of two distinct strategies to induce people to join. First, it can increase the benefits that arise from being a member, or even make certain crucial benefits contingent on membership. For example, individual protection in grievance, disciplinary and redundancy situations, and the ancillary benefits such as legal services and cheap mortgages that many trade unions now provide, are confined to members. To some extent there is evidence that this actually works. Risk-aversion is known to be a strong motive for joining trade unions (Jones, 1981; Guest and Dewe, 1988).

Another strategy is to find ways of either reducing the costs of membership or increasing the costs of non-membership. A traditional way of doing the latter is the device of the 'agency' or 'closed' shop. This makes union membership a condition of employment, and effectively raises the cost of non-membership by the simple expedient of 'no union card, no job'. However, the current legal position on closed shops is extremely complex, and it has now become near impossible for one to exist unless it is with an employer's connivance. Whilst many employers value the stability that a trade union brings, the closed shop is a source of power that few, if any, would willingly pass into a union's hands. Perhaps most important of all, in addition to the relative costs and benefits associated with membership, there is an even more basic factor which has a bearing on the willingness of people to join. This is the union's potential usefulness to them, which is perhaps most easily understood if it is expressed as a question. Given that people have interests which they need to advance or protect, to what extent is the trade union a potentially useful vehicle for doing so?

Usefulness, which has been explored extensively by Crouch (1982), is really a function of two factors that are largely independent of each other. The first is the capability of employees to use other means to advance or protect their interests, or to put matters another way, the extent to which they are dependent on acting collectively to do so. The second is whether a trade union is easily accessible for use by employees. The two factors are shown diagrammatically in Figure 3.3, and can be applied to different groups of employees to explain what Crouch describes as 'the logic of joining'.

Starting at the top left-hand corner and moving clockwise, *professionals* have a powerful position in the labour market, and thus have little dependence on their associations to protect their interests. Nevertheless, their organizations are extremely easy to use, and joining often gives access to useful resources. *Skilled craftsmen*, who do not have quite such a powerful market position, are

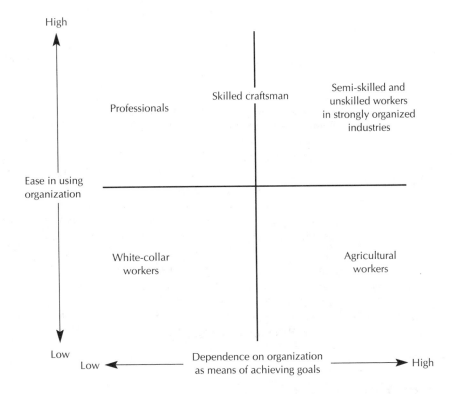

Figure 3.3 Usefulness of collective organizations (C. Crouch, 1982).

somewhat more dependent on their union. Like professionals, their unions are highly restrictive about entry criteria and are therefore comparatively easy to use to advance their interests. The *semi-skilled and unskilled* have a fairly weak position in the labour market, and, therefore, a strong need to act collectively. In situations such as mass-production industries where they are found together in large numbers, and can easily organize themselves, the union is relatively easy to use. At the bottom right are *agricultural workers*, who once again have a weak position in the labour market and a strong need for unions to protect and advance their interests. However, because they are dispersed, they find access to the union very difficult. Indeed, it is for this reason that the State found it necessary to sponsor the formation of the Agricultural Wages Board to provide a facility for their collective representation. Since this is one of a number of wages councils, the functions of which will be described in more detail in Chapter 5, its role will not be elaborated here. Suffice it to say that there are many other employees who are also in a weak labour market position and, like agricultural workers, are highly dispersed. They also find it extremely difficult to organize themselves in order to be able to work out terms and conditions of employment on a collective basis. Wages councils provide circumstances where this can happen by bringing together employee's and employer's representatives at the State's behest. Finally, at the bottom left are *white-collar workers* who, because their prospects as individuals were traditionally much higher than other groups, had a low dependence on unions. Moreover in the past, except in the public sector, they were seldom to be found together in large enough numbers to make the accessibility of the union easy. However, in the past two decades things have changed somewhat. Their traditional individualized career expectations have not been so easily realized, and white-collar unions have grown accordingly (Bain, 1970; Childs, 1985).

The two factors in the model only indicate a general predisposition for employees to see trade unions as more or less useful, and irrespective of usefulness there is another factor which can influence the decision to join. A lot can depend upon the prevailing attitudes of an employer. If an employer encourages or shows no opposition to union membership, employees have little to lose by joining. Indeed, the crucial factor in white-collar union growth was almost certainly a period of employer assent and encouragement (Bain, 1970). However, employers can sometimes feel the opposite, and to inhibit employees from joining, it is seldom necessary for them actually to oppose trade union membership. It can simply be enough, as in the case of IBM, to indicate that no need is seen for a trade union (Dickson *et al.*, 1988).

CASE-STUDY 3.1

Trade unions: attraction and recruitment of members

Explaining levels of membership

1. The following groups of workers are amongst those where trade-union membership is usually very high. What factors do you feel account for this?

   Manual workers in the public services
   White-collar workers in the public services
   Manual workers in shipbuilding
   Manual dockworkers
   Coal mining
   All manual workers in metalworking trades

2. The following are amongst groups of workers where union membership is often very low, and sometimes non-existent. What factors do you feel account for this?

> Hotels
> Catering
> Retailing
> Textile workers
> Insurance, banking and finance
>
> 3. Assume that you are a full-time officer of a national trade union that represents non-manual workers. You are about to embark on a recruitment campaign designed to attract middle and junior managers in private industry into membership. What attributes and policies do you feel that the union would need to emphasize to make membership appeal to these people?
>
> ### Pursuing objectives
>
> 4. Consider the five types of collective associations of employees shown in Figure 3.3. Assume that all the groups wish to protect and if possible advance their interests in terms of earnings and working conditions. Which of the following tactics do you feel are likely to be the most successful in pursuit of these aims, and how might the tactics be used?
>
>   i   Complete individualism – every man for himself.
>   ii   Restricting entry to the occupation to maintain a market scarcity of that occupational skill.
>   iii Agreeing job boundaries with other occupational groups so that each performs its own functions.
>   iv   A cooperative working relationship with the management of employing organizations.
>   v   Mild industrial action such as overtime bans.
>   vi   Mass striking.

Trade unions in the enterprise

There can often be a significant difference between trade unions as national institutions and the trade-union organization that is found in the workplace. To most employees, the real trade union is not some remote national body, but the organization found at work (Goldthorpe *et al.*, 1968). For a great many, if not the majority, any attachment they have to it is mainly for instrumental reasons; that is, in terms of the pay-offs that it delivers. At this level workgroups are in face-to-face contact with their union, can shape its actions, and therefore can determine what particular pay-offs it pursues. More importantly, the rank-and-file membership can, if necessary, call its leadership to account, and if there is any possibility of a clash between their interests and those of the wider trade union, workplace officials can usually be persuaded to take the side of the workgroup

(Clack, 1966; Hemingway, 1978). For these reasons, workplace trade unions can often take on a totally different nature from their national parent bodies, and what tends to characterize them is an almost exclusive concern with bread-and-butter issues. Other than to a few dedicated activists, wider social matters, which are often major objectives of national bodies, tend to be of little concern. There is often a fair measure of parochialism, and for reasons which will be explained presently, sometimes a degree of detachment from the parent trade union as well. Having said this, the parent trade union is still the main source of information and support, and so most workplace organizations will usually try to stay within national union guidelines.

The major functions of a workplace trade union are largely those which its membership determines; usually to protect and advance the interests of individuals, workgroups or those of the workforce as a whole *vis-à-vis* the employing organization. Because employing organizations can vary widely, the activities in which a workplace trade union engages to do this can vary considerably from place to place. In the public sector, where pay rates are determined nationally, efforts are usually concentrated more on domestic conditions of service, such as local changes, reorganizations and the protection of individuals. Where pay is determined at plant or enterprise level, as in a great deal of manufacturing industry, negotiations over pay can obviously become a major function as well. Because of these differences in scope, the way that workplace trade unions organize themselves can also vary widely. At the shop-floor or office level, most will make use of a shop-steward system of some sort. The expression 'shop steward' is, however, a rather general term. As used here it describes all forms of lay representative elected by specific groups of members in the workplace, and the term is not in universal use. For example, in print unions 'father or mother of the chapel' is common. With draughtsmen the title used is 'corresponding member', and in some white-collar unions they are called 'office representatives'. Because it is common to find that elections go uncontested, 'elected by the membership' can also be something of an overstatement. Nevertheless, stewards will usually be selected in some way by those that they represent, even if it is only because nobody else can be found to do the job (Nicholson, 1976).

As can be gathered, the steward's job is not a popular one. Often it is only filled out of a sense of desperation by some individual who cannot tolerate the disorganization which results from ineffective or non-existent occupancy of the role (Moore, 1980). In addition, because the job can be a difficult one to fill, shop stewards come in many varieties. For example, one distinction that has been drawn is between leader and populist stewards (Batstone *et al.,* 1977). Leader stewards are those who are usually more committed to trade-union principles and seek to shape the opinions and actions of the membership, whilst populists are often more content to let their constituents lead them by the nose. Having said this, what the steward wishes the role to be is only one factor that shapes its nature. One important influence is the role that the membership wants its stewards to perform. Another is the amount of discretion that the larger workplace trade-union organization allows to them. Indeed, one study points to the idea that shop stewards gyrate between a number of overlapping roles, and which one is occupied at a particular time varies according to the demands of the situation (Pedler, 1973). Nevertheless, whatever style the steward adopts, the job is essentially one of representing the interests of constituent members in a specific workplace, usually by dealing directly with supervision and management. However, very few stewards actually negotiate agreements. Rather they administer and police agreements made by more senior workplace union officials (Schuller and Robertson, 1983). The important point is that they are usually in daily face-to-face contact with those that they represent, are knowledgeable about their concerns, preferences and interests, and are therefore able to articulate them (Lawler and Levin, 1968; Howells and Brosnan, 1970, 1972).

In a larger enterprise stewards will be part of a union structure, and an important distinction that can be made is between establishments where there is a workplace branch (or branches) of the trade union or unions concerned and those establishments where there is a steward organization which is not an official organ (or subdivision) of the trade union. This, for example, is common in most of the public sector, and in some parts of private industry as well. In most British trade unions, the branch is traditionally the fundamental unit of organization, and union constitutions endow it with certain sovereign rights. Within certain specified limits it is usually allowed to formulate its own policies and choose its own approach to the issues that it deals with. Thus it can make and ratify agreements in its own name, discipline its own members, and in some unions levy additional subscriptions (Boraston *et al.,* 1975). However, whether or not there is an enterprise-based branch, except in very small firms there will commonly be a hierarchy of stewards. In larger establishments there will often be one or more full-time stewards, who are released from work duties and continue to be paid as normal by the employer. Survey evidence (Daniel and Millward, 1983; Millward and Stevens, 1986) indicates that two-thirds of establishments of over 2000 employees have these officials, and in a large organization where there are several unions, it would not be uncommon to find that each one had its own full-time senior shop steward or convenor, often with a joint shop stewards' committee (JSSC) chaired by a works convenor. In a firm which has several large plants, there may well be a body of lay trade-union officers from all unions and all locations, a 'combine committee'. As can be seen therefore, trade-union organization at the level of the enterprise is often highly organized, and can have a very sophisticated hierarchical structure.

Structure is one thing, and the use to which it is put can be altogether different. This gives rise to important considerations about the nature of these organizations, and perhaps more importantly, the factors which influence their patterns of action. This is an extremely large subject, and one that has fascinated industrial relations researchers for some time. Although there is insufficient space to give an extended description of the research evidence here, it is important to mention some of the more prominent influences at work.

To some extent the *nature of existing collective agreements* will play an important part. Nationally negotiated agreements which are framed very tightly and leave little room for local variation clearly restrict the scope of a workplace union (Boraston *et al.,* 1975). Moreover, *national trade-union policies* can be influential in this respect as well. They can be framed in a way that either restrains or facilitates autonomy (Boraston *et al.,* 1975). In most trade unions, workplace organizations are serviced in some measure by a full-time officer of the union, and the way that this role is performed can affect autonomy. However, since the ratio of trade-union members to full-time officers is often extremely high, and in the order of 5000 to 1 (Clegg, 1979, p. 56), it would be near impossible for most unions to bring the activities of all workplace organizations under the direct supervision of these officials. For the most part therefore, although full-time officials usually like to be kept informed of what goes on inside firms, they are usually far too busy to become involved with the minutiae of day-to-day dealings between stewards and managers. Thus it is hardly surprising to find that where a well-developed and competent workplace organization exists, full-time officers often play little part in the formulation or negotiation of agreements and tend to become involved only when deadlock occurs (DOE, 1971; Daniel, 1977).

This is not to say that there are no tensions and problems in the relationship between full-time officers and lay activists. Both parties often have dissimilar frames of reference which arise in the different responsibilities of their roles. In most larger unions, full-time officers are appointed by a higher official of the union, and therefore are employees of the union itself. It is to the wider union rather than to a specific group of members that they owe their primary allegiance, and this requires that one of their major concerns is to promote its policies and try to see that lay activists observe them. Conversely, workplace officials and stewards are elected by, and subject to direct pressure from, the rank-and-file members that they represent. Irrespective of wider union policies, they are likely to feel that they are far more competent to define and articulate the interests of their members than any full-time officer (Batstone *et al.,* 1977). Because of this, they can sometimes feel that a full-time officer who tries to be a guide and mentor to lay officials is highly intrusive, and that her or his proper role is only to give advice and help when it is specifically requested. However, it would be comparatively rare to find that workplace activists shun full-time officers completely. Often relationships are very close indeed (Batstone *et al.,* 1977), and where a workplace organization is well developed and competent, full-time officers, whilst keeping an eye on things, will only become involved in matters when requested to do so.

Perhaps the most important factor which shapes the nature of workplace trade unions is, however, the *management of the employing organization.* There is a great deal of evidence to show that autonomy in workplace trade unions exists where it has been fostered by a firm's management. In many organizations managers seem to prefer to deal with lay officials, perhaps because they have a knowledge and understanding of the firm, and so it is easier to develop bargaining relationships with them than with externally based full-time officers. In addition, in a multi-union situation, where a problem arises that involves several unions it is obviously easier for a manager to bring stewards together than it would be to get three or four full-time officers to attend the same meeting. This has led to some speculation about the potential outcomes of these relationships. One viewpoint is that it could be the first step towards a form of company unionism, or at least as close as management is able to get within the structure of British trade unionism (Terry, 1983). Another sees it in somewhat stronger terms, as containing an element of danger that stewards could be socialized into accepting management's viewpoint (Willman, 1980). An even more severe version points to the possibility of the emergence of lay élites that could come to operate against rank-and-file interests (Hyman, 1979). With the exception of the first, however, all the available evidence suggests that these things are extremely unlikely. Although bargaining relationships between stewards and managers undoubtably get stronger with time, there is nothing to suggest that members' interests are not represented. Closer bargaining relationships should perhaps be seen in a simpler light as something that stewards cultivate to pursue their members' interests more effectively (Edwards and Heery, 1985; Rollinson, 1991; Shafto, 1983).

More recently there has been a strong influence on the behaviour of workplace trade unions which mostly originates from *environmental sources*. Legislation and economic recession with its associated high levels of unemployment have both passed power into the hands of management, and to some extent management's support, acceptance, and even promotion of strong workplace trade unionism has diminished. This does not, however, mean that managers have necessarily set out systematically to destroy trade unions in the enterprise. Although some trade-union power has undoubtedly vanished, workplace organization has held up very strongly (Terry, 1986; Kelly, 1987). To have exerted control in a highly visible way would have carried the attendant risk of provoking a trade union backlash, and in order to avoid this, managers may well have found it prudent to hold back from measures which could be interpreted as too Draconian (Ogden, 1981; Spencer, 1981). Instead they have used their bargaining advantage to modify the nature of workplace relationships; for example, by promoting such activities as direct communication with employees and other schemes of involvement. Whilst it is possible that these could ultimately affect the ability of workplace organizations to mobilize their memberships, there is as yet nothing to suggest that trade-union attitudes have undergone the sea change that some commentators such as Roberts (1988) speak of. In the long run it may well turn out that management has found a new set of tools which allows it to continue the process in which it has been engaged for some time: a degree of shaping of the way in which workplace trade unions develop.

CASE-STUDY 3.2

Identifying the nature of collective associations

Consider the two firms described below. In each case try to identify what you feel would be some of the characteristics of the employee association that might emerge.

Organization A

This organization is a long-established light-engineering company that employs approximately 5000 workers on three sites, all of which are within two miles of each other. There are separate trade unions for staff and manual workers, and all employees below the level of departmental manager are normally members. Pay and conditions are negotiated at company level, and across the years unions and management have negotiated a comprehensive set of agreements covering most aspects of employment. Trade unions are given full facilities to operate within the different plants, and have developed stable systems of shop-floor or office representation. At company level there is a joint negotiating committee consisting of management and trade union sides, which has four scheduled meetings each year. However, it usually meets more frequently than this, often to deal with matters arising in the different plants. Summary statistics for the three plants are as follows:

	Plant A	Plant B	Plant C
Total no. of employees	1700	2050	1200
Managerial staffs (non-union)	16	28	12
Non-manual employees			
Clerical	43	57	29
Technical	41	62	30
Supervisory	32	51	27
Manual employees			
Production craftsmen	55	66	37
Maintenance craftsmen	32	44	22
Semi-skilled and			
unskilled production	1462	1715	1028
Ancillary (canteen etc.)	19	27	15

Organization B

This is a large building society located in the north of England. It has a large headquarters complex and 63 branch offices which vary in size from five employees in the smallest to over 20 in the largest, with an average number of 12 per branch. A staff association is recognized, and there is a joint consultative committee which meets quarterly to discuss matters of mutual interest to management and employees. Pay, holidays and other service conditions are fixed by management, but prior consultation with the staff association usually takes place before any announcement is made. The typical breakdown of staff for an average branch employing 12 workers would be as follows:

Branch manager	1
Assistant manager	1
Secretaries and typists	3
Counter assistants	7

There are approximately 1000 staff at head office, made up as follows:

Directors	5
Senior managers	9
Middle and junior managers	72
Clerical and typists	848
Porters, security staff and maintenance workers	64

Conclusions and preview

This chapter has dealt with collective associations of employees as organizations, mainly with the most significant form – trade unions. Because what they are and how they behave are to some extent functions of their past history, their origins and development have been described, together with some of the effects on current structures and government. Of necessity this has meant that they have been dealt with in isolation, which is not how things happen in the real world. In some ways this is reflected in the latter part of the chapter, where the focus moved from national institutions to trade unions at the level of the enterprise. Here it can be seen that the trade union in a firm is essentially an organ of representation that interfaces between employees and managers about those parts of the employment relationship which are handled collectively. Therefore, although trade unions exist as institutions, it is not as institutions that they are important to employees. Rather their importance lies in the process of representation, and this means that they are part of a dynamic social situation.

Successive chapters in the book will consider these processes in more detail. For example, some of the methods of participation and involvement covered in Chapter 8 can only take place if employees are represented collectively, and in Chapters 9 to 11, the processes of bargaining, negotiation and protest, all of which are essentially collective, are dealt with. It is also important to bear in mind that the activities of collective associations are not always collective in the sense of involving large numbers of employees acting in unison. Thus in Chapter 6 where the individual processes of discipline and grievance are covered, the reader should bear in mind that in many, if not most, of these cases, the employee would be represented by his or her trade union.

In the past decade there has been a great deal of legislation which has put limits on the actions of trade unions. This has not been covered in this chapter, but is dealt with in Chapter 5. Finally, it should be noted that in the latter part of this chapter it has been stressed that at enterprise level, management can have a huge influence on the behaviour of a trade union. As such there is a very clear link between this chapter and the one that immediately follows, where management as a party in employee relations is dealt with.

Further reading

Pelling H. (1987). *A History of British Trade Unionism* 4th edn. Harmondsworth: Pelican

> A very readable and comprehensive account of the development of British trade unions from the time of their origins to the present day.

Coates K. and Topham T. (1982). *Trade Unions in Britain*. Nottingham: Spokesman

> A comprehensive account of the structure, functions and activities of British trade unions.

Batstone E., Boraston I. and Frenkel S. (1977). *Shop Stewards in Action: The Organization of Workplace Conflict and Accommodation*. Oxford: Blackwell

> A very thorough study of the activities of white-collar and manual trade-union shop stewards in the same factory. Contains very comprehensive details of steward activities, relations with their members, and bargaining relationships with managers.

4

Management in employee relations

Introduction

In this chapter the focus moves away from employees to the other party in an organization's system of employee relations: its management. Because the word 'management' has two rather different meanings, the chapter starts by defining the way in which it is used here – to distinguish a group of people within an organization. The structuring of the modern enterprise, and the way that this gives rise to management positions, is then described, together with some of the potential employee-relations issues and problems which can be associated with structure. Management's role in employee relations is then discussed. Its claims to authority are examined, and some of its available methods for influencing employee behaviour without the overt use of power are noted. Flowing from this, the all-important topic of management's behavioural style is examined, and a number of different ways of categorizing styles are given. Finally, the implications of style are briefly explored, with particular reference to its potential effect on strategy and policy in employee relations.

Management defined

The word 'management' can be used in two different ways: first, to distinguish those members of the organization who usually have some formal authority over other employees; second, the word can be used to describe a set of activities that are concerned with running an organization, usually the responsibility for achieving one or more objectives and using certain specified methods of doing so. In employee relations, the term is more often used in the first way, and here the same convention will be followed. In addition, the term will be used to encompass those people who, whilst they do not necessarily have subordinates, are still designated as part of management. Often they are specialists who advise other managers, or make decisions on their behalf; in employee relations an example would be personnel and industrial-relations specialists. Wherever it is necessary to refer to the activity of management, the word 'managing' will be used.

Management in the modern enterprise

To some extent, the emergence of management as a group and managing as an activity are both products of the modern form of industrial organization. The modern enterprise is often large and complex. Size and complexity usually mean that planning, coordinating and controlling the activities of an organization become much more formidable tasks. The main feature used to address these problems is an organization's structural design (Child, 1986). Whilst this clearly does not mean that all organizations are structured in the same way, size generally gives rise to structures which are more elaborate in two crucial ways, both of which can have some impact on employee relations.

Horizontal differentiation

To some extent, all organizations are differentiated into specialized departments and functions, for example production, marketing, finance, research and development and so on. Although all of these functions perform their own specialist tasks, all the tasks should mesh together to achieve objectives set for the whole organization. To try to achieve this, each one usually has its own objectives that are set by top management. However, they also operate in their own sub-environments, each of which has its own set of constraints (Dill *et al.*, 1962; Lawrence and Lorsch, 1967). For example, customer and competitor pressures usually have a more immediate impact on marketing departments, and trade-union and supplier problems on the production function. Although they all have their own constraints, at the same time they are required to achieve their own objectives. An important consequence of this is that each one will almost inevitably look inwards to some extent, and focus on its own problems and tasks. The more specialist and differentiated are their tasks, the greater is the tendency for them to develop their own outlook and values, and for the objectives of the department to displace the overall goals for the organization (Wilson, 1966). The structural remedy for this is to assign specific responsibility for achieving objectives to an individual rather than to the group as a whole, that is, someone is placed over the department or function and charged with meeting objectives – a manager. Problematically, since this person then becomes the one who is also charged with overcoming the constraints, it is more than likely that he or she can become as wrapped up as anyone in departmental or functional objectives, and tend to lose sight of those for the organization.

One of the most pronounced problems this can give rise to in employee relations is that different informal practices can spring up throughout the organization. If objectives are not met, managers tend to be the ones who come under the most immediate pressure from above. Their subordinates can sometimes be one of the most powerful constraints on meeting objectives, and so they have a very real incentive to make their own informal agreements with them. This informality can have its positive side, and is highly valued by many managers as a way of dealing with changing situations. As was pointed out in Chapter 2, the contract of employment can only be specific about an employee's duties when they join the firm, and cannot foresee every future contingency. Thus if there is a necessary change about which subordinates are apprehensive, an informal deal can sometimes be a useful way of making adjustments to working practices. It can keep things in motion, and permit experiments without too much commitment on either side, and is therefore valuable to both parties. In some firms there is a frequent need to make informal adjustments to working practices (Terry, 1977), and eventually some of these can become incorporated into formal agreements. This, however, is not inevitable, and informal arrangements that have existed for some time can, in the minds of employees, become an established part of everyday life or 'custom and practice' (Brown, 1972). This is particularly the case if they are made with departmental stewards or representatives acting on behalf of subordinates. From an organizational point of view, this sort of thing can tend to get out of hand and lead to serious problems. For example, concessions gained by stewards in one department can be quoted as precedents by stewards in another.

CASE-STUDY 4.1

The shift-pay incident

Throughout the 1960s and 1970s increased attention was paid to acoustic and thermal insulation, and asbestos was a widely used building material. However, in the 1980s the health hazards of certain types of asbestos became fully recognized. To conform with health and safety legislation, many firms with premises that contained asbestos had to have it removed. One such case that had interesting employee-relations implications took place in a geographical region of one of Britain's largest companies. This company discovered that it had a large number of buildings containing asbestos, some of which were used by both employees and the general public. Accordingly, plans were made to remove the material, but owing to the inherent health hazards of doing so, it was necessary to close the building completely while this took place. To try to minimize the disruptive effects, contractors worked 24 hours a day to remove the material, and the renovation of each building needed between two and five days. Legislation also required that whilst the work was in progress, and for shortly afterwards, chemists would be in attendance around the clock to monitor the building atmosphere for the presence of asbestos fibres, a highly specialist task which contractors could not perform for themselves. Fortunately the organization itself had a small chemical laboratory with chemists qualified to do the work, and crucially who were able to sign the required documentation that gave premises a 'clean bill of health' when the jobs were completed.

Shortly after the first job was completed the departmental steward representing the chemists approached the laboratory manager and claimed the payment of shift allowances for chemists involved in this work. The organization had a comprehensive set of nationally negotiated pay agreements, one of which contained a provision for shift pay. However, according to the wording of the agreement, additional shift payments could only be made where the nature of a job involved shift working as a permanent duty. The laboratory manager therefore explained this to the steward and stated that he was unable to authorize shift allowances. After consulting with his members, the steward informed the manager that they would refuse to work around the clock on this work, and might also exercise their prerogative to inform both the contractors and the Health and Safety Executive, which would probably result in 'closure orders' on the buildings concerned.

This placed the manager in a difficult position. To start with, if he authorized shift payments, this would be spotted by the salaries department, who would refuse payment. Moreover, whilst his own superior had told him to stand firm on this lest it be used as a precedent by other groups who also had occasionally to work around the clock when emergencies occurred, other managers, including his boss, made it clear that they would hold him responsible for any loss of business or disruption that resulted from closed premises.

Question

If you were the laboratory manager how would you go about resolving this situation?

In large complex organizations, another important consequence of horizontal differentiation is the existence of line and staff management roles side by side. The former are managers concerned with the core activities of the organization, for example production, marketing and (at the very top) general managers. Specialist or staff members of management are usually considered to be the technical advisers to the former, for example work study, planning and so on. In employee relations an important group of specialists are the personnel or industrial-relations staff of the organization. This has been a constantly evolving role, and in its early form, it was little more than an implementer of the welfare policies. Later, as mass-production techniques became more widespread, it was more associated with administration of employment policies laid down by top management. In the postwar years, when full employment and buoyant markets gave trade unions greater bargaining power, its main task was industrial peacemaking (Torrington and Hall, 1987). All these roles were mainly concerned with activities at the operational level. More recent changes in organizations, some of which were discussed in Chapter 1, have resulted in yet another shift in emphasis.

There is an increasing interest by organizations in the use of a human resource management approach. This is dealt with in greater detail in Chapter 12 and therefore will not be discussed here. Suffice it to say that if it is widely adopted, it would almost certainly mean that personnel specialists became much more involved in strategic and policy levels of decision making (Tyson, 1987; Gowler and Legge, 1986). In any event, at whatever level they operate, an important task of this group is to advise on, and sometimes to completely formu-late, the policies and strategies for the relationship between an organization and its employees, and in addition to try to ensure that these are uniformly applied.

These days personnel specialists tend to regard personnel work as a profes-sion in its own right. Like all professions, they can lay claim to a monopoly of cer-tain types of expertise and knowledge, and assert that their objectives for the use of human resources are vital to the organization's success. However, as noted above, line managers also have objectives to achieve, and their subordinates per-form tasks that can be crucial to achieving the objectives. Thus they can also claim a responsibility for evolving and implementing employee relations prac-tices appropriate to their own areas. Predictably, this can result in tensions and potential conflicts within the management group itself. Line managers can come to feel that personnel specialists should not exercise too much influence, and that they (the line managers) should handle employee-relations matters. It can even lead to an element of subterfuge and secrecy creeping into the way these things are handled, and make the fragmentation problems outlined above much worse.

Vertical differentiation

Within all organizations, and usually within their departments and functions as well, there is a hierarchy of authority which goes hand in hand with differences in scope of decision making. Managers lower down are more involved in the day-to-day operations of the enterprise, and general managers at the very top are usually concerned with policy and strategy matters affecting the whole organiza-tion. Rewards get larger as the hierarchy is ascended and in addition, increased decision-making authority results in decisions that affect subordinates and oth-ers in the organization. Often those below the level of supervisor can have little or no authority or self-determination, and this can result in them feeling the need to challenge any proposals and decisions that they perceive will affect them adversely. Since they have little or no individual power in the organization, an obvious way in which they can do this is to act in concert. Trade unions, which were covered in the previous chapter, are an obvious vehicle for doing this. Indeed, the effect can spread to within the management hierarchy itself. In some organizations it is not unusual for junior and middle managers to be excluded from all but the most minor of decisions, and to become little more than a sub-group of employees. If they come to see themselves this way, they too can start to see advantages in collectivizing to protect their own interests, and this has been advanced as a major reason for the growth of managerial unions (Bamber, 1976).

The management role in employee relations

Although many managers would argue that they too are only employees, most would also assert that because they are given control of more resources and made responsible for their efficient and effective utilization, this differentiates them from other employees. Whichever way we look at things, a manager's subordinates are part of the resources of the organization, and to some extent she or he will be held responsible for the manner in which they are used. In addition, it is sometimes all too easy for both scholars and students of the subject to forget that managers have other things to attend to than employee relations. To put matters another way, from management's point of view, effective employee relations is more likely to be a means to an end, rather than an end in itself. Their prime aim in employee relations is therefore likely to be to ensure that the part of the organization for which they are responsible runs smoothly. Nevertheless, an important implication of the view that subordinates are resources is that management will fairly obviously lay some claim to a right to command their actions. To use a phrase which is common in employee relations, they will to some extent feel that this right of command is part of their 'legitimate prerogatives'. Indeed, their behaviour can often be a reflection of the ferocity with which they assert or defend these claimed prerogatives. As such, it is important to have some understanding of the arguments that can be used to assert them in the first place.

One basis for asserting the right to command has been called the 'property rights' argument. The ultimate property rights for a business belong to its owners, but in a large modern enterprise they are usually shareholders who play no active part in the day-to-day running of the firm. Thus managers deem themselves to be agents who exercise these rights on behalf of the owners, and argue that they have the delegated authority to do so (Storey, 1976, 1983). The idea is a very old one whose roots are lost in history. However, it is still prevalent today and, for example, in a comparatively recent survey most managers asserted that the managerial role is one of stewardship, and that the interests of the owners should take precedence over all other groups in the enterprise (Mansfield *et al.*, 1981). In recent years an additional and somewhat different claim to authority has been asserted: the so-called 'professional manager' argument. Increasingly, organized groups of managers, such as the British Institute of Management, have suggested that the occupation of managing should be regarded as a profession. In essence it is argued that managers have emerged as an occupational group with unique skills, knowledge and expertise. Because of this, they, and they alone, have the necessary competence to conduct the affairs of the enterprise, and to make decisions about the best use of resources (Salamon, 1987).

Whichever argument is the most prevalent – and probably both are used to some extent – they give rise to a very powerful set of ideologies and values, which can lead management to take the view that its role in employee relations is legitimately that of the dominant party, a view which is likely to be reinforced by the authority conferred on managers by the organizational structure. However, from what was said in the previous chapter, where there is a trade-union presence in an organization it also has a source of authority: that conferred on it by its members. Wherever there are separate sources of authority in an organization there is a risk of conflict, in this case arising from a clash of ideologies. Managers might assume that any change they propose should automatically be adopted and implemented by their subordinates. Trade unions on the other hand could see things somewhat differently. They might be prepared to agree to only those changes that benefit their members, or at least those which do not have an adverse affect on their interests. The subject of power and politics is far too extensive to cover here. However, it can be noted that authority is really a special form of power. Wherever power exists, the use of politics as a means to pursue, maintain and exercise it is seldom far away. As such both sides can engage in political behaviour to try to enhance their own power relative to the other. For example, under the guise of keeping all employees well informed, managers sometimes seek to undermine trade-union authority by communicating directly with the workforce about matters which are normally handled collectively with trade-union representatives. Similarly trade unions can deliberately 'misunderstand' management communications in order to mobilize bias in their members. Indeed, as will be seen later in the book, where communication and participation are covered (Chapter 9) and where negotiation and bargaining are discussed (Chapters 10 and 11), these are areas where different ideologies can also mean that union and management can be approaching the same issue in fundamentally different ways, and with quite different frames of reference. This in turn can mean that a dialogue between the two sides is difficult because they simply do not see the same issue in the same way. It is no accident, therefore, that they are often the most politicized activities in employee relations.

For these reasons management's ideology and the behaviourial style which it gives rise to can be a major factor influencing the nature of a firm's employee relations. Style is a topic that will be covered in greater depth presently. Before doing so, however, it is important to explain how, in addition to simply asserting a right to be obeyed, there are many other ways for management to influence the behaviour of employees. One of these, structure, has been discussed in outline already, and its use as an influence on behaviour will be covered further in Chapter 12. Therefore, discussion will be confined to two other important ways: technology, and job design and its motivational effects.

Technology

Technology is generally taken to denote the means by which tasks are accomplished. This is usually considered to be a management choice, and can have a huge effect on management's ability to exercise control. For this reason, what is chosen is unlikely to be dictated solely by considerations of rational economic efficiency. It can often owe as much to management's desire to control people's activities as anything else (Child, 1972). A fairly obvious example of this is the machine-paced nature of work on a mass-production assembly line, where it is the speed at which the line moves that dictates how much effort employees have to expend. Using mass-production methods also de-skills work, which not only lowers labour costs but also makes labour more easily replaced. Employees can of course be well aware of this, and if a change in technology has too dramatic an effect, its introduction may very well be opposed. Indeed, it is unlikely to be a coincidence that the most highly organized and cohesive union organizations are often found in the mass-production industries.

Job design and motivation

Another way in which management can attempt to influence efficiency and effectiveness of employees is to design jobs with an eye to their motivational content. How to get the most willing work performance from subordinates has long been a concern of management, and across the years there have been a whole string of theories about what motivates employees. The oldest of them all, the so-called scientific management approach (Taylor, 1947), whilst basically a theory and method of job design involving simplification and specialization of tasks, nevertheless contains the assumption that employees are primarily motivated by money; an idea which is a lot older than the theory itself. Somewhat later, and arising out of a series of studies in the General Electric Company in the USA, it was discovered that social interaction between people in a working environment could be a source of motivation (Roethlisberger and Dixon, 1939). The implication is that if people are responsive to the social milieu rather than just to the carrot-and-stick techniques of scientific management, then more effective and efficient work performance could be obtained by meeting their needs. Later still, a stream of theory emerged which emphasized the needs of humans to use their inherent capacities and skills in a mature and productive way. Examples here are Maslow's hierarchy of human needs (Maslow, 1970), McGregor's theory X and theory Y (McGregor, 1960), and Herzberg's theory of hygiene factors and motivators (Herzberg, 1966). Broadly speaking, the implications of these theories are that jobs should be designed to permit a degree of autonomy and challenge, and that if this is done, people are more productive because they find work meaningful and self-fulfilling. In addition there are other approaches to work motivation. Unlike the above theories which emphasized a somewhat universal set of motivators, these approaches assume that individuals make highly complex mental judgements about the nature of their work. For example, Vroom's valence expectancy theory views work motivation as a function of an individual's perception that behaving in a certain way will lead to particular outcomes. Thus if the outcomes are valued enough, the motivation to produce them is increased (Vroom, 1964). Another example is Adams' equity theory, which views motivation in terms of the comparisons that individuals make between their own ratio of work inputs to rewards and the inputs to rewards ratios of colleagues or others performing similar tasks (Adams, 1963). Where individuals perceive themselves to be under-rewarded in comparison to others, then their motivation is reduced, and they may well reduce their level of effort. Conversely, being over-rewarded is likely to lead to an increase in effort.

Since human motivation is extremely complex, it is likely that none of these theories is more than a partial explanation. However, most of them have received some support from research, and if their principles are applied in appropriate circumstances, they can give management some capability to influence the behaviour of employees. For example, techniques such as job rotation or enlargement can be used to remove some of the monotony of performing a single repetitive task. Similarly, jobs can be enriched to give a measure of autonomy and satisfaction.

CASE-STUDY 4.2

Motivation and job design at work

Paul and Robertson (1970) provide an example of an experiment in the use of job-enrichment techniques to influence employee behaviour. This took place at Imperial Chemical Industries in the 1970s.

The exercise involved sales representatives who, although having a high degree of job satisfaction, were given very little discretion over the way they operated. The company was carrying out a number of job-enrichment studies, and despite their products being fully competitive, sales for 1967 showed no improvement over those for 1966. Thus the representatives were seen as a suitable group for the changes. The changes were generated by managers above the supervisors of the sales representatives, and were introduced, gradually, by the methods normally used for introducing change.

In the changed situation sales representatives were allowed to pass on or request information at their own discretion instead of writing a report of every customer call. They were also allowed to determine calling frequencies and how to deal with defective or surplus stock, to request calls from the technical service department and, if they were satisfied it would not prejudice the company's position, to settle customer complaints by payments of up to £100. They were also given a 10 % discretion on the prices of most of the products sold.

As a matter of deliberate policy, representatives whose jobs were enriched were not informed that they were part of an experiment. This was to avoid any artificial effect of simply knowing they were under observation. For comparison a control group who were not subject to the changes, and also kept in ignorance of their role in the experiment, was used.

Question
What do you feel would be the likely results of these changes?

Although motivation theory can be a useful tool, it is important to realize that there are limitations on the freedom with which these techniques can be used. To start with, both the task itself and the technology used clearly impose some limitations. In addition, choice is likely to be influenced to some extent by management's own values. Management can be just as much a captive of its own ideologies and values as anyone else; in particular those about what it is that motivates employees. For example, managers who assume that employees are only likely to be motivated by money are probably more likely to apply a scientific management philosophy, and reserve all planning and directing as strictly part of their prerogatives. Conversely, managers who feel that intrinsic motivation is more important are likely to incline towards enlarged and enriched jobs.

A somewhat new twist to the story is that in today's conditions, where management is searching for even more effectiveness and efficiency in the use of human resources, enlargement and enrichment techniques may well be enjoying an increased use for other reasons altogether. It will be remembered that in Chapter 1 it was noted that there is an increasing tendency to move towards a flexible, multi-skilled workforce, rather than one where jobs are designed around the principle of task specialization. Almost by definition, a multi-skilled, highly flexible workforce has enlarged and possibly enriched jobs. The reason for these changes, however, is to achieve more efficient use of labour and keep manpower levels to a minimum, not to make jobs more intrinsically satisfying, although this may well happen. There has been a tremendous amount of work redesign of this type in the USA (Cappelli and McKersie, 1987), and almost certainly in the UK as well (Brown, 1986). Recession has enabled management to reassert its power to push through these changes, often with little or no concern for whether they were viewed favourably by employees. It would therefore be unwise to assume that just because jobs have changed in a way that could make them more interesting, those who perform the jobs are more highly motivated as a result. Neither would it be safe to assume that they are unaware that they are probably doing more work for the same money. Thus whilst job design is one way in which managers can attempt to improve efficiency and effectiveness, a lot will depend on how the changes are brought about. Changes which are forced on employees, even if they do result in jobs which are potentially more satisfying, could in the long run have an effect which is exactly opposite to the one predicted by the motivational theories. A great deal is bound to depend upon the way management goes about these things, or to put matters another way, management's behaviourial style. This is such an important topic for employee relations that it deserves the separate consideration which follows.

Management style

Style defined

The expression 'management style' has a particular meaning in employee relations. This is quite different from the way it is used in other subjects such as organizational behaviour, where it is most often employed to distinguish between different leadership styles; for example, democratic/participative versus autocratic. In employee relations, however, style is used in a more global way to refer to management's overall approach to handling the relationship between the organization and its employees. Whilst their leadership style can be part of handling this relationship, employee-relations style is much more a reflection of their approach to their own position in the organizational hierarchy *vis-à-vis* that of their subordinates.

As noted above, managers have a variety of ways of influencing the actions of their subordinates, and to some extent which ones they use will be influenced by their assumptions about what motivates employees. They are also likely to have preferred ways of managing human resources which in part arise from their beliefs about the legitimate role of management in the enterprise, and these preferences can be reflected in employee-relations styles. Nevertheless, there are all sorts of internal conditions and arrangements in an organization which can exercise a mediating influence on style. There is a great deal of pragmatism in management behaviour, and so style should not be taken as an infallible indication of the way managers will behave in all circumstances. Rather it is their preferred way of doing things, and two simple examples will serve to illustrate the point.

In the 1960s and much of the 1970s, when managers in certain industries had to deal with powerful and highly unionized workforces, they adopted a style of behaviour which involved a great deal of consultation and negotiation with employees and their representatives. In those very same firms, in the recession of the 1980s, the idea of managerial prerogatives emerged – or possibly re-emerged – as a dominant line of thinking, and gave rise to what has been called confrontational 'macho management' techniques (Marchington, 1982). This perhaps represents a situation where the underlying style, or preferred way of doing things, could only emerge when conditions were ripe. In contrast, there are organizations where, because management were acting out altogether different philosophies, the recession produced little or no change in their behaviour, and consultation and negotiation continued in a relatively unaltered way. This perhaps reflects the idea that in employee relations as in other matters, managements are sometimes less concerned with short-term gains than with safeguarding the long-term security of the firm. Just as they have a need to seek external stability by forging bonds with market environments, some managements have attempted to build up systems of jointly agreed rules with the workforce to ensure long-term internal predictability and security (Gospel, 1973).

In summary, although management style is a very useful concept and can tell us what might occur given the right set of circumstances, it needs to be used with some care. Underlying values and philosophies almost certainly give rise to patterns of behaviour that managers would prefer to use. Nevertheless, visible behaviour can sometimes be a poor indicator of the underlying style. Having said this, style can be a very useful concept to explain why managements differ widely in employee-relations strategies. However, one problem is that because managers are individuals, and by definition individuals are unique, potentially there are as many different styles as there are managers. Clearly this is not very helpful in trying to understand the implications of different styles. Therefore, it is easier to have a somewhat simpler scheme of classification that portrays different styles as 'ideal types', that is, the distinctive patterns of behaviour that can be expected from managers who hold a number of clearly defined and characteristic views.

A basic scheme for describing style was devised by Alan Fox (1974), who drew a fundamental distinction between two contrasting management frames of reference: unitarist and pluralist. Managers with a unitarist frame of reference make the assumption that an organization is basically an integrated and harmonious whole. At heart all organizational members – both management and employees – are seen to have a common purpose, embrace a single set of organizational aims, and everyone is on the same side. Managers with this set of beliefs and values are likely to see any conflict in the organization as unnecessary, unnatural, and probably the result of otherwise loyal employees having been led astray. Conversely, with pluralist managers the organization is assumed to consist of a number of competing groups, all of whom legitimately have different interests to pursue. As such, there is always some potential for conflict. However, because the view also contains an assumption that if sensible institutions and procedures are evolved conflict can be managed and contained, it is not necessarily regarded as a harmful phenomenon. So long as it is controlled and managed in an orderly way, conflict often generates a wider and more creative range of solutions to problems, and can therefore have potential benefits. Here it is important to point out that whilst there can appear to be some similarities, the unitarist–pluralist style distinction is quite different to the autocratic–democratic one used in leadership theory. Unitarism and pluralism are ideological frames of reference about whether or not an organization is made up of members who have unity of goals and purpose, or at least one common goal and purpose that transcends all others and makes them all pull in the same direction. The autocratic–democratic distinction is much more a reflection of the style a leader uses to try to get her/his followers to pull in the same direction.

CASE-STUDY 4.3

Management ideology

We deplore the use of the terms 'industrial relations' and 'labour relations'. We prefer 'human relations', by which we mean a recognition of the essential human dignity of the individual.

An employee, at whatever level, must be made to feel that he is not merely a number on a pay-roll but a recognized member of a team: that he is part of the company and an important part; and 'company', not in the sense of some inanimate thing possessing no soul, but rather in the sense of a goodly fellowship.

We reject the idea that amongst the employees of a company there are 'two sides', meaning the executive directors and managers on the one hand and the weekly-paid employees on the other. Executive directors are just as much employees of the company as anyone else. We are all on the same side, members of the same team. We make no secret of our belief that any employee, from executive director to office boy, who does less than his best, while drawing his full salary or wages, is morally indistinguishable from a thief who helps himself to the petty cash.

We recognize that the tone of any organization depends primarily on one man, on the executive head of it: on his philosophy, on his outlook, on the standards which he sets, on his example: in short on his leadership.

(Reddish, 1967)

Question

Which of Fox's categories, unitarist or pluralist, do you feel is most reflected in these statements? Whichever one you choose, try to write a statement of similar length to reflect the opposite philosophy.

Fox later elaborated his basic scheme, which has been more explicitly articulated by Purcell and Sisson (1983), who point out that there are different shades of unitarism and pluralism, and that both can exist within the same organization. For example, personnel specialists might well hold pluralist views, whilst line managers might be more likely to have a unitarist frame of reference. They point out that Fox's scheme essentially describes attitudes and values of individual managers, whereas style is much more useful as a way of describing their overall behavioural approach.

Starting from this basic distinction, Purcell and Sisson develop a typology of management styles as follows:

Traditionalists, where the style hinges on the idea of legitimate management prerogatives. Often there is open hostility and a refusal to negotiate with trade unions because they are seen to interfere with a legitimate right to manage.

Sophisticated paternalists are managers who also refuse to recognize or negotiate with trade unions, but differ from traditionalists in a very important way. Rather than adopt an openly hostile stance, they use a number of tactics to keep them out of the organization. For example, by the use of careful selection and training methods, offering superior conditions of service and higher pay, management attempts to create a set of conditions in which employees see no benefits in collectivizing.

A **sophisticated modern** style recognizes that the presence of trade unions somewhat limits management's freedom of decision. However, because trade unions give stability in relationships and facilitate communication and change within the workforce, this is seen to have a positive side. In these organizations, there is a strong emphasis on developing effective procedures to handle potential differences of interest, and two subtypes are said to exist:

Constitutionalists where agreements are usually framed to draw clear distinctions between issues that are bargainable and those which are reserved for management discretion. Although the frontier of control between management and workforce on these matters is somewhat movable over time, it tends to remain fixed for long periods.

Consulters in which the aim is to minimize conflictual bargaining. Instead, mechanisms of cooperation and joint determination are strongly emphasized, and these often contain provision for lengthy and extensive consultation procedures.

Standard moderns are by far the largest group. In these organizations, employee relations is essentially fire fighting, and is characterized by pragmatic and opportunist behaviours. The frontier of control can be very fluid, and its position at a particular time depends upon whether management or employees hold the balance of power.

A more recent and rather different method of describing styles is one developed by John Purcell (1987), who argues that ideologies and frames of reference may not be the only factors, or even the most important ones, in determining which particular style is adopted. He points out that style in employee relations can be much more a matter of strategy and policy. Thus as a matter of conscious choice, management can focus on either one or both of two different aspects of

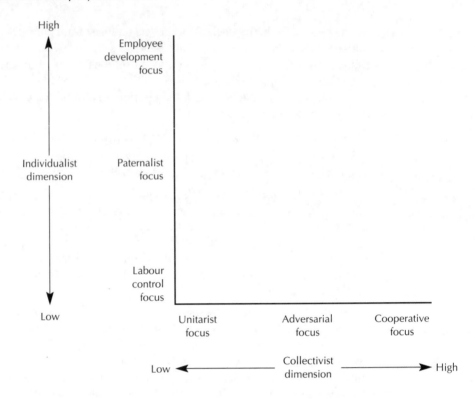

Figure 4.1   Purcell's scheme for mapping management styles (Purcell, 1987).

the relationship between an organization and its employees. These are quite different dimensions of the relationship, and each one can be thought of as a continuum along which there are a range of behavioural options. Purcell's scheme is shown diagrammatically in Figure 4.1.

The *individualist dimension* is concerned with the extent to which employees as individuals are regarded as important within the organization. At one end of the continuum is what Purcell calls an 'employee development' focus, which strongly emphasizes making the most of individual employees as organizational resources. Usually this involves giving them a great deal of encouragement and help to expand and develop their talents and work capabilities, and in addition, reward systems are often designed to encourage individual contributions to the organization. At the other extreme are firms who are said to adopt a 'labour control' focus. Employees tend to be viewed simply as one of the overhead costs of the business, and are essentially seen as a commodity which can be acquired or dispensed with as necessary. In the middle of the continuum is what Purcell calls a 'paternalist' focus. Although there is little emphasis on employee development and career progression, these firms nevertheless have a strong sense of social responsibility and caring towards individuals.

The *collectivist dimension* describes the extent to which an organization adopts the idea that employees should be involved in decisions that affect them. Purcell stresses that because there are other methods, such as joint consultation or worker directors, this does not necessarily mean negotiating with trade unions. Nevertheless, where an organization recognizes trade unions, they are the most readily available mechanism for employees to participate in decision making. At one end of the continuum are firms with a 'unitarist' focus, where the word is used in much the same way as in Fox's scheme. At the other end are firms with a 'cooperative' focus, which involves very strong attempts to build constructive working relationships with collective organizations of employees, and to involve them in a wide range of decisions. In the middle are firms who are said to have an 'adversarial' focus. Whilst trade unions are recognized and negotiation takes place, there is also an emphasis on managerial prerogatives. Therefore, strict attention is paid to agreements and procedures, which are designed to limit the range of issues on which employees can influence decisions.

The implications of management style

The Fox and Purcell schemes for describing style contain somewhat contradictory implications. Fox of course implies that although management has business objectives to achieve, the employee role in achieving the objectives is at least partly determined by management's ideology and values. This in turn implies that any employee-relations policies and strategies that exist are largely determined by preferred behavioural style, or at least they have to be commensurate with it. These implications are illustrated in Figure 4.2(a).

Purcell, on the other hand, accords far less prominence to ideology as a direct driving force on behaviour. Style is seen much more as a way of achieving policies and strategies, as shown in Figure 4.2(b). Although policy and strategy are dealt with later in the book, this is a point which is highly germane to the management role in employee relations, and so cannot be completely deferred until then. Purcell's scheme, for example, implies that management's behaviour is most likely to be a reflection of the planned and preferred way of using the organization's human resources, Fox's that the planned way of using the resources is derived from an imperative to behave in a preferred way. Thus it is pertinent to comment briefly on which of the two is most likely to be the case.

At the present time the evidence is mixed and it would hardly be wise to make a definitive statement on a trend in either direction. On one hand there are firms who for a long time have had very highly developed employee-relations policies and strategies, which are translated into definite patterns of behaviour that their managers are expected to observe in dealing with employees. Examples in this category would be Marks & Spencer and IBM (Dickson *et al.,* 1988), who lean very much towards what has now become known as the human resource management approach. This is a perspective which has aroused a great

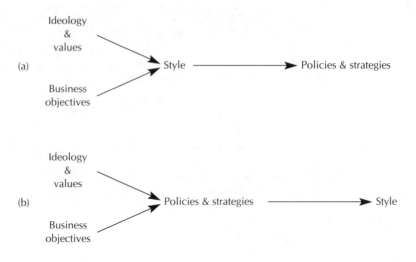

Figure 4.2   (a) Implications of Fox's scheme of styles. (b) Implications of Purcell's scheme of styles.

deal of interest, and since it is geared to trying to obtain a measure of employee commitment to organizational goals, it is an approach which has been argued to have a strong appeal to British management because it is basically underpinned by a unitarist philosophy (Guest, 1987).

What is perhaps more interesting is that its underlying philosophy, aims and methods are not dissimilar in some respects to those prevalent in Japanese industry. In the West, and in particular in the USA, the impressive performance of Japanese industry has created an intense interest in its management methods, especially those concerned with the use of human resources. Some of these ideas have been adopted by American firms (Walton, 1985), and there are also some signs that the practices may be becoming more widespread in the UK. One example of this is the increased use of schemes of workplace involvement such as quality circles (Bradley and Hill, 1987). British-based subsidiaries of American organizations seem much more likely to use these methods (Hamill, 1983; Purcell *et al.,* 1987). Thus it may even be the case that they are imported practices. Since a strategic human resource management focus is much more prevalent in the USA, this may be evidence of the beginnings of an increasingly strategic focus by British industry. However, these moves are by no means universal, and there are also signs of a more ideologically driven approach. Since a unitarist frame of reference still runs very deep in British management (Poole *et al.,* 1982), it seems more likely that both strategy and ideology shape behaviour, and a pragmatic appreciation of the prevailing circumstances dictates which of the two has the major influence in any particular time and place.

CASE-STUDY 4.4

Piers Mail Order Plc

Piers Mail Order is a long-established company with its headquarters in the North West of England. It recently took over a slightly smaller rival (Greenwell Ltd) located in the same town, and although this will continue to operate under its own name, it is intended that the operational activities of the two organizations will be closely integrated as soon as possible. Since both firms employ large numbers of people, Piers' Director of Personnel (Ms Clark) is in the process of comparing their manpower levels and employee relations policies. The essential statistics for the two organizations are as follows:

	Piers	Greenwell
Total employees	2372	1843
of whom:		
Directors	6	11
Senior departmental managers	19	36
Middle managers, and supervisors	48	44
Clerical	874	651
Warehousing (manual operatives)	1021	882
Transport and distribution	404	219

On meeting with her counterpart at Greenwell, a number of features emerged which seemed to point to more dramatic differences between the two companies. To start with, she found that the personnel function, if there could be said to be one, came under Greenwell's Warehousing Director, who had a small clerical section of five people in his office to look after these matters. So far as could be determined these people mainly kept personnel records. There was no training or development of employees, and although Greenwell recognized trade unions for its manual employees, it was clear that this was a step that had been forced on the company in the 1970s. There was no consultative or negotiating committee that met on a regular basis. Any industrial relations activity was conducted on an *ad hoc* basis by the Warehousing Director, and from what he said this mainly consisted of annual pay negotiations that frequently came near to a stand-up fight. Unionization of clerical workers was actively discouraged, and it was made clear to any prospective staff employee that this was the case. However, there was a contributory pension scheme for all employees.

All this contrasted sharply with Piers, where there was a policy of recognizing trade unions, and almost all but senior managers were members.

Indeed there was a very active joint committee of management and union representatives that met regularly. Management also put a great deal of effort into workplace communications. Perhaps the most disturbing difference, however, was in the training and development of employees. Ever since Piers had invested heavily in computerization of its warehousing and customer service facilities, the company had pursued an active policy of continuous training. This had now developed to the point where in addition to updating on new products and technological developments that affected their jobs, employees were actively encouraged to prepare themselves for promotion. For example, an in-house supervisory management training programme was run in conjunction with the local technical college.

Tasks

Using an appropriate framework, evaluate the management styles at Piers and Greenwell. What employee relations changes do you feel might be necessary to integrate the operational activities of the two firms, and what steps might the Personnel Director of Piers have to take to bring these about?

Conclusions and preview

There seems little doubt that managers will continue to occupy a dominant position in the modern enterprise, a position which will, if anything, become even more dominant in the future. Thus management's influence on employee relations will continue to be highly important, and arguably the most important influence of all. Two reasons are given for asserting this. First, it will be recalled that at the end of Chapter 3 it was noted that there are strong grounds for suggesting that management has been able to mould the nature of workplace trade unionism into the form it finds the most acceptable. Second, as has been explained in this chapter, management has a number of ways at its disposal of shaping employee behaviour. Taken together, these give management a far greater capability to shape the nature of an organization's employee relations than anyone else. For this reason management's style is likely to be an extremely important factor in what emerges.

As has been noted, there are two divergent views on style, which have rather different implications. One implies that it will be a reflection of the planned and preferred way of using the organization's human resources, the other that it has its origins in values and ideologies about management's legitimate role in the organization, and that this gives rise to an imperative to behave in a preferred way. Whilst there is no definitive answer as to which is the more likely, the implications for the topics covered in subsequent chapters should be clearly understood. An ideologically driven style, particularly if it veers towards unitarism, is likely to have a highly significant effect on how the processes described in Chapters 6 to 10 are handled. For example, the disciplinary regime in an organization could be very harsh, grievances could be regarded as an affront to managerial authority, and communications, involvement or participation virtually non-existent. In an extreme case, it could also be expected that the processes of bargaining and negotiation might be conducted by managers with a frame of reference that is perhaps best expressed by the statement 'the answer's no – now what's the question?'

If style is more a matter of conscious thought, and directed at an effective use of human resources, the implications could be rather different. These will not be elaborated here, but the reader is asked to give the matter some thought in future chapters. For example, in Chapter 12, which deals with some aspects of what has become known as the human resource management approach, the whole matter can depend on a well-thought-out strategy. Similarly style is also a relevant consideration for what is covered in Chapter 13: the topics of policy and strategy in employee relations.

Further reading

Hawkins K. (1978). *The Management of Industrial Relations*. Harmondsworth: Penguin

> A useful and easily understood book which details some of the major pressures and constraints that management has to deal with in employee relations.

Poole M. and Mansfield R., eds. (1980). *Managerial Roles in Industrial Relations*. Aldershot: Gower

> A book of readings by different authors which gives a good overview of factors which could influence thinking and strategy in employee relations.

Thurley K. and Wood S., eds. (1983). *Industrial Relations and Management Strategy*. Cambridge: Cambridge University Press

> A book with somewhat similar coverage to the previous one.

5

The State in employee relations

Introduction

Employees and managers who were discussed respectively in the last two chapters are the parties that interact directly in employee relations. There is however a third important player, the State. In Britain the State is seldom involved directly in day-to-day employment matters, but nevertheless has an important influence. The laws which it passes affect many of the rights and obligations of employers and employees, and these establish a basic set of rules which strongly influence the way that the two parties relate to each other. In the last three decades there has been a progressive increase in State intervention of this type, and the UK currently has a far more legally bound system of employee relations than ever before.

It is important for the reader to understand why the State feels compelled to exercise this role, and how this intervention constrains the behaviour of employees and managers. Therefore the chapter starts with a brief examination of the role of the State, and its reasons for intervention. As will be seen, although its aims are essentially economic, it also seeks to mould society in a way that is in accordance with the social and political philosophies of the government of the day, and this inevitably influences what actions it takes. Therefore, the range of methods that the State can use to intervene in employee relations is the next topic to be considered, and this is followed by a description of the way in which philosophies towards intervention have changed.

Enacting legislation is the main vehicle used by the State to regulate employee relations. To explain the ways in which legislation can be used, an outline scheme which depicts laws as affecting one or more of five different aspects of the employment relationship is given, and recent legislative changes are described. This is followed by a brief overview of the various institutions and agencies of labour law, in order to explain how the law operates in practice.

The final section of the chapter is somewhat more speculative. Since the future framework of British labour law could be strongly affected by membership of the European Community, the chapter concludes with a brief examination of proposed EC social legislation, the Social Chapter.

The role of the State

For the purposes of the discussion the State is taken to be the government of the day, together with all those other institutions such as the civil service, the police, armed services and judiciary, that carry out its will. Only the government in Parliament has law-making powers, and it is the sole body that can bring about substantial changes to many of the rules affecting employee relations (Crouch, 1982). For the purposes of administering the law, the judiciary is theoretically independent of the State. However, whilst it has the power to interpret legislation, it does not have law-making powers, and for this reason it is more convenient, and arguably more logical, to view it as an arm of the State.

Until comparatively recently most British governments tried to avoid any involvement in the employment relationship, and up to the 1950s there was probably no industrialized country where the State was less interventionist in terms of its industrial-relations laws (Kahn-Freund, 1960). However, from the mid 1960s onwards, the pace of State intervention has accelerated significantly, and today there are many statute laws which regulate the actions of both employers and employees.

The objectives of the State

In broad terms, it is often reasoned that the State's aim in intervening in employee relations is to achieve its economic goals. One of the prime tasks of government is to manage the national economy so that it is prosperous, stable and productive. This means that it has to try to achieve four objectives that can easily conflict with each other: to maintain a high level of employment, to ensure price stability, to maintain a favourable balance of payments, and to protect the exchange rate (Crouch, 1982). To a large extent, the desire to achieve these goals is the same for all political parties, and in this respect their economic ends are largely the same. However, political parties in Great Britain have significant differences in their ideologies and philosophies about the way society should be ordered, and these give rise to social goals which become entwined with economic ones. For this reason, a government's policy with respect to employee relations is not only directed at achieving its economic ends, but is also an expression of its ideology and philosophy about the desirable nature of society. Thus the laws which it passes tend to reflect both of these aims (Lewis, 1983).

As was noted in Chapter 3, whilst the relationship between trade unions and the *Labour Party* has its own tensions, there is an ideological affinity between them. Theoretically they are different wings (industrial and political) of the same working-class movement, and therefore they have a consensus about political, social and economic justice for working people. For this reason organized labour has traditionally had a strong, although by no means a decisive, voice in formulating Labour Party policy, and this is reflected in its labour legislation. In broad terms the *Conservative Party* sees itself as the champion of free enterprise and a market economy, and although its political tentacles are much less easily discerned, it has an equally strong bond with private business. The connections usually take place through strong social networks which deliver a considerable amount of financial support from employers, mainly from the banking, insurance and manufacturing sectors. However, many of these donations are hard to pinpoint, and are channelled via bodies which are ostensibly non-political. For example, organizations such as British United Industries, The Centre for Political Studies, The Economic League, and Aims of Industry are all known to be conduits for private industry contributions to the party (LRD 1985a), and about two-thirds of Conservative Party funds come from company donations (Ball, 1981). Although the *Liberal Democratic Party* receives some donations from private enterprise (LRD, 1985b), to a large extent it is purposely non-aligned with either side of industry.

It is important to recognize that these differences in affiliation go well beyond financial support. They tend to reflect ideologies about how society should be ordered. Thus the two major political parties have quite different social goals, philosophies and beliefs about the most appropriate ways in which national economic ends should be achieved. These are reflected in their programmes of labour legislation, which tend to define the roles that different groups of citizens should play in society, and in particular, the respective roles of employers and employees. Having said this, enacting legislation is by no means the only way for the State to intervene in the employer–employee relationship. Thus it is appropriate to examine the complete range of alternatives it has at its disposal.

The scope and means of State involvement

The ways that the State can involve itself in employee relations can be many and varied. However, a convenient framework for examination is provided by Armstrong (1969) who identifies seven overlapping roles, each of which constitutes a way of influencing the employer–employee relationship.

As an *employer* the State either directly or indirectly funds the employment of almost 30 % of the workforce of the UK. The Civil Service and National Health Service are both funded centrally, and whilst local authorities, police and fire services are under local control, they are financed largely by grants from central government. The traditional understanding in the UK has been that the State would be a responsible employer, and in return for this, public-sector employees and trade unions accepted a reciprocal obligation to avoid conflict (Winchester, 1983). The major effects on employee relations were that trade unions were accepted and encouraged, and in most of the public sector formal consultative and negotiating machinery was established. In the interests of fairness and to avoid conflict, pay was often based on comparisons with the private sector, sometimes using pay review bodies as a valuable adjunct to bargaining machinery.

Problematically, because the State has a role as an employer, it is also the *paymaster* to a large proportion of the working population. Thus the policies and procedures it operates with respect to its own employees can set a clear benchmark for others. For this reason it can feel that it must set an example to private industry, particularly in times when it is exhorting the need for pay restraint in the national economic interest. This occurred in the 1970s, when the public sector came to be seen as the major culprit in a trend towards economic instability and inflation. Public-sector employment was growing at a significant rate, and was thought to be diverting resources from the wealth-creating private sector. In addition, large public-sector pay increases were seen to be fuelling aspirations in private industry. All these factors led to increasingly severe public-sector wage policies (Thomson and Beaumont, 1978). In 1977 and 1978 there was a glut of major private-sector disputes, most of which resulted in significant wage rises. By then there had been several years of public-sector wage restraint. The private-sector increases caused an eruption of indignation in the public sector, which culminated in widespread industrial action: the so-called winter of discontent of late 1978 and early 1979.

In its role as a *buyer* the State has a potential effect on employee relations in many organizations. The 1891 'Fair Wages Resolution' of the House of Commons expressed a philosophy that whilst public money should normally be spent in the most economical manner, the State should extend the obligation to be a responsible employer to all of its contractors. Clearly a contractor who pays low wages, or uses other inferior or unfair employment practices, is likely to be able to make a lower bid for a government contract than one who does not. To discourage this, the resolution established that government contracts would not automatically be awarded to the lowest bidder. Since then the resolution has been reaffirmed on numerous occasions, and in 1946 several additional requirements were introduced, namely that government contractors should pay wages not less favourable than those prevailing for the particular trade or industry in the district concerned, that a contractor's workers should be free to join trade unions, and that anyone who subcontracted to the contractor should also observe these conditions. These provisions were widely adopted by almost all public-sector organizations, and their contracts usually contained a clause requiring the contractor to undertake to abide by the terms of the resolutions. These resolutions gave an incentive to many employers to pay decent wages, and also provided a measure of legitimacy for trade unions. However, the resolution was rescinded in 1983. This, as will be seen later, was indicative of an underlying philosophy in the government of the day.

Yet another role identified by Armstrong is that of *manpower manager*, in which the State promotes effective manpower utilization, for example by operating employment exchanges to link those seeking work with those who have employment to offer. One extension of this role has been to encourage labour mobility where it is deemed necessary. This can be seen in the Redundancy Payments Act, 1965, one of the major purposes of which was to ease the relocation problems of those made unemployed in declining industries. In addition, the State plays an active part in promoting industrial training, and recent examples are the schemes introduced from 1980 onwards to give training or retraining to the unemployed.

The remaining three roles all heavily involve the State in enacting legislation. As a *protector* it has imposed minimum standards from the beginning of the 20th century onwards. For example, the Employment of Women and Young Persons and Children Act of 1920 and successive Factories Acts have all established basic standards on health and safety matters. More recently there has been a great deal of legislation to try to outlaw unfair discrimination, and the Race Relations Act, 1976, Sex Discrimination Acts of 1975 and 1986 and Equal Pay Act of 1970 are all directed at this aim. Perhaps the most visible protective action of the State, however, has been the creation of *Wages Councils*, which have their origins in the Trade Boards Act of 1909. Here the government took action to protect workers in the so-called 'sweated trades', primarily by fixing minimum and binding wage levels and establishing a wages inspectorate to police the Act. A number of other trade boards were created as a by-product of a parliamentary committee – the Whitley Committee – which was set up in 1917 to enquire into ways of bringing about peaceful methods of settling wages and conditions in industry. It was fairly easy for the committee to identify suitable structures and processes where trade unions and employers were well organized enough to be able to set up collective bargaining arrangements. However, if either or both parties were poorly organized, there was more of a problem. Therefore, the Trades Boards Act, 1918 empowered the Minister of Labour to set up new trade boards in those industries where no adequate bargaining machinery existed. Nevertheless, since the tradition in British industrial relations is that voluntary methods are superior to compulsion, the aim in doing this was primarily to encourage trade unions and employers to develop their own arrangements. By 1938 there were approximately 50 trade boards in operation, and subsequent legislation in 1946 and 1959 renamed them Wages Councils. It also extended their responsibilities beyond those of setting basic pay rates, by enabling them to cover matters such as overtime pay and holidays. Again, the underlying philosophy was that they should work towards their own demise, and that the two sides would develop their own system of collective bargaining. For this reason, the Wages Councils Act, 1979 introduced measures to make them more effective and independent of the State. Instead of the government appointing all of a council's members, designated trade unions were empowered to nominate persons to membership directly. Their composition was fixed at equal numbers of representatives from unions and employers' associations, plus three independent members. In addition, their powers were extended to enable them to determine a wider range of service conditions, together with the right to make their own wage-regulation orders.

By the early 1980s, over 2.5 million workers were subject to pay determination in this way. For the most part these were, and continue to be, in industries such as agriculture, retailing, catering and clothing manufacture, where employees are so dispersed it is difficult for unions to become well organized. When a wages council issues a regulation order, a notice is sent to all relevant employers, who then have a legal responsibility to display it and observe its conditions. If there is a failure to do so, employees can make a complaint to the Wages Inspectorate, and this can result in a court order to comply. It is important to note that government philosophy towards Wages Councils has recently moved in the opposite direction, and has reduced their role. The Wages Act, 1986 removed their entitlement to set anything other than basic minimum pay rates. In addition, the government argued that since young people were being priced out of jobs by national minimum rates, wages council awards should not apply to anyone under the age of 21. Perhaps most significant of all, in November 1992 the government announced that its next piece of labour legislation (which at the time of writing has not yet been placed before Parliament) will contain a provision to abolish all the remaining Wages Councils.

Another State role involving it in legislating is that of *incomes regulator*. Since the end of World War II governments of both parties have at times used the law to regulate both price and wage increases with the aim of controlling inflation. Whilst the current government rejects this policy in public, it is arguable that the past thirteen years have seen its use in a less visible way. Control of interest rates and the money supply have both been used to influence consumer demand. This is turn has had an effect on employment levels, which has lowered the pressure for pay increases and the rate of inflation. As such these steps could just be prices and incomes policies in another guise.

The State's most visible use of legislation in employee relations is in its role as a *rule maker*. The first comprehensive attempt to regulate the actions of employers and employees was the ill-fated Industrial Relations Act of 1971. This set out to completely reform collective labour law, and had it succeeded in its aims, it would have imposed on British industrial relations many of the features of the American system. That is, collective agreements would have become legally enforceable unless they included a specific disclaimer clause to the contrary. The Act also gave employers a wide variety of legal remedies against trade unions, who were deemed to be legally responsible for the unofficial actions of their members. In order to be able to claim the important legal immunities described in Chapter 3, trade unions were also required to register themselves, and to subject their rule books to external scrutiny. However, except for inserting disclaimer clauses in their agreements, the majority of employers and trade unions simply ignored the Act, and preferred instead to rely on the traditional nature of British bargaining relationships (Weeks *et al.*, 1971). The Act itself was repealed by the Labour government which came to power in 1973, and since 1979 when a Conservative government was elected, the rule-making role has continued unabated. This, however, has relied more on a stealthy, step-by-step approach than on a grand design introduced in a single piece of legislation. These measures will be described presently. Meanwhile, in order to show that the history of State involvement is one of changing philosophies, it is more important to examine events over a somewhat longer period.

The changing nature of State intervention

Until the beginning of this century the prevailing belief was that employers and employees were the best judge of what form their relationship should take. For this reason the State mostly sought to abstain from intervention in the employment relationship. This does not, however, mean that it ever completely ruled out intervention. Rather the position was that intervention was appropriate for some aspects of the relationship, and not for others (Clegg, 1979). Indeed, the Coal Mines Regulation Act, 1860 was introduced explicitly to bring more fairness into the basis on which miners were paid, and to improve the inspection of pit safety. Thus what has changed more than anything else is the definition of what is an appropriate area of intervention, and this in turn is a reflection of changes in the State's underlying philosophy. One way of explaining this is through a descriptive scheme developed by Crouch (1982), who links the nature of State intervention with changes in two other variables. The first is the dominant political ideology of the day, and the second is the emergence of strong, autonomous trade unions. The way these variables interact can be plotted to give four 'ideal type' patterns of intervention. These are shown in Figure 5.1.

Except for very briefly during wartime, full *corporatism* has not existed in

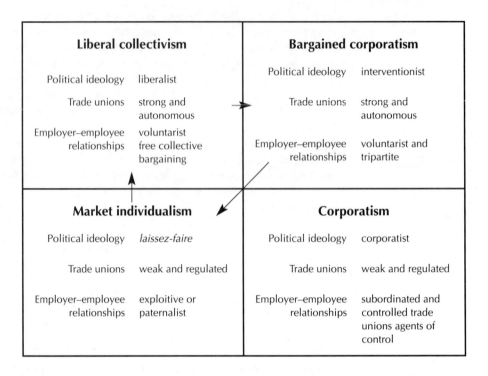

Figure 5.1   State approaches to industrial relations (after C. Crouch, *The Politics of Industrial Relations*, Fontana, 1982).

Great Britain and it is of little concern here. The corporate state is one which is associated with totalitarian regimes, and if trade unions are allowed to exist, they become incorporated into the State apparatus, as, for example, was the case in eastern-bloc communist counties (Porket, 1978).

In *market individualism* the dominant economic philosophy is *laissez-faire*, and trade unions are comparatively undeveloped and weak. This was the situation in Great Britain until late in the 19th century. The market was seen as the supreme arbiter of competitive interests, and this gave a legitimacy to social inequalities. Indeed, the relationship between an organization and its employees was interpreted very strictly as that which exists between master and servant. Whilst the State avoided direct involvement in employee relations, its laws reinforced the social values of the ruling classes, the most sacred of which was their 'property rights'. Moreover, trade unions were only just inside the law, and operated in a precarious way, which gave employers a free hand to be highly exploitative. As Crouch points out, the whole situation subordinated the individual to the control and authority of the owner, which at best was paternalistic, and most of the time was downright repressive. Thus it was inherently unstable, and employees had a strong incentive to collectivize in order to redress their disadvantaged position.

More widespread collectivisation and a higher degree of organization in trade unions prompted the State to change its stance to one of *liberal collectivism.* It recognized the potential power of independent trade unions, and they came to be seen as an opposition force with separate and distinct interests from those of employers. With the partial recognition of the idea of a plurality of interests, the State passed laws to maintain a balance of power between the two parties, primarily by encouraging them to find ways of voluntarily reconciling their differences. A result of this was that whilst legislation largely ensured that the dominant party remained dominant, it also made it possible for employees to challenge the domination in a limited way.

This mode of thinking continued for over half a century. However, after the Second World War another stance, *bargained corporatism,* began to emerge. During the war trade unions had been co-opted into the power structure. When it ended all the major political parties adopted full employment as a major policy objective and both of these features tended to increase the bargaining power of organized labour. In an attempt to control inflation and bring about stable prices, governments increasingly consulted on a regular basis with both employers' associations and organized labour. Thus the State virtually became a third party in the bargaining process. In one form or another this lasted up to the end of the 1970s, and many aspects of the employment relationship which are now the subject of legislation first became incorporated in this era.

However, direct intervention by the State as a party in the bargaining process inevitably means that the principle of voluntarism becomes more and more questionable.

Paradoxically, while both major political parties continued to involve themselves in this way, governments were still nominally committed to free collective bargaining. However, the British way of conducting industrial relations was increasingly seen to have a number of defects, and the three decades up to 1978 saw the periodic use of statutory prices and incomes policies to try to control the economy. A sign of increasing concern was the setting up of the Royal Commission on Trade Unions and Employers' Associations (the Donovan Commission) in 1964. Whilst its 1968 report strongly defended the principle of voluntarism, it also acknowledged many weaknesses in British industrial relations. Therefore, the commission recommended a more professional approach both by trade unions and management and also that a Standing Commission on Industrial Relations be established to oversee the necessary reforms. Despite this, government continued to press for further intervention. In 1969 a government White Paper (*In Place of Strife*) appeared, and this proposed even stronger powers of intervention by giving the Secretary of State the right to enforce solutions for unconstitutional strikes and inter-union disputes. Since this struck at the very roots of voluntarism, it was met by an uproar from the trade unions, and the proposal was dropped in return for an undertaking from the TUC that it would deal with these matters.

As mentioned earlier, in its 1971 Industrial Relations Act the Conservative government made a concerted attempt to affect a wholesale revision of labour law. Without repeating what was said, the Act reflected a philosophy that the abstinence of the law gave trade unions a positive encouragement to behave irresponsibly (Clegg, 1979). Thus it defined certain of their actions as unfair industrial practice, and gave legal remedies to employers and employees who felt themselves unfairly treated. The Act was repealed by the incoming Labour government in 1974, and from then until 1979 bargained corporatism reached its zenith. A 'Social Contract' was struck, and in this trade unions agreed to give assistance to the government in resolving some of the country's economic problems, in return for which the government delivered a number of reforms to promote social and economic equality: the so-called 'social wage'. This resulted in a number of laws, all of which were designed to improve individual and collective rights. In addition, there was a parliamentary enquiry into the introduction of industrial democracy (the Bullock enquiry). This however, turned out to be an ill-fated venture, and will be described in more detail in Chapter 8.

Recent trends and developments

Since 1979 when the Conservative Party took power, there has been a radical break with the ideas of industrial and economic consensus which are part of bargained corporatism. The first two casualties were full employment as a national economic objective, together with market intervention by the government to promote a buoyant economy. Instead a return was made to *laissez-faire*, free-market economics. In theory the government has continued to favour voluntarism, but in practice there has been a great deal of legal regulation which has been informed by an ideology that economically and socially trade unions are a 'bad thing'. Conservative election manifestos of 1979, 1983 and 1987 all contained the same message – that trade unions had abused their privileged position, were controlled by a politically motivated leadership who coerced a reluctant rank and file into action, and had pursued their ends regardless of the national interest. However, instead of adopting the wholesale reform tactics of 1971, there has been a step-by-step 'ratchet' approach, to try to achieve a permanent change in the culture of employee relations, and shift the balance of power firmly back into the hands of employers (Mackie, 1989).

Much of the legislation has been aimed at freeing employers from what has been portrayed as an excess of union power, and has been directed at weakening unions in order to 'free the market'. For example, the employment legislation of 1980, 1982, 1984, 1988 and 1990 has all introduced measures to reduce significantly trade-union power, and restrict the capability of unions to take action to advance their members' interests. In addition, employers have been positively encouraged to use the legislation to prevent industrial action. To date, however, except for a few well-publicized cases, they have shown little appetite for doing so (Evans, 1987). It has been an avowed aim of government to introduce what it calls a 'new economic realism' into wage bargaining, and to this end it has set out to emasculate collectivism. In addition, whilst it has promoted the evils of collectivisim and virtues of individualism, the government has shown no reluctance in reducing the individual rights established by previous legislation (Denham, 1990; Hendy and Eady, 1991). As one commentator has remarked, 'if it were not for the Clean Air Act, the government would reintroduce child chimney sweeps' (Keegan, 1991). Again the stated aim has been to free employers from what are argued to be unwarranted controls on a 'free labour market'. Overall there has been intervention in almost every aspect of the employment relationship, either by revoking or modifying previous legislation, or by passing new laws to regulate some hitherto untouched area. This is reviewed in the next section, where the law is considered in a more specific way.

The law in employee relations

An overview of sources

The laws which impinge on employee-relations matters come from a number of different sources. One fundamental distinction that can be made is between *criminal law* and *civil law*. The former deals with unlawful acts that are offences against the public at large, and the latter deals with the rights of private citizens and their conduct towards each other. For the most part, the most significant laws affecting employee relations are civil laws, although there are elements of criminal law which also have some relevance. The most importance civil source is *statute law,* which results when a bill is introduced in Parliament, is passed by both Houses, and is then given royal assent by the monarch. Sometimes, however, an Act of Parliament grants powers to a minister to modify certain details of a law through a *statutory instrument.* For convenience these can be regarded as part of statute law, as can *EC laws* that are adopted in the UK. Another important source is *common law,* which results from decisions made by judges and tribunals, and creates binding precedents on judgments in subsequent cases.

A typology of employee-relations law

In law, both trade unions and employing organizations are treated as individuals. Thus either one can be taken to law in a criminal prosecution or a civil lawsuit. Whilst the laws affecting employee relations are numerous and come from diverse sources, they all have one thing in common: they all serve to regulate relationships of some sort. Thus they can all be placed into one or more of five

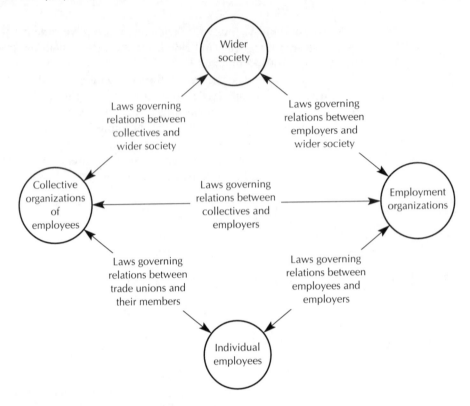

Figure 5.2   Laws affecting employee relations.

categories according to the relationships which they influence. These are shown in Figure 5.2.

Laws affecting the relationship between individual employees and their employers

In Chapter 2 it was explained that the law assumes the relationship between individual and employer to be a personal one. Thus the main body of law which is relevant in this area is that which affects the contract of employment. A summary of the major legislation in this field is given in Table 5.1, and this also gives a note of the major changes introduced since 1979 which affect the rights of employees and employers.

Laws affecting the relationship between individuals and their collective organizations

Joining a collective association is a voluntary act, and in so doing, the individual usually undertakes to abide by the association's rules. Nevertheless, there is a legal framework which defines the mutual rights of collective associations and their members, the vast majority of which has appeared since 1979. The major provisions are shown in Table 5.2.

Laws affecting the relationship between collectives and employers

To some extent the relationship between collectives and employers have always been constrained by the law, usually to the heavy disadvantage of trade unions.

Table 5.1   Major legislation affecting the relationships between individual employees and employers.

Legislation	Matters covered
Employment Protection (Consolidation) Act 1978	Entitlement to written particulars of contract, time off for public duties, minimum notice periods, time off for trade-union activities.
Sex Discrimination Act 1975 amended by Sex Discrimination Act 1986	Maximum hours of work for women repealed. Sexual discrimination in relation to employment, retirement pensions, promotion and training.
Equal Pay Act 1975 as amended by Sex Discrimination Act 1986	Maximum hours of work for women repealed. Sexual discrimination in relation to employment, retirement pensions, promotion and training.
Equal Pay Act 1970 as amended by Equal Pay Regulations 1986	Equal pay for work of equal value, equal pay procedures with independent expert to conduct job evaluation studies.
Social Security Act 1986, and Maternity Pay Regulations 1986	Maternity pay replaced by maternity allowance, rights to reasonable time off for antenatal care with pay, right to return to work.
Race Relations Act 1976	Racial discrimination in relation to employment, retirement, promotion and training.
Rehabilitation of Offenders Act 1974	Right to have 'spent' convictions discounted.
Industrial Tribunal Regulations 1985	Burden of proof about 'reasonableness' of unfair dismissal placed equally on employer and employee, not solely on employer. Size and administrative resources of employer to be taken into account when assessing reasonableness. Pre-hearing assessments of cases introduced with warning on costs or possibility of awarding costs to employer for frivolous, unreasonable or vexatious claims. Summary judgements possible.
Employment Acts 1980 and 1988	Employer immunity for selective dismissals for industrial action extended. Dismissal or victimization for non-union membership unfair. Special compensatory awards for dismissals for union membership or non-union membership reason.
Employment Act 1982	Minimum length of service to be able to claim unfair dismissal increased to 2 years for employees working over 16 hours per week and 5 years for those working between 8 and 16 hours.
Transfer of Undertakings (Protection of Employment) Regulations 1981	Protection of contract of employment when whole company transferred to new owners as a going concern.
Wages Act 1986	Wages Councils; powers to set wage levels for workers under 21 abolished; also non-wage conditions for all workers. Truck Acts (1831–1840) rescinded to allow cashless pay and rights of employers to make deductions defined.
Data Protection Act 1984	Safeguards for personal information held about individuals on computer. Rights of access to, and amendment of, data.
Health and Safety at Work Act 1974	Comprehensive legislation defining mutual rights and obligations of employers and employees and operation of safety enforcement procedures.

This is because the law accords a paramount position to the individual contract of employment, and takes little account of the fact that many employee-relations matters are essentially collected in nature. Therefore, much of the law in this area aims to prevent trade unions from cutting across what is deemed to be an individualized contractual relationship. Again, this is an area in which there have been significant changes since 1979, and the major items of legislation are shown in Table 5.3.

Table 5.2   Major legislation affecting the relationship between individuals and their collective associations.

Legislation	*Matters covered*
Trade Union Act 1984	Requirement to conduct ballot of all members at least once every ten years to continue with political fund. Definition of political activities for which ballots required for all union-supported action.
Employment Act 1988	Non-union members given right to join trade union, industrial action to enforce union membership made unlawful, ballots required for principal executive officers of unions every 5 years or less. Right to join or not to join a trade union. Rights for union members to:
	• prevent industrial action without a ballot • avoid being disciplined by their trade union in most circumstances • inspect union accounts • prevent misuse of union funds • pursue grievance against union in courts.
	Commissioner for Trade Union Rights established

Table 5.3   Major legislation affecting the relationship between collective associations of employees and employing organizations.

Legislation	*Matters covered*
Trades Disputes Act 1906	Established trade union immunity from civil suit for inducing breach of contract when calling out members on strike.
Transfer of Undertaking (Protection of Employment) Regulations 1981	Requires transfer of collective agreements where organization transferred to new owners as a going concern.
Employment Protection (Consolidation) Act 1978	Requirement to consult with recognized trade unions prior to redundancies taking place and minimum periods of recognized consultation according to numbers involved.
Employment Act 1980	Rights for trade unions to claim recognition by employers abolished. Secondary or sympathetic industrial action made unlawful unless employer has contract with primary employer. Secondary picketing made unlawful. Rights to use employers premises for certain trade-union ballots established.
Employment Act 1982	Definition of trade dispute considerably narrowed to wholly or mainly related to industrial-relations issues. Industrial action to compel union membership or non-membership or trade union recognition made unlawful.
Trade Union Act 1984	Trade union liability for damages established, enabling unions to be sued for unlawful industrial action in certain circumstances.

Table 5.4 Major legislation affecting the relationship between collective associations of employees and wider society.

Legislation	Matters covered
Employment Act 1980	Public funds made available for trade-union ballots.
Trade Union Act 1984	Political objects of trade unions defined for which a political fund necessary.
Highways Act 1980 Police Act 1964 Conspiracy and Protection of Property Act 1875 Prevention of Crime Act 1953 Criminal Law Act 1977	All contain clauses which pertain to the conduct and actions of pickets in industrial disputes.

Laws affecting the relationship between collectives and wider society

For the most part, law in this area is aimed at ensuring that the actions of trade unions do not affect the well-being of society at large. Therefore it is an area in which certain aspects of criminal law are relevant. The major legislation, some of it of quite a respectable age, is shown in Table 5.4, again with a note of more recent changes since 1979.

Laws affecting the relationship between employers and wider society

Law in this area falls mainly into two categories. First there is a huge volume of company law, which regulates the activities of firms as commercial organizations. In certain cases this falls within the field of criminal law, and is designed to protect shareholders and investors against fraud and malpractice. Secondly, there are more specific laws governing the responsibilities of organizations to

Table 5.5 Major employee-relations legislation affecting the relationship between employing organizations and wider society.

Legislation	Matters covered
Employment Act 1982	Requires companies of over 250 employees to record in annual reports any progress towards employee involvement, including schemes of financial involvement.
	Rescinded 'fair wages' resolutions of House of Commons (1891 onwards) which obliges government subcontractors to observe terms not less favourable than those agreed between trade unions and employers in that locality.
	Union (or non-union) labour only clauses in commercial contracts made void.
Companies Act 1985	Defines company law and responsibilities of company to shareholders.
Health and Safety at Work Act 1974	Defines companies' safety responsibilities towards general public and customers.
Finance Acts 1978, 1980, 1984, 1987	Tax incentives to promote employee share ownership and profit sharing schemes.

the public at large; for example, those concerning toxic waste and atmospheric pollution. As such, few of these laws are directly concerned with employee relations, and are merely noted here for completeness. Having said this, when either type of law is contravened, there can sometimes be a strong effect on employee relations. One example is where a firm becomes insolvent, and is either wound up or sold off as a going concern by the official receiver. Another is where a takeover or merger occurs. In this area there is also a body of EC legislation, which, if it were adopted in Britain, would have a significant impact on employee relations. Although this has yet to be adopted in the UK, it is relevant to acknowledge its potential, and the matter will be addressed separately at the end of the chapter. The major current legislation is shown in Table 5.5.

How the law operates

Figure 5.3 illustrates in outline the relationship between the various courts and institutions that deal with employee-relations cases. As can be seen, each leg

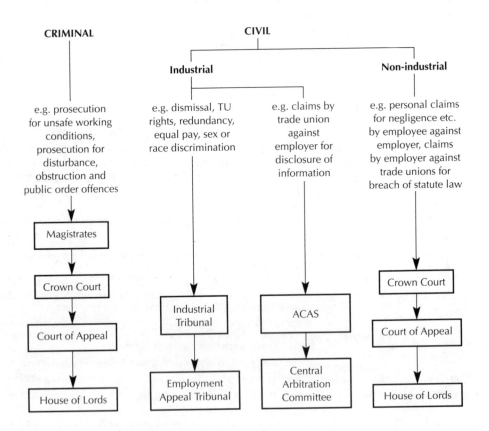

Figure 5.3   The legal system for employee-relations cases.

consists of at least two levels. The general principle is that attempts are always made to resolve a case at the lowest level possible, and only when a decision is not accepted by the parties, or it is beyond the jurisdiction of that level, does it pass to the next one.

Criminal cases involve prosecution by an agency of the State such as the police or one of the various industrial inspectorates. Thus health and safety violations can be dealt with in this way, and can result in prohibition orders, and fines or closure if these are ignored. Prosecutions can also be brought by the police for obstruction, assault, and public order offences in industrial disputes.

Industrial tribunals are the first recourse for a great deal of employment legislation. They usually consist of a legally qualified chairperson appointed by the Lord Chancellor, plus two other people, one from either side of industry, who are selected from panels nominated by the TUC and management organizations. Tribunals are bound by the decisions of higher bodies such as the *High Court* and *Employment Appeal Tribunals.* The latter hears appeals on points of law from tribunals, or on matters arising from a decision of the Certification Officer. They are composed of a High Court judge and people from panels nominated by the TUC, and the Confederation of British Industry (CBI).

Non-industrial civil courts can deal with a vast array of issues. For example, claims for compensation for injury resulting from an allegation of negligence would be handled in this way. It is also the route which would be used by an employer seeking to restrain a trade union from taking industrial action.

The Advisory, Conciliation and Arbitration Service (ACAS) is an independent body established by Parliament in 1975, and has its origins in the passing of the 1971 Industrial Relations Act, when both trade unions and employers called for an independent conciliation and arbitration service to be established. Its primary functions are to:

- Advise employers, unions and individuals on industrial relations and legal matters.
- Conciliate at the request of either party in a dispute. All individual legal claims to tribunals are automatically notified to ACAS who, if requested, will attempt to conciliate.
- At the request of both sides in a dispute, arrange arbitration, that is, ACAS itself does not arbitrate, but appoints the arbiter.
- Deal with the first stages of claims for disclosure of information by trade unions.

This, however, is simply a summary of its responsibilities, and perhaps conceals its extremely wide range of services. As its name indicates *conciliation* is one of the most important of these. At the request of one or more parties to a collective dispute it can intervene to try to bring about a resolution, a service highly valued by both employers and unions (Jones and Dickens, 1983). ACAS also offers conciliation in cases where individual employees have complained to an industrial tribunal about an infringement of their rights under employment law. Indeed ACAS is automatically informed of these cases and, in the interests of expediency, must try to settle them before they are heard by a tribunal. *Mediation* and *arbitration* are two of its most important services. The former is a process in which a potential solution to a dispute is recommended to the parties, but they still carry on negotiating to find their own details for a settlement. Arbitration, which has to be at the request of at least one party, and at the express consent of both, is where a third party adjudicates and sets the terms of a settlement. Here it should be noted that ACAS does not actually arbitrate itself since this would affect its ability to conciliate. Rather it appoints an arbiter on request.

In addition to these highly visible activities, ACAS provides a wide range of *advisory services* for both employers and trade unions, and again these are well valued by both parties (Armstrong, 1985). Yet another function is a duty explicitly delegated to ACAS by Section 6 of the Employment Act, 1975. This is to produce codes of good practice in order to promote improvements in industrial relations. Whilst these do not have the status of laws, they are submitted to the Secretary of State for Employment and are placed before Parliament. As such they are 'approved' codes of practice, and conformance with them can be taken into account by industrial tribunals. ACAS also undertakes *enquiries,* usually in an attempt to improve industrial relations in specific industries or firms. Finally, it also undertakes a good deal of *research*, either directly or commissioned by others, to provide commentaries on new and current issues relating to the nature of British industrial relations.

Finally mention should be made of three bodies which, for reasons of simplicity, are not shown in Figure 5.3. The *Certification Officer* (in Northern Ireland the Registrar of Friendly Societies) is required to oversee the rules and accounts of trade unions, and in the case of new applications for registration, to make judgement on their claim to be independent of employers. The *Registrar of Companies* is required to check their accounts filed annually at Companies House, and take action (including criminal proceedings) against defaulting companies and their officers. Finally, the Employment Act, 1988 established a *Commissioner for the Rights of Trade Union Members.* The function of this official is to help individual trade union members take out cases against their own unions, and this can include providing them with a measure of financial help to do so.

The potential effects of EC legislation

The background to the legislation

Great Britain is a member of the European Community, and at the end of 1992 EC legislation came into force which began the process of creating a single

European market. This has long been an aim of the Community, and was an explicit commitment in the Treaty of Rome signed by West Germany, Italy, France, the Netherlands, Belgium and Luxemburg in 1957. Great Britain, Denmark and Ireland joined the original six states in 1973, and more recently, Spain, Portugal and Greece have become members. However, the movement towards a fully integrated internal market did not gain real momentum until the 1980s. In 1987 the Single European Act was signed, and this aims for a strengthening of economic cohesion in the community by removing all technical and physical barriers to competition. As well as economic integration, the original Treaty of Rome and the Single European Act both contain clauses which make social cohesion an integral part of the Community's aims. For example, it has long been envisaged that the EC would become a large internal labour market with complete freedom of movement of employees and employing organizations. For this reason it is felt that the rights and opportunities to be enjoyed by working people should be harmonized. Indeed, for many years most member states have recognized the need for social and economic objectives to go hand in hand (Roberts, 1992). One example is the idea of minimum levels of remuneration, which has been argued to be in accordance with the original Treaty of Rome. Proposals were advanced in 1974, which were subsequently endorsed by the EC Council of Ministers (EEC, 1974). Since then, discussions and negotiations about a number of other employment matters have resulted in the formulation of definite proposals, and several EC directives have been issued (EEC, 1983a, b). From time to time the Commission has brought enforcement proceedings against member states for non-compliance with its social directives. For example, in 1983 the UK was forced to amend its Sex Discrimination Act, 1975, which was deemed to be in violation of the EC Equal Treatment Directive (Mazey, 1988; Bridgford and Stirling, 1991).

In 1989 a draft Community Charter of Fundamental Social Rights of Workers, the Social Charter (subsequently renamed the Social Chapter), was presented to the European Council of Ministers. This contained an array of proposed legislation, and despite British opposition, was adopted by the Commission's Labour and Social Affairs Committee, and endorsed by the Heads of State at the Strasburg summit of that year. In addition a comprehensive 47-point action programme was prepared, which lays out measures that need to be taken to implement the Social Chapter.

Whilst the British Conservative Government has always been an enthusiastic supporter of a single European market, it has consistently opposed the social dimension. Problematically, the vast majority of other community states view it as a crucial part of the single market (Roberts, 1992). To some extent this is because there are considerable differences in the prosperity of the different member countries, and unless employment rights and conditions are levelled up, it is seen that the single market could create a situation which would give some states an unfair competitive advantage over others. For example, those countries that have fewer social provisions usually have lower labour costs, and this could result in a migration of investment from the more prosperous areas: the so-called 'social-dumping' effect. Clearly it might also imperil workers' rights in the areas where they are now the most advanced.

Under the Treaty of Rome the principle of 'unanimity' was deemed to be necessary for the adoption of community laws. Thus any single state could exercise a power of veto. However, to accelerate progress towards the single European market, 'qualified majority voting' was introduced on some issues. This is a complex formula in which the member states have a total of 74 votes apportioned between them according to their size. For a majority to exist on any issue, 54 votes cast in favour are needed. Strictly speaking, the provision only applies to the establishment and functioning of the single market, together with health and safety provisions. Thus the unanimity principle still applies for such matters as taxation, movement of labour, and the rights and interests of employees. Up to the Maastricht summit of December 1991, the UK was therefore able to avoid introduction of a great many of the provisions of the Social Chapter. However, at the summit, which was intended to set the final agenda for greater integration, Britain opted out of the Social Chapter and the single currency provisions. Therefore, although for the time being its full implications are unlikely to become law in the UK, the feeling is extremely strong amongst other community members that the social dimension is part and parcel of the single market. For this reason it is hard to see how it can be resisted indefinitely, whichever political party is in power in Great Britain. Indeed, the other eleven member states have fully embraced the Chapter, and a number have made it plain that the matter is not dead, just dormant. Several now take the line that in opting out, Great Britain has forfeited all rights to consultation and voting on EC social legislation. Moreover, there are real fears that there could be many developments about which Britain has no say, but will eventually have to accept (Wolf, 1991; Towers, 1992; Mill, 1992).

Provisions of the Social Chapter

The Social Chapter and its attendant action programme are complex. It falls into twelve articles, each one dealing with a specific aspect of labour law. The major provisions of each article are given in what follows.

Article 1: Freedom of movement

The right of freedom of movement is restricted only on grounds of public order, safety, or public health.

Workers from any Member State working in another Member State have the right to engage in any occupation on equal terms with the same working conditions and social protection as nationals of the host country.

The right to freedom of movement also implies establishment of common rules on entitlement to residency across Member States for workers and their families; removal of barriers to movement by recognizing diplomas and equivalent qualifications granted in other jurisdictions; and improvement in the living and working conditions of frontier workers (those working in one country but residing over the border in another).

In accordance with the aim of avoiding 'social dumping' there are two major requirements of the action programme which are considered particularly important. First, to avoid 'distortions of competition between undertakings', foreign workers, especially those providing subcontracting services in a host country, would be required to have conditions of employment no less favourable than nationals of the host country. Second, a labour or 'social' clause would be required to be inserted into public contracts. In order that the collective agreements of the host country would be respected, this would guarantee equal treatment to employees of firms tendering for public contracts.

Article 2: Employment and remuneration

In each Member State, all employment shall be fairly remunerated. Workers to be assured of an equitable wage sufficient to enable them to enjoy a decent standard of living. Such provision is also to apply to part-time workers, and those on fixed-term, temporary, and seasonal work contracts. Every worker to have access to public placement services free of charge.

Although the Commission recognizes that the setting of wages is largely a matter for the two sides of industry within member states, it also considers that a level of remuneration which gives a decent standard of living should be guaranteed as a right. It is also important to note that it explicitly makes provision for part-time and fixed-term contract workers to have equal rights in this matter. As was explained in Chapter 2, in the UK people employed in this way are often excluded from some of the protection given by employment legislation.

Article 3: Improvements of living and working conditions

Completion of the internal market must lead to an improvement in the living and working conditions of all workers in the Community. Specific reference made to harmonization of the duration and organization of working time and to forms of employment other than 'open-ended' contracts (that is, part-time work, fixed-term contracts, and temporary and seasonal employment). The improvement is to cover the development of procedures in the event of collective dismissals and bankruptcies.

> Workers are also to have the right to a weekly rest period and annual leave, the duration of which is to be harmonized in accordance with national practices.
>
> Conditions of employment of each worker are to be stipulated in laws, in collective agreements, or individual contracts of employment, according to the arrangements applying to each Member State.

The intention here is that all employees should have clear, explicit and fair contracts of employment, also that there should be a requirement to consult beforehand with trade unions about collective redundancies, especially where these result from a firm transferring its operations across national borders. Perhaps the most controversial proposal, however, is the one about working time, where the intention is that a maximum working week should be defined, together with statutory rights to rest days and holidays.

Article 4: Social protection

> Each worker to have the right to adequate social protection and, irrespective of his status and the size of the enterprise, to be entitled to an adequate level of social security benefits. Those unable to enter or re-enter the labour market and without means of subsistence are to receive sufficient resources and social assistance in keeping with their particular situation.

The main objective here is to harmonize social security provisions across member states, and in particular to bring up standards in those countries which currently have the lowest level of development. This owes much to a desire to prevent the 'social dumping' effect that was mentioned earlier.

Article 5: Freedom of association and collective bargaining

> Workers (and employers) should be free to join or not to join trade unions or other associations so as to defend their economic and social interests.
>
> Workers' organizations (and employer associations) have the right to negotiate and conclude collective agreements under the conditions laid down by national legislation and practice. The dialogue between the two sides of industry at the European level must be developed and might result in contractual relationships at interoccupational and sectoral level.
>
> The right to collective action also includes the right to strike, again subject to the obligations arising under national regulations and collective agreements.

The aim is to promote a dialogue between the two sides of industry, and in some industries the potential for European-level collective agreements to be derived is recognized. In an earlier draft an unqualified right to strike was recognized, but it is now accepted that this is a matter where national legislation will have supremacy.

Article 6: Vocational training

> Every worker shall have access to vocational training and receive such training throughout his working life, without discrimination on the grounds of nationality. Continuing and permanent training systems to be set up by the competent public authorities, undertakings, or the two sides of industry, enabling every person to undergo retraining (particularly through leave for training purposes) to improve skills or acquire new skills.

Here it is intended that provision should be made for continuous training, especially through the 'leave for training' provision. Indeed, the need to enhance current training standards is emphasized, and this should include provision for all young people to follow supplementary vocational training courses during working time. The aim is that member states should give all interested young people the opportunity to follow a course of vocational training of at least one year's (and if possible two or more year's) duration, after completing their compulsory education.

Article 7: Equal treatment for men and women

> Equal treatment and equal opportunities for men and women. Action should be intensified to remove discrimination against women in access to employment, wages, working conditions, social protection, education, vocational training and career development. Measures should also be developed to enable men and women to reconcile their occupational and family obligations.

Here the measures which are proposed are mainly specific ones to enhance women's opportunities. Some of these rights are currently enshrined in UK legislation, but those proposed by the EC are considerably more ambitious; for example, improved facilities for child care, maternity benefits and so on.

Article 8: Information, consultation and participation

> Information, consultation, and participation for workers must be developed along appropriate lines, having regard to the practices in force in Member States. Procedures must be implemented in due time, particularly with respect to technological changes that

have major implications for the workforce; restructuring activities and mergers affecting the employment of workers; instances of collective redundancy (that is, mass lay-offs); and trans-frontier workers affected by employment policies pursued by the undertakings in which they are employed.

Participation and consultation are discussed at greater length in Chapter 8, and it is sufficient to note that implementation would require firms to put in place some method of consultation and/or participation in decision making. It is also intended that provisions should be developed to encourage the financial participation of employees.

Article 9: Health, protection and safety at the workplace

All workers are to enjoy satisfactory health and safety conditions in the working environment. Appropriate measures to be taken to ensure a further harmonization of conditions while maintaining improvements already made. The measures are to take account, in particular, of the need for the training, information, consultation, and balanced participation of workers as regards the risks incurred and the steps taken to eliminate or reduce them.

The commission's intention here is to build on the existing provisions in the Community, and a number of directives laying down minimum standards are envisaged. In addition it is proposed to establish a Safety, Hygiene and Health Agency to assist and coordinate implementation.

Article 10: Protection of children and adolescents

The minimum employment age should not be lower than the minimum school-leaving age and, in any case, not lower than 15 years. Young persons in gainful employment are to receive equitable remuneration in accordance with national practice. Appropriate measures must be taken to adjust labour market regulations applicable to young workers so that their special needs for vocational training and access to employment are met. The duration of working hours (including overtime) must be limited, and night work is to be prohibited for those under 18 years except for certain jobs stipulated in national legislation.

Following completion of their compulsory education, young people are entitled to receive initial training sufficient to enable them to adapt to the requirements of their future working life. For young workers, such training is to be undertaken during working hours.

Measures to be implemented in this area are largely intended to prevent exploitation of those least able to protect themselves. For example, a minimum employment age would be established, and the working hours and requirement to work nights would be restricted for young people.

Articles 11 and 12: Elderly persons and disabled persons

According to the arrangements applying in each country, every worker of the Community must, at the point of retirement, be able to enjoy resources affording a decent standard of living. Those not entitled to a pension upon retirement or without other means of subsistence must be entitled to sufficient resources and to medical and social assistance specifically suited to their needs.

All disabled persons, irrespective of the source and nature of their disablement, must be entitled to additional concrete measures aimed at improving their social and professional integration. The measures in question encompass vocational training, ergonomics, accessibility, means of transportation, and housing.

These provisions largely encompass such matters as establishing a threshold level of retirement pension which would enable people to enjoy a decent standard of living. In addition, it is intended that there should be a commitment to safeguarding access to employment opportunities for disabled people.

CASE-STUDY 5.1

A situation of radical change

The time is the late 1990s and you are the Human Resources Director of one of the UK's largest integrated manufacturing concerns. The company employs approximately 70 000 people on over 20 different sites, and its products range from electronics to heavy engineering and armaments. The national economy has not really improved since the recession of 1992, and a sterling crisis just before the general election this year has resulted in a change of government. During this time Great Britain has continued to be a member of the EC, but has also vigorously resisted adopting the common currency provisions and most of the articles of the Social Chapter that it opted out of at the Maastrict summit of 1991. Meanwhile, after some initial murmurs of dissent from one or two, most of the other 11 member states of the EC have shown more and more inclination to adopt the provisions of the Social Chapter. In some areas they have made considerable progress in their national legislative programmes to bring this about.

The new UK government has announced that it intends to embrace fully the provisions of the Social Chapter and will introduce a crash parliamentary timetable over the next six months to put the legislation in place. In fact informal opinion on the matter suggests that it has little choice. It is the price it must pay for economic support from the rest of its EC partners.

Whilst your organization could hardly be called a poor employer it is only about average in terms of its employee-relations policies and practices. Trade unions are recognized, and collective bargaining over pay and service conditions takes place. However, the exigencies of the economy in the past four years has meant that the company has had to watch costs closely. For this reason, whilst keeping within the law, it has pursued a policy of giving no more than the necessary minimum of ground to its employees; a policy which has resulted in a hardening of union attitudes within the organization.

Clearly there are likely to be some significant implications for the firm from the legislative changes, and the chairman of the board has asked you to make a presentation highlighting:

(1) What legislative changes the government will have to introduce, and in particular how this will affect current legislative provisions.

(2) Bearing in mind that the company is 'middle-of-the-road' in terms of its employee-relations practices, which of these legislative changes is likely to result in it having to make substantial internal adjustments.

Question

What will you say in your presentation?

Note: Assume no major legislative changes in employment law in the UK after 1992.

Conclusions and overview

Whilst the State in Britain is not officially a direct player in employee relations, by virtue of its law-making powers it is able to exert a significant influence on the relationship between organizations and their employees. The intervention of the State in this way has been a continually unfolding process which has changed direction according to the underlying ideologies and philosophies of those in power. At the present time the government is one which has a rampantly anti-union philosophy. This is reflected in much of its legislation, and is nowhere more evident than in its rejection of the Social Chapter of the European

Community. This step, incidentally, was one which flew in the face of the considered professional opinion of British personnel management (Mill, 1992).

Since the State is such an influential player, its actions have clear implications for some of the topics already covered in the book, and those that will follow in subsequent chapters. The rights enshrined in the individual contract of employment described in Chapter 2 have been reduced by some of the legislation described here, as have the activities of trade unions, which were described in Chapter 3. For this reason, the topics of bargaining, negotiation and industrial action which will be covered in Chapters 9 to 11 also have significant legal dimensions, which will be highlighted then. Finally, there are also legal aspects to the topics of communication, participation and involvement which will be covered in Chapters 7 and 8.

Further reading

Baglioni G. and Crouch C. (1991). *European Industrial Relations.* London: Sage

A book which surveys the field of industrial relations in almost every EC country, each one being covered in a separate chapter.

Crouch C. (1982). *The Politics of Industrial Relations* 2nd edn. London: Fontana

A penetrating and highly readable analysis of the growth of government intervention in industrial and employee relations in postwar Britain.

Towers B., ed. (1983). *A Handbook of Industrial Relations Practice.* London: Kogan Page

Chapters 13, 14, 15 and 16 give excellent summaries of changes in labour law since 1979.

Wedderburn, K.W. (Lord) (1986). *The Worker and the Law* 3rd edn. Harmondsworth: Penguin

A very comprehensive text which, amongst other things, gives extensive coverage to the topics of voluntarism versus state intervention.

6

Discipline and grievance

Introduction

This chapter deals with two very important individual issues, the handling of which can strongly affect the tone of the relationship between an organization and its employees. Whilst they are very often bracketed together, in practice most organizations try to keep discipline and grievance apart. This is usually for reasons of administrative simplicity, and in order to bring to the reader's attention that there are considerable conceptual and practical differences as well, the chapter starts by defining the two processes, and then examining them from first principles. The remainder of the chapter examines each process separately and in detail. The aims of each one are explored, and their legal implications are explained. For each process, a scheme for effective handling is given, together with an explanation of some of the factors that can influence effectiveness. Finally, and somewhat more speculatively, the chapter highlights the potential role of both processes in the light of more recent human resource approaches to employee relations.

Discipline and grievance: a theoretical perspective

Whilst both processes can be described in many different ways, for discipline the definition adopted here is 'some action taken against an individual who fails to conform to the rules of an organization of which they are a member' (Wheeler, 1976); and for grievance it is 'with respect to conditions of employment where a situation appears contrary to the provisions of collective agreements, the individual contract, work rules, laws or regulations or custom and practice' (ILO, 1965).

These definitions point to an apparent similarity; the idea that when one party in the employment situation fails to abide by the rules of the relationship, the other can bring a procedure into play to get them to adjust their behaviour, that is, managers can use disciplinary procedures, and employees can use grievance mechanisms. This does not necessarily mean that the procedure is a formalized one and, as will be seen in the early stages of both discipline and grievance, informal methods are quite common. Nevertheless, as an alternative to informal methods, or perhaps after using them without a resolution of the matter, formal procedures can be entered.

Once procedures are entered, matters can become very formal indeed, and this gives rise to another apparent similarity. Because formal processing of disciplinary and grievance matters usually consists of hearings which are quasi-judicial and quasi-legalistic in nature, both processes are often referred to in the same breath, and bracketed together as complementary faces of industrial justice (Salamon, 1987; Torrington and Hall, 1987). This argument, however, can be extremely misleading. It is not safe to assume that because they look similar, the two processes are directed at anywhere near the same ends.

In reality there is no overarching theory, be it justice or something else that can be used to encompass both discipline and grievance. They are two different processes, which exist for distinctly different purposes, and after this brief conceptual examination will be treated as such for the remainder of the chapter. However, perhaps because it is appealing in its simplicity, the 'two faces of justice' idea is extremely widespread, and it is important to examine it in somewhat greater depth. Essentially it rests on the idea that organizations can be likened to societies in miniature. That is, just as societies have rules of behaviour for their members, and use due process and formalized legal procedures to establish whether the rules have been breached, discipline and grievance are taken to be parallel processes used in organizations. Just how misleading this comparison is can be illustrated by examining some of the features of the two processes.

Criteria of justice

Discipline has a superficial resemblance to society's system of criminal justice and the guides to good practice (ACAS, 1977, 1987) reinforce this idea. They stress that people should not be accused or arraigned until the matter has been investigated, and that in arraignment, evidence should be presented to substantiate the accusation. There should be considered judgement before sanctions are decided, and it is usually considered fair that there should be a right of appeal against the judgement. However, there are huge problems with comparing wider society and organizations in this way. Criminal laws exist to protect all of society's members. Moreover, they are drawn up in public (in Parliament) and society has an opportunity to choose the lawmakers every five years. Imperfect as the system is, it still contains features which are largely absent in organizations. Here management are the lawmakers. They draw up the laws in private, and largely to protect their own interests rather than those of all the members of the organization. It is hardly surprising, therefore, that discipline has been called a very private system of justice (Henry, 1987).

Grievance has no similarity to this whatsoever, and the concept of justice is much more akin to that used in civil law. This is apparent in the definition given earlier, where the words *appears contrary to the provisions of* are used. As was noted in Chapter 2, the employment relationship is full of obligations which are implied rather than specific, and for this reason the parties often have expectations of each other that are unstated. Employees' expectations of management are often the result of a lack of explicit rules. Thus there are often no definite rules or criteria against which it can be judged whether an employee has been wronged by some action of management.

Capabilities to control behaviour

Discipline is much more a method of control than grievance. Indeed, current theories stress its use for this purpose (Ashdown and Baker, 1973). For example, in most organizations there are rules of behaviour which employees are expected to follow, and their actions are monitored by supervisors. Thus two important requirements for a system of control (objectives for performance and performance monitoring) are present. Grievance, however, has little claim to being a system which can control management's behaviour. It more often deals with situations where no prior rule for a manager's actions exists. Thus the only thing that can be asserted with any certainty is that something unanticipated has happened. At best this is saying that there should have been a rule in the first place. Therefore, it is less concerned with bringing management's behaviour within predetermined limits than with establishing what the future rules for behaviour should be. As such it is essentially a rule-making system, rather than a system of control.

Different effectiveness criteria

Although the idea of using discipline to control behaviour can be viewed as unethical, this at least gives one clear criterion against which the effectiveness of the process can be evaluated, that is, does it control employee behaviour? Since grievance is essentially a rule-making process, matters are far more difficult. Effectiveness can only really be evaluated in terms of whether both parties are satisfied with the rules that result, a much more ephemeral criterion. Indeed, employees and managers are likely to have different conceptions of what constitutes a fair rule of behaviour in the first place. This can make the handling of grievance a highly problematic affair.

As can be seen therefore, discipline and grievance are very different in a number of important ways. For this reason the remainder of the chapter deals with them in a very practical way. No employee will like being disciplined, and no manager is likely to enjoy a subordinate saying that he or she is so dissatisfied with the manager's treatment that grievance procedures will be invoked. However these things do happen. Therefore, perhaps the major consideration should be to try to ensure that when it does, there is mutual satisfaction with the outcome and the way matters have been handled, or at least that dissatisfactions are minimized as far as is possible.

CASE-STUDY 6.1

The scrap bin incident

You are the newly appointed manager of the Service Department of Terrondel Ltd, an organization which manufactures a wide range of domestic appliances. Your department services and rebuilds appliances which have been returned from dealers as imperfect, and also rectifies faults on those that have been rejected by inspection on the production line. This morning when you came into work, you found a note from the production manager referring to one of your subordinates, Gerry Green. This instructs you to look into what has happened with a view to disciplinary action.

On leaving work at the end of the night shift, Mr Green was approached by a security guard who ordered him into the office and instructed him to turn out the contents of the small duffel bag he was carrying. Mr Green at first declined, at which the guard snatched the bag and emptied its contents onto a table. Amongst the contents were two small items of decorative trim from a washing machine. When this was pointed out to Mr Green, he protested that there was nothing wrong. The items had been removed from the scrap bin, and it was normal practice for people in the department to retrieve these components for their own use. Nevertheless, the security guard reported the matter to the night superintendent, who instructed Gerry to report to your office at 2.00 p.m. this afternoon. He also telephoned the production manager, which resulted in the note you received.

You know that there are firm company rules about removing things from the premises, but suspect that they have not been strictly enforced in the past. Perhaps more importantly, you were approached first thing this morning by the shop steward who told you that what had happened had also been reported to him by Mr Green. Although as yet you have no idea what he will say, the steward has made an appointment to see you about the matter at 10.30 this morning.

Questions

i If you were the shop steward, what concept of justice would you be emphasizing most, and what would you be seeking as a 'just' solution.

ii In your role as the manager, what conception of justice might you be emphasizing, and what would you be seeking as a 'just' solution.

Discipline

General considerations

Perhaps the most pragmatic approach, and one which is in accordance with current thinking, is to view discipline as a process for adjusting employee behaviour.

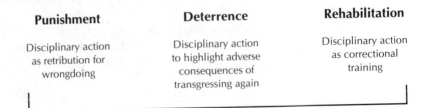

Figure 6.1 Alternative philosophies of discipline.

This implies control of behaviour, and gives rise to two questions. What aspects of behaviour does it seek to regulate, and how does it try to do this? Without going into too much detail, it is probably safe to say that the aspect of behaviour it ultimately aims to regulate is an employee's mental processes, so that they are prompted to behave in a way that is more acceptable to management. The question of 'how' it seeks to do this is much more complex, and is connected with the philosophy underpinning disciplinary action. There are a whole range of philosophies that could be at work, but for the sake of simplicity the three main perspectives can be expressed along a continuum as illustrated in Figure 6.1.

Punishment has little to do with shaping future behaviour, and it is more concerned with taking retribution against the employee for breaking the rules, that is, the 'eye for an eye and tooth for a tooth' philosophy. *Deterrence* is only a short way from punishment, and by using disciplinary action as an unpleasant consequence that follows a transgression, it is hoped that the employee will be deterred from transgressing again. *Rehabilitation* uses the disciplinary process to show the employee that certain behaviour is unacceptable. The aim is that in the future she or he will voluntarily adopt patterns of behaviour which are acceptable. Clearly, whichever one of these philosophies is at work is likely to have a strong impact on how disciplinary issues are handled. As will be seen later, this has strong implications for the success of the process in terms of modifying the employee's future behaviour. To illustrate the point the two extremes of the continuum will be considered.

Space precludes an extensive discussion of the use of punishment as a way of conditioning behaviour, but suffice it to say that it requires extremely stringent conditions for its effective use. In practice these requirements are difficult to achieve, even in a well-designed psychological experiment, and within the confines of disciplinary procedures they can hardly be met at all. Perhaps more importantly, unless these stringent conditions are met, even mild punishment is likely to give rise to emotional reactions (Kadzin, 1986). This can set up forces that actually resist conformity (Zipf, 1960), and punishment can quickly become a self-defeating action.

It is for these reasons that the rehabilitation approach currently receives the strongest endorsement. In this approach there are different stages of the procedure. Sanctions get progressively more severe for repeated transgressions, and the idea is that an employee is given every chance to modify his or her behaviour. Even here, however, it is important to note that aversive stimuli such as rebukes and other sanctions are used. These are delivered after a transgression has taken place, and purposely associated with the transgression. Thus even where a manager's philosophy is truly correctional, unless very great care is taken about how matters are handled, it is almost certain that the recipient will interpret the sanction as a punishment. For these reasons, whether or not a person's behaviour changes can depend as much on the way matters are handled, as on what sanctions are used.

Codes of practice and the legal implications

Whilst there are a whole range of sanctions up to and including dismissal that can be used, the law gives most employees a statutory right not to be dismissed for unfair reasons. It also gives them the right to challenge a dismissal before an industrial tribunal. Therefore, a fair and effective disciplinary procedure is as vital to management as it is to employees. Wherever possible it is advisable that the procedure should conform as closely as possible to the code of practice formulated by the Advisory, Conciliation and Arbitration Service (ACAS). Broadly speaking, this stresses the rehabilitation approach, and emphasizes that procedures should:

(1) Be in writing.

(2) Specify to whom they apply.

(3) Provide for matters to be dealt with quickly.

(4) Indicate the disciplinary actions which may be taken.

(5) Specify the levels of management which have the authority to take the various forms of disciplinary action, ensuring that immediate superiors do not normally have the power to dismiss without reference to senior management.

(6) Provide for individuals to be informed of the complaints against them and to be given an opportunity to state their case before decisions are reached.

(7) Give individuals the right to be accompanied by a trade union representative or by a fellow employee of their choice.

(8) Ensure that, except for gross misconduct, no employees are dismissed for a first breach of discipline.

(9) Ensure that disciplinary action is not taken until the case has been carefully investigated.

(10) Ensure that individuals are given an explanation for any penalty imposed.

(11) Provide a right of appeal and specify the procedure to be followed.

The code does not lay down universal procedures, but recognizes that they need to be tailored to the circumstances of each organization. It also notes that rule

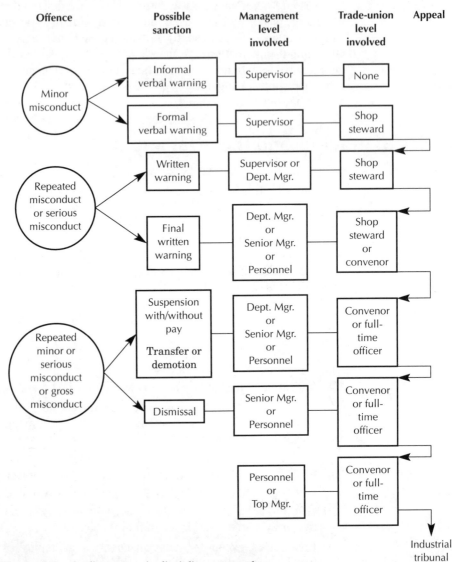

Figure 6.2 Outline stages in disciplinary procedures.

transgressions vary in severity, and that some invite more severe sanctions at an early stage according to organizational circumstances. An example could be that a first incident of smoking in a no-smoking office might be dealt with as a minor misdemeanour, but the same behaviour where there is a risk of explosion might well be viewed as gross misconduct. Nevertheless, a specimen set of stages can be inferred from the code, and these are shown in Figure 6.2.

Problematically, employment law has little to say about the matter of discipline, and it only approaches clarity in the case of the severest sanction of all – dismissal. Nevertheless, whilst the law gives management a great deal of discretion about lesser penalties, even some of these have contractual implications. For example, unless the contract of employment specifies (perhaps by referring to disciplinary procedures) that penalties such as fines, deductions, suspensions or demotions can be exacted, these can be *ultra vires*, that is, beyond the employer's contractual rights.

The Industrial Relations Act, 1971 and the Trade Union and Labour Relations Act, 1974 define that an employee can only be dismissed without fear of redress if dismissal is deemed to be fair. However, certain categories of employee are not protected in this way; for example, those with under two year's consecutive service if they work for 20 or more hours per week (five years if working for less than ten hours), and those who have reached statutory retirement age. In addition, certain occupations such as police and registered dockers are excluded. Dismissal itself is defined in the Employment Protection (Consolidation) Act, 1978 as occurring in one of three ways: by the employer terminating the contract with or without notice, by constructive dismissal, or by non-renewal of a fixed-term contract. Failure to renew a fixed-term contract would not generally be deemed as unfair. Constructive dismissal does sometimes arise in tribunal cases resulting from the use of discipline, and also has some implications in grievance handling, which will be considered later. Thus the first situation, termination by the employer, is the one of main concern here.

Like many legal terms 'unfair' is a word that is open to interpretation in the light of specific circumstances. Until the 1985 Industrial Tribunal Regulations came into force, the burden of proof was on the employer to show that:

(1) dismissal had occurred for one or more of a number of reasons that were considered 'reasonable and fair' in the specific circumstances;
(2) these were sufficient reason for dismissal.

Under current legislation, however, the onus is as much on the employee to show that the employer did not act reasonably. It is therefore impossible to give hard and fast rules for what is deemed fair. Given appropriate circumstances, however, the following are some of the general guidelines that can apply.

The *incapacity* of an employee to perform the job for which she or he has been employed. This can be for reasons of lack of skill, qualifications, inefficient or ineffective work performance, or health. In the case of the latter, management generally has to demonstrate that reasonable efforts have been made to establish the employee's state of health, that it noticeably affected performance, and that suitable alternative work is not available. With poor performance, the employer is usually required to demonstrate that this has persisted in spite of giving reasonable support to enable improvement.

Misconduct, which can encompass a wide range of behaviours, such as unauthorized absence, poor timekeeping, fighting, drinking, swearing, insolence and rudeness, and wilful disobedience. Again the onus is equally on the employer and employee to show whether or not dismissal was fair in the circumstances. In the case of drinking, for example, it is not the act of drinking but its effects on work performance that count, and bad language is sometimes part of the working culture of certain groups of employees.

Breach of statutory duty, where the employer could not continue to employ the person in their designated job without breaking the law. For example, where a driver loses their licence for some reason.

Other substantial reasons. This can potentially be a catch-all reason because tribunals can sometimes view things solely from an employer's perspective (Dickens, 1982; Aikin, 1984). It is frequently used where an employee refuses to agree to changes that management attempts to impose unilaterally. As was stated in Chapter 2, the employment contract is deemed to be individual in nature and, strictly speaking, it needs the consent of both parties for its variation. Thus, if one party unilaterally seeks to impose changed terms, the other can allege that the contract has been broken, and that constructive dismissal has taken place.

Whatever the reason that is given for dismissal, there is another point that is important. It can be hard to demonstrate fairness unless certain procedural aspects have been observed. The law not only looks at why dismissal took place, but also how the employer went about it. In the case of dismissal for incapacity or repetitions of mild misconduct it will, for example, often require proof of thorough investigation of the circumstances, and that prior warnings of future consequences were given. If an employee challenges dismissal, the case can ultimately be heard by an industrial tribunal. There is, however, a facility for conciliation through ACAS prior to a tribunal hearing. In 1989, for example, 56 % of such claims were settled in this way, and only 18 % went to tribunals (ACAS, 1989). In the event of a tribunal finding in the employee's favour it can make one of two basic awards: reinstatement or compensation. Where matters have gone as far as a tribunal, it is usually assumed that the relationship between employer and employee has irretrievably broken down, and so reinstatement orders are comparatively rare. In practical terms they are more in the nature of a recommendation. However, if a firm fails to comply with one, the tribunal has the right to increase compensation by up to 26 weeks' pay.

Compensation, when awarded, is in two parts. The *basic award* is based on age and length of service, and is equivalent to the amount the employee would have received if made redundant. The *compensatory award* is for loss of benefits and earnings, and within limits, is discretionary. Therefore, tribunals have the power to reduce compensation if the employee's actions are felt to have contributed to her or his dismissal. Indeed, since an employee is under a duty to mitigate her or his loss as much as possible, the tribunal can reduce this element if it believes the employee has not sought work after dismissal, or was not prepared to accept it if offered.

An outline scheme for the effective handling of discipline

'Effective' is defined here as handling which results in future observance of rules by an employee. To be effective it must also be fair and just; not only because there are legal implications if it is not, but because these are important aims in their own right. Because it is also necessary for the process to be seen as fair and just, effectiveness also means being systematic and consistent in the way issues are handled. Thus matters need to be handled in an appropriate way from the start. Indeed, if the initial stages are not conducted in a fair and just way, everything from then on can be called into question. Because these stages are usually handled by first line supervisors, what follows is largely directed at this level of management, and the scheme is shown in outline in Figure 6.3.

In the initial stages it is crucial that the issue is viewed as one which is only *potentially* a disciplinary matter. Thus the process is essentially one of tentative exploration, and its overall aim is to reach a *decision* about whether or not to enter disciplinary procedures.

Awareness and clarification

When first becoming aware of an issue it is important to avoid falling into the trap of assuming a proven case. Since the primary aim of discipline is to encourage an improvement in behaviour, the first step is to clarify whether or not a case exists. Answering the four questions shown in Figure 6.3 can be a useful step, and from these it should be possible to decide whether or not a potential infringement of rules has occurred. To do this, it is obviously necessary to know what the rules are, and how they are applied in practice. Moreover, it is important to take note of any custom and practice arrangements or precedents that could condone what has happened. These things should all be taken into account before deciding whether or not matters will be taken further. If (after doing so) it is decided that a problem or issue exists, in fairness and justice the next step is to see the person concerned.

Preparation

Although it is advisable not to make the initial interview too formal and intimidating, to ensure that it serves its purpose of clarifying matters it is important that it is preplanned to some extent. It needs to be held somewhere that is free from interruption, and big enough to accommodate all those who need to be present. These people (for example, the individual concerned, representatives and witnesses) should all be notified, and it is also advisable to make some enquiries about the contextual circumstances surrounding the situation. For example, whether there are any current employee-relations issues and problems which might escalate as a result of action which is decided, or whether the problem itself is part of a wider employee-relations issue.

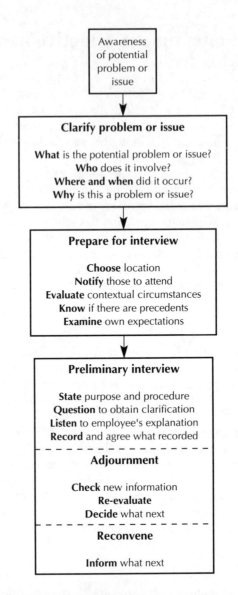

Figure 6.3 Outline of stages in initial handling of potential disciplinary issue.

An important note of caution should be sounded here. It can be tempting to look at the past record of the person involved to see whether there is a history of disciplinary matters. However, the purpose of seeing her/him is essentially exploratory and tentative. Thus it can be inadvisable to look into the past, because if disciplinary action does eventually occur, it can result in accusations that the individual's past record caused matters to be viewed in a biased way.

The interview

In fairness to the employee concerned, and in the interests of getting to the root of the matter, it is helpful to put her/him at ease by opening with a statement which outlines the purpose of the interview, and how it will be conducted. This should make it clear, in a non-threatening way, that the interview is being held with a potential for matters to progress into disciplinary procedures. The purpose of other people being present should also be explained. The facts of the matter as they are known should then be stated, and fairness and justice dictate that the employee should be given a chance to state her/his version of matters. Since the aim is to clarify and gain further information, witnesses called by either employee or supervisor who can shed further light on matters can be important. In the interests of clarity what both they and the employee say should if necessary be questioned. Indeed, only through intelligent questioning is it likely that the matter can be fully explored. Throughout the interview, the most important skill which is needed is listening, and this seldom happens of its own accord. Thus if the person who is conducting the meeting summarizes what has emerged at fairly frequent intervals, it can help her/him to listen actively, particularly if she or he tries to make the summaries reflect whether the key points of the issue are still the same, or have changed. It is also important that a record be kept of what is said at this meeting, and that the record is agreed by both parties.

At the end of the interview it may be the case that there is some difference between the way the employee and supervisor perceive the situation. If so, it is important that the supervisor should not try to enforce her/his perceptions of the meeting on the employee. Conversely, a conclusion could be reached that there is no case to answer. In this eventuality it should be remembered that the experience will almost certainly have been a harrowing one for the employee. An honest admission at this stage that matters were not as they originally appeared can do a great deal to win the employee's respect and improve future relationships.

In the situation where there still appears to be a difference in perceptions, it is important to avoid making a hasty decision. Thus it can be sensible to call an adjournment which is long enough to enable further investigations to be made. If this is done the matter should not be left hanging in mid-air, but a definite time, date and venue should be fixed for the meeting to be reconvened. The adjournment should be used constructively, to review outstanding issues from the interview; for example, the real status of the rule which it is claimed has been broken. It can also be useful to look into the circumstances surrounding the case, particularly if any claim for mitigating circumstances has been raised. Having done this, the next important thing to do is to decide whether a case still exists, and if so what it is. Whichever of these happens, the fairest place to say so will be at the reconvened interview.

Where it is decided that the matter needs to be handled through disciplinary procedures, it is now fair to examine the employee's past record. Indeed, it can be important to do so. If there have been previous incidents of the same nature, it may well be that procedures dictate that they should be handled at a level above that of the supervisor, and if the case appears to be one of serious or gross misconduct, it could involve sanctions heavier than she/he is allowed to impose. In these circumstances, more senior levels of management such as the departmental head or a personnel specialist should be consulted. It should be pointed out, however, that those consulted need to be selected with a great deal of care. The next level of management upwards would almost certainly be the one that has to deal with the matter if a sanction is taken and the employee subsequently decides to appeal against it. Therefore, it is important that a future judge of the issue does not become an unwitting party to the sanction.

Where the supervisor can handle the matter further, it is important that any action she or he takes is both consistent and fair. Checking with other supervisors, managers and personnel specialists could still be useful, particularly if there are circumstances which might mitigate the normal penalty in some way. Again, however, and for the reasons given above, any consultation needs to be done with a great deal of care. It is also important to plan the conduct of the reconvened interview, and many of the points made earlier about clarity with respect to its aims and objectives also apply.

The reconvened interview

Here the basic purpose is twofold: to conclude the investigation, and to take any action which is deemed necessary. The structure of this meeting will be similar to the previous one. It should start with a statement of how things stood at the adjournment of the first interview, and then any new information that has come to light should be presented. Again the employee should be given the opportunity to raise questions and to state her/his point of view. When this has happened the interview should be brought to an end by the supervisor stating what conclusions have been reached, and what action it is proposed to take. If this does not involve a sanction, but simply consists of a warning that the employee's conduct must improve, it is important that the employee be told:

(1)   what should be achieved;

(2)   whether that standard is normal;

(3)   whether help can be expected from management and supervision in meeting that standard (that is, training);

(4)   the time-scale over which the improvement is to take place.

It is clearly much better if the subordinate understands the reasons for what has happened, and that if an improvement is made matters will go no further. Where he or she does not agree with the outcome, and irrespective of whether a sanction has been imposed, fairness and justice dictate that the employee be informed of any rights of appeal against the decision, and how to proceed with this.

Factors influencing the effective handling of discipline

The list of things that can interfere with the effective handling of discipline is potentially endless. Some of these result from misuse of procedures, and others from human fallibility. Indeed, some are not actually concerned with handling itself, but are as a result of the contextual circumstances that play a part in shaping handling styles. There is only space to describe some of the more prominent factors here, and for convenience these can be grouped under four general headings.

Contextual factors

Clearly unless *substantive rules* exist it is hard to demonstrate that a transgression has occurred. What is perhaps more important is to recognize that managers are virtually the sole authors of these rules, and that their *attitudes and ideologies* can play a part in how they are framed. Managers can jealously guard what they see as their legitimate prerogatives (Fox, 1974), and one problem that can arise is where a manager uses the process to establish a new rule that reinforces his or her authority. Problems can also arise because managers have a tendency to link an employee's observance of formal rules with vaguer expectations, such as having a willing and cooperative attitude. For example, an employee who is found guilty of breaking a minor substantive rule can sometimes be subject to a sanction which is out of all proportion simply because they are also judged guilty of not conforming to these vague expectations.

Another problem can arise from informal custom and practice arrangements, which play a strong part in determining whether formal rules are observed in practice (Terry, 1977). Substantive rules can easily get out of date, and those who formulate them need to ensure that they are explicit, realistic, and above all acceptable. It is probably as well to remember that if everybody is breaking a rule, it is probably high time it was changed anyway. Under no circumstances should the disciplinary process be used as a matter of convenience to resurrect a long-dead rule that has remained unenforced for some time. Notice should be served that the rule is to be reintroduced, and that future observance is required. Finally there is the all-important problem of communicating the rules. Instead of making a vague assumption that employees know the rules, or at best posting them on a notice board, it would arguably be more cost effective to devote some attention to explaining rules, and the reasons why they exist. Nevertheless, rather than informing them beforehand, the disciplinary process is sometimes abused by using it to teach people the rules after they have been broken.

Subordinate factors

Awareness of rules does not of course guarantee their acceptance. Whilst there is some evidence that people's *personal characteristics*, such as personality (Mulder, 1971) and lack of prior socialization (Gough, 1948), can influence their willingness to flout substantive rules (Hogan and Hogan, 1989), great care needs to be exercised in branding people in this way. To make these judgements and then use the process to bring people into line can lead to a charge of victimization, and quickly escalate what is an individual matter into a collective dispute. Indeed, great care needs to be exercised where a subordinate has a prior history of being disciplined. Although there is some evidence that anticipation of the adverse consequences of rule transgression can result in a tendency to conform (O'Reilly and Weitz, 1980), poor handling on a prior occasion can have the reverse effect. It can, for example, result in an emotional reaction which affects the relationship between subordinate and supervisor, and this in turn can affect rule conformity (Greer and Labig, 1987).

Supervisor factors

One of the biggest problems here lies in what are technically known as *causal attributions*. When a supervisor perceives a rule transgression has occurred, the perception is inevitably accompanied by a judgement about why this happened. On one hand the subordinate's internal psychological characteristics such as ability, aptitude, effort, intelligence and attitudes can be attributed as the cause. Alternatively, external factors in the subordinate's environment such as the task, its difficulty or clarity of instructions are seen to be responsible. Unfortunately people are all too ready to assume that internal factors have prompted a particular act of behaviour, and external factors tend to be ignored (Mitchell and Wood, 1980). Clearly this problem is much more likely where vague expectations about the right attitudes are linked to overt behaviours. The important point, however, is that internal attributions have been shown to be much more likely to attract severe disciplinary actions (Larwood *et al.*, 1979; Bemmels 1991), and this is something against which supervisors and managers need to be on their guard.

Another factor of some importance is that of the supervisor's *position*, where evidence suggests there is a greater tendency to use disciplinary procedure where position power is high (Beyer and Trice, 1981). In addition discipline seems to be used much more where supervisor spans of control are very large; perhaps because time is short, relationships are less personal, and informal methods are less convenient (Goodstat and Kipniss, 1970). Again it can be noted that it is an abuse of discipline merely to use it to enhance personal power.

Issue-handling factors

This can perhaps be the most crucial aspect in terms of obtaining rule observance. It is not easy to shape employee attitudes in a way that gives conformity to rules, and the use of discipline is not something that is likely to endear a subordinate to the supervisor. Thus methods of handling which emphasize a genuinely corrective problem-solving approach rather than one which has even a hint of being punitive can be highly important (Maier and Danielson, 1956). Non-threatening methods, for example those that explain matters to the subordinate so that the diagnosis of their behaviour is seen as accurate, are far less likely to result in resentment and emotional reactions (Greer and Labig, 1987). Moreover, there is some evidence that early transgressions are best handled by counselling, and warnings of sanctions which could follow (Huberman, 1975).

CASE-STUDY 6.2

The night-shift supervisor

You are Tony Edwards, Customer Enquiries Manager for Gasco PLC. The organization supplies gaseous fuel to a wide variety of customers, and under its public liability provisions is required to have a bank of telephones manned around the clock so that customers can make contact in the case of emergency. Some three months ago you appointed James Kerr as night-shift supervisor, on three month's probation. Although he is only 27, you spotted him some time ago as a sharp, intelligent man, have talked with him regularly since his promotion, and he has given you no grounds for concern. When you arrived for work this morning you found a note on your desk from a night-shift supervisor in another department, the computer room. This was in a sealed envelope marked 'Confidential'.

The computer-room supervisor reported that he had tried to see Kerr the previous night at about 3.40 a.m., to inform him of a temporary malfunction which would have affected the capability of telephone operators to access customer records on the computer. He had gone first to Kerr's office, and although the telephone operators were working normally, Kerr was not there. On asking an operator where Kerr was, he was told that he was trying to find the duty technician as there was some trouble in accessing customer records on the computer. The computer supervisor thought no more of it, but on the way back to his own department had noticed a light on in another office. He looked through the window in the door and saw Kerr asleep. Kerr was aroused and apologised and left almost immediately. The computer supervisor also reported that there were rumours from his own staff that Kerr had been seen asleep on several other occasions.

You telephoned the Computer Department manager, who stated that his night-shift supervisor is a fair man, and not given to exaggeration. Therefore you telephoned him at home, and he confirmed everything he had put in the note, and said that he had also recorded the information in the incident book which he is obliged to complete at the end of every shift. You thanked him, came back to your office, and wrote to Kerr asking him to come in and see you at 5.00 p.m.

Grievance

Definition

In British industrial relations, grievance can be a notoriously unspecific expression that embraces both individual and collective issues (Marsh and Evans, 1973), and so the line between grievance and dispute is often a blurred one (Singleton, 1975). Some writers also distinguish between complaints and grievances. Torrington and Hall (1987), for example, consider the former to be simply written or verbal dissatisfactions brought to the attention of a supervisor or shop steward, and the latter a dissatisfaction which is formally presented. This, however, can be very misleading. It implies that complaints are merely issues which are raised, and grievances are those which are actually pursued. As will be seen later, there is a great deal of support for the idea that a dissatisfaction which is dealt with informally, and as close as possible to its point of origin, has the best chance of being resolved to the satisfaction of both parties. Formal procedures usually recognize this by specifying that grievant and superior should have made every attempt to resolve the matter directly between themselves before recourse is made to the formal process. Therefore, a complaint can often be the essential preliminary step in grievance handling, and this makes any distinction between complaint and grievance a misleading one. For this reason it is important to distinguish how the word 'grievance' is used here. Following the example of Thomson and Murray (1976), grievances are taken to be expressions of dissatisfaction by an individual. How an issue is initially raised, or for that matter how it is subsequently handled, is considered to be of less significance than the fact that it exists in the first place. Therefore, no distinction is made between complaints and grievances, and the discussion covers any situation where an individual considers it important enough to express a dissatisfaction to her/his immediate superior with the aim of resolving it.

The legal implications of grievance

Unlike discipline where there are legal implications if fair and just procedures are not developed, for the most part there is no similar imperative with grievance. However, it is clearly in an organization's interests to have a grievance procedure; a point recognized by the Industrial Relations Code of Practice (1972), which offers the following guidance:

> 'All employees have a right to seek redress for grievances relating to their employment. Each employee must be told how he can do so.
>
> Management should establish, with employee representatives or trade unions concerned, arrangements under which individual employees can raise grievances and have them settled fairly and promptly. There should be a formal procedure, except in very small establishments where there is close personal contact between the employer and his employees.
>
> Individual grievances and collective disputes are often dealt with through the same procedure. Where there are separate procedures they should be linked so that an issue can, if necessary, pass from one to the other, since a grievance may develop into a dispute.
>
> The aim of the procedure should be to settle the grievance fairly and as near as possible to the point of origin. It should be simple and rapid in operation.'

The procedure should be in writing and provide that:

- the grievance should normally be discussed first between the employee and his immediate superior;
- the employee should be accompanied at the next stage of the discussion with management by his employee representative if he so wishes;
- there should be a right of appeal.

Two points can be noted here. First, although the code recognizes that individual grievances can sometimes turn into collective disputes, the overwhelming tendency these days is for organizations to distinguish between the two types of issue by having separate procedures for each one (Millward and Stevens, 1986).

Whilst there is no legal requirement to have a grievance procedure, there are a number of situations which could put an organization at a distinct disadvantage if it did not have one that was demonstrably fair and just. There is now a considerable body of legislation designed to prevent sexual and racial discrimination in organizations, and an employee who feels aggrieved in this way has the right of access to an industrial tribunal. An organization that had no grievance procedure through which an employee could try to resolve an issue of this type could be at a disadvantage should a case reach a tribunal. Another situation is where an employee claims constructive dismissal before a tribunal. As an example consider the case where the management of a firm has attempted to impose a complete and radical revision of an employee's job. If the employee had been given no opportunity or facility to raise the issue as a grievance and to work out a mutually satisfactory resolution with management, she or he might decide walk out, and claim constructive dismissal. In these circumstances it could be construed that the lack of a formal procedure for handling matters of this type had forced the employee's hand, and this could sway matters in her or his favour in the eyes of a tribunal.

Effectiveness in grievance handling

It is also important to note another point made in the code: the aim is to *settle* or *resolve* a grievance. Grievance is not simply the reverse of discipline, and often there are no explicit rules which make the issue clear-cut. Therefore, the simple criterion of 'rule observance' used for discipline is not an appropriate one to judge the effectiveness of grievance. After Briggs (1981), the two criteria used here are:

(1) *Conflict management* Does the process enable peaceful settlement of dissatisfactions without recourse to other protest behaviours, such as, individual action, for example absenteeism or quitting or escalation in which the individual seeks group level support?

(2) *Agreement clarification* Does the process permit clarification (and where appropriate redefinition) of the terms of the reward–effort bargain in a way that ensures both parties have satisfaction with the outcomes?

At first sight these may seem stringent, but there is no reason why a well-constructed grievance process should not be capable of meeting them. Having said this, it is extremely important for the procedure to put boundaries on what it can and cannot deal with. Collective matters, which are more appropriately handled through disputes procedures, are an example of what should normally be outside individual grievance processes. There are also other issues that could more appropriately have their own separate procedures. Indeed, in large organizations it is not uncommon to find that there are several variants of the grievance procedure, each of which deals with a specific type of issue. For example, health and safety matters and pay/salary appeals might have their own mechanisms for handling dissatisfactions. For these reasons, grievance procedures need to be tailored even more closely to the specific needs of an organization than do those for discipline, and it is correspondingly more difficult to be specific about an ideal procedure. However, a model which can illustrate the outline principles involved is given in Figure 6.4.

The first thing to note is that the employee initially raises the dissatisfaction with the supervisor in an informal way. Because subordinate and supervisor are attempting to resolve matters between themselves, strictly speaking, matters have not yet entered procedure. This parallels the same step in disciplinary procedures where, except in the case of serious or gross misconduct, it would contravene the principle of natural justice to issue a formal verbal warning unless an employee had first been told that her/his conduct was unsatisfactory, and given

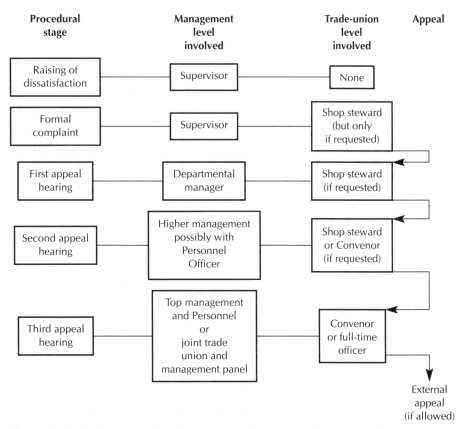

Figure 6.4 Outline stages in grievance procedure.

time to improve it. The same principle applies here, and where a subordinate is dissatisfied with her/his supervisor's conduct, the supervisor should be the first to hear of it, and have an opportunity to remedy the situation.

It can also be noted that in all the steps that follow, 'trade union' involvement is strictly on the basis of request. This is a feature which helps distinguish between individual grievance and disputes procedures. In the UK the owner of a grievance is the individual concerned, and so there is nothing inevitable about a trade union becoming involved. However, most procedures allow an individual (if they so wish) to put matters in the hands of their trade union, and if there are prospects of the issue going beyond the first stage, many employees would take advantage of this feature.

After the first informal step matters become much more specific to the organization. Clearly if at any stage the employee receives an answer which satisfies her/him, the grievance no longer exists, and the procedure automatically terminates. Usually at least one level of appeal exists, and the number of appeals allowed can sometimes be equivalent to the number of levels in the management hierarchy. However, particularly where formal negotiating machinery exists, a joint committee of management and trade union will sometimes hear appeals, and some procedures allow the case to be heard outside the organization in front of an independent third party as the final stage. In organizations which are members of an employers' association, it is sometimes this which provides the final stage. For example, an appeal hearing convened by an employers' association might happen where a grievance procedure has no stage involving a joint trade union and management panel within the firm. Without recourse to an outside arbiter it will always be management that judges the fairness of its own actions. Thus, although eventual recourse to an external and independent judge is by no means universal, it can do much to encourage fair and just decisions earlier on.

An outline scheme for the effective handling of grievance

To meet the criteria of effectiveness in grievance means that fairness, justice and systematic handling are just as necessary as they are in discipline. Similarly, the initial stages can be the crucial ones, and these will also inevitably be handled by first-line supervision. There is, however, an important difference between discipline and grievance in terms of the potential after-effects of the process. In discipline, even though a supervisor is scrupulously fair and just, she or he can hardly expect the process will have endeared her or him to the subordinate. Grievance on the other hand presents a positive opportunity to build good working relationships. This does not mean that the supervisor has to give ground on every occasion, but simply that people usually prefer to work for someone who is fair, just and understanding. Handling a subordinate's dissatisfaction in an appropriate way is an unrivalled opportunity for a supervisor or manager to demonstrate that they possess these attributes. For this reason, the first stages of grievance should also be regarded as tentative and exploratory. Above all, it needs to be remembered that the aim is to *resolve* the employee's dissatisfaction, and an outline scheme is shown in Figure 6.5.

When first becoming aware that an employee has a dissatisfaction, some managers and supervisors have a tendency to feel that their authority is threatened. However, it is important to remember that unless the dissatisfaction is brought to their attention and dealt with, it could fester beneath the surface. Thus a supervisor needs to curb any feelings of defensiveness or annoyance that the dissatisfaction has been raised. In order that its nature and origin can emerge in clear and unambiguous terms, it is crucial that the first informal approach is handled in an open-minded and open-ended way. Since it is the subordinate who will be informing the supervisor about these things, it is difficult to plan the detailed conduct of the initial interview beforehand. Nevertheless, details such as where it is to be held and notifying those who have to be present obviously need prior attention. Similarly, some thought should be given to any surrounding circumstances. For example, whether there are any current problems that

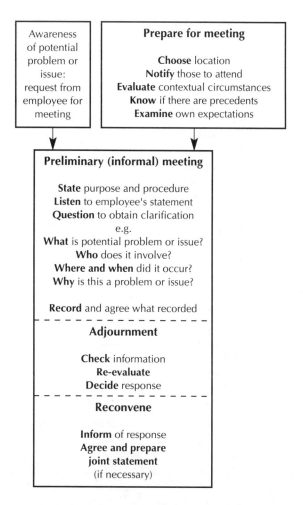

Figure 6.5 Outline of stages in initial handling of potential grievance issue.

might be associated with the issue, or indeed, whether the issue itself is part of a wider employee-relations matter.

The interview

In a grievance situation it is unlikely that a full awareness of the nature of a dissatisfaction can emerge until this very first stage has taken place. Since the employee has to state the case, the roles in this interview are broadly the reverse of those in the disciplinary procedure. However, this does not mean that the supervisor has to be totally reactive. The subordinate can well feel that what he or she has to say challenges the supervisor's judgement in some way, and this can make it difficult for him or her to articulate matters clearly. However, the issue is hardly likely to be capable of resolution unless the full details do emerge, and for this reason the supervisor has an active part to play in helping the employee to state the case. Clearly this needs to be done in an unobtrusive way, by putting the subordinate at ease and encouraging a free flow of dialogue. Thus an opening statement is needed which outlines the purpose of the meeting and how it will be conducted. It should be made clear that it is being held at the employee's request, and she/he should then be given full rein to state the way that she/he sees matters. In the interests of encouraging him or her to express the issue clearly she/he should, if necessary, be questioned. Questioning however, does not mean interrogation. It is extremely important that it should not be done in a way that leaves the impression that there is an attempt to sweep the matter under the carpet. The aim is to clarify and to gain further information. Thus many of the questions that were used to prepare for the disciplinary interview can be used as a guide. It is also important to remember that there could be custom and practice arrangements or precedents in the organization that might have a bearing. Needless to say, the skills of active listening and summarizing are important as well.

At the end of the meeting the supervisor may be able to make a decision that removes the dissatisfaction. If this is not the case, it is vital that the supervisor does nothing to enforce her or his own perceptions on the employee. The meeting should be brought to an end by summarizing where matters stand, and if there seems a possibility that the dissatisfaction could be resolved by seeking higher authority, the meeting should not be closed, but adjourned, and a date and venue fixed for it to be reconvened.

At any reconvened meeting, the supervisor should open by briefly restating matters, and whether there has been any change in the position since the last meeting. If there has not, the employee should then be informed of her/his rights to enter formal procedures. In these circumstances perhaps the most suitable way to bring matters to a close is to agree to draw up a concise but accurate statement of the matter. Whilst this does not have to be done there and then, what will go into the statement should be agreed; for example, the exact nature of the employee's dissatisfaction as it emerged from the meeting, and the supervisor's response.

Factors influencing the effective handling of grievance

As with discipline there are factors which can affect the successful use of procedures, and the same four headings will be used for the purposes of discussion.

Contextual factors

Having a grievance procedure is one thing; whether or not employees know it exists and can be used to resolve their dissatisfactions can be something altogether different. Grievances can be extremely rare in some organizations.

Torrington and Hall (1987) suggest that this is because few people would wish to risk antagonizing their superior by questioning her or his judgement, lest it result in them being branded as a troublemaker. For this reason it can be extremely dangerous to infer that a low number of grievances indicates a situation where there are no dissatisfactions. Indeed it may mean just the reverse, that is, that the climate is so threatening that nobody dare challenge management decisions. Perceptive managers will therefore look upon grievance not only as a method for dealing with dissatisfactions, but also as something that can stimulate upwards communications. Thus to make grievance procedures effective, employees must not be made to feel guilty if they seek to have dissatisfactions remedied. This means that the first essential is for higher managers to ensure that appropriate *rules and procedures* exist, their existence is advertised, and lower levels of supervision make the procedures work (Swann, 1981). This last point can be particularly important. It is only at lower levels that procedures can be made to work effectively, and for this reason, whilst senior managers would obviously not wish to encourage frivolous complaints or undermine supervisors, they should not be surprised if they have to repeat the message several times before it takes effect. To put matters another way, if a firm has to announce, and then keep announcing, that it has an open-door policy, it needs to be asked whether the doors are really open (Beck and Beck, 1986).

It should also be noted that custom and practice rules also play a crucial role in the raising of grievances. These influence the nature and traditions of workgroups, which could affect the willingness of their members to contest supervisory decisions (Sayles, 1958; Ronan, 1963). Thus it is important that senior management do not automatically assume that a supervisor who appears to handle a high number of grievances is ineffective. It could very well be a sign of the reverse.

With grievance, *ideologies and attitudes of managers* can be just as influential as in discipline. It is their actions that usually give rise to employee dissatisfactions in the first place, and perhaps more important, ideologies and attitudes can give rise to distinctive ways of dealing with dissatisfactions, if and when they arise. For example, it will be recalled that in Chapter 4 two contrasting management philosophies, unitarist and pluralist, were described. Predictably, those who hold a unitarist frame of reference are much more likely to make arbitrary and frequent changes which give rise to dissatisfactions in their subordinate's work milieu. What is more of a problem is that unitarist managers are almost certainly those who are most likely to consider that employees have no justification for feeling aggrieved.

Just as management ideologies and attitudes can be important, so can those of the *trade union*. Whilst there is nothing inevitable about trade-union involvement, a tendency for formal handling of grievances has some connection with two important characteristics of employee relations. The first of these is the *nature of workplace representation*. Although grievants are those who have the dissatisfactions, whether or not they pursue them through formal grievance procedures could well depend upon whether they are prompted to do so by representatives

(Bemmels *et al.*, 1991; Dalton and Todor, 1981). Where this happens, it should not prompt defensive reactions, or the assumption that stewards are trouble-makers. Bringing matters out into the open clearly lowers any tendency for things to lie hidden beneath the surface, and erupt in more disruptive ways. Thus in the long run stewards may well be performing a valuable service. The second characteristic, *industrial-relations climate,* is much more intangible, but can be an extremely important factor in grievance handling. The topic of climate will be explored in depth in Chapter 10, and for simplicity it will be used here to denote the quality of the relationship between trade union and management. This can be thought of as a continuum stretching from hostile at one extreme to cooperative at the other. A cooperative climate does not necessarily mean that trade union and management have no differences. Rather it indicates that they view each other in a way that permits differences to be resolved, and that differences can be aired openly in a spirit of trust and compromise. Conversely, in a climate which is laden with hostile views, trust and compromise are less likely.

There is a considerable body of evidence to show that hostile climates are associated with high rates of grievance activity (McKersie, 1964) and low morale in employees (Norsworthy and Zabala, 1985), and therefore tend to produce handling methods which are of low effectiveness. For example, in hostile climates there is less likelihood that grievances will be handled informally. Those which are not upheld at early stages are then doggedly pursued through all the successive levels of appeal in the procedure (Turner and Robinson, 1972). Thus rather than becoming a problem to be solved, both trade union and management use grievances as an opportunity to do battle, and tend to see matters in terms of winning or losing.

Subordinate factors

One factor which can be extremely important in the raising of grievances is the *subordinate's perceptions*. Dissatisfactions can often arise where a person makes a comparison between their own efforts and rewards and the efforts and rewards of others. Indeed the perceived degree of inequity together with the extent to which the supervisor is considered to have used fair methods in allocating rewards and effort have both been shown to affect the likelihood of using grievance processes (Barrett-Howard and Tyler, 1986; Fogler *et al.*, 1983).

Just as supervisors are likely to make *attributional judgements* in discipline, with grievance subordinates are likely to attribute motives to supervisors for their actions. For example, if a subordinate attributes some internal factor such as attitude, personality or mood to be the reason that a supervisor allocated her/him a particularly unpleasant task, then she/he is much more likely to interpret the action as a personal punishment and retaliate by using grievance procedures (Gordon and Bowlby, 1985).

Supervisor factors

There is some evidence that certain supervisory styles are associated with higher rates of grievance activity in subordinates. For example, supervisors who do not adequately explain or justify changes to subordinates seem much more likely to attract grievances as retaliatory action (Fleishman and Harris, 1962; Kulick and Brown, 1979). Moreover, how a supervisor reacts to prior grievances can give rise to even more dissatisfactions. One recent piece of work shows that if a subordinate successfully pursues a grievance, there is a tendency for the supervisor to retaliate by giving the subordinate a lower than normal performance appraisal at the next opportunity (Klass and De Nisi, 1989).

Issue-handling factors

There is a great deal of evidence to show that trade unions and management both feel that individual dissatisfactions should initially be handled informally and at the lowest possible level. No matter what the procedural rules specify, managers and stewards often handle matters in this way, and this has a great many benefits. Indeed the evidence suggests that organizations where low-level settlement is common are those that tend to have more cooperative industrial-relations climates (Turner and Robinson, 1972). This, as was noted above, is likely to have an effect on the subsequent rate of grievance activity.

Conclusions and overview

Despite their apparently straightforward nature, discipline and grievance issues can be extremely complex to handle, and there are a large number of factors which can affect whether the processes work effectively. Problematically, it is the early stages of the procedures which are most crucial, and these are often left to supervisors to handle, many of whom are untrained and ill-equipped to do so. However, providing sensible, consistent methods are used, it is possible for the matters to be handled effectively.

Both processes are, and continue to be, a fundamental part of traditional industrial relations. However, new approaches to employee relations are beginning to emerge, notably human resource management, which is the topic of Chapter 12. This places a strong emphasis on employee self-discipline and commitment of employees to the goals of management, and to do so makes extensive use of processes of communications, involvement and participation which are covered in the next two chapters. This raises the question of whether effective grievance and discipline handling will be as important for this newer approach as it has been in the past. Although any answer must obviously be speculative, there are strong grounds for reasoning that if anything, effective handling of discipline and grievance could be even more vital.

To start with, although the adoption of a human resource management approach is a top-level strategic decision (Guest, 1987), it can only be delivered in a practical way if there is a strong focus on employees as individuals lower down (Walton, 1985). Moreover, the approach is underpinned by philosophies which are basically unitarist (Guest, 1987), and where these are present the notions of managerial prerogative and imposed discipline are never far beneath the surface. Thus, although human resource management might hope that discipline will only have to be used as a regrettable long-stop, there seems little doubt that it will be used to extract compliance if need be. Indeed, there is some evidence that firms may well be tightening up their disciplinary regimes (Edwards and Whitston, 1989). As noted, the other side of the coin is that the approach also has a strong emphasis on gaining employee commitment to management's goals, and on promoting employee self-discipline. However, unless there are readily available methods to bring employee concerns to the surface so that they can be resolved, it is hard to see how this can happen. For these reasons the effective handling of grievance and disciplinary issues could be even more crucial in the human resource management approach than in traditional industrial relations.

CASE-STUDY 6.3

Overlooked

You are Mr Tree, the manager of an area Industrial/Commercial sales department in a large national organization which supplies fuel and fuel burning equipment to domestic, commercial and industrial users. You have only been in this post for about one month. Before that there were separate Commercial and Industrial sales departments, and you were the manager of the latter. As part of a major reorganization which combined the two functions throughout the whole organization, the two departments in your area were merged. Structures for the area Commercial and Industrial departments prior to the reorganization are shown in Figures 6.6(a) and 6.6(b), and for the new combined department in Figure 6.6(c).

Combining the two departments involved redesign of all jobs, and so new job specifications were produced, and the jobs themselves were advertised internally. Staff from the two previous departments were guaranteed that if they did not get the job for which they applied, they would be found a post somewhere in the new structure, and also that existing salaries and

Departmental structures

(a)

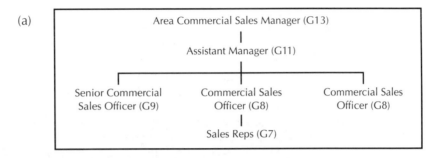

(b)

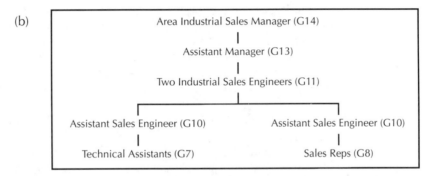

(c)

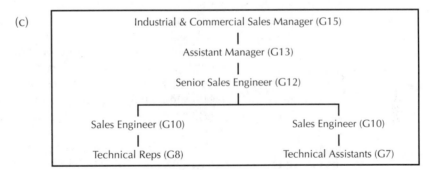

Figure 6.6 Case-study 6.3: Departmental structures. (a) Commercial Sales Department prior to reorganization. (b) Area industrial Department prior to reorganization. (c) Industrial and Commercial Sales Department.

conditions would be protected. You have been extremely busy across the past month interviewing staff and sorting out details of the posts. The final appointments were only made last week.

Obviously, in a situation like this everybody hopes they will get promoted but there are never enough promotions to go around. Anyway, as you see things, these occasions have to be used to give a leg-up to the deserving. In making the appointments you were able to do this for one bright young man from your old department who was promoted from a Technical Assistant job on grade 8, to a Sales Engineer on Grade 10. Obviously you could not do this for everybody, but at least you were able to ensure that none of your old staff went into jobs on a lower grade. After all, loyalty needs to be rewarded, and many of the people whom you have learned to know and trust over the years are probably better qualified and of higher calibre than those from the Commercial department.

The last appointments were announced three days ago, and immediately afterwards you received a request from a Mr Ivor Bennett to see him. Although you do not know exactly what this concerns, you are pretty sure that it is about his recent appointment and the way it was handled.

Bennett was the Senior Sales Officer in the previous Commercial department. He had applied for both Senior Sales Engineer and Sales Engineer posts in the new structure, and was unsuccessful in both applications. Since these were the only jobs he had applied for, he had eventually been placed as a Technical Assistant. This is a Grade 7 job, and therefore two grades below his previous status. He will be working directly for the young man from your previous department who has now been promoted.

His interview for the Sales Engineer's job was rather a disaster. For one thing, your boss Mr Square was on the interview panel, and he arrived late owing to traffic problems. Bennett's interview was the first scheduled for that day, and despite delaying the start to wait for Mr Square, it eventually commenced at about 9.30 a.m. Mr Square arrived at about 9.45, and this rather flustered Bennett. Mr Square's style of interviewing tends to veer towards the 'pressure' technique, and this he proceeded to do from his first question. He perhaps tended to use a little more pressure than normal, but in your view this could have been because he was frustrated at having been delayed. Since you always tend to take your tone from the senior panel member, you followed suit. The net result was that Bennett, unlike all the other candidates, rather went to pieces.

When Bennett had left the room and his performance was discussed, you did get some hint that there might be rather more to things than met the eye. Mr Square had said 'he suspected that Bennett was a poor judge of character, and therefore, he had grave reservations about his capability to be in charge of others; he added that 'indeed he does not know who his friends are'. Although you could not be sure, you felt that this was connected with a salary regrade claim that Bennett had pursued some nine months previously, in which he successfully obtained a regrade from G9 to G10.

Mr Square had been on the grading appeals panel, and before it actually met, had taken Bennett on one side and advised him that there were several G10 vacancies likely to be advertised when the reorganization occurred, so why bother with the grading claim. It appeared that Bennett had ignored this, and went ahead with the claim, which he won.

From what you know of Bennett, he has been a keen, loyal worker, and is probably upset about the drop in status. However, what can you do? Although the decision was officially yours, Mr Square obviously did not want to see him get the job. The last thing you wanted to do was start off by annoying your new boss. Anyway you could not promote everybody, or even guarantee them no drop in status. Apart from which, Bennett has not dropped in salary and conditions, and in your view should be thankful for that. Indeed, when you compare things with your own position he has been treated very fairly. You are now managing a department of nearly twice the size, and only received one extra grade for it. You do not want to see Bennett become demotivated because he is a good worker and you will need everybody's cooperation. This is a big opportunity for you, and somehow you have to get the combined department welded together. However neither do you want to annoy your staff by changing things now; nor Mr Square for that matter.

Question

How will you handle matters when you see Bennett?

Further reading

Thomson A.W.J. and Murray V.V. (1976). *Grievance Procedures*. Farnborough: Saxon House

> A comprehensive study of the operation of grievance procedures and mechanisms in a sample of UK firms. Gives valuable insights into the ways in which managers and shop stewards view and use procedures to resolve dissatisfactions.

ACAS (1987). *Discipline at Work: The ACAS Advisory Handbook*. London: Advisory, Conciliation and Arbitration Service

> A brief but useful handbook, which contains many practical points about disciplinary handling, with reference to the ACAS code of practice.

Steinmetz L. (1984). *Managing the Marginal and Unsatisfactory Performer.* Reading MA: Addison-Wesley

A thought provoking book that examines the problems of unsatisfactory performance in employees and explores a range of potential ways that these can be handled, only one of which is through disciplinary procedures.

7

Communications in employee relations

Introduction

A flow of information is vital for an organization to be able to coordinate its internal activities. For this reason there is a very real sense in which information can be thought of as the life blood of a firm. This can be particularly true in employee relations, and so the chapter opens by explaining the importance of communication, but also cautions that it will not on its own ensure that employee relations are effective. Following this a model is given which explains the dynamics of the communication process, and how it can be used for problem solving. The different methods of communicating information to employees are then examined, and their respective advantages and limitations are highlighted. Finally, the topic of a firm's communications policy and strategy is explored, and an outline set of criteria is developed for the design of an employee-relations communications system.

The importance of communications in employee relations

In general terms communication can be described as a process which conveys information between people. Simple as this sounds, it is important to recognize that communicating involves much more than simply sending information. If it has not been transmitted clearly, and in a form which can be understood by the receiver, it can hardly be said that communication has taken place. This can be a particular problem in employee relations. In some organizations employees do not get to hear about even minor matters which affect them until they are overtaken by events. This can result in employees developing an extremely poor opinion of management, and they sometimes impute a sinister motive for them being kept in the dark, that is, that something unpleasant is about to happen. Ineffective or inadequate communications can quickly lead to speculation and rumours. If all employees are starved of information, they are only too ready to listen to these rumours, and before long they become accepted as the truth.

Perhaps more important, certain processes in employee relations are unlikely to work at all unless considerable attention is devoted to making communications effective. For example, any scheme of involvement or participation hangs crucially on effective communication. Having said this, it is important to recognize that sharing information is not the same thing as sharing power or decision-making authority. Whilst there can obviously be no sharing of decisions unless information is shared as well, simply keeping employees informed does not mean that they have been invited to help run the organization. Thus, even where communications are excellent, it should never be assumed that this is a form of participation.

A case in point is team briefing, which will be described later in the chapter. Whilst this is potentially a highly effective scheme of face-to-face communications, it is nothing more. Despite this, managers often refer to themselves as being participative simply because they pay attention to communications. Even worse, the top management of an organization sometimes asserts that because it has developed effective methods of communicating with employees, a form of employee participation is being used. Nevertheless, where involvement or participation are real aims, both are processes which crucially depend on mutual trust and cooperation. Unless there is a process which allows ideas and feelings to be shared or compared so that other people can be taken at their word, trust and cooperation are unlikely to occur.

As can be seen therefore, it would probably be no exaggeration to suggest that communication is probably the least understood, and most heavily misquoted, word in employee relations. Indeed, there is a popular mythology about the process which probably does more to stand in the way of effectiveness in employee relations than to bring it about. All too frequently the very existence of problems is attributed to misunderstandings or inadequate communications. From this it is but a short step to portraying improved communication as a panacea to all employee-relations difficulties. Unfortunately it is not. No matter how much integrity and openness lie behind the telling, nothing in the world will transform an unpalatable message into a palatable one. Neither will an unlimited amount of effective communicating remove the basic differences that exist between employees and managers. This was pointed out forcibly some twenty years ago, and to quote: 'it would be wrong to overestimate the significance of communications as a cause of problems facing management and employees . . . communications cannot in themselves remove conflicts of interest and values' (CIR, 1973b).

For this reason it is better to regard effective communication as a process which allows the differences between employees and managers to surface and be dealt with. More optimistically, it will perhaps go further by helping employees and managers to better understand each other's viewpoint and find mutually acceptable solutions to their differences. Therefore whilst having a vital role to play in employee relations, effective communication is no more than a necessary lubricant, without which feelings of insecurity and mistrust can all too easily arise. Nevertheless, if managers do communicate effectively with employees it can increase trust between them and trade unions and employees, and help to reduce misunderstandings (ACAS, 1990). The resulting feedback that they receive can also help managers to perform better, and improve their decisions.

Despite this, it is important to point out that even where there is an adequate flow of information, and the information itself is relatively uncontroversial, there can still be communications difficulties in employee-relations matters. Often this is because of problems that arise in the actual process of communicating. These will be considered later with the aid of a general model, and for the present it is sufficient to note that there are three important features of any information that is transmitted.

First, information is not simply facts. The way that it is transmitted and the way that it is received usually mean that it is a mixture of both fact and opinion. The sender and the receiver are likely to have different opinions about what is factual, and so they will put their own interpretations on what is transmitted. A simple example will perhaps illustrate the point. Imagine a situation where management, as part of a process of regular briefing, informs a group of employees that the planned output for a department was 2000 units, but only 1800 units had been produced. In the same briefing, the manager also mentioned that in the last month, absence owing to sickness had been higher than usual. The bald facts may very well be that output is down and sickness absence is up. Indeed, the manager might well feel that they are both associated, and that could have been his reason for mentioning both points. Employees, on the other hand, might interpret things quite differently. For example, they could consider that 2000 units of output was too high a target anyway, especially since it is winter and a high level of sickness is to be expected. Moreover, they might well impute another reason for the manager's remarks. They could take them as a lightly veiled threat that attendance will be under scrutiny from now on, and that those with a less than perfect record could expect action of some sort to be taken against them.

A second point which flows from this is that information is transmitted for a purpose. Sometimes the purpose can be simply to inform others, and on other occasions it is intended to persuade and influence as well. People are well aware of this. It is the reason why they have opinions about whether what they hear is strictly factual, and look behind the words that are written or uttered to impute a meaning into them.

The third point is somewhat different, and concerns the way people vary in what they see as the reasons or purposes for communicating. In employee relations there can be significant differences between management and trade unions in this way. With managers the major purpose in developing effective communications can go well beyond informing people about what is going on. It is often to persuade them that management's solutions to problems are the only viable options. In other words, the aim is to legitimize management's aims, including those of directing the workforce as it sees fit. Trade unions, on the other hand, can see the whole process of effective communication and the value of information in a different light. For them the main purpose in acquiring information can be to strengthen their hand in negotiating on behalf of their members. For this reason, they put their own interpretation on the information that is transmitted, and also have fundamentally different views about what information should be made available.

The law and communications

There is an old adage which can be particularly true in employee relations, that 'information is power'. To some extent it has long been recognized that unequal access to information can be one of management's most potent sources of power (Moore, 1980). For this reason there are certain legislative provisions for disclosure of information, notably in the Employment Protection Acts of 1975 and 1978, both of which place a legal obligation on management to disclose information to recognized trade unions for the purposes of collective bargaining. That is:

(1) information without which trade union representatives would, to a material extent, be impeded in carrying on such bargaining

(2) information which it would be in accordance with good industrial-relations practice to disclose for the purposes of collective bargaining.

(EPA, 1975, Section 1)

These however, are rather vague requirements, and there are further guidelines for employers on what they can reasonably be expected to reveal. For example, the ACAS code of practice (ACAS, 1972) suggests that the following could all be reasonably expected to be made available.

(1) Information concerning pay and benefits

(2) Information on conditions of service

(3) Information on manpower levels

(4) Information on performance and productivity

(5) Certain financial information.

Whilst these recommendations and legal requirements exist, it is important to note that they place the onus on trade unions to identify what information is needed and explicitly to request its disclosure. Moreover, the obligation to disclose only extends to information which is relevant to issues covered in collective bargaining, not, for example, to those which are dealt with in non-bargaining forums such as joint consultative committees. Perhaps more importantly, the Acts specify certain types of information that management is legitimately entitled to refuse to disclose, namely:

(1) where national security would be jeopardized;

(2) where the employer would be breaking the law to do so;

(3) where the employer has obtained the information in confidence;

(4) where for reasons other than its use in collective bargaining, disclosure would cause substantial loss to the employer's undertaking;

(5) where the employer has obtained the information for the purposes of pursuing or defending legal proceedings.

Moreover, even where the information is germane to collective bargaining, employers cannot be required to:

(6) produce, or allow, documents to be copied or inspected;

(7) involve themselves in an amount of work or expenditure which is out of proportion to the value of the information for the conduct of collective bargaining.

It can be noted therefore, that whilst there are provisions which enable disclosure to be claimed, there are also a number of ways in which management can avoid doing so. In practice, although trade unions have brought a number of claims for disclosure before the Central Arbitration Committee, their record of success is not high (Hussey and Marsh, 1983).

Another relevant piece of legislation, which gives an oblique encouragement to employers to develop systems of employee communications, is Section 1 of the Employment Act, 1982. This requires limited-liability companies employing more than 250 people to include a statement in their annual report which describes any action taken during the financial year to introduce, maintain or develop arrangements aimed at:

(1) systematically providing employees with information on matters which concern them;

(2) regularly consulting employees or their representatives in order to take into account their views on matters which affect them;

(3) encouraging employee involvement in the company's performance through an employee share scheme or some other means;

(4) achieving a common awareness on the part of employees of financial and economic factors which affect company performance.

Although stopping well short of requiring firms to take these steps (that is, they are only required to include a note of changes), the Act could be said to provide an indirect incentive to develop communications. Whether this actually results in communications being improved is, however, another matter. For example, an investigation of companies whose annual reports proclaimed a commitment to doing one or more of these things showed that managers were much more committed to a window-dressing exercise than anything else (Mitchell *et al.*, 1987).

CASE-STUDY 7.1

Disclosure of information

Given below are a number of situations in which a trade union has requested the disclosure of information for the purposes of collective bargaining. The management of the firm in question has refused, and the matter has been taken to the Central Arbitration Committee (CAC) for a ruling.

    i A white-collar union is recognized for negotiating a range of conditions including salary scales at five factories and laboratories of a major chemical company in north-east England. It also has the right to make representations on behalf of its members within the procedure for challenging job evaluation. The union sought information about the detailed way in which the job evaluation scheme works to place specific jobs within pay groups.

ii In one firm four unions negotiate separately for different groups of employees. In order to prepare a claim for semi-skilled workers the TGWU has sought information about skilled workers' bonuses.

iii A white-collar union which negotiates for junior staff grades 1–6 has endeavoured to persuade an employer to introduce a productivity scheme. It sought details of the schemes used for senior staff above grade 6, whose work is sometimes covered by more junior staff.

iv A major credit-card company and a union have agreed to salary reviews based on a survey conducted by an independent firm of consultants. The company has agreed to give the relevant information from the survey, but not to hand over the actual report for scrutiny by the union.

v A trade union, suspecting that a company operates the criteria for progression through grades either incorrectly or using discrimination, has asked for minimum and maximum salaries and the spread of pay rates according to sex and hours worked. The company refused, and said if it gave these details, individuals' salaries could be identified.

Tasks

In each case decide:

i Whether or not the CAC is likely to rule in favour of the trade union.

ii The likely grounds for the decision of the CAC.

A scheme for analysing communication

Even in its simplest form, communication will involve two individuals. Because individuals differ in the way they interpret words and their meanings, the process is beset with potential difficulties. To illustrate some of these problems and provide a tool for analysis, a generalized model of the communication process which is based on the early work of Schramm (1953) is given in Figure 7.1. For simplicity the model shows one way of communication, and the reader needs to bear in mind that it is a two-way process. That is, the originator of a message and its recipient usually exchange roles to produce a dialogue.

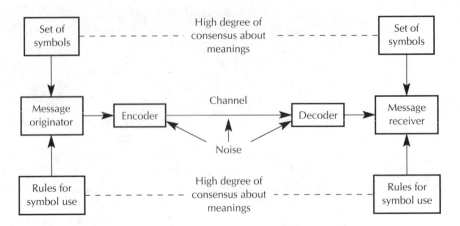

Figure 7.1   General model of the communication process.

The two basic requirements for communication are first the transmission of a set of signals along a suitable medium or channel, and second, its reception at the other end. This requires that the message be conveyed as a set of symbols (or a language) which gives them meaning. Starting at the left-hand centre of the model, it can be seen that the basic process begins with the originator of a message encoding it into symbols. It is transmitted along a channel, and for the message to be received, the recipient needs to decode it. In a telephone conversation, for example, thoughts are transformed into words, which are encoded into electrical impulses in the mouthpiece of the telephone. The impulses are transmitted along telephone lines and unscrambled into audible words in the earpiece of the telephone at the receiving end. In a written communication the originator's thoughts are encoded into words, transmitted by sending a piece of paper containing the words, and the words are interpreted by the reader. The model also shows that *noise* can be a factor of some importance. This can be conceived of as any extraneous unwanted signals which enter the channel. In the telephone system this could occur if the mouthpiece is held too close, and the sound of breathing distorts the words. Alternatively noise can enter where the transmission wires are in a bad state of repair, or if the earpiece at the receiving end is malfunctioning. As will be seen below, noise of one sort or another can also interfere with face-to-face and written communication.

If the model is now applied to the process of workplace communication, and each one of its component stages is examined, it can be used to identify some of the things that can go seriously wrong.

Symbols and coding

All messages originate in the minds of their senders, and have to be encoded from thoughts into a set of symbols. Thus the first essential is a set of symbols which are in common use by both sender and receiver. In order that the symbols convey common meanings, a second crucial essential is that there is a consensus about the rules for using them. A lack of consensus can often arise when specialist or technical language is used. Whilst it can have a very clear meaning to the sender, it can be highly ambiguous as far as the recipient is concerned. An example is the word 'credit'. To an accountant this means the amount of money at a firm's disposal, but to other people it can mean something altogether different, for example belief, trust or even kudos. What can be an even bigger problem in employee relations is that some messages can be notoriously hard to encode into symbols that are widely understood. For example, in trade-union circles an outburst of temper or show of emotion can be interpreted by other trade unionists as a sign of integrity and deeply held convictions. The same behaviour displayed by a trade-union official at a negotiating table could well be interpreted by managers as a lack of self control, or that they had the trade union 'on the run'.

Channels of communication

Here, a wide variety of problems can arise. To start with the channel must obviously be capable of conveying the symbols, and for this reason a great deal of thought needs to be given to whether it is the most appropriate one for the message. Spoken channels are best for some messages and written ones for others, and for some, a mixture of both is more appropriate. Indeed, certain symbols can be notoriously difficult to encode in written form. Sincerity, integrity and trustworthiness are all much more difficult to detect on paper than they are in the face-to-face situation. It is also important to realize that certain types of message can seriously overload a channel. For example, confusion can quickly arise if a manager attempts to describe verbally something very complex, such as details of new organizational structures or methods of work organization. This can often be done much more easily on paper, with the aid of diagrams. Nevertheless, face-to-face communication is much richer than the written form. It therefore gives a more personal focus, and many clues that aid understanding. For this reason it is often the most useful channel for messages where the sender needs to check that the receiver has correctly interpreted matters (Lengel and Draft, 1988).

Noise on the channel can also pose huge problems. At the transmission end, if a verbal message is too long, latter parts of it can interfere with what was said earlier on. With face-to-face communication, a significant source of noise can be an unintended clash between what is said and the non-verbal signals given out by the speaker. For example, a manager might say that she/he is interested in a subordinate's problems, but the manager's posture, eye movements and general demeanour can signal the opposite. Only about 7 % of the impact or meaning of a message comes from its actual content. More is conveyed by vocal inflection, and a huge 55 % from non-verbal signals such as facial expression and posture (Keltner, 1970). It is as well to remember that where this happens, it is the non-verbal message that is usually taken to be the factual one (Ekman and Friesen, 1975).

Another significant source of noise arises from the distortions which can occur in extended communication channels. If information is relayed through several different people, each time the message changes hands perceptual distortions can be introduced. In a very long chain, what is transmitted by the original sender can be totally unrelated to what is taken in by the final receiver. Noise can also interfere with the message at the receiving end. To some extent, recipients are likely to have preconceived ideas about what they 'expect' to receive as a message. This distorts their perceptions and interferes with receiving the sender's intended meaning. Because it is instantaneous, face-to-face communication can suffer particularly from noise at the receiving end. Whilst in terms of the total information that can be conveyed it is a far richer channel than the written one, the receiver has little opportunity to run his or her eye over the words a second time. One potential problem is of course the receiver who is so eager to make a response that he/she does not listen attentively, that is, some people listen and others 'wait to talk'. However, even where listeners are attentive, there can still be problems. For fear of conveying the impression that they were not listening, or that they are lacking in comprehension, people can misunderstand but still be wary of asking for clarification. To compound the problems, message originators are often so eager to get the message out that they fail to check whether it has been received as it was intended.

All of these sources of noise can be present in written channels as well. Readers can have preconceptions that lead them to make interpretations quite unintended by the author. Moreover, written material is devoid of the inflections of speech and the non-verbal signals that can help to ensure understanding in a face-to-face situation (Argyle, 1973, 1975; Cook, 1979). As an example, consider the following statement that emblazoned a bulletin sent out by a sales manager to his staff: 'Visiting customers can be a pleasure'. Is he exhorting his staff to pay more calls on the customers, or asking them to extend an invitation to customers to come and look around the firm?

Finally, it is necessary to mention a factor that can become a serious source of noise common to both verbal and written channels. The timing of a message can often have a huge impact on how it is received and interpreted. Announcing a drop in profits can be interpreted in different ways according to when the message appears. If it is said at one time it could be taken by employees to mean that productivity needs to be improved. If, however, it is said in the middle of wage negotiations, it can be interpreted as an underhand trick by management to pave the way for a meagre offer.

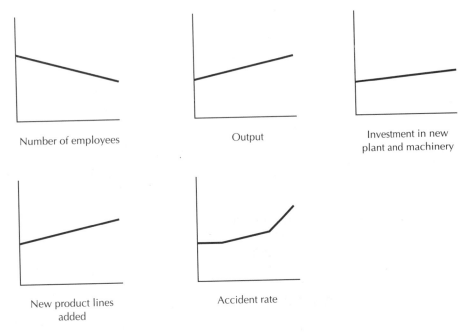

Figure 7.2   Case-study 7.2.

CASE-STUDY 7.2

Plush Limited

The Plush company manufactures domestic furniture, and employs about 1000 people. Management has always prided itself on good employee relations in the firm, but since it has grown dramatically in the past five years, there is a concern that things could be more difficult to handle in the future. Accordingly the managing director formed a 'Human Resource' Committee, and one of its first considerations was to find ways of improving communications with employees. After some discussion it was decided that there should be an ongoing attempt to keep employees informed about the company and its operations, and that a simple way to do this would be to display a number of large charts in a prominent place. Initially it was intended that there should be four of these, but at the insistence of the Works Manager, who was extremely safety conscious, a fifth one was added showing accident rates. The initial charts showing the position in the previous twelve months looked as shown in Figure 7.2.

Shortly afterwards it was brought to the attention of the Human Resource Committee that because employee turnover was on the increase, there appeared to a substantial number of vacancies in the firm. It was also noted that shop stewards in the company were taking an increasingly tough line with supervisors and managers about the payment of allowances for waiting time when machinery was adjusted to change from one product to another. They were also being particularly obstructive about the allocation of work duties, and were threatening that if the time allowance for some jobs was not improved, there could be a 'work to rule'. The Works Manager stated that one steward had told him that rumour about an impending shakeout was rife on the shop-floor, and that the general mood amongst employees was that they should make hay whilst the sun shone. To cap it all the Managing Director reported that at the meeting of the Joint Negotiating Committee on the very same morning, the trade-union side had tabled a claim for the biggest rise ever, well over twice the current inflation rate.

Question

How do you account for these reactions?

Methods of workplace communication

In employee relations the two most frequently used methods of communicating are written and verbal, and sometimes both are used for the same message. However, the responsibility for making communications effective is a matter about which there are varying opinions. The Trades Union Congress has for many years placed the onus firmly on management to communicate with employees about matters which affect them (TUC, 1971). Conversely, the Department of Employment Code of Practice (DOE, 1972) suggests that in unionized organizations effective communications should be a shared responsibility. More recently the Advisory, Conciliation and Arbitration Service has suggested that it is primarily top management's responsibility to ensure that arrangements for an effective system of communications are put in place, and gives two main reasons to support this argument. First, it is top management who sanction most of the changes about which employees need to be kept informed. Second, top management controls the actions of lower-level managers and supervisors, and it is through these people that information will usually be relayed (ACAS, 1990). The position taken here is similar to the ACAS stance, but with one important addition. It must be recognized that collective bargaining and consultation both result in communication with trade-union representatives. Thus they sometimes get to hear about things before managers and supervisors. Since one of the prime responsibilities of representatives is to keep those whom they represent informed, they will almost inevitably become a communication channel. This is not to say that management should ever assume that it is a trade union's responsibility to carry out the communications task. Rather it means that managers should recognize the inevitability of union representatives reporting back to their members. For this reason management should be at pains to ensure that the information conveyed to representatives in bargaining and consultation forums is accurate and clearly understood. The other side of the coin, of course, is that it places a responsibility on trade unions to ensure that they have a clear understanding of what management has said, and to guard against distortion when they report it back to the members.

Information to be communicated

A general guide to the type of information that management should make provision to communicate to employees is given in an ACAS advisory booklet (ACAS, 1990). This groups information into three main categories:

(1) *Information about conditions of employment* where in addition to the written statement of the main particulars of employment, which was explained in Chapter 2, management should ensure that other matters are made known. Specific reference is made to matters such as organizational or works rules, and arrangements for trade-union representation.

(2) *Information about their jobs* is considered to be vital to all employees, and falls into a number of subcategories:

    (a) *Operating and technical instructions*, which includes the work to be carried out, the standards to be met and how machinery and equipment should be used.

    (b) *General information* about the workplace can be vital to employees, particularly those who are new to the firm. In addition, it is considered advisable that employees should be given background information about the organization, and each individual should know their work objectives, together with the standards of performance expected of them.

    (c) *Health and safety* information should be given so that employees are made aware of any particular working rules which concern this matter.

(3) *The organization's performance, progress and prospects.* Here it is recommended that there should be a regular flow of information which keeps employees updated on financial performance, management and manpower changes, the state of the market and the order book, changes in products or services, new technical developments, and investment.

Channels of communication

As noted earlier there are two main methods of communicating in employee relations, verbal and written, and depending on the issue, a mixture of both is sometimes needed.

Verbal methods

Face-to-face methods are now strongly emphasized verbal communications. However in large organizations videos, films, or tape/slide presentations can be useful, and have the advantage of enabling the same message to be given by the same person to widely dispersed groups of employees. The great advantage of any face-to-face method is that if it is done well, communication is direct and rapid. It also gives the opportunity to check that the message has been accurately received, and to discuss its content or answer questions.

One method which is now much in vogue is **team briefing**. Essentially, this is a cascade system which commences at the top of the organization. Managers at each level brief the next level below about relevant matters, and this continues down through the whole organization. It is important to note that although there is some communication of information about company-wide matters, the main emphasis is on issues relevant to those being briefed. Therefore, at each level much of the information is specific to the workgroup. The operational guide to the process produced by the Industrial Society (Middleton, 1983) lays down the six cardinal principles on which it is based.

(1) *It is face-to-face*: although time is left for questions at the end, this is primarily to check that the message has been understood and general discussion is discouraged.

(2) *Small briefing teams*: usually not less than four, and no more than 15 people.

(3) *Leaders*: briefing is by the line manager or supervisor responsible for the team.

(4) *Regularity*: it should occur regularly, preferably at fixed intervals of about a month, and briefing itself should last no more than thirty minutes including questions.

(5) *Relevance*: it concentrates primarily on local information which is considered to be most relevant to the team. The 'core brief' which comes from higher levels of management should occupy no more than one third of the session.

(6) *Monitoring*: leaders need to be trained on how to brief others, and it is usually considered important for higher levels of management to monitor the effectiveness of supervisor's briefings.

As can be seen, although there is a built-in check that those who are briefed understand what is said, team briefing focuses heavily on one-way communication. The benefits claimed for it are:

- It reinforces the role of line managers and supervisors because as the providers of information, it differentiates them from their subordinates.
- By giving work a purpose and relating people to the organization as a whole, it increases the commitment of subordinates.
- It reduces misunderstandings by avoiding the assumption that people know what is going on, and instead, explicitly sets out to ensure that all employees receive a common message.
- Because the early provision of information can assist in people's understanding of why changes are necessary, it helps with the acceptance of change.
- Because employees receive a common official message, it helps control the grapevine.
- Although it should not be used for consultative or decision-making purposes, because people are better informed this can promote feedback to management via other channels, and thus improve the flow of upward communication.

(Grummit, 1983)

Having noted these points, whether the stated advantages are obtained in practice is a contentious point. Whilst most employees would rather be better informed than kept in the dark, the ideas underpinning team briefing are aimed at reinforcing managerial prerogatives, and are therefore highly unitarist. As such, employees might well be suspicious that the information conveyed is rather one-sided and selective. Indeed, what evidence there is on the outcomes of communication schemes such as these tends to show that the expected benefits of improved employee attitudes are largely unrealized (Ostell *et al.*, 1980; Marchington *et al.*, 1989).

Written methods

Written forms of communication are usually most effective where:

- There is a need for employees to have a permanent record of the information.
- Accuracy or precise wording is vital.
- A detailed explanation is desirable.
- There are large numbers of employees dispersed over several locations.

Again there are several ways that this can be done. Some firms develop *employee handbooks*, which can be particularly useful for new entrants as a source of reference for information such as company rules, policies and holiday arrangements and so on which does not change frequently. Many companies now provide summary annual reports, and these are used to inform employees about the activities and performance of the enterprise. Whilst they are generally considered interesting and valuable, survey evidence shows that employees tend to view them as presenting a biased picture that only shows management's view of things.

Moreover, they are often regarded as out of date, and only tell employees what they have already heard through other channels (Hussey and Marsh, 1983).

Bulletins and notice boards are probably the most widely used methods, and in the case of the latter are sometimes the only form of written communication. The great problem with notice boards is that not everybody stops to read them, and so it can never be guaranteed that the message has been received. For more regular dissemination of information, many large organizations also produce in-house journals and newsletters, which often contain social as well as organizational items.

One feature of most organizations which has not yet been mentioned is that informal channels usually exist alongside formal ones. This is often referred to as 'the grapevine', and whilst its existence is not officially recognized, almost everyone in an organization acknowledges that it operates. Indeed, as the saying goes, 'most organizations do not have grapevines – they have whole vineyards'. For the most part, managers tend to deprecate the very existence of these informal channels, but at the same time deliberately make use of them when it is convenient. An example would be the practice of leaking information about declining profits to try to structure people's attitudes whilst wage negotiations are in progress. Moreover, whilst formal methods such as team briefing are aimed at controlling the grapevine, it is unlikely they will ever eliminate it altogether. For this reason, it has been argued that no attempt at eliminating it should take place. Instead, management should take greater pains to ensure that official channels match the informal ones, and in this way both will reinforce the same message (Foy, 1983). However, the whole matter of using informal channels in this way needs to be considered with some care. In informal communications networks, individuals often attribute a rumour to a prestigious person in order to give it more credibility (Rostnow, 1980). Therefore, if official channels subsequently confirm that these people are accurate sources of information, they can quickly become the most credible sources in the whole organization. Since message content and its subsequent effect on the behaviour of recipients is strongly connected with the credibility of its source (Secord and Blackman, 1964), management can soon discover that they have fostered a means of undermining their own influence.

Communications: policy and strategy considerations

Effective communication is unlikely to happen of its own accord, and it requires effort and enthusiasm to bring it about. Because modern organizations are large and complex, the matter needs to be preceded by a great deal of thought and planning. Nevertheless, the problem of poor communications is not confined to large organizations. It can be a grave mistake to assume that because managers or owners in small firms are in day-to-day contact with employees, communications are naturally good and no formal arrangements are necessary. Indeed, the whole idea that employee relations are much more harmonious or that employees have a commitment to the goals of the employer in small firms is a gross overstatement (Goss, 1988; Rainnie and Scott, 1986).

To bring about effective communications in an organization, a positive impetus from top management is needed. Indeed ACAS have identified this as an area in which top management should most urgently develop an explicit policy and an active strategy (ACAS, 1990). The policy is needed so that there should be a clear expression of the employer's intentions and objectives, and the active strategy to ensure that these intentions and objectives are realized. Like any other area in which policy and strategy are developed, ACAS also recommends that they should periodically be reviewed and, if necessary, revised in the light of changing circumstances.

Since a system of workplace communications in an organization needs to be tailored to its particular requirements, it is impossible to give a universal scheme here. However, an outline set of steps for the development of policy and strategy can be derived from the ACAS guide. This is given in Figure 7.3, and shows the major considerations necessary.

The first need is to give consideration to two features: first, what is to be communicated, and second, the aims in doing so. Although both are obviously connected they probably need to be considered separately. For example, if management simply has the aim of keeping employees well informed, different considerations can arise compared with the situation where management has the additional aim of promoting an upwards flow of information as well. In both cases a great deal of thought will need to be given to what is communicated, but in the latter case there is a further consideration of how this will be done so that it stimulates communication in the reverse direction. To put things more bluntly, unless employees are kept informed about matters which interest and affect them, it is unlikely that they will have much to say themselves.

In terms of what should be communicated, this has been covered earlier in the chapter. Nevertheless, whilst it is important to stress that communications should stimulate interest, this does not mean that the range of issues on which employees are kept informed should be unduly narrow. For example, if matters are confined solely to task-related issues, communication or briefing sessions can all too easily become a vehicle for task allocation and performance review. Arguably these are matters which are much more appropriately dealt with on a one-to-one basis between supervisor and subordinate, where the motivational effects of feedback are much higher (Pincus, 1986).

As part of considering strategy and policy, ACAS recommend that firms should audit their existing arrangements. Here there are a number of interconnected questions that need to be considered. There is little point in implementing

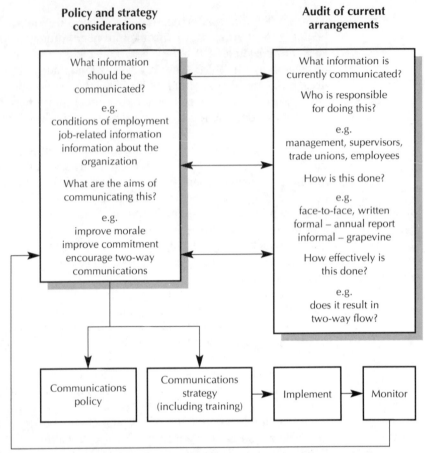

Figure 7.3   Outline of method to construct a system of workplace communications.

a grandiose communications plan if there are already serious impediments to effective communications. The one which is of perhaps most significance concerns the effectiveness of current methods and processes. Here the most important source of information for management is the employees themselves, and/or their representatives. Indeed, a firm seriously wishing to audit the effectiveness of its current practices could perhaps consider an employee opinion survey which taps attitudes to three major features of workplace communications:

(1) What is communicated: is it too much? too little? is it considered relevant and interesting or irrelevant and dull?

(2) Is the way it is communicated considered to be appropriate? For example, is the information communicated in a way that is most easily digested and understood by employees?

(3) What improvements could employees suggest about information which should be communicated to them, and the ways in which this takes place?

Clearly there is a need for the results of the audit to be compared with management's policy and strategy considerations. From this a new policy can be constructed, and a strategy derived for its implementation. Inevitably this will be organization-specific, and should cover both 'what' is to be communicated and 'how'. Perhaps as important, it should not neglect the vital matter of training the communicators to improve their abilities, and make them more aware of the importance of the task. As well as this, some thought should also be given to those who will receive the messages. For example, if financial information is to become a regular feature of bulletins or briefing sessions, it needs to be recognized that the recipients may need some initial training to show them how to interpret the statements. Finally, it is simply not enough to implement the strategy and leave it at that. The communications activity must be monitored to ensure that the strategy meets the policy objectives and is cost effective. It is for this reason that Figure 7.3 shows a feedback loop to the consideration of policy and strategy.

Conclusions and overview

Whilst communication is a very important consideration, it should not be thought of as an activity which on its own will ensure effective employee relations. Since it is essentially concerned with employees receiving information rather than sharing in decision making, neither should it be regarded as synonymous with participation. Having said this, whether or not it involves an element of involvement or participation, an effective system of communication can be an essential prerequisite of good employee relations. Moreover, because it seldom, if ever, happens by itself, management needs to develop coherent policies and strategies to make it happen.

Different management styles in employee relations and the philosophies which underpin them usually result in different views about the aims and purposes in communicating with employees. Thus there is a strong connection between the topic of this chapter and the material in Chapter 4. In addition, because there is some tendency to consider communication as a form of participation or involvement, there is also a connection between this chapter and the one that follows. For this reason the reader is particularly asked to remember that none of the methods described in Chapter 8 will work unless communication is effective.

What has been covered here also has a strong bearing on the topics covered in Chapter 12, where a number of initiatives which have become associated with the human resource management approach are described. Most of these are aimed at increasing employee commitment, and once again, their success can crucially depend on effective communications. Finally there is a direct link between what has been covered at the end of this chapter and the subject of Chapter 13, which considers employee relations policies and strategies in a more detailed way.

CASE-STUDY 7.3

Swallow Insurance Services

Swallow Insurance Services is a fast-growing insurance brokers. It has quadrupled in size in the last five years and has plans for significant future expansion. It deals with all types of insurance for both personal and property risk in industrial, commercial and domestic sectors. Currently it employs approximately 1000 people; 100 at the head office in Liverpool, and the rest in branch offices. It is structured into five regions, each with a small regional office of about 30 staff. Each region has up to 20 branch offices with about 10 staff in each one.

Because of new developments and modifications to existing products, insurance is a fast-changing business. For this reason the company is aware of the need to foster a customer service ethos in its staff, and to this end it pays great attention to employee-relations matters. It is currently reviewing its communications policy, and wishes to ensure that all employees are kept up to date with information on matters that affect them. In addition, it is particularly keen to encourage feedback from employees about conditions at the sharp end of operations, together with any information that they gather about customer needs. As a matter of policy it has been decided that the following types of information should be disseminated:

- For all new employees full details of conditions of service; and for everyone, full information on changes that are made from time to time, for example holiday entitlements.
- Job-related information such as new product developments, promotions within the company, new offices opened, and internal vacancies.
- Changes in organizational policy on such matters as health and safety.
- Company objectives, performance, and progress towards objectives.

Question

Taking into account the nature of the business and the company structure, what do you feel are the most appropriate ways for this information to be disseminated? Give reasons for your choice and state how the company should go about putting its communications aims into effect.

Further reading

Bland M. (1980). *Employee Communications in the 1980s: A Personnel Managers Guide*. London: Kogan Page

> A comprehensive book covering most aspects of communication in employee relations.

Hussey R. and Marsh A. (1983). *Disclosure of Information and Employee Reporting*. Aldershot: Gower

> Reports the results of an extensive survey in British firms on disclosure of information to trade unions, communication of information to employees, and the communication process.

8

Involvement and participation

Introduction

Involvement and participation are both very prominent words in employee relations at the current time. Involvement is in vogue because it is one of a number of practices which have been associated with the increasingly influential human resource management approach. The word 'participation' is prominent for two reasons: first, because the word tends to be used interchangeably with involvement, and second, because EC legislation, if adopted, would make some form of participation mandatory in all member states. However, the two words really mean different things and for this reason the chapter commences by distinguishing between them. It then gives a brief review of the recent events affecting employee participation in Great Britain, and argues that at present involvement is on the increase, and any trend towards participation is very weak. Following this, different methods which can be used to implement schemes of involvement and participation in organizations are described, together with some of the evidence and arguments concerning each one. The focus then moves to proposed EC legislation on participation, and some of its implications for firms in the UK. Finally, a brief review of the Institute of Personnel Management's guidelines for selecting an appropriate scheme for an organization is given.

Involvement and participation defined

Because there is a tendency for the words to be used interchangeably when discussing involvement and participation in employee relations, it can be vital to define the way in which they are used. As will be seen, participation in particular is a word that is used in a very loose way, and it is not uncommon for two people to discuss the subject and to find that they mean totally different things. In this book, the words participation and involvement are taken to refer to distinctly different processes. After Pateman (1970), participation is defined as 'a process in which employees, either directly or indirectly through their representatives, share equal power over decision-making outcomes, in the organizational decision-making process which management normally reserves to itself' and involvement as 'the various means used to harness the talents and cooperation of the workforce in the common interests that they share with management' (Farnham and Pimlott, 1987, p. 69).

As can be seen, the essential feature of participation is that it gives employees or their representatives a share in the process of management. With involvement, although a degree of common interest between employees and management is acknowledged, this does not necessarily mean that management invites them into the decision-making process. As such there is a clean distinction between the two and this will be maintained throughout the rest of the chapter.

An overview of involvement and participation

As will be seen presently, in practice involvement is much more in vogue in employee relations than participation. Nevertheless, in one form or another participation has been on the employee-relations agenda for a long time. Indeed, one writer has wryly observed that when conditions are severe enough for managers to have a strong need for employee cooperation, they tend to rediscover the word, only to forget it very quickly when the emergency has passed (Ramsay, 1977). However, the pressures for some form of participation have almost certainly grown stronger across the past four decades. In the Second World War even married women were conscripted into industry, and this brought about fundamental changes in social values and the way society is organized. After the war, greater economic prosperity and security, together with the higher levels of awareness and education in the working population, all helped to fuel rising aspirations. Moreover, in the 1960s and 1970s, when trade-union power was at its greatest, there was an increasing willingness to question traditional patterns of deference in industry. Thus politicians and managers alike looked in new directions for solutions to industrial-relations problems. In the mid 1970s a parliamentary committee of enquiry was set up, chaired by Lord Bullock. This included members from both sides of industry and was charged with looking into the whole question of industrial democracy. By then, several countries in Europe had made provision for some form of worker participation in decision making, the most notable example being West Germany. In Great Britain the prevailing mood in the government of the day was that some move in this direction had become inevitable. Thus the terms of reference of the Bullock Committee, as it subsequently became known, were quite explicit: to identify a way in which some form of worker representation on the boards of directors of firms could best be achieved; not (it can be noted) whether it should occur.

The final (majority) proposal of the committee contained a recommendation which has some similarity with the scheme of worker directors used in German industry, that is, that company boards should be reconstituted to consist of equal numbers of directors appointed by shareholders and employees. In addition a smaller number of independent directors should be co-opted onto the board; the so called $2x + y$ formula (Board of Trade, 1977). However, there was fierce dissent amongst some management members of the committee, who were totally opposed to the idea of worker directors, so much so that they produced their own recommendations which were appended to the main report. Since most British managers were also vehemently opposed to the whole idea of worker directors, this minority report was almost certainly an accurate reflection of their feelings. Therefore, the debate continued for some years without legislation ever being placed before Parliament. In 1979, when a Conservative government was elected, the proposals were firmly shelved.

Since then, apart from a few isolated examples about which more will be said later, the idea of boardroom representation as a form of participation has largely withered away. Having said this, the word 'participation' has not disappeared from the vocabulary of either trade unionists or managers. Indeed, there are people from both sides who consider themselves to be 'progressive', and continue to endorse the idea of participation as a 'good thing'. However, what they mean by the word can vary considerably. When managers use the word they tend to be referring to a completely different process from the one envisaged by trade unions. Therefore, it is extremely important to recognize that the word 'participation' is generally used in a value-laden way that reflects the aims of the user as much as anything else.

Progress question 8.1
Different perceptions of participation

In view of the aims and purposes of trade unions described in Chapter 3, and the effects of management ideologies given in Chapter 4, in what ways are the perceptions of the two parties about participation likely to differ, and what aspects of the process would they be likely to emphasize?

Except in a highly restricted way, participation, as the word is defined here, is seldom an aim of British management. In practice what managers usually aim for is a limited form of involvement, and even this is highly defensive of managerial prerogative, and can often be used to enhance managerial control as much as anything else (Dickson, 1981a; Ramsay, 1991). This does not of course mean that it is harmful, or that it fails to benefit employees by increasing their extrinsic and intrinsic satisfaction from work. However, the tendencies of a decade and a half ago, which were in the direction of a democratization of industry, have now largely disappeared. The schemes of involvement which are now in vogue are much less concerned with avoiding the adversarial industrial relations of the 1960s and 1970s and more directed at obtaining employee cooperation and commitment to the success of the enterprise (Guest, 1987; Long and Warner, 1987; McKersie, 1987; Walton, 1985).

Different forms of involvement and participation

A scheme of classification

Since the distinction between involvement and participation has been strongly emphasized, and within either process there are different approaches that can be used, it is useful to have a way of classifying the different methods. One way of doing this is to compare the different methods along a number of dimensions, each one of which describes some aspect of the process in use.

Involvement or participation is the first dimension, and distinguishes between the different methods in terms of the degree of participation in decision making each one provides for. The next and perhaps most significant distinguishing feature is whether the form uses **direct or indirect methods**. Direct methods are those which bring managers and subordinates into face-to-face contact as part of the process, and indirect methods are those in which representatives deal with management on behalf of employees. For matters which affect the whole organization, it would be a practical impossibility for the whole workforce to engage in face-to-face processes. Therefore the distinction is an important one. By their very nature direct methods almost inevitably limit the issues that are dealt with to task- or work-related matters and take place at low level. Moreover, since it results in a sharing of decision-making power about matters which affect their interests, participation in the sense that it is used here favours the interests of employees. Low-level involvement much more strongly favours managerial interests because it can be confined to matters which divert employee attention away from strategic issues (Drago and Wooden, 1991). It is perhaps for this reason that low-level direct methods are strongly favoured by managers but viewed with some suspicion by shop stewards, who tend to favour indirect methods which they see as giving the possibility of more real influence in decision making (Dickson, 1980, 1981b; Warner, 1983). Interestingly, what evidence there is suggests that employees at shop-floor level overwhelmingly favour direct methods, and have little interest in wider forms of joint decision making on company-wide issues (Hanson and Rathkey, 1984).

Another dimension of some importance is **scope**. This is conceptually distinct from the previous one, but in practical terms tends to be connected. It can be defined as the 'range of issues or managerial functions embraced by the process'. A process which is narrow in scope allows management to define certain matters as totally reserved for their consideration, whilst one with a wide scope has few, if any, reserved issues. **Depth of decision making** describes the extent to which employees or their representatives jointly determine with management the outcomes of matters with which the process is concerned. A shallow process would allow employees or their representatives little or no real say in decisions, and one which was deep would involve decisions that were jointly made.

In what follows, five major forms of involvement or participation will be described: collective bargaining, boardroom participation, joint consultation, task-related methods and financial methods. For each one, some of the evidence will be given which allows them to be characterized along these dimensions.

Collective bargaining

Since the next chapter will deal with the theory and practice of collective bargaining it is not the intention to present a detailed picture here. Nevertheless, because the popular view of collective bargaining is that it is merely concerned with haggles over money, the assertion that it is a form of participation needs to be justified. There are powerful arguments that collective bargaining serves at least three distinct functions: economic, governmental and decision-making (Chamberlain and Kuhn, 1966). The first of these, the *economic* function, represents the popular view of the process, that is, one which is used to determine the substantive terms on which employees will continue to supply their labour. However, the *governmental* function draws attention to the idea that collective bargaining is essentially a political process. It comes about because the two parties are mutually dependent on each other. Importantly, when they engage in the process, they also reserve the right to take any action which they deem necessary to veto decisions that the other might attempt to make unilaterally (Chamberlain and Kuhn, 1966, p. 121). Finally, the *decision-making* function allows employees (though their own representatives) to play a part in determining policies and actions which guide and rule their working lives (Chamberlain and Kuhn, 1966, p. 130).

Progress question 8.2
Collective bargaining and participation

> In what ways could it be asserted that collective bargaining is a form of employee participation?

In practice the extent to which all three functions are served together will clearly depend upon a number of factors. Employees and their representatives can vary in their desire to be involved in managerial decision making, and managers can have views on whether this involvement is legitimate. For this reason, one important factor is the relative power of the two sides. Nevertheless, when it takes place in good faith, it would not be exaggerating matters to assert that of all the processes described in this chapter, collective bargaining is the one most likely to approximate to the definition of employee participation given earlier. Thus it is with some validity that it has been argued to be an extremely practical form of industrial democracy (Clegg, 1974), and is by far the most favoured route to employee participation for most shop stewards and trade unionists (Dickson, 1980). Moreover, because the relationships built up in collective bargaining usually bring about a willingness to compromise, its potential as an effective form of employee participation is much greater than other forms where the commitment by either party to reach agreement is often absent. For these reasons, it can be argued to be an indirect form of participation which is potentially of wide scope and depth.

Boardroom participation

As was described earlier, the recommendations of the Bullock Committee were greeted by most managers in the UK with intense hostility. They also prompted a very mixed response amongst trade unionists, and the principle of worker directors is not one which has ever received wholehearted support from the British trade-union movement. Thus it is hardly surprising that this form of participation has been comparatively rare.

In private-sector enterprises, the evidence suggests that schemes which have been introduced have not been successful (Chell and Cox, 1979; DOE, 1987). Of seven which were extensively studied, all were introduced at management's initiative, and the scheme was dominated by management from the start. For the most part, worker directors found themselves isolated from shop stewards in the firm, and also from the real decision-making processes of other board members. Thus the schemes tended to reinforce management control over decision making rather than share it.

In the public sector there were two notable schemes. The first, at the then British Steel Corporation, appointed 12 worker directors to the boards of its regional operating groups in 1965 (Brannen *et al.*, 1976). Initially worker directors were appointed by management, and were required to vacate any union position on appointment. However, these requirements were relaxed in 1973 and in addition, trade unions became involved in the selection of directors. Nevertheless, it could hardly be said that the experiment was a great success. The functions of directors were very unclear, and the scheme encountered a great deal of hostility from middle managers, which in some cases amounted to obstruction. As in the private-sector schemes, worker directors largely found themselves excluded from much of the real decision making, which tended to take place by functional directors outside board meetings, with decisions simply brought to the board for ratification. It can also be argued that as a form of worker participation its aims were subverted. On some issues there was a tendency for worker directors to be socialized into adopting the viewpoint of management members of the board. Thus they became primarily directors, and only secondarily representatives of the workforce.

The second public-sector experiment was a short-lived initiative that took place in the Post Office between 1978 and 1980, and was abandoned in the face of management opposition to its extension (Brannen, 1983). Here the Bullock formula for numbers of management and union nominees to the board was followed, and worker directors were present in a greater concentration and, importantly, at main-board level. For this reason they were somewhat more assertive, and were sometimes highly outspoken and critical when industrial-relations issues were debated. In time, management appointees came to view their contributions as somewhat parochial and obstructive and, as a result, resorted to the time-honoured practice of conducting their business outside the boardroom. Thus the presence of worker directors had a reduced impact in terms of employee participation.

Overall therefore, the evidence from both private- and public-sector schemes tends to indicate that boardroom participation has been less than successful in Great Britain. In some measure this is because there has usually been a great deal of hostility to the idea amongst managers. Nevertheless, the idea that boardroom participation could become a viable method to exert employee influence at a level where important decisions are made is not a totally forgotten one. Indeed, it is one of the preferred methods in legislation currently proposed by the EC and this could have an impact on the matter in the UK. As such the topic will be referred to later in the chapter.

Joint consultation

This can be defined as a process which 'involves employees through their representatives in discussion and consideration of relevant matters which affect or concern those they represent, thereby allowing employees to influence the proposals before the final management decision is taken' (IPM, 1981, p. 8).

Progress question 8.3
Joint consultation

From the definition given, what reasons could you give for joint consultation finding much more favour as a process with managers than with trade unionists?

In one form or another joint consultation has existed in British industry for nearly sixty years. It therefore has the longest pedigree of all the methods covered here, but has waxed and waned in popularity. It enjoyed an increased use in World War II, during the late 1940s and early 1950s, and there has been a revival from the early 1980s onwards. However, in between these periods, it tended to fall into disuse. The reasons for these fortunes are hard to identify, and there are three competing explanations which have been neatly described by Joyce and Woods (1984) as the McCarthy thesis, the accommodation thesis and the external threat thesis. In outline the McCarthy thesis, which is also underwritten by several other authors (Chadwick, 1983), holds that joint consultation withers as workplace trade unions gain in power, primarily because shop stewards consider the process an inferior one to normal bargaining arrangements.

The accommodation thesis views consultation as a management ploy which is used to contain trade-union power; that is, by seeming to engage in meaningful discussion, but in reality only giving a form of pseudo participation or involvement, management retains its authority. Whilst the idea is plausible, empirical support for the idea is somewhat harder to locate. Nevertheless, it can be noted that there has been a more widespread use of joint consultation from the recession of the early 1980s onwards. This, it is argued, has been a strategic move aimed at a long-term reduction in the power of trade unions in a period when they have been least able to resist (Bassett, 1987).

Finally, the external threat thesis reasons that, normally, neither management nor union would wish to collaborate with each other openly. Therefore, when there is an external threat or pressure, for example the possibility of the firm's demise, this can bring them together in willing cooperation. However, because of their prior roles, an 'arms-length' relationship such as joint consultation, in which differences are temporarily put aside, is the most useful. There is little evidence either to refute or support this argument directly, but there has been a revival in the use of joint consultation since the early 1980s (Daniel and Millward, 1983; Millward and Stevens, 1986). Some of this could well have been at management's behest, and has been aimed at enlisting employee cooperation in recessionary conditions.

In all likelihood the position is more complex than any of the three theses allows for. A great deal will depend upon the spirit in which both sides enter the process, and the degree of clarity that exists about what it sets out to accomplish (Bate and Murphy, 1981). In some organizations management will have used it to resist collective bargaining, or at best pay lip service to the idea of meaningful consultation (Marchington and Armstrong, 1986). In others it will be valued by management and trade unions alike as a valuable adjunct to collective bargaining and used in this way (Marchington and Armstrong, 1981, 1983). Nevertheless in strict terms, joint consultation, whilst potentially wide in scope, is essentially shallow in depth and is at best an indirect form of involvement.

Task-related methods

This term is used to embrace a wide variety of schemes in which groups of employees become involved in identifying and solving problems concerned with task performance. Whilst there are a number of variants on the basic form, by far the most widely used in recent years has been the quality circle, on which discussion will be focused here.

In essence quality circles are small groups of employees, usually up to 12 in number, who meet voluntarily on a regular basis under the guidance of a group leader. Their role is to identify, analyse and find solutions to work-related problems. More often than not the circle leader is the supervisor of the workgroup from whom the circle members are drawn. Thus circle processes involve and are perhaps under some degree of direction from a person in the management hierarchy. Since they deal only with immediate work-related problems they are essentially a method of direct involvement. Moreover, they are one which is narrow in scope, shallow in depth, and which has little to do with a sharing of power or decision making on organizational issues. Indeed, it is probably because they are what has been referred to as **parallel participation**, which leaves the conventional power structure of an organization relatively untouched, that they have an appeal to top management (Mohrman and Lawler, 1988).

Although the original idea for quality circles was an American one, their first widespread use was in Japan. Thus, their adoption in the West, first in America and more recently in Europe, is something in the nature of an imported practice. In some organizations circles deal purely with quality problems, and in others they tackle a mixture of quality and quantity-of-output matters. When they work well, it is more than possible that circles could foster a degree of bottom-up decision making and sense of involvement which could release some of the creative talents of employees that remain untapped in many organizations.

Having said this, there is no unified body of theory on which the design of task-related methods can be based (Griffin, 1988). In Europe, if there is a philosophy which informs their use it is probably that of the 'human relations' school of management. This reasons that a participative work organization which gives some degree of autonomy to workers to decide how they perform tasks will lead to a greater degree of job satisfaction, and this in turn will result in more committed and productive employees. As will be noted later, there could well be a problem in terms of the theory. For the present, however, it is more important to note that any benefits received by quality-circle members are explicitly assumed to be derived in only one way. This is the increase in intrinsic satisfactions that they get from taking part in the process, and there is no suggestion that they should share financially in the savings that could result from quality or productivity improvements. Thus circles are essentially a way for managers to get more output for the same cost (Wilson, 1989). Indeed, management aims in introducing quality circles are invariably in terms of organizational performance, and any other outcomes, such as individual development or increased intrinsic satisfactions, tend to be viewed more as desirable by-products than anything else (Burpa-Di Gregoria and Dickson, 1983).

Whether quality circles actually benefit organizations or their employees is still an open question. They have been investigated extensively, mainly in the USA and to a lesser extent in Great Britain, and the findings are very mixed. Some studies report an increase in intrinsic satisfactions of participants but not in productivity (Steele and Shane, 1986), and others an increase in productivity but not satisfaction (Marks *et al.*, 1982). Many of the accounts which extol the virtues of quality circles are of dubious validity. They often report matters in highly anecdotal terms, and frequently the work turns out to have been written by managers or consultants whose job it was to introduce circles into an organization (Steele and Lloyd, 1988). Thus it is hardly surprising to find that one review of the published evidence concluded that the less rigorous was the design of the research, the more likely it was to report positive results (Barrick and Alexander, 1987). Having said this, the more rigorous work reveals some very interesting features. Many quality-circle initiatives fail almost as soon as they start (Drago, 1988), and a number of reasons for this have been identified, for example insufficient training for circle members (Steele *et al.*, 1985) and perceptions by middle managers and supervisors that circles are a threat to their positions, which results in them inhibiting the functioning of circles (Bradley and Hill, 1983, 1987; Russell and Dale, 1989). Perhaps more importantly, there are strong grounds to question some of the theoretical assumptions that underpin task-related methods.

It is important to recognize that as well as having a current relevance to employee relations, the effects of participation have long been of interest in the behavioural sciences. The human-relations school of management, which came into prominence in the 1930s, contains a basic assumption that employees who are happy and satisfied will work harder. Flowing from this, management theorists such as Bennis (1966) and Likert (1967), and motivational theorists such as McGregor (1960), Maslow (1970) and Herzberg (1966) all reason that employees derive a great deal of job satisfaction from having a degree of autonomy and personal decision making. In addition, expectancy theory (Vroom, 1964), which deals with motivation at a more individual level, explicitly acknowledges that employees who have a say in selecting their own goals will be more committed to achieving them. These ideas are all reflected in a practical way in the theories of job design (Hackman and Oldham, 1980) that stress the need to incorporate a degree of autonomy into work as a means of enhancing motivation, commitment and performance.

Notwithstanding these ideas, the evidence that more involvement in task-related decisions has effects on employee attitudes towards the organization as a whole is somewhat harder to locate. It has been known for a long time that if someone shares in a decision he or she tends to become more committed to seeing it translated into action (Lewin, 1951). Thus sharing in task-related decisions could lead to a general type of satisfaction and acceptance of difficult goals. However, it is by no means certain that this will result in greater performance (Mitchell, 1979), or that the effects will be anything other than short-lived (Ivancevich, 1977). A great deal seems to depend on whether people desire to be involved in decision making in the first place (Alutto and Belassco, 1972; Alutto and Acito, 1974; Driscoll, 1978). Indeed there is work which suggests that any evidence for the links between participation and satisfaction, and satisfaction and commitment, is very flimsy (Lischeron and Wall, 1975, Wagner and Gooding, 1987).

Most problematic of all is the conceptual leap that is made when involvement in minor decisions about task-related matters is equated with participation in a wider sense. It is not impossible that motivation and commitment to task performance is enhanced if decisions about tasks are shared. However, it could be little more than wishful thinking to assume that a process which triggers motivation and commitment at this level also unlocks a more general type of commitment to the organization as a whole. Nevertheless, management motives for introducing most current schemes of task-related involvement are usually in the hope that they will result in this type of attitude change. However, since they are usually introduced in a way which does not remove any of the basic features which create the 'us and them' attitudes in organizations, they may well be doomed to failure (Kelly and Kelly, 1991). Therefore, the whole idea that task-related methods on their own will inevitably lead to greater commitment can be called into question (Levitan and Johnson, 1983). Even where they are successful, there seems to be a limit to the time for which they continue to produce results, and for this reason, it has been suggested that they might only be of value as a stepping stone to deeper and more extensive forms of shared decision making (Lawler and Mohrman, 1987).

Financial methods

The idea of profit sharing or employee share ownership is by no means a new one. However, a positive encouragement was given by the Finance Acts of 1980, 1984 and 1987, which has added an impetus for these schemes to be adopted. Whilst methods of financial participation can vary considerably in detail, three basic forms can be identified. In **profit sharing** there is some distribution of profits amongst employees, usually annually or twice yearly as a supplement to normal salary or wages. Payment systems such as the Scanlon plan and Rucker plan can be grouped with these. In the former, a supplement which is based on the ratio of total payroll cost to sales value of production is paid, and with the Rucker plan the supplement is based on value added in production. The second form is **employee share ownership schemes** (ESOPS). These distribute a proportion of profits as shares, either directly to employees or into a trust which holds them on their behalf. Finally, there are **profit-related pay schemes** (PRP) in which a set proportion of pay is made up of profits.

Despite the fact that these methods are generally referred to as 'financial participation', none would qualify as participation in the sense that the word is used here. In share ownership, which nominally makes employees part-owners of the enterprise, the total size of the employee shareholding is usually so small that employees would be unable to influence company decision making. Indeed in many schemes of this type the shares are non-voting shares anyway. As such, so-called financial participation is at best little more than a very limited form of involvement.

The economic theory behind profit sharing, and in particular PRP, was originally stated by Vanek (1970), and was later elaborated by Weitzman (1984). This is quite complex, but the essential thrust is that profit sharing is likely to have macro-economic benefits such as reducing unemployment and inflation and increasing economic growth. It argues that this will happen because wages can only rise with profits, which will make employees more committed to the goals set by management. However, it also argues that for this to happen direction of the enterprise must be left completely to management, and that employees and trade unions must be strictly excluded from organizational decision making. However, the whole theory has been hotly criticized by a number of other writers who argue that Vanek's and Weitzman's theorizing completely ignores the human dynamics of the employment relationship, and therefore schemes of this type are doomed to failure unless trade unions and/or employees are involved in decision making (Mitchell, 1987; Duncan, 1988; Nuti, 1987).

Progress question 8.4
The State and financial participation

Referring back to Chapter 5, what reasons can you give for State encouragement for schemes of financial participation from 1980 onwards?

Perhaps the bigger problem is that whilst there has been considerable debate on the subject, empirical evidence is comparatively sparse, and what there is illustrates a potential conflict between theory and practice.

There is a strong suggestion in the theories of Vanek and Weitzman that because the schemes will work best where employees and unions are excluded from decision making, the strongest appeal would be to an autocratic management, or perhaps one that has a strong unitarist frame of reference. Paradoxically it is mainly those with a consultative or participative style of employee relations that have the strongest tendency to adopt the schemes (Poole, 1988). A second discrepancy appears in terms of the effects of these schemes on increased employee commitment. Since most schemes are voluntary and employees have to opt to take part, management's motive for introducing a scheme would probably be in the hope that it would raise commitment in the less committed. However, the evidence suggests that it is those who are already the most committed who decide to take part, and others tend to stay well away; a clear case of preaching to the converted (Dewe *et al.*, 1988). However, by far the most interesting findings concern the potential effects on organizational performance. Although these schemes have a slight positive effect on their own, the greatest increase in productivity seems to occur where they are used in conjunction with other forms of involvement or participation (Rosen and Quarrey, 1987; Rosenberg and Rosenstein, 1980, Wilson *et al.*, 1990). This gives a strong possibility that the schemes are most useful in producing the intended effects in certain specific circumstances, that is, where other forms of participation or involvement are used to raise initial commitment, and financial methods give employees a share in the results of any increased productivity.

The implications of EC legislation

Clearly any form of involvement or participation is heavily dependent on the ideologies of interest groups. The current mood amongst the most influential parties in the UK comes down heavily in favour of limited forms of involvement in which employees help implement management decisions, but do not participate in the setting of policies. However, in Chapter 5 it was pointed out that changes in EC legislation are on the horizon, and that these could have a strong impact on what happens in Great Britain in the future. The two most important proposals are both aimed at harmonizing company law throughout the EC, and are explained in what follows.

The Fifth Directive, which first appeared in 1973 and was substantially modified in 1983 to give a more flexible approach, would make it mandatory in all companies with 1000 or more employees for some form of employee participation to be adopted. To do this, it is envisaged one of four basic options would be used:

(1) Between one-third and one-half of the membership of either a supervisory board or of a unitary board would be worker directors elected by employees of the firm.

(2) Co-option of the same proportion of employees onto the supervisory board.

(3) By having an employee body such as a works council separate from company organization.

(4) To use some other system agreed through collective bargaining mechanisms.

The proposed legislation also makes it clear that if either of the last two options is used, it should result in a form which gives employee rights no less favourable than those obtainable if worker directors are appointed. These, for example, would be access to information, the rights to be consulted on major decisions affecting employees, and the right to undertake internal investigations.

In the UK companies only have a unitary board and so the second option would not be viable. In any event, bitter opposition to worker directors by most British management, together with trade-union preferences for an extension of collective bargaining, would almost certainly mean that only options 3 or 4 would be practically acceptable.

As explained in Chapter 5, the British government continues to fight a vigorous rearguard action against these measures, and in any event, since there is a diversity of practice amongst EC members, progress towards reaching agreement has been slow. No doubt the present British government will continue its spirited opposition, and as things stand it has opted out of the Social Chapter. However, the Social Chapter and this directive were adopted in principle by 11 of the member states at the Maastrict summit of 1991. Thus the issue cannot be postponed for ever.

The second piece of legislation, the **Vredling Proposal**, is still formally under consideration. It applies to multinationals that have large undertakings in Europe, but whose head office could be anywhere in the world. The proposal recognizes that information and consultation rights of employees are normally determined mainly by national legislation, but that the international aspects of multinationals tend to render national legislation ineffective. For this reason it calls for these multinational organizations to provide information to employees or their representatives at least half-yearly on a wide variety of subjects. In addition to this, they would be legally required to consult on matters which substantially affected employee interests; for example, plant closures.

Although the proposal has received substantial support from the European Trade Union Confederation, it has encountered fierce opposition from US and Japanese multinationals, who have been prominent in lobbying against its adoption; so much so that there are fears that if it were adopted there might be curtailment of inward investment by multinationals into the EC, or even worse, a degree of divestment. For this reason its adoption is unlikely for some years, and even then it might only occur in a much altered form.

Current guidelines for selecting and implementing schemes of involvement and participation

Short of a legislative change, an increase in employee participation in the UK seems unlikely. However, various forms of involvement are being adopted in a more widespread way, often by organizations with no prior experience in this area. To aid them in the selection, development and implementation of appropriate schemes, the Industrial Participation Association and the Institute of Personnel Management have jointly produced a set of guidelines. These recognize that any scheme has to be tailor-made to an organization's particular circumstances. Therefore, a prescriptive design which purports to be universally applicable has purposely been avoided. The guidelines come in two parts: a statement of principles which sets out what is considered to be good practice (IPA/IPM, 1983a), and an action guide consisting of questions that organizations which are considering adopting these methods should ask themselves (IPA/IPM, 1983b).

The document dealing with principles and standards of practice reflects much that is current in terms of British management thinking in the area. It makes clear that *best practice* (author's italics) is to provide for direct involvement in task-related matters. Whilst it acknowledges that this inevitably means that managers will need to communicate and consult more often, it stresses that this does not mean that management shares its responsibility for business decisions. Indeed, consultation is seen as a process in which management allows employees to express their views and contribute their ideas *before the final decision is taken by management* (author's italics). Therefore, despite its title, which includes the word 'participation', it deals exclusively with 'involvement', and defines the aims of this as:

(1) Generating the commitment of all employees to the success of the organization.

(2) Enabling the organization better to meet the needs of its customers and adapt to changing market requirements, and hence to maximize its future prospects and the prospects of those who work in it.

(3) Helping the organization to improve performance and productivity, and adopt new methods of working to match new technology, drawing on the resources of knowledge and practical skills of all its employees.

(4) Improving the satisfactions employees get from their work.

(5) Providing all employees with the opportunity to influence and be involved in decisions which are likely to affect their interests.

In terms of general principles it stresses that *involvement* (author's italics) is applicable in a wide variety of organizations, but that successful implementation depends crucially on attention to a number of factors:

(1) Finding the form most suitable to the enterprise.

(2) Identification and development of the form should take place through discussions with employees and/or their representatives.

(3) A lead needs to be given at the very top of the organization to get things moving.

(4) A recognition that employees of all levels may need training for the scheme to be a success.

(5) That no matter what type of scheme is adopted, management still remains responsible for making business decisions.

The action guide, which reinforces many of the points made in the standards of practice, is perhaps more likely to be of practical use in organizations. It stresses the need for management to agree with others the form that the scheme shall take, and to allow sufficient time for people to adjust before the full results will be realized. A very comprehensive checklist of questions that organizations should ask themselves about current arrangements and the intended form of the scheme is provided, and these cover such matters as:

(1) The organization's aims and objectives for the scheme.

(2) The extent of direct involvement that currently exists and is intended.

(3) The arrangements that exist and which will be made for communications within the organization.

(4) The policies and arrangements with respect to consultation.

(5) The representational arrangements that exist and which will be necessary for the scheme to operate together with any arrangements for profit sharing that are in place or will be introduced.

As noted, despite the titles of the two documents, they have little if anything to say about participation. Nevertheless, for schemes of involvement, which are their major concern, they give a well-developed set of considerations that would be of considerable use to any firm which is new to the area.

Conclusions and overview

Whilst the two words 'involvement' and 'participation' tend to be used interchangeably there is a significant difference between the two processes. Management ideologies in Great Britain make it extremely unlikely that participation can exist, or ever has existed, in a widespread way in the UK except through collective bargaining. Moreover, despite the use of the word 'participation' in their titles, the current guidelines for implementation of these schemes come down strongly against participation, and in favour of involvement. However, the direction in which matters will move in the future will depend a great deal on whether EC legislation is adopted.

For the present, therefore, the only form of participation which is likely to be used in the UK is collective bargaining. In this sense there is a clear connection between this chapter and the one that follows. There is also an important connection with the previous chapter where a distinction was drawn between communications and processes of involvement or participation. Involvement and participation clearly go well beyond the simple transmission of information, and it was for this reason that team briefing, which is essentially a method of communication, was dealt with in the previous chapter. However, to work effectively, participation and involvement both require that a correspondingly effective system of communications is installed at the same time. For this reason, the previous chapter and this one should be viewed as complementary.

Further reading

Brannen P. (1983). *Authority and Participation in Industry*. London: Batsford
    A useful description and short history of worker directors schemes in the British Steel Corporation and the Post Office in the 1970s.

Middleton J. (1987). *Consultation*. London: The Industrial Society
    A general guide to joint consultation and its introduction in organizations.

Robeson M. (1988). *Quality Circles: A Practical Guide* 3rd edn. London: Gower
    A general, if somewhat prescriptive, book which covers the subject of this method of task related involvement.

IPA/IPM (1983). *Employee Involvement and Participation: (a) Principles and Standards (b) Action Guide*. London: Industrial Participation Association/Institute of Personnel Management.

9

Collective bargaining

Introduction

Collective bargaining is the primary method used by British trade unions to exert an influence on employers, and can, therefore, be a vital part of employee relations. Although this chapter only deals with this topic, it is important to stress that it is strongly connected with the topics of negotiation and industrial action. These last two topics are dealt with in subsequent chapters, but the reader is asked to remember that there is a connection when reading this one. The chapter commences by defining collective bargaining and describes some of its major functions and purposes. It is a feature of employee relations which can exist in many forms, and so the next part of the chapter describes the different types of bargaining arrangements that can exist. The aims of the parties in collective bargaining are then considered, and attention is drawn to the idea that these can have important longer-term effects on the bargaining relationship itself. The focus then moves to the outcomes of bargaining, in which the various types of agreement that can result are described, together with some of the recent trends in this area. Finally, the chapter considers what has historically been one of the more controversial issues in British industrial relations: the State's attempt to bring about a reform of the nature of collective bargaining.

The role of collective bargaining

Definition

The essence of any collective organization of employees is that, as individuals, its members are relatively powerless *vis-à-vis* an employer. Thus it marshals their collective strength to redress the power disadvantage. In Great Britain this has traditionally been the mainstay of trade-union activity, and gives rise to several important features of the relationship that ensues.

First, it becomes part of the ongoing way in which an organization and its employees relate to each other, the purpose of which is to regulate the terms and conditions under which their relationship will continue. This implies that both parties have a vested interest in reaching agreement over the matter. Whilst this does not mean that reaching agreement will always be easy, it is important to note that finding a way to continue the relationship is a definite aim.

Second, in collective bargaining employees are represented with 'one voice'. Thus certain aspects of the relationship between an organization and its employees are determined through an intermediary. This, in turn, means that the bond between employer and employee inevitably becomes more remote and detached about some things.

Third, the method most frequently used to identify and agree the terms for continuing the relationship is the process of negotiation. This will be dealt with in detail in the next chapter, and therefore is not explored here. Nevertheless, it is important to stress that collective bargaining and negotiation are not the same thing. The expression 'collective bargaining' essentially describes the nature of a relationship, and negotiation is simply a process used to settle its terms.

With these points in mind, collective bargaining is defined here as:

> a relationship existing between employees and employer(s) in which the interests of the former are represented collectively by an association, and the latter by either organizational management

or a collective association of employers, and which primarily uses the process of negotiation to reach agreement about the terms and conditions of the relationship.

Before moving on to consider collective bargaining in more detail, it is important to mention briefly a point which will be explored more extensively in subsequent chapters. The use of negotiation tends to make the collective bargaining relationship a highly political one. As in all relationships where terms and conditions are settled by negotiation, processes other than negotiation itself can be used by one side to exert pressure on the other. A prime example in employee relations is industrial action, and it is for this reason that the topics of collective bargaining, negotiation and industrial action cannot be divorced.

The functions and purposes of collective bargaining

There are many perspectives on the functions and purposes of collective bargaining. The traditional view is that the prime function is an economic one. That is, by substituting collective action for individual action, trade unions act as a form of labour cartel (Webb and Webb, 1902). Whilst it would be hard to deny this idea, to view things completely in these terms is to relegate the relationship to one which is concerned only with economic exchange. As explained in Chapter 2, in the employment relationship there are very powerful social factors at work as well. Thus it is much more complex than a simple economic transaction. This point is recognized by Flanders (1968) who draws attention to the idea that collective bargaining is a political process, the outcome of which is a wide variety of rules governing social as well as economic aspects of the employer–employee relationship. Indeed in Flanders' view, since the two parties become joint authors of the rules, it is more appropriately called a process of 'joint regulation'. Having said this, Flanders' viewpoint is not without its critics. Fox (1975), for example, criticizes it for underplaying the economic aspects, and in turn re-emphasizes the traditional view by stating that 'It is as a bargaining agent that the union finds the major justification in the eyes of its members, and issues of financial reward are still, whether for material or symbolic reasons or both, among its major bargaining preoccupations' (Fox, 1975, p. 157).

What is perhaps more likely is that both of these arguments are true. Collective bargaining tends to serve the purposes that those involved want it to serve. Thus it can be either one or both of these things. This is reflected in Chamberlain and Kuhn's (1965) analysis of purposes, where three different functions are described, with each one representing a sequential stage in the development of the relationship. The **market or economic function** fixes the price at which labour will be bought and sold, and is similar to the traditional economic view. The **government function** is concerned with establishing a constitution, and the constitution itself consists of rules which become the foundation of an ongoing relationship between management and employees. Thus although negotiation about substantive economic issues is still important, agreement on this aspect of the relationship is by no means the only end product. It is just part of a continuous and ongoing dialogue in which trade union and management become joint authors of rules on many more aspects. This is the view expressed in Flanders' notion of 'joint regulation', and also finds favour with other analysts. For example, Dubin (1954, 1957) stresses that management and employees both need predictability, and since it fixes boundaries on the behaviour of both parties, collective bargaining gives this stability to their relationship. The **decision-making function** gives a system of industrial government or industrial democracy; a view also echoed by Clegg (1951). That is, because employees through their representatives participate in making decisions on matters which affect their interests, this results in them and the organization becoming bound together in a pattern of mutual accommodation.

Chamberlain and Kuhn stress that the three functions are stages of development. Thus where the third exists, so will the first and second, and the nearer the relationship gets to the third stage, the more likely it is that decisions which were once regarded as the sole prerogative of management become joint ones. Clearly where this happens collective bargaining is capable of dealing with such a wide range of topics that it would virtually embrace everything in the employer–employee relationship. Therefore a move in this direction is likely to go hand in hand with a fundamental change in the way that the parties approach most issues. Here a useful distinction which will appear again in the next chapter is one that can be drawn between distributive and integrative bargaining (Walton and McKersie, 1965). Distributive bargaining is essentially a zero-sum affair, and both sides approach an issue as if it were a cake of a fixed size to be split up. Thus both have the view that what one party gains, the other one will lose. Integrative bargaining can be likened to a joint effort to make the cake bigger. Both parties accept that they have more to gain by working together than by simply arguing about fair shares of a fixed sum. This, however, does not mean that they have no differences of interest, but rather that they have come to recognize that their separate interests are more likely to be achieved through cooperation than by remaining in opposition.

A bargaining relationship which has progressed to serving the decision-making as well as other functions will clearly need an approach which is mainly integrative. However, even where this progression has been made, the nature of the issues that arise can have a strong bearing on whether an integrative approach is possible. With some it can be quite easy; for example, where the existence of an organization is threatened by external market conditions, and both sides collaborate to make changes that are necessary for survival. Others, such as pay, naturally lend themselves to a more distributive approach. Thus because there are always likely to be some distributive issues in the background, the move towards joint decision making in collective bargaining is seldom complete, and is never an easy one in the best of circumstances. Moreover, it can only ever reach this stage if both parties want it to, and feel comfortable with the situation when it is reached. For example, it would require that management be willing to extend the scope of bargaining into areas where it has traditionally reserved the decision making for itself. Similarly, it would require a trade union to become the joint author of decisions, and this means giving up its prior role of challenging management's decisions. Since past habits die hard neither of these are easy positions for the two parties to adopt.

CASE-STUDY 9.1

Corehart Engineering PLC:

Extracts from the minutes of the Joint Negotiating Committee Meeting of 19th March 1992

92/10 Pay and conditions

Following previous special meetings of the committee to deal with negotiations on pay and service conditions, the Industrial Relations Manager and Works Convenor reported jointly on their discussions to produce a document setting out proposed new terms. This was presented to the meeting in draft form, the major points of which were:

(1) Pay rates: to be increased by 6.7 % across the board.

(2) Shift premium rates: to be increased by a like percentage.

It was noted that management had felt unable to agree to a reduction of one hour in the working week on this occasion, and also the trade-union side stated that it reserved the right to pursue this matter at a later date as a separate item. The agreement was then signed by the Works Convenor on behalf of the trade unions, and the Industrial Relations Manager on behalf of management.

92/13 Proposed procedural agreements

The trade-union side formally submitted its proposals in the form of outline draft agreements to establish procedures to deal with the following:-

(1) Regrading of individuals.

(2) Monitoring of health and safety in the workplace.

The management side agreed to consider the documents and to produce a detailed response at or before the June meeting of the committee.

92/17 Quality circles

Concern was raised by the trade-union side that suggestions for improvements to working methods made by quality-circle members were subject to extremely long delays before a response was received from senior management. Management replied that these delays were undesirable and could jeopardize enthusiasm for circles. It was agreed that in the event of a delay of more than six weeks, senior stewards should approach departmental managers to investigate the reason.

92/18 Communications

Concern was expressed by the management side that employees appeared to be misinterpreting the content of discussions between management and trade unions at joint consultative and negotiating committee meetings. The trade-union response to this was that the only formal measure adopted to acquaint employees with discussions was placing of minutes on notice boards. This did not occur until some time after the meeting, by which time rumours had inevitably begun to circulate. The trade-union side also stated that great care was taken after each meeting to ensure that stewards were accurately briefed, and that management should do likewise for supervision.

After some discussion it was agreed that in future short workplace meetings of no more than 15 minutes' duration would be allowed in the week following joint consultative and negotiating committee meetings. These would allow accurate briefing of employees and would be conducted by supervisors, where necessary with the aid of stewards.

92/21 Smoking and health

There was some discussion on whether or not in the interests of the health of all the workforce, the establishment should become a 'no-smoking' organization as a matter of policy. Management stated that this was a somewhat delicate issue, and whilst they would wish to discourage smoking on the grounds of health, there was the additional problem of impinging on the freedom of the individual. After further discussion it was agreed that trade union and management would collaborate on producing a questionnaire to be sent to all employees to canvas their views on this matter.

Questions

i Classify the issues reported in the above as falling into market/economic, governmental, decision-making functions of collective bargaining.

ii From your answer to Question 1 what conclusions would you draw with respect to the state of development of the collective bargaining relationship at Corehart?

Alternative patterns of collective bargaining

In Britain arrangements for collective bargaining display a bewildering diversity. There are variations between industries, between firms within a given industry, and sometimes within a particular firm. Nevertheless, there are a few general rules that can be applied. Public-sector organizations are more likely to recognize and negotiate with trade unions. In the private sector the size of an organization can be an important factor, and usually the larger it is, the more likely is a bargaining relationship. Collective bargaining is more likely to be used to set conditions for manual than for non-manual workers. It is also more frequently found in manufacturing than in the service sector (Daniel and Millward, 1983; Millward and Stevens, 1986). There is, however, no legal compulsion to recognize a trade union for bargaining, and even when this occurs there is a great deal of evidence to indicate that management is the dominant partner in choosing the bargaining structures that will be used (Clegg, 1976; Deaton and Beaumont, 1980). Thus even in quite large organizations there are situations where although there are collective associations of employees, they are not recognized for bargaining purposes; for example, in private financial services, such as some banks and building societies. Clearly without recognition there is little likelihood of a collective bargaining relationship. Indeed the Employment Protection Act, 1975 defines recognition as 'recognition of a union by an employer or employers to any extent for the purpose of collective bargaining' (EPA, 1975, c. 71, ss. 11.2 and 11.3).

Historically, this was often only conceded unwillingly by employers, and after a struggle, the classic method adopted by trade unions being to increase the level of membership to the point where they could legitimately claim to speak for the majority of a workforce, and then to take strike action if recognition was refused. Some attempt to avoid this was made in the Employment Protection Acts of 1975 and 1978, in which provision was made for a legal procedure through which independent certified trade unions could claim negotiating rights. This usually involved a properly conducted ballot of the employees concerned, and in the light of the result, a recommendation to the court by the independent Advisory, Conciliation and Arbitration Service. This procedure was repealed in the Employment Act, 1980, and since then the position has reverted to one where the matter is left totally to employers and trade unions to sort out for themselves.

Since full recognition is a fundamental and probably irreversible step which, once taken, will inevitably result in attempts by trade unions to expand the boundaries of collective bargaining, it is not one which management ever takes lightly. For this reason recognition is often something which develops by degrees over a period of time. For example, the first stage might only provide for a trade union to represent employees on individual matters such as grievance and discipline. Later on it could progress to a right to be consulted on matters, but not to negotiate, and only in time will it progress to the stage where the trade union has a right to fully represent the employees' interests by negotiating procedural and substantive agreements. Whilst this might sound very long-drawn-out, it has the advantage of allowing the parties to become more familiar with each other, and more comfortable with the relationship.

Because there is such a wide diversity in bargaining relationships, in what follows a number of dimensions will be used to characterize the different arrangements that are found. These are level of bargaining, bargaining units, scope of bargaining, and bargaining form. As will be seen, whilst they are discussed separately there is a close connection between them all.

Levels of bargaining

This is used to describe where bargaining normally takes place. It can vary anywhere between the limits of bargaining at national level on behalf of all firms in a particular industry or group of industries (multi-employer bargaining), and bargaining for a workgroup within a department of a single firm (shop-floor bargaining). Until the Second World War, multi-employer bargaining was the normal practice in the UK, and in certain industries in the private sector where it has certain advantages to employers, this is still the case. These are usually in highly competitive industries such as hosiery or footwear which are made up of small firms. In these there are obvious cost advantages in allowing an employers' association to deal with trade unions, and the standardized terms and conditions which result put all firms 'in the same boat'. It is perhaps for this latter reason that it also has some adherents in large organizations as well; for example, in the clearing banks (Purcell and Sisson, 1983). Nevertheless, whilst multi-employer bargaining still takes place in the private sector, it has now lost a great deal of its importance. In the public sector, however, it is still very much the norm. The pay and service conditions for employees of central government, local authorities, and most industries that until privatization were in the public sector are still determined this way.

Wherever national bargaining takes place, some degree of supplementary bargaining at lower levels can become virtually inevitable. This is as true in the public sector as in private industry, and is needed to work out the local details of higher-level agreements. Nevertheless, in a great deal of manufacturing industry, because the real determination of pay and conditions takes place at employer level, multi-employer agreements are little more than a token. Most of the private sector is subject to a fairly rapid rate of change, and so managers have an understandable tendency to feel that they need agreements which are specific to the firm. Indeed, some large manufacturing firms, such as Ford and the General Electric Company, conduct all their affairs at organizational level or below, and are not even a party to multi-employer agreements. Nevertheless, there is a considerable degree of diversity in the way that single-employer bargaining is conducted. In multi-plant firms a distinction which can be drawn is between bargaining that is conducted at an organization level for all sites and that which is at the level of each individual plant.

Management has by far the greatest say in setting the level of bargaining, and since the level at which agreements are made can crucially affect a trade union's ability to mobilize its bargaining power (Hawkins, 1979), the choice could well be prompted by strategic considerations. For example, multi-plant or organization-wide bargaining enables management to separate the trade union from its major source of power, the shop-floor. In addition, where there are several plants, some of which are better organized and perhaps more militant than others, the mild ones can outvote those that are more militant. Moreover, multi-plant bargaining can give more uniform and predictable labour costs, and lowers the likelihood of different plants making parity or leapfrogging claims (Purcell and Sisson, 1983). Nevertheless, despite these advantages, the majority of multi-plant firms conduct their bargaining at the level of individual plants. To some extent this could be a matter of tradition or habit; for example, where the different plants have been acquired over some time by mergers or takeovers, and well-established methods have been inherited. However, plant bargaining has certain strategic advantages of its own. It denies trade unions access to the level where strategic policy decisions are made, and where they might insist that these matters become bargainable issues. In addition, it enables management to argue that each plant must be able to stand on its own feet financially, and thus fits well with other management control systems such as cost or budget centres (Purcell and Sisson, 1983). The most interesting idea of all, however, is that appearance is very different from reality in plant-level bargaining. Just because bargaining takes place at the level of each individual plant, it does not necessarily mean that managers have a great deal of freedom to make agreements. They may very well sit at the negotiating table and bargain but they could still be working to very strict guidelines from above. Here there is some evidence that this situation is quite common, and that the real decisions about what is agreed are made at corporate level (Kinnie, 1985, 1986, 1987; Purcell and Gray, 1986).

Bargaining units

These are defined as the groups or categories of employees that are covered by the agreements which are made, and clearly have some relationship to the level at which bargaining takes place. However, perhaps the most important point is that they have a bearing on which trade unions are involved, and for this reason, their selection also has strategic implications. If bargaining units are narrow, for example, and white-collar workers, skilled manual workers and unskilled employees all have different agreements, there is some facility for management to use divide-and-rule tactics. However, this type of arrangement also makes negotiating much simpler for the trade unions because they do not have to reconcile their different policies. Conversely, if there are too many bargaining units, one problem that results for management is that negotiating or renegotiating agreements can become a long-drawn-out affair, which can pose particular problems in times of rapid technological adjustment. Therefore, because status-based differentials can obstruct an organization's ability to react quickly and flexibly, some firms are attempting to move in the opposite direction, that is, towards a 'single-status' workforce, with 'harmonized' working conditions for manual and staff employees (Roberts, 1985). This is never easy to achieve, and removal or revision of bargaining units can pose significant difficulties (ACAS, 1982).

Bargaining scope

The scope of bargaining refers to the number of topics or issues which are the subject of negotiations for a given bargaining unit. Theoretically it can vary between the extremes of a very narrow scope, for example one which is strictly confined to wages and hours, to the other extreme where everything is negotiable. There are some grounds for reasoning that if management unduly restricts the scope of bargaining, it tends to result in a more militant workforce (Dubin, 1973). Whilst there is a small amount of evidence to support this (Rollinson, 1987), it must also be remembered that managerial prerogative starts where bargaining scope ends (Farnham and Pimlott, 1987). Thus scope is not usually something that either side can change at will. It is often heavily influenced by the history of the bargaining unit and by established frontiers of control. Therefore, although trade unions at enterprise or workplace level have a long pedigree of attempting to widen the scope of bargaining, their ability to do so tends to depend on the preconceived ideas of both sides about what should be legitimate bargaining issues (Storey, 1976).

Bargaining form

Strictly speaking, this is usually thought of as the way that agreements are recorded. Where bargaining is conducted at a high level, it is more remote from the place where agreements have to be implemented. Therefore, to avoid ambiguity, it is more likely that the agreements will be formally documented, and for this reason there is likely to be a correspondence between bargaining form and the level at which bargaining takes place. However, the greatest significance of formality is likely to be its effect on a whole host of other things, not the least of which is the industrial-relations climate. Whilst climate will be referred to in the next section of the chapter, it is important here to trace its links with the degree of formality in the bargaining relationship.

Purcell (1979), for example, has distinguished between two important characteristics of the bargaining relationship: formality and trust. Of the two, trust is by far the more important and tends to result in more cooperative climatic conditions. Nevertheless, the degree of formality has important effects as well. Too much formality can result in a pedantic and highly bureaucratized bargaining relationship, in which observing protocols becomes more important than anything else. Formality without a degree of trust can be particularly prone to produce this effect. However, given that there is an appropriate degree of trust, some formality is, in effect, an acknowledgement that there are rules to the game, and a public proclamation that the rules will be honoured. Therefore, its importance is not so much in formal writing down of agreements, but in the mutual trust and constructive behaviour that it brings. Purcell also points out that a degree of formality has other advantages. Although a high degree of trust is often found in very informal bargaining arrangements, it is likely to be there because of the good interpersonal relationships that individuals have developed. Therefore, it can quickly vanish if one of them moves on to something else. A degree of formality, however, allows the bargaining relationship to become more constitutional, to transcend the effect of dominant personalities, and to survive changes in the occupancy of bargaining roles.

CASE-STUDY 9.2

Bargaining arrangements

Consider the arrangements for bargaining in each of the following organizations:

Organization A

Size (no. of employees)	8000
Managers	425
Other salaried staff	3175
Manual – skilled	4200
– unskilled	nil
Number of locations	A region of a former nationalized industry with headquarters office, stores complex, and 14 depots.
Negotiating committees	3 at national level – managers – white-collar – manual
Nature of agreements	Pay levels negotiated nationally. Procedural and policy agreements of paving type and subjected to more detailed agreements locally. Separate sets of agreements for each negotiating committee.

Organization B

Size (no. of employees)	5000
Managers	40
Other salaried staff	760
Manual – skilled	1000
– unskilled	3000

Number of locations

1 in West Midlands – mass production engineering.

Negotiating committees

3 at organizational level
– white-collar
– skilled manual
– unskilled manual

Nature of agreements

For each negotiating committee a wide range of substantive and procedural agreements.

Organization C

Size (no. of employees)	150
Managers	3
Other salaried staff	15
Counter assistants	132

Number of locations

1 in West Midlands – independent supermarket.

Negotiating committees

None.

Nature of agreements

Observes movement in nationally negotiated pay rates, but pays well above this level to attract and retain suitable employees. All matters agreed on *ad hoc* basis between departmental managers and shop stewards.

Questions

i In each case what is the bargaining level, the bargaining units used, the scope of bargaining and the bargaining form?

ii Why do you feel this is the case – does it have particular advantages or disadvantages for the parties involved?

The objectives of the parties

There is something of a paradox in the very existence of a collective-bargaining relationship. Whilst it usually indicates that there are underlying conflicts of interest between employer and employees, it also reflects that they recognize that they have something in common and must find ways of reconciling their differences. Essentially neither of them can exist without the other, and so neither one really has the freedom not to seek a point of reconciliation. Moreover as noted above, because the relationship is one of mutual dependence, both parties need predictability from each other. The easiest way to achieve this is to construct agreements which fix the acceptable limits of either party's freedom of action. In Britain the vast majority of issues in collective bargaining tend to be dealt with like this, and a fairly straightforward way of viewing the objectives of the parties is by using the idea of 'frontiers of control' (Goodrich, 1975). This is shown in Figure 9.1.

Almost all collective bargaining is concerned with fixing, ratifying or moving the frontiers of control for some feature of the employment relationship. For simplicity, assume that as a result of a custom and practice, or perhaps because of a prior negotiated agreement, some detail of the employment relationship is already defined. This could specify the activities that management can instruct employees to perform, the minimum level of pay for performing the duties, or the extent to which management has freedom to change the ways in which they are performed. This is shown as the line down the centre of the diagram which is the current frontier of control. Any shift of the line to the right would reduce the employees' area of control over the job, and correspondingly increase management's discretion. A shift to the left would have the reverse effect. Clearly both parties have a vested interest in advancing their frontier of control, or at least preventing it being pushed back. Here a number of important points should be noted.

First, control is usually sought over several aspects of a job at the same time. Thus frontiers are multiple. In the example above the aim would probably be to exert control over *what* duties are performed, *how* they are performed, and the *pay rate*. Second, frontiers of control are situation-specific. Different features of the employment relationship tend to have different degrees of importance attached to them by different groups of employees and managers in different places. Again using the example given in the diagram, in one workplace *how* duties are performed for a given rate of pay can be the dominant issue for employees, whilst *what* is performed can be the most important one for management. In this case the frontier is likely to be fixed at a point where so long as employees do what they are told, how they do it is left to them. Third, once established, frontiers have to be defended. The ability to do this can ultimately depend on whether sanctions can be taken against the other party as and when

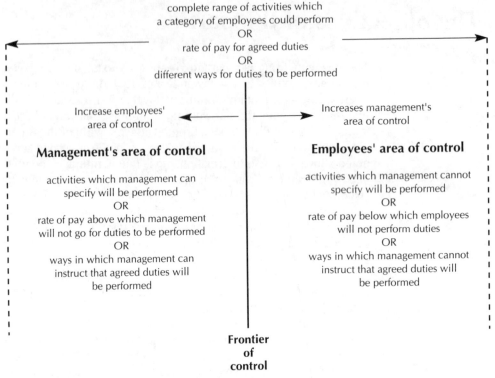

complete range of activities which
a category of employees could perform
OR
rate of pay for agreed duties
OR
different ways for duties to be performed

Increase employees'
area of control

Increases management's
area of control

Management's area of control

activities which management can
specify will be performed
OR
rate of pay above which management
will not go for duties to be performed
OR
ways in which management can
instruct that agreed duties will
be performed

Employees' area of control

activities which management cannot
specify will be performed
OR
rate of pay below which employees
will not perform duties
OR
ways in which management cannot
instruct that agreed duties will
be performed

**Frontier
of
control**

Figure 9.1 Frontiers of control.

they attempt to encroach on territory. For this reason the balance of power between the parties can affect where frontiers lie, and this tends to change from time to time. For example, in recessionary periods employers have a tendency to roll back the frontiers of control and enlarge managerial prerogatives (Brown, 1987). Fourth, control over one or more aspects of the employment relationship can become sacrosanct to one of the parties. Thus some frontiers are more fiercely defended than others.

Having made these points, it should not be inferred that a collective-bargaining relationship is always simply a matter of one side grabbing territory in an opportunist way when they hold the balance of power, merely to relinquish it when power passes back to the other side. Whilst there are bargaining relationships that are like this, in the long run those that are effective are usually characterized by a much greater respect for the other party's territory. This, however, requires that certain conditions are necessary. To start with, both sides must enter into the relationship with the aim of resolving their differences, and this means that they must bargain in good faith, with the aim of reaching an agreement which both accept as binding. Although this does not require that the agreement will stand for ever, it does mean that it will be scrupulously honoured for the foreseeable future, and stand until it is replaced by another agreement. Second, to make agreements, and then make them stick, both sides must also have a minimum degree of organization. Management has many advantages in this respect, and therefore, it needs to give employees the freedom to organize themselves into a collective association which is genuinely independent of the employer. Moreover, management must recognize that this collective speaks for employees, not just when management hears what it wants to hear, but when the unpalatable happens as well. Finally, the ongoing relationship as reflected in the 'industrial-relations climate' of the organization needs to be such that these conditions are not undermined.

More will be said about the effects of climate in the next chapter, and it is sufficient to point out here that it has some very significant effects on the bargaining relationship. One which can be very important is the influence that climate has on the capability to deal with issues in an integrative way. Even where the nature of issues makes an integrative approach possible, this is unlikely unless there is a cooperative climate (Dyer *et al.*, 1977; Martin and Biasatti, 1979). More importantly, those organizations with a cooperative climate tend to bargain integratively about a wider range of issues, and are much more able to accommodate change (Cooke, 1989; Dastmalchian *et al.*, 1982; Schuster, 1983). However, a cooperative climate does not occur of its own accord. Trade unions are essentially reactive organizations, and tend to respond in like fashion to the way that management behaves towards them (Tracy and Peterson, 1977). Thus the overwhelming evidence is that to move climate in a cooperative direction management has to be the instigator (Harbison and Coleman, 1951). Indeed, an uncooperative one can usually be traced back to managers who refuse to discuss issues which they see as impinging upon their prerogatives (Martin, 1980).

CASE-STUDY 9.3

Westmid PLC: Service engineers

Westmid PLC is a geographical region of a national organization which installs and maintains gas distribution systems and appliances in domestic, commercial and industrial premises. The actual work is undertaken by service engineers, who are located in one of 12 depots throughout the region. There are approximately 80 service engineers per depot, working in teams of 10, each team having its own supervisor.

Although there is a basic hourly pay rate, the majority of a service engineer's work attracts a bonus. A very wide variety of different jobs fall within the engineer's remit, each one of which has an allowed time. Bonus is paid according to a ratio of actual time to allowed time. Because of this, certain formally agreed allowances are payable. For example:

(1) Engineers must arrive at a depot each morning to collect their day's work, and return in the afternoon to report that which is completed. A daily allowance of one hour, paid at hourly rates, is made for this.

(2) Engineers are not always able to complete a job on the same day; for example, where there is no part in stock. Waiting time at hourly rates is paid for this.

(3) When training an apprentice, an engineer's speed of work can be slowed down. An instructor's allowance is paid for the days when they are accompanied by an apprentice.

In addition there are informal practices observed in most depots. For example:

(4) Because bonus is more readily earned on some types of work than others, supervisors generally ensure an equitable distribution of different types amongst their engineers.

(5) Where engineers have to travel considerable distances between individual jobs, this would interfere with bonus earnings. So long as they telephone in to the depot to formally 'clock off', it is normal practice for them to go home directly from the last job of the day.

(6) If a particular job turns out to be problematic, and a fault takes a great deal of time to diagnose before rectification, the supervisor can authorize 'average bonus' for the job.

(7) When called out after hours to deal with an emergency, service engineers informally have the option of receiving additional payments or having time off in lieu.

(8) If a job has been signed off as completed but subsequently turns out to be defective, the engineer returns and completes the job without further payment.

Questions

i In what areas have frontiers of control been established and where do the frontiers lie?

ii About what aspects might the parties wish to expand their frontiers and why?

The outcomes of collective bargaining

The definition of collective bargaining given earlier stresses that its purpose is to reach agreement on the rules that regulate the employment relationship. Broadly speaking, rules can be of three types, each of which has its own corresponding type of agreement. These are working arrangements, substantive agreements and procedural agreements, each of which will be considered in turn.

Working arrangements

These are usually the result of very informal processes at shop-floor level. At times they are very temporary in duration, and at others a highly permanent feature of the relationship between workgroup members and their supervisor (Brown, 1972; Terry, 1977). Because they are highly variable in nature, and rather specific to the circumstances in which they are made, they are virtually impossible to discuss in a general way. However, some examples can be discerned in the case-study above.

Substantive agreements

These govern the rights and obligations of the two parties in terms of an exchange of rewards for services. They can cover all types of direct and indirect remuneration such as pay rates, hours, holiday entitlement, and maternity and sick leave. A recent trend with some employers is to try to obtain substantive agreements that are more comprehensive and of longer duration; for example, pay deals which are pegged to some external indicator such as the retail price index and run for two or three years. This can give management an element of much needed predictability about future wage costs (Brewster, 1989).

Procedural agreements

Agreements of this type are the cornerstone of collective bargaining in Britain (Jenkins and Sherman, 1977). When a trade union is recognized for collective bargaining, in addition to making substantive rules on pay and so on, both parties have an interest in establishing machinery for the ongoing rule making and for the application and reinterpretation of rules. Procedural agreements allow this to be done. They usually establish the ways in which any differences between the union(s) and the employer(s) will be reconciled, and thus become

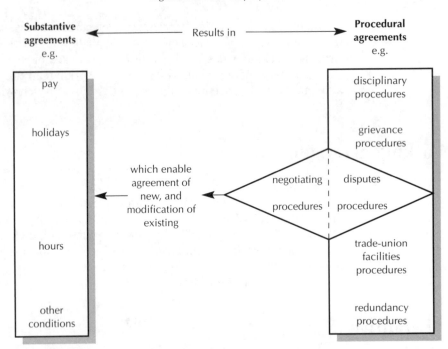

Figure 9.2   Relation of substantive and procedural agreements.

both treaties of peace and devices for the avoidance of war (Marsh, 1966). For this reason there is a virtually limitless scope for procedural agreements to deal with different matters. For example, procedural agreements commonly exist on trade-union recognition and representation, grievance, discipline, redeployment and redundancy, introduction of new technology and working methods, and procedures for handling disputes.

Whilst they have a different function to substantive agreements, procedures should not be thought of as something completely separate. It is quite common for a substantive agreement to contain procedural elements. A (substantive) agreement on job evaluation, for example, would probably also define how grading anomalies would be resolved, if and when they arose. Another way in which procedural and substantive agreements are related arises in the renegotiation of new substantive terms. This is shown in Figure 9.2.

A procedural agreement about negotiating will sometimes specify that there are regular intervals at which trade-union and management representatives will meet to consider matters of mutual interest. Where this is the case a party wishing to bring about some alteration to an existing substantive agreement can simply table an agenda item and present a claim. Where negotiating committees meet on a more *ad hoc* basis, the way of seeking this alteration could be to lodge a dispute about the substantive terms that currently exist.

Although it is possible to construct procedural agreements on virtually any aspect of employee relations, two types have come into prominence fairly recently, and deserve a special mention. In the popular press they tend to be regarded as synonymous but since this is by no means inevitable, they will be considered separately.

Single-union agreements are simply a special type of recognition agreement. There is nothing new about the idea of an organization recognizing only one union for bargaining purposes. Indeed, the evidence suggests that of those establishments recognizing trade unions, over 60 % recognize only one for manual workers, and nearly 40 % only one white-collar union (Daniel and Millward, 1983; Millward and Stevens, 1986). Nevertheless, because this type of arrangement is seen to overcome many of the difficulties inherent in multi-unionism, and probably makes flexibility and cooperation easier to obtain, it is of increasing interest to employers.

What has perhaps made them more prominent in the UK is that a number of foreign-owned companies, notably Japanese firms, have insisted on single-union arrangements as the price of trade-union recognition. In almost all cases this has been part of an integrated package of conflict-handling measures; the so-called 'no-strike' and/or 'pendulum arbitration' clauses. However, whilst these agreements have clearly caught the attention of the popular press, very few actually exist. So far less than half of one per cent of the unionized workforce in the UK is covered in this way (Gregory, 1986).

Although trade unions are not opposed in principle to these agreements, they do pose some difficulties. The idea of exclusive representation rights is attractive to any union, particularly to those which have been badly hit by a contraction of their traditional strongholds in manufacturing industries. Nevertheless, the idea has met with a mixed reception. Until recently, some unions such as the AEU were not willing to enter into such an agreement if it meant foregoing the right to strike, but others such as the EETPU, had no such inhibitions. These two unions have recently merged, and it remains to be seen what the new policy will be.

Whilst there are few problems where there has been no history of trade-union recognition in a firm, the introduction of a single-union deal in an already unionized plant is fraught with potential tensions. From a trade-union point of view, the most controversial cases have been those where an employer has sought to move from the recognition of several unions to a single-union situation. This usually happens when the employer builds a new plant on a greenfield site, and there have been cases where signing a single-union agreement would have excluded other unions which had previously held bargaining rights in the firm. In more controversial cases there have been situations where employers have used the move to try to escape from agreements with unions on other existing sites as well. Perhaps the most distasteful practice of all has been the way that some employers have encouraged trade unions to outbid each other to obtain recognition. In the eyes of most trade unions these 'sweetheart deals' encourage a dilution and betrayal of some of the strongest-held principles of trade unionism.

To prevent inter-union rivalries the trade union movement has operated a set of guiding principles since the mid 1930s: the TUC Disputes, Principles and Procedures, more commonly known as the Bridlington rules. These reflect two fundamental principles.

(1) Unless it is by arrangement with that union, no union should undertake new organizing responsibilities for specific categories of workers in an organization where another union already represents the majority of workers employed.

(2) No TUC-affiliated union should accept into membership a member of another affiliated union without first investigating why that person wishes to change unions.

If a union enters into a single-union agreement, it can violate either or both of these, and a Congress decision in 1985 requires unions to refrain from doing so where other unions would be deprived of their existing recognition rights. This in turn has led to further problems, and at present the TUC operates a code of practice which requires affiliates to supply it with prior notice, and full details of any single-union deal it is in the process of negotiating. Perhaps more importantly it requires them to refrain from entering into agreements which remove, or are designed to remove, the basic right to strike. This raises the issue of the second procedural development.

No-strike deals are simply no-strike clauses in recognition agreements. They have also caught the imagination of the popular press, and the suggestion has been made that they herald a completely new form of conflict-free industrial relations (Bassett, 1986). However, a so-called 'strike-free deal' only really consists of a package of measures to minimize conflict and promote cooperation between management and employees. Typically, it contains an explicit provision to restrict industrial action, often by making the final stage of a disputes procedure one of binding, 'pendulum' arbitration (Lewis, 1990). Whilst there seems little doubt that this can succeed in minimizing disruptive industrial action, it is a gross overstatement to assert that it can eliminate it altogether. Moreover, a very penetrating analysis of a large number of these agreements and the way that they work in practice has concluded that they are not really very different to normal disputes procedures (Lewis, 1990). A genuinely strike-free agreement, for example, would need to be legally binding, and this is seldom, if ever, the case. Thus the clause referring a dispute to arbitration is really no more than an agreement to avoid industrial action until the procedure is exhausted; a feature found in most disputes procedures.

However, many disputes procedures also provide for matters to be referred to an arbitrator, and what is perhaps more innovative is the use of 'pendulum' or 'final offer' arbitration. Although this is common elsewhere, for example in the

USA (Treble, 1986), it is comparatively new in Britain. It requires an arbiter to make a straight choice between the final offers of management and the trade union, whereas conventional arbitration allows any difference to be split. The argument for having a pendulum arbitration clause is that it is likely to make the necessity for arbitration somewhat less. That is, it encourages both sides to adopt a more realistic stance from the outset, and to be more ready to move to the middle ground when negotiating. However, unless an agreement contains an arbitration clause which is binding in law (and almost none are), it does nothing to prevent either party from giving a suitable period of notice to withdraw from the agreement, and then take industrial action. For these reasons it is hard to see how any agreement made within the voluntarist framework of British industrial relations can guarantee a completely strike-free situation. Having said this, so far as can be determined, the parties to these agreements show few signs of discontent, and so it seems likely that their use will spread.

Collective bargaining and the public interest: legal attempts at reform

As was noted in Chapter 5, although there is a long tradition of voluntarism in British industrial relations, since the 1960s this has been strongly eroded. If left unchecked, voluntary collective bargaining has increasingly come to be seen as something which can inevitably produces inflationary wage settlements. However, any inflationary effects are perhaps more a symptom of the issues which have to be bargained, rather than the nature of bargaining itself. After World War II there was a progressive increase in the use of piece-work and other 'payments by results' methods in industry. Piece-work rates can only ever be negotiated at the place where the work is done, and this tends to result in real earnings being determined at enterprise or shop-floor level. Nevertheless, industry-wide bargaining was still the official way of setting pay rates, and because bargaining power at shop-floor level was usually much greater than in national forums, the gap between actual pay and official pay rates got progressively wider, and severe wages drift set in. In the 1950s and 1960s, it must be remembered, the vast expansion of a consumer society meant that manufacturers had little difficulty in passing on cost increases to customers. However, price rises inevitably resulted in further wage demands, and Britain became progressively less competitive in international markets. A number of attempts were made to pull away from the inflationary effects of piece-work bargaining, primarily by trying to link wage settlements more firmly with productivity. Indeed, in the early

1960s many employers sought self-financing 'productivity deals', in which restrictive practices were bought out for a share of the resulting cost savings (Flanders, 1964; McKersie and Hunter, 1973). Whilst, to some extent, this moved pay determination away from the shop-floor, changes of this type can still only be negotiated at enterprise level by those who fully understand their implications. Thus it had the effect of strengthening even further the trend towards workplace bargaining.

In 1964, and as a result of the concern with the inflationary effects of British industrial relations, a Royal Commission on Trade Unions and Employers' Associations (the Donovan Commission) was established. Its report which appeared in 1968 strongly defended the principle of voluntarism, but acknowledged its shortcomings. One of its major conclusions was that Great Britain had two systems of bargaining. There was a 'formal' system of national bargaining between trade unions and employers' associations, and the 'informal' system, which was based on relationships between managers, shop stewards and workgroups. In manufacturing industry at least, the latter system was where real earnings were determined. The remedies it proposed were that management should re-establish control, and link pay more firmly with productivity. In recognition that trends in payment systems meant that national bargaining was far less significant, it recommended that management and trade unions should adopt a more professional approach at workplace level. This was to involve less reliance on informal methods of pay determination, and instead, formal plant or company-wide agreements should be developed. It also recommended the establishment of a Standing Commission on Industrial Relations (the CIR) to oversee the reforms.

It is now widely recognized that the reforms of the Donovan Commission produced tensions of their own. It greatly encouraged the emergence of strong and autonomous workplace trade unions, which probably stood in the way of management reasserting control over labour costs and working practices (Ogden, 1981). Even if organizational practices are formalized, informal rules quickly re-emerge (Terry, 1977) and if this occurs in a situation where a workplace trade union has become more strongly entrenched and its role legitimized, other procedural changes quickly lead to an overall shift in the balance of power (Hawkins, 1978). As such, in some government circles the Donovan reforms came to be seen as having failed to bring the needed sea change in British industrial relations, particularly in respect to the basic nature of collective bargaining.

Following the election of a Conservative government in 1970, a concerted attempt was made to bring about a wholesale revision of labour law and collective bargaining. The 1971 Industrial Relations Act, which was briefly referred to in Chapter 5, was underpinned by a belief that trade unions were responsible for the defects in British industrial relations, and also for the nation's economic ills. Moreover, the abstinence of the law was viewed as a positive encouragement for them to behave in an irresponsible way (Clegg, 1979). The act therefore defined certain actions as 'unfair industrial practice', and gave legal remedies to employers who felt themselves to be hampered in this way. In the American style, it made provision for collective agreements to become legally enforceable contracts, which gave grounds for legal proceedings against trade unions and strike leaders in the event of industrial action. To reduce the effects of multi-unionism, the idea of a 'sole bargaining agent' was also borrowed from the United States. The Act also imposed a set of emergency procedures to enforce compulsory ballots, and a cooling-off period of up to 60 days in the case of major strikes or those affecting national interest. Perhaps the only remarkable feature of the Act, in practical terms, was the hostility it engendered amongst trade unions, and to some extent in management as well. It was repealed by the incoming Labour government in 1974, and (in nominal terms at least) since then there has been a return to the principle of voluntary collective bargaining.

In some quarters, however, the belief that legal reform (including binding agreements) is a 'good thing' has not completely disappeared. For example, in 1991 the government published a Green Paper which outlined the next proposed tranche of labour legislation. This included a proposal to make agreements legally enforceable, and so it is relevant to examine the arguments for and against this step.

The first argument in favour is that legally enforceable agreements would need to be far more explicit and comprehensive which means they would define the respective rights and obligations of employers and employees much more precisely. This, it is argued, would leave less room for ambiguity, and the inevitable conflicts that it gives rise to. In rebuttal it can be argued that no agreement can be so comprehensive that it specifies every detail of the arrangements that have to be made on a day-to-day basis. For this reason some degree of informality is both inevitable and necessary, simply to enable managers and employees to accommodate to each other at shop-floor level.

The second argument is that trade unions would be forced to ensure that their members honoured agreements, and this would reduce the possibility of unconstitutional industrial action. Against this it can be pointed out that in recent labour legislation such as the Trade Union Act, 1984 and the Employment Act, 1988, these safeguards are already given. Moreover, in countries where the law makes agreements legally enforceable, levels of industrial action are often higher than in the UK. Two examples will perhaps illustrate the point. In Australia, which has had a system of compulsory arbitration for many years, all agreements are ratified by the courts, and become legally binding. One of Australia's principal aims in introducing this system was to make strikes of any type unnecessary, and strictly speaking they are illegal (Lansbury and Davis, 1987). Nevertheless, Australia has a great many short strikes at plant level. Usually these strikes are over very local issues, the details of which could never be specified in legally enforceable national agreements. Indeed, in terms of days lost per thousand workers, Australia usually comes fairly high in the international strike league. For example, in the years 1973 to 1982, during which strike action in Britain was at its highest, the average days lost through industrial action in Australia were one and one-half times those of the UK (Creigh and Makeham, 1982).

Another example is Canada, which in terms of days lost per 1000 workers between 1973 to 1983 had a strike record twice the level of that in the UK, and indeed had the highest level of all Western industrialized nations. The Canadian system of industrial relations is very similar to that of the USA. Firms have comprehensive, legally enforceable agreements. Within the duration of an agreement, grievance or disputes procedures which include third-party arbitration are designed to handle any conflict, and strictly speaking, this makes striking illegal. Nevertheless, Canada has many long and bitter strikes, and thirty per cent of all stoppages occur whilst an agreement is in force (Thompson, 1987).

The third argument for legal enforceability is that it would promote long-term responsibility and change attitudes on both sides. It would give management stability, and enable it to get on with the job of managing the organization secure in the knowledge that agreements would be honoured. In return it would give employees greater security and earnings. Against this it can be argued that the dangers of moving away from a voluntarist system could by far outweigh any advantages. In a voluntarist system agreements are binding in honour. Whilst reaching agreement can be difficult, when it is reached, it is for the most part scrupulously honoured by both sides. Indeed, a lack of honour on one side merely invites the other one to behave dishonourably as well. For this reason conflicts are usually handled peaceably, and the system only tends to break down where one party perceives that the other is behaving unfairly. Thus, honour acts as a very strong (perhaps the strongest) normative glue. This binds the whole system together, and makes it possible to have high-trust bargaining relationships. If an agreement is made legally enforceable, it removes any necessity for the parties to operate on the basis of 'my word is my bond'. Instead, it becomes fair game to look for, and exploit, the smallest loopholes in what has been agreed. The only remedy to this is to make agreements so detailed and comprehensive that any loopholes are closed. As the evidence from Australia and Canada shows, this is hardly practical, and even if it were, there is another potential drawback. Legal enforceability applies to both sides. Thus in a situation where management seeks a change for very necessary reasons, the *status quo* can be legally enforced until employees agree. The result would be a very elongated process of change and adaptation.

Perhaps the most damning condemnation of the idea of legal enforceability, however, is the satisfaction which the parties find with a voluntarist system. There is nothing in law which says an employer must recognize a trade union for bargaining purposes. Therefore the reduction of trade-union powers of resistance in the recessionary periods since 1980, coupled with the overtly anti-trade-union legislation of the same period, has given any employer who so wished an ideal opportunity to withdraw recognition. Despite this, de-recognition has been extremely rare, and what has occurred has been highly selective (Claydon, 1989). Thus the vast majority of employers would seem to be well content with the present nature of collective bargaining, and the stability that it brings.

Conclusions and overview

Whilst collective bargaining makes extensive use of negotiation, the two should not be regarded as the same. Collective bargaining is essentially a relationship, and negotiation a process to set the terms of the relationship. The bargaining relationship itself can take many forms. Some of these are reflected in the structural arrangements made for it to continue, and others are more a reflection of its quality; for example, the industrial-relations climate that it engenders, and its outcomes in terms of the agreements that result. However, whatever form the relationship takes it is essentially used by the parties to draw a line that specifies their rights and obligations. Thus it is a highly significant method for determining the ways in which organization and employees relate to each other.

Although collective bargaining is essentially a relationship between employers and employees, from time to time the State has taken the view that it is not always a responsible one in terms of the national interest. For this reason, attempts have been made to reform the nature of collective bargaining, usually by passing laws which limit the freedom of the parties to act as they see fit. Thus, what has been described at the end of this chapter has strong connections with what was covered in Chapter 5. However, the strongest links are clearly with the two following chapters. The one that comes next considers the topic of negotiation, and as noted above, this is the major vehicle of interface for the two parties in the collective bargaining relationship. The chapter after that then goes on to consider the subject of industrial conflict which, in the eyes of some people, has tended to be an inevitable by-product of collective bargaining.

Further reading

Chamberlain N.W. and Kuhn J.W. (1965). *Collective Bargaining*. New York: McGraw-Hill

A very thorough and scholarly examination of the collective bargaining process.

Clegg H.A. (1979). *The Changing System of Industrial Relations in Great Britain*. Oxford: Blackwell

A very detailed examination from an author who is arguably the greatest authority on the place of collective bargaining in British industrial relations. It contains particularly relevant chapters on the changing role of the State and its attempts to reform the nature of collective bargaining in the UK.

Basset P. (1986). *Strike Free: New Industrial Relations in Britain*. London: Macmillan

A highly influential if somewhat optimistic text, which gives an account of the changing nature of collective agreements in the UK and their potential effects on industrial relations.

10

Negotiation

Introduction

This chapter deals with negotiation, and follows on from the previous one, where it was noted that the dominant way of deciding the details of the relationship between an organization and its employees in collective bargaining is the processes of negotiation. It was also pointed out in the previous chapter that there is a sense in which the topic of negotiation cannot be divorced from that of industrial action. Therefore, the chapter starts by tracing this link. It then examines negotiation from a theoretical perspective, and explains how the process can be strongly influenced by its surrounding contextual circumstances. Next, some of the important behaviourial aspects of negotiation are described, and its practicalities are explored by considering the negotiating process in three stages: preparation, face-to-face negotiations, and post-negotiating activities. The final section explains the scheme of 'principled' negotiation, which gives some guidelines and prescriptions for constructive negotiating behaviour.

Negotiation: a conceptual perspective and definition

Whilst almost everybody engages in some form of negotiation on a daily basis, in employee relations the term has a rather special meaning. It is the main way of resolving issues within the collective-bargaining relationship, and the relationship itself gives negotiation certain characteristics that make it different from negotiating in other circumstances. To start with, in the employment relationship there is a basic and sometimes quite stark inequality of power. An employer's ability to withstand the loss of a single employee is far greater than the employee's ability to withstand the loss of the job. It is for this reason that employees choose to be represented collectively, that is, to speak with one voice.

Second, although the collective-bargaining relationship redresses the imbalance of power to some extent and reflects the dependence of employers and employees on each other, there are some matters in which their aims are significantly different. As in other situations where it is recognized that differences exist, discussing the differences and trying to reconcile them is usually the first step. However, in employee relations this first step is taken in the knowledge that either party has an alternative: it can withdraw from the relationship and thus inflict harm on the other one. This makes it quite different from commercial negotiations where, for example, a firm that fails to find satisfactory terms of doing business with another has not actually been harmed. Both parties entered into negotiations with the anticipation of gain and, if one withdraws, the outcome is that the other suffers a lost opportunity rather than a harm.

There are two important implications of these features. First the very thing that brings the two sides around the table into a negotiating process is the knowledge that each one can suffer harm at the hands of the other party. Second, the very fact that negotiations are in progress is an expression that the parties have conflicting aims. Thus negotiation is no less of an expression of conflict than is strike action. For this reason it is a gross oversimplification to think of negotiation as peace, and industrial action as war. They are simply different ways of pursuing the same end. That is, the purpose is that of finding an acceptable resolution to their differences. They are both processes of persuasion in which one party attempts to get the other to see things their way, and the only difference is that whilst one uses the force of argument, the other uses the argument of force. Moreover, when negotiations are concluded it seldom means that no conflict remains. It is unlikely that both parties achieved all that they desire. Therefore a concluded negotiation simply means that for the time being a situation has been reached where the major differences have been resolved. For how long this will persist tends to depend upon the nature of the differences that have been resolved, and the agreement that has been reached. For these reasons negotiation is defined here as a process of handling conflict, which is used by two or more parties to reconcile their interests, and with the aim of producing an agreement that both, for the time being, are able to live with.

The theory of negotiation

Negotiation is a very dynamic process. Thus one set of negotiations is never quite the same as another. There are many factors at work, and even in stable bargaining relationships they can vary quite considerably. Often the process can take place over days, weeks or even months, rather than in a single session which lasts a few hours. In reality it consists of several processes, all of which are usually at work together. However, like all human interaction it can take its tone from the contextual circumstances in which it takes place, and these can influence the process before it even starts. Therefore, before exploring the internal dynamics of negotiation, it can be useful to understand the effects of this contextual backdrop.

The contexts of negotiation

In what follows, it needs to be remembered that all the contextual factors interact with each other and this means that it is always hard to isolate the effects of one. Thus they are only described separately for the sake of simplicity, and can be expressed as the four general groups shown in Figure 10.1.

The *relative power of the parties* is an important (many would argue the most important) contextual factor (Walton, 1969). It is perhaps not so much who actually has the most power that is important, as what the parties 'perceive' their power positions to be. Magenau and Pruitt (1979), for example, argue that this is what most influences a negotiator's motivation to maintain demands and press them home. In essence, and even if it is only a subjective one, each negotiator is likely to have an evaluation of what it will cost the other party to agree or not agree to what is demanded of them, and in this lies their evaluation of relative power. For example, if a trade-union negotiator perceives that management's costs of not agreeing to the union's demands will be greater than the costs of conceding the claim, she or he will evaluate the union's power position as the greater, and will therefore be prepared to doggedly press home the case. Clearly the management negotiator will also have an evaluation of his own power and that of the trade union. Thus it is perfectly possible for both sides to enter negotiations perceiving that they have a power advantage. Whilst the process of negotiation

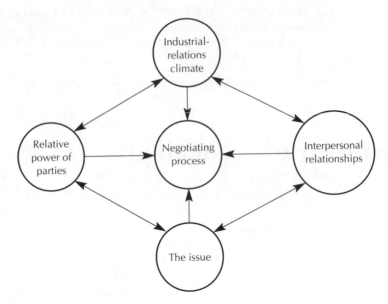

Figure 10.1   The contexts of the negotiating process.

will refine these perceptions to some extent, those that the parties start with can have a huge influence on how matters progress. Therefore, negotiation is not so much the use of power as the exploitation of potential power (Morley, 1979).

It is for this reason that threats of sanctions, either by implication or more openly, are a fundamental part of the process (Hawkins, 1979). This, however, is to portray negotiation as simply a matter of coercion, which it is not. Ultimately, negotiating power is the capability to get the other side to change their view. Whilst having the capability to harm them is one source of power that can bring this about, it can be a particularly expensive and dangerous one to use (Fisher, 1969).

A second contextual factor is the *issue* itself. Negotiators represent others, and are not free agents. Whilst they can exert some influence on their constituents, they are also subject to a great deal of pressure in return. Generally, the greater is the importance of an issue to the constituents, the greater is the pressure on a negotiator. Thus the negotiator will be concerned to demonstrate publicly a strong commitment to achieving what the constituents want. In practice this often means taking a stand in negotiations, which in turn can mean that it takes longer to reach agreement (Morley, 1984). In most negotiations, however, there are usually a number of issues on the table at the same time, and some of these are more important than others. The fact that there are multiple issues also tends to have a strong effect on the tactics that negotiators are likely to use. For example, the least important of them can be sacrificed to achieve those that are paramount, and for this reason it is vital for a negotiator to know the relative importance of the issues in the eyes of the constituents that they represent

(Balke *et al.*, 1973). It is also important for the negotiator to have some idea of their importance to the opposing side. If, for example, a negotiator wrongly estimates this, it can become a major source of hostile interactions, crossed communications and misunderstandings during the negotiation (Bonham, 1971).

Industrial-relations climate can be an all-pervasive context. It was mentioned briefly in the previous chapter, and was noted to have a strong effect on the whole bargaining relationship. It is a reflection of the way that the two sides see each other (Rim and Mannheim, 1979), and once formed, these views can be extremely resistant to modification. Because each party treats the other one in a certain way, they tend to respond to this by behaving as expected, and the whole matter can become a self-fulfilling prophecy (Biasatti and Martin, 1979). Nicholson (1979), for example, shows that memories die hard. Because of this the issues climate, which is connected with memories of the way issues have been handled in the past, can strongly affect interpersonal climate, the personal relationships between the two sides, and this in turn can strongly affect behaviour in negotiations. If, for example, the climate is harmonious, issues tend to be approached by both sides in a joint problem-solving way (Harbison and Coleman, 1951), and where it is hostile, it can result in an extremely frosty atmosphere, where each side tries to undermine the other.

The final context is that of *interpersonal relations* between negotiators. If negotiators have dealt with each other for some time, they are likely to have developed a rapport, and appreciate that their counterpart is subject to pressure from her or his constituents. Usually this means that a constructive negotiator will have a fairly accurate idea of what can be achieved as the final settlement point (Walton and McKersie, 1965). Where climates are particularly good, negotiators are also likely to accept each other's standards and expectations, and to avoid behaviour which irritates the other side or impedes progress. The outcome of this is that irrespective of their constituent's demands, certain things are never said, and certain things are never asked for (Anthony and Crichton, 1969). Therefore, whilst good interpersonal relationships on their own are not sufficient to result in a successful negotiation (Marsh, 1974), they can have a huge impact on the way the process is conducted, and the length of time it takes. On the shop-floor, for example, negotiators are in almost continuous contact with each other and have a vested interest in maintaining a long-term relationship of goodwill (Gottshalk and Mee 1972). This can sometimes have an effect when they meet in more formal negotiating arenas, and can be used constructively to explore positions without having to take too rigid a stance (Morley and Stephenson, 1977). Perhaps most important of all, good relationships enable negotiators to 'get off the record' and explore potential solutions outside the formal negotiating arena.

These then are the most important contexts of negotiating, and it must be stressed again that they are connected. An example will perhaps illustrate the point. The nature of an issue has effects on the relative power position of the parties, and this in turn will influence the way it is pursued. Thus the issue puts limits on the relationship between bargainers. However, their relationship also plays a part in the way that they approach an issue, and so there is some effect in the reverse direction.

CASE-STUDY 10.1

The signs of climate

Consider the following statements made by managers and trade union officials in different organizations.

1 *Manager* We know how the union got into this firm: management was short-sighted and made a lot of mistakes, and if we had been on our toes it would never have happened. Now it's here we can't get rid of it, and the best we can do is to contain it by an intelligent and aggressive personnel policy.

2 *Union officer* This company is in a really difficult market and managers have a tough time. Whilst the members obviously all want security and better pay and conditions, they know you can't have a prosperous firm just by wishing for it. We have to work to make the company prosperous, but at the same time take care that the results of prosperity are fairly shared out.

3 *Union Officer* If the company could find an excuse they would sack every steward in the place. The only reason they deal with us is that ten years ago we had a stand-up fight to get a decent pay deal, and this led to a long and bitter strike. Since then management deal with us because they have to, but they have never got over the bloody nose we gave them then.

4 *Manager* Working with the union is not giving up control. In reality by working with them and enlisting their help in difficult times, management has more control over the future destiny of the firm than ever it has had before.

5 *Manager* In the past because we felt we were doing the right thing we fought the unions tooth and nail. Eventually, we saw that this was getting us nowhere. Bit by bit we have found that the union has a job to do the same as we have. In a sense, by keeping management on its toes, the union has made most of us better managers.

6 *Union officer* Although the trade union should never try to take over management's job, we have a vested interest in cooperating about some things. I suppose you could say that we have stopped seeing management as the enemy; the real enemy is out there in the market place. So

far as getting the best of the real enemy is concerned, management and union are generally on the same side.

Questions
i In each case, what sort of industrial-relations climate do you feel that the statement indicates?
ii In each case, what do you feel that the aims and policies of management and union would be with respect to each other?

The internal dynamics of negotiation

Whilst it has been criticized as being somewhat rigid in the way that it classifies different processes (Morley, 1979), by far the most comprehensive and explicit description of the complexities of negotiation is that given by Walton and McKersie (1965). The Walton and McKersie scheme points out that negotiation consists of a number of activities rather than just one. The actual interface where negotiators act on behalf of their respective groups is classified as *inter-organizational bargaining*, and this can take place in one of two basic forms: integrative or distributive. In *distributive bargaining* the issues are dealt with by attempting to reach agreement on how a fixed amount should be divided up, while *integrative bargaining* involves negotiators in adopting a joint problem-solving approach. It must be noted however, that some authors consider this distinction to be too rigid. Morley and Stephenson (1977), for example, argue that these are not different processes, but different types of task. Moreover, Anthony (1977) has pointed out that even if the two sides have a collaborative approach, negotiation in employee relations is seldom concerned with anything other than dividing up a cake of a fixed size. Notwithstanding these points, because the aims and behaviour associated with integrative and distributive bargaining tend to be very different, the distinction between them is still a useful one. Thus, rather than discount the idea altogether, it is perhaps more realistic to note that negotiations often contain a mixture of both distributive and integrative bargaining, a point acknowledged by Walton and McKersie when they allude to *mixed bargaining*.

Another activity, but this time one about which there is less controversy, is *intra-organizational bargaining*. The groups that negotiators represent usually consist of subgroups and individuals with a diverse mixture of priorities and objectives. In addition, the group as a whole is often far more optimistic than the negotiator about what can realistically be achieved (Anthony and Crichton, 1969; Rackham and Carlisle, 1978). Therefore, before negotiators ever face each other, in intra-organizational bargaining they usually have to negotiate with their own constituents to try to bring the expectations of the group into line with their own. This can be a vitally important activity. An effective negotiator will always try to ensure that her/his formal mandate allows maximum room for manoeuvre. For

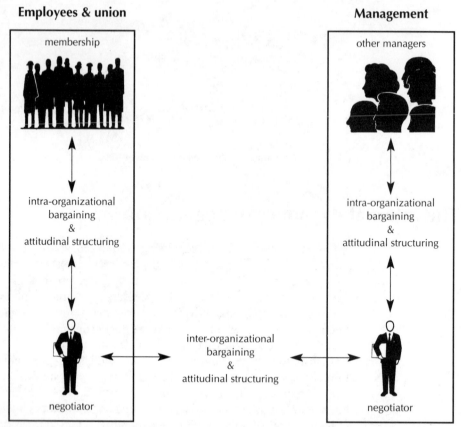

Figure 10.2   Processes in negotiation (after R.E. Walton and R.B. McKersie, 1965).

this reason there is often an additional need for intra-organizational bargaining later on in negotiations, when aims and priorities may have to be revised.

The final activity described by Walton and McKersie is that of *attitudinal structuring*. This consists of attempts by negotiators to persuade each other and/or their own constituents to see things differently, usually by attempting to modify or reinforce their perceptions of the situation. For example, a trade-union negotiator might try to persuade his constituents to lower their aspirations by pointing out that these can only be achieved through strike action. A similar tactic that is often used on the other side is to hint that they have grossly overestimated their power position.

As well as giving a way of describing different activities, the Walton and McKersie framework also fits neatly with the reality of negotiation as a multi-stage process. This will be described presently, but Figure 10.2 gives some idea of the way in which the different activities link together and come into play at various stages of negotiating.

CASE-STUDY 10.2

Hillside District Council

Hillside District Council serves an expanding rural and urban area in which unemployment is well above average. The council is an extremely progressive one that has expanded its activities and been highly innovative in developing new services to the community. Three months ago central government passed legislation which could be used to force local authorities to shed a number of their functions. This authorizes the Audit Commission to investigate a council's activities and order a council to divest itself of services which are considered unnecessary. The Audit Commission is also able to instruct that activities be put out to tender where it decides that these could be performed more cheaply by private enterprise.

The Commission will be conducting an investigation of the authority in four months' time, and the chief executive's estimate of the effects on council departments is that to avoid adverse comments from the Commission, the Community Services department would need to lose about 40 members of staff, and the Operational Services department about 20. If the council could avoid an adverse report, other departments would probably be allowed to remain unaltered.

The ruling political group on the council like to think of themselves as responsible employers in the best traditions of local government. They are very proud of the range of services provided by the authority, and above all, would wish none of them removed.

The trade union has also estimated that the same departments would be most at risk, and if the worst were to happen it would pose problems for some members. Those most likely to be affected are specialists in their own fields, and are fairly well paid. Cutbacks in other authorities would make it hard for them to find new jobs. Some would probably be prepared to take enhanced early retirement, and a scheme to give up to ten years' pensionable service exists. However, in the event of drastic cuts, the numbers opting for early retirement would be unlikely to be sufficient to cope. As such the membership can be expected to call for a strong resistance to any proposed cuts.

The distribution of council manpower is given below.

Department	Function	Staffing	
		Establishment	Actual
Chief Executive's (inc.ITEC)	Personnel		
	Legal services		
	Central typing services		

Department	Function	Staffing	
		Establishment	Actual
	ITEC – training centre for rehabilitation of unemployed	87	66*
Community Programme	Long-term job and skills training for the unemployed	60	39*
Finance & Admin.	Accounts	135	119*
Housing	Maintenance of housing stock, rent collection etc.	145	145
Leisure and Community Services	Parks, recreation centres, social services	105	102
Operational Services	Refuse collection, street cleaning etc.	64	65
Planning and Environmental Services	Urban and rural planning, architects etc.	112	83*

* Recruitment difficulties due to national shortage of qualified personnel.

Questions

i What do you feel will be the objectives of council and trade union in this matter?

ii What type of bargaining between council and employer is likely to take place?

iii Can you identify an integrative solution to the difficulty? What is it, and how should it be proposed?

Practical negotiation

Perhaps the easiest way to consider the practical aspects of negotiation is to view it as a process with three main stages: preparation, the face-to-face encounter(s), and post-negotiating activities. In each of these, however, there are usually a number of phases. To simplify matters a number of assumptions will be made in the following description of the stages. First, as is normal in employee relations, it is assumed that employees and management are represented by a team of negotiators. The management side would probably consist of line managers and a personnel specialist, and for employees the team would be made up of representatives of the groups most affected by the issue. Second, each side has a spokesperson, who is referred to here as the negotiator.

Stage 1: Preparation for negotiation

Preparation is seldom something that can be done quickly, and to assemble the information to put forward a convincing case takes time. However, until the party raising the issue puts forward its claim or an opening proposal, the preparatory activities of the other side are limited. Thus if a trade union presents a wage claim, there will be little negotiation at the first meeting of the two parties. Management would probably hear the claim, ask questions to obtain clarification, and then the meeting would be adjourned. The adjournment might be for several weeks, in which time management would undertake its own detailed preparation. If management were the proactive party, say in presenting a proposal for an extensive revision of working practices or a major reorganization, then the trade union would listen and retire to commence preparation.

Clearly negotiators on both sides have to prepare their own case. They also have to be able to defend it, and if necessary launch a counter-attack if and when the opposition tries to undermine it (Torrington, 1972). Clearly this means that a great deal of consideration has to be given to the opponent's likely position. However, it is just as essential for a negotiator to know the objectives, constraints and limits of manoeuvre imposed by her or his own side. To this end, and before the first formal negotiating meeting, negotiators will probably take part in some initial skirmishing, both with those that they represent and with the opposing side's negotiator.

Skirmishing with the opposing side often takes the form of preliminary meetings to set an agenda for formal negotiations. Obtaining a suitable agenda can be a part of negotiating tactics, and allows a negotiator to include throw-away issues that can be conceded to achieve the more important objectives (Anthony and Crichton, 1969). As well as settling procedural details, this initial skirmishing inevitably includes attempts to structure attitudes. Where negotiators have dealt with each other for a long time these initial meetings often include an element of tacit negotiation as well. That is, negotiators communicate to each other what is achievable and what is not.

In parallel with this, negotiators will also meet with their own side to prepare the case, and inevitably information gained in meetings with their opposite number will spill over into what takes place. In order to avoid being saddled with aims where only a fight will win the day, a negotiator is likely to bargain with her or his own side to attempt to reshape their attitudes and aspirations. This

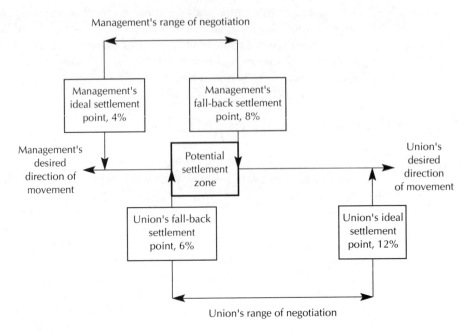

Figure 10.3 Negotiating positions.

shaping of aims is a fundamental part of working out *bargaining positions and objectives*. Often there will be multiple objectives, some of which are more important than others. Thus a negotiator will try to get them ranked in order of importance to give some idea of the issues which can be conceded in the interests of reaching agreement (Kennedy *et al.*, 1980). A crucial part of formulating these objectives is to establish the bargaining range for each one, and this usually involves estimating the likely bargaining range for the other side as well. The importance of the bargaining range can be explained with the simple diagram shown in Figure 10.3.

For every one of its bargaining objectives, each side will need to know what it ideally hopes to achieve, and also the fall-back point below which a settlement would be considered unacceptable. For example, in Figure 10.3 assume that the trade union has lodged a claim for a 12 % across-the-board pay increase. This is the ideal, but it has a fall-back point of 6 %, which is the minimum its members will accept, that is, they would be prepared to take industrial action to improve an offer of below 6 %. Thus its bargaining range is 6–12 %. Management would ideally like to settle for 4 %, but to avoid disruption, and if pressed hard enough, it would be prepared to go up to 8 % but no further, and its bargaining range is 4–8 %. The potential zone of settlement achievable by negotiation, and without recourse to industrial action, is therefore somewhere between 6 % and 8 %.

With multiple bargaining objectives it is even more crucial to establish these limits. Effective negotiators are those who build an element of flexibility into their strategy and try to avoid having objectives which are so rigid that they are incapable of modification (Rackham and Carlisle, 1978). Whilst they are aware that the two sides will probably not come close to settlement until very late in the negotiating process, they also recognize the crucial need to maintain momentum once convergence starts. This is far easier for a negotiator if he or she knows which objectives can be lowered or abandoned in order to achieve others (Magenau and Pruitt, 1979).

Preparation will also involve establishing a clear system of roles within each team, and this can be vital in ensuring its effective performance. Usually the chief negotiator or spokesperson will already have been decided, and vital though this is, there are other important roles as well. If, for example, some things can be left to other team members, it enables the chief negotiator to concentrate on interacting with the other side. For this reason, it can be important to have someone who records what is said; not only its substantive content, but also any non-verbal signals that either reinforce or contradict the message. In complex negotiations, where several different groups could be affected by the outcome, it can also be vital to have members of the team who keep an eye open for the way in which developments can affect each group.

Stage 2: Face-to-face negotiations

The face-to-face part of negotiating tends to take place in different phases. How long each phase lasts and what takes place within it can depend crucially upon the skills of the negotiators. In all of them there are periods of very circular activity that achieve little or nothing, and these tend to be followed by changes in behaviour that come in spurts (Douglas, 1962).

The first phase tends to be one of *opening moves*. The proposing side will normally present their case, together with supporting arguments. If it is complex, and it often is, an adjournment is sometimes necessary to allow the receiving side the opportunity to study what has been proposed. The phase can be very formal, with each side attempting to convince the other of the justice of their case (Douglas, 1962), and in these opening moves, it can be very important that neither side conveys a 'take it or leave it' attitude.

When the receiving side presents its response, or perhaps later when a 'response to the response' is made, negotiations are likely to move into the second phase, that of *developing the case*. In this phase negotiators will attempt to argue the strength of their own proposals, and to reduce the validity of the opposing argument. Thus it is a phase of thrust and parry, and argument and counter-argument. Negotiators will often try to reconnoitre the opponent's position and undermine it, and at the same time make their own case more legitimate. It is also the one in which the more subtle tactics of bargaining are most likely to be used. Sometimes these are negative tactics that are designed to divide the opposition, or to intimidate them with lightly veiled threats of what will happen if they do not adopt a more 'realistic' view. However, positive tactics are also likely to be used, for example, offering an olive branch to the other side in return for concessions. In a strange way even the apparently hostile behaviour can have a positive purpose when looking at the negotiation process in its entirety. Much of it is cosmetic and is therefore designed to identify the future direction of the bargaining dialogue and areas where concessions might eventually be exchanged (Morley and Stephenson, 1977).

Because new information is appearing fairly rapidly, in this phase it is quite likely that each side will occasionally wish to adjourn in order to reconsider its position. It is also likely that negotiators will meet more frequently in private, for 'off-the-record' conversations; a process sometimes referred to in less complimentary terms as 'corridor bargaining'. In the author's experience, and this is confirmed by other negotiators, it is quite common here for the two principals to agree privately what the terms of the substantive settlement will be, and then to persuade their constituents to accept them. Overall, the phase is one of progressive refinement, in which those areas where agreement has been reached are put out of the way, to focus on those which will prove to be the crux of the final settlement.

The third phase is that of *agreement seeking*. The previous phase was one where in public there was a high degree of polarization, but in private a search for points of convergence took place. This one, however, often contains more public signs that the parties are moving towards agreement. Its opening can often be detected by one of the parties making concrete proposals for a settlement. In addition, the process tends to become more formal again, and negotiators step back more firmly into their representative roles.

The final phase is that of *closing*. Even where negotiators have worked out in private where they will agree, they have to demonstrate that they are still fighting on their constituent's behalf. Therefore, formal negotiating is unlikely to end just yet. Indeed the phase is almost bound to commence with what appears to be a continuation of the previous phase of agreement seeking. It sometimes opens by one side offering in public what they have already offered in private, perhaps by presenting it as a new concession, and asking for something in return that has also been conceded privately. On other occasions the phase will simply consist of a summary of what has been agreed in previous meetings, and then the privately agreed terms will be proposed as a final offer. If and when the terms are formally accepted, it then remains to detail every point, and check that it is understood. This can be vital for two reasons. First, it is a public demonstration that an agreement has been reached, and that both sides have a common view about its terms. Second, in the relief of having come to the end of what can often be a stressful process, there is always a tendency for exhaustion to take over, and for details to be overlooked. Thus a detailed review of everything can help reduce the possibility of future misunderstandings, and perhaps the best advice is therefore to 'summarise what has been agreed, and get agreement on what has been summarised as agreed' (Kennedy *et al.*, 1980, p. 113).

Before giving a description of the last stage it is important to make a final point about this one. It has been portrayed as a process which leads inevitably to a peaceful settlement. This is not always the case, and sometimes it can be punctuated by the use of tactics which are designed to exert pressure in other ways. For example, employees can take industrial action, and employers can withdraw from negotiations and attempt to impose changes. Whilst it is important to note that this can happen, these matters are covered in the next chapter, and so details are deferred until then.

Perhaps the more interesting case is where no agreement is reached and the parties record a 'failure to agree'. In essence this means that the negotiators recognize that there is little likelihood of further concession or compromise on either side, and mutually agree to withdraw from the process. Because prolonging the negotiations could well lead to a hardening of attitudes and increase the possibility of acrimony, if an impasse is reached this is usually a wise decision. What happens from then on, however, can depend a great deal on whether negotiating procedures allow for this contingency. Sometimes disputes procedures make provision for third-party conciliation, mediation and/or arbitration. These processes, which can be provided by the Advisory, Conciliation and Arbitration Service, were described in Chapter 5 and will not be covered again here. Suffice it to say that if the parties have had the good sense to realize that an impasse has been reached, seeking the help of an outside third party is not a sign of either incompetence or weakness. Indeed, because it can tend to take the heat out of matters and can do much to safeguard the longer-term bargaining relationship, it is probably more a sign of wisdom than anything else. Otherwise one or other of the parties may resort to pressure tactics, and this can have severe climatic repercussions. Perhaps the most important point to make is that if a withdrawal is necessary, both sides should agree the position they have already reached, and preferably set down in writing the remaining areas of disagreement. This way the task of conciliators, arbitrators or even higher-level negotiators is made much clearer.

Stage 3: Post-negotiation

When a satisfactory agreement has been reached there is a natural tendency to regard matters as having ended. However, no agreement in the world can deal with every possible contingency, and there is always the likelihood that minor points of detail will need to be sorted out. Sometimes these are not identified for days or even weeks after agreement has been reached. Thus they are frequently left to the principal negotiators or individual managers and shop stewards to resolve on an *ad hoc* basis. Indeed, there can be as much effort devoted to this tidying-up work as there was to reaching the agreement. It is not, however, a matter which can be neglected. Unless these issues are brought to light and resolved, the two sides have not achieved the clear understanding that they perhaps assume they have reached. Moreover, until these things are finally cleared up, it cannot really be said that the new agreement has been fully implemented.

The scheme of 'principled' negotiation

Negotiation can clearly be a daunting and somewhat intimidating process for those who have not experienced it at first hand. However it is a skill, and like most skills it can be polished and improved. Skilful negotiators understand that there are both risks and opportunities in the process. They also have an awareness of the resources available to pursue or protect the interests of those that they represent (Morley, 1981). An important resource is the skill of the negotiator, and this is really a whole range of skills that may need to be used at different times in the negotiating process. For example, social and interpersonal skills can be important, as can those of information handling and judgement. These may be called for at different times. Fortunately, however, to some extent all can be enhanced by practice and application (Kniveton, 1974).

With this in mind it can be helpful to have guidelines to follow, and a useful set is given by Fisher and Ury (1987) in their scheme of *principled negotiation*. These are not focused specifically on negotiations in an employee-relations context. Nevertheless, there are many similarities in the negotiating process whether it occurs in industrial relations, commercial, or international fields, and the scheme was constructed after research and practice in a wide diversity of negotiating circumstances at Harvard University in the USA. Although it is ethical, the word 'principled' is not used in this sense, but refers to a number of guiding principles that deal with the preparation and face-to-face aspects of negotiation. Prime importance is given to avoiding what the authors call 'positional bargaining', that is, taking up an initial position, doggedly defending it, and then reluctantly conceding points to reach a compromise. As they point out, whilst this can serve the useful purpose of conveying to the other party what is wanted, it can all too easily lead to a regressive spiral in which the harder a position is defended, the greater is the likelihood that the negotiator will become locked into a situation from which there is no retreat. Thus four guiding principles are offered, principles that experienced and effective employee-relations negotiators probably use unconsciously without realizing it.

The first principle is *separation of the people from the problem*. The issue to be dealt with needs to be separated in the mind of the negotiator from the person on the opposing side who is handling it. Only by doing this can conflicting goals be dealt with in a way that allows a good working relationship to be maintained with the other negotiator.

Flowing from the first one, the second principle is to *focus on interests and not positions*. The first reaction on hearing a proposal from the other side is often to focus purely on the threat to one's own interests. To do this, however, tends to result in a lack of understanding about exactly what it is that the other side is seeking to achieve. Thus applying the principle involves identifying clearly what the opposing side proposes, what their interests are in proposing it, and how things look from their position. For example, when employees submit a wage claim it is all too easy for management to assume that it is merely prompted by a desire to maintain living standards. It probably is this, but it might also be because workers in a nearby firm, with whom they have traditionally had comparable pay rates, have just received a pay rise. In part, therefore, the claim could be concerned with regaining self-respect.

The third principle, *inventing options for mutual gain*, can be the hardest to put into practice, and means that quite subtle thinking is needed. It is an attempt to look for ways in which both sides can achieve their objectives, and at first sight this might seem to be simply a plea for integrative bargaining. Whilst this is true to some extent it is, however, a lot more. The authors make the point that it is all too easy to assume that every available option lies between the two extremes of one or other of the parties having all their objectives satisfied. To avoid this they advocate a conscious search for a whole range of alternative solutions, which clearly involves understanding very clearly what the opposing side's interests are. It can also mean that creative decision-making techniques such as brainstorming need to be used.

The fourth and final principle is to *insist on objective criteria*. Essentially this means that there must be a clear understanding with the opposing side about the criteria which will be used to judge when agreement has been reached. Moreover, this must be done before negotiating starts. Clearly the criteria have to be seen as fair by both sides, but the very process of establishing them can be a valuable step towards the two sides understanding each other's interests. Without the criteria, however, it can be extremely hard for innovative solutions to be accepted. As an example, suppose that management proposes a reorganization of some sort, and that it is resisted by trade-union negotiators because their members perceive that the changes will upset cherished status and position privileges. Assume that management has costed the proposal as giving a 10 % efficiency saving, but has not revealed this. Had the trade union been in possession of this information, it might well have been able to suggest alternatives that would still give a 10 % saving. The 10 % criterion would also be a very objective benchmark against which its counter-proposals could be evaluated.

In addition to these four guiding principles, Fisher and Ury offer some very useful advice on the tactics of making the scheme more workable. For example, they acknowledge that negotiation often takes place against a background of unequal power positions, and for this reason they suggest that it is always necessary to develop a *best alternative to a negotiated agreement*. In employee relations, this might perhaps consist of the trade union identifying the level at which an offer from management is so unacceptable that it warrants taking action of some sort to bring about an improvement. The authors also recognize that negotiations can be acutely affected by what has gone on in the past. This can make either side wary about joining in the use of constructive tactics, and even worse, one or both might have a tendency to resort to a whole series of underhand manoeuvres. Although Fisher and Ury offer no panacea to this situation, and in any event there is probably no such thing as a foolproof negotiating formula, they give extremely useful hints on how to push negotiations in a more constructive direction. Thus in a very pragmatic way, their scheme reinforces a great deal of what makes for effective negotiating behaviour.

Conclusions and overview

In employee relations negotiation is a complex process. Although the parties have some things in common, there are many occasions when their aims are diametrically opposed. Thus it is not always possible for the process to take place within an integrative, joint problem-solving framework. Indeed, reaching a solution which reconciles the different aims of the parties sometimes means travelling a long and tortuous path.

In reality negotiating is not a single process. Rather it is one which consists of a number of different activities, each of which tends to be more prominent at a different time in the proceedings. In addition, although it is not always immediately obvious, the overall process can be subdivided into a number of stages which need to be traversed before agreement is reached, and the rate at which it is possible to move through them will tend to depend on a number of factors; for example, the contextual circumstances surrounding the negotiations and the skills and abilities of the people at the negotiating table. Finally, it is important to stress that even prolonged negotiations sometimes fail to progress to agreement without interruption. One or both of the parties can exert pressure in other ways, and this links negotiation with the topic of the next chapter, industrial action.

CASE-STUDY 10.3

Highmore Ltd

Highmore is a fast-growing warehousing and distribution company that is located in the West Midlands. Over the last few years it has expanded significantly, first by absorbing several other warehousing and distribution firms within a fifty mile radius, and more recently by branching out into a number of other services such as local deliveries and a national express parcels service. Pay has been based on the nationally negotiated rates for the various types of job performed by its employees. However, to some extent Highmore inherited rates within the different firms which it has absorbed, and the growing need for new and different skills has allowed shop stewards plenty of scope to exert pressure in negotiations, all of which has produced many anomalies in pay structures. For example, despite the fact that a joint negotiating committee was formed some time ago to cover the whole firm, pay has usually been settled separately on each site. As a result some differentials between different jobs have widened and others have narrowed. Employees with similar skills and doing the same job on different sites are sometimes paid different rates. Management has therefore decided that both organizational structure, and with it pay structure, need some attention. They have given notice at a recent meeting of the joint negotiating committee that they are looking closely at these matters, and are currently producing a new structure plan for the company, together with serious consideration of the introducion of a scheme of job evaluation.

Over the years a focal figure who acts as full-time convenor for all the sites has emerged on the trade-union side. The industrial-relations manager has developed a good working relationship with this person, and it is their practice to meet at least once per week on an informal basis to review issues that are current. Their most recent discussion mainly concerned the fact that the new structure plan and job evaluation would be tabled by management at the next scheduled meeting of the joint negotiating committee in six weeks' time. The convenor, who had done his homework on the subject, outlined a number of potential issues and problems which had been raised with him by stewards:

- Arbitrary management decisions about duties and grading could influence pay levels;

- The possibility of a rigid, inflexible wage system that was not responsive to the wide variety of new areas being entered by the company;

- An overemphasis on the rate for a specific job at the expense of rewarding people for their flexibility;

- Apprehension that there would be no increase or benefit to employees, or even worse, it could be used as an excuse to reduce the total wages bill.

Whilst the industrial-relations manager admitted that these problems could exist, he expressed the hope that by working together to iron them out, management and union could find a solution that benefited both. The convenor replied that he hoped that this would be the case, but in the meantime he would have to reserve his position until definite proposals were made by management. In any event the membership would never consent to accepting either the new structure or job evaluation results in advance, and would therefore reserve the right to negotiate acceptable job classifications and a level of pay that was not dependent on the results of a job-evaluation exercise.

The manager said that he noted what the convenor had said, and proposed that management should put forward suggestions at the next meeting of the joint negotiating committee on both the new structure and how any job-evaluation exercise would be undertaken. The convenor replied that the trade-union side would examine any proposals with an open mind. However, just as he was leaving he mentioned that management might like to consider the idea of bringing in an outside organization, preferably from an academic institution that would be completely neutral, to study the matter.

Questions

i What has taken place here, and how is it likely to affect matters at the meeting of the joint negotiating committee when management produces its proposals?

ii What will be the likely negotiating aims, positions and opening proposals of both sides at this meeting?

Further reading

Walton R.E. and McKersie R.B. (1965). *A Behavioural Theory of Labour Negotiations*. New York: McGraw-Hill

> A seminal work which gives a very thorough examination of the strategies and tactics of negotiation.

Stephenson G.M. and Brotherton C.J., eds. (1979). *Industrial Relations: A Social Psychological Approach*. Chichester: Wiley

> A very scholarly work which contains a number of chapters dealing with the psychological influences on the bargaining process.

Fisher R. and Ury W. (1987). *Getting to Yes*. London: Arrow Books

> Although something of a 'how to do it flavour' is reflected in the book, it gives a very readable explanation of principles which can be followed to try to develop negotiating skills.

11

Industrial action

Introduction

This chapter deals with the subject of conflict in employee relations. In the vast majority of cases the negotiating process described in the previous chapter will be successful in resolving differences between employees and managers. However, there are times when it is temporarily suspended because agreement cannot be reached. On these occasions, in an attempt to reinforce its bargaining position, one party might take action against the other, and a conflict episode takes place. It is because conflict episodes usually occur in this way that industrial action can most sensibly be viewed as an extension of the negotiating process. Seldom, if ever, is it used as an end in itself, but rather as a means to an end. Indeed, whilst its use is by no means inevitable, there are times when industrial action, or perhaps just the threat of it, seems to be a necessary prelude to finding a basis of agreement.

Having said this, the nature and volume of conflict in employee relations is mostly misunderstood and often grossly overstated. The very nature of organizations means that they are virtually arenas of conflict, and industrial action is almost certainly the smaller part of what takes place. For this reason, and in order to place employee relations conflict within this wider context, the chapter commences with a brief examination of the conflictual nature of organizations.

Attention then turns to the subject of industrial action in Britain, and a number of essential definitions are given which are important in understanding the topic. The different forms of industrial action are then described, together with the circumstances which constrain the use of each one. To illustrate some of the characteristic patterns of industrial action in Britain, strike trends are examined across the last 30 years, and following this, some of the explanations of different patterns of industrial action are given. The focus then moves to the conduct of industrial action. A model is used to explain some of the factors that can influence the decision to take action and the way that it is conducted, and finally the chapter concludes with a short description of the effects of the law in this area.

Conflict: theories and perspectives

Conflict between an organization and its employees is an emotive topic, and in some eyes it is considered to be unwarranted and outside the bounds of reasonable behaviour (Hutt, 1973). Employee-relations conflict, however, is just one of many forms of inter-group conflict that can take place in organizations. Far from being the exception, conflict of one form or another is very normal in organizations (Alderfer and Smith, 1982; Edwards, 1987a), but until fairly recently any form whatsoever was regarded as highly dysfunctional. Currently, however, both theory and research tend to demonstrate that this is a very naive view.

Most organizations are structured into units and departments, and goals are set for each one. Whilst these units are dependent on each other in order to achieve their goals, they usually have to compete with each other to obtain the necessary resources to make goal attainment possible, a feature which on its own produces some potential for conflict. On top of this individuals and groups put a great deal of effort into pursuing their own ends, and often use a range of highly subtle political tactics to do so (Katz and Kahn, 1978; Pfeffer, 1981). For these reasons there is usually a great deal of continuous conflict in organizations, most of which goes on beneath the surface. However, employee relations is often a highly visible activity, and because of this any conflicts which occur tend to assume a significance out of all proportion to their place in the wider picture.

Nevertheless, the view that conflict, and particularly employee-relations conflict, is unnatural is still the dominant one in organizations. One reason for this could be the effect of other social institutions in shaping attitudes. Many of the important institutions in our society – the home, the Church, and so on – are founded on the premise that harmony is the natural state of affairs, and this has a powerful effect on the way conflict is regarded (Robbins, 1979). Another and perhaps more influential set of ideas comes from classical theories of management, such as those of Fayol (1949) and Urwick (1943), which are still held to be essential truths in organizations. In these, the epitome of a well-managed organization is one which has unity in goals and purposes. The role of management is portrayed as the four key activities of planning, organizing, directing and controlling, all of which are designed to ensure that overall corporate goals are met. The planning activity ensures that the resources to achieve the goals are available when required, and organizing and directing are intended to ensure efficient resource utilization. Finally the controlling activity monitors things to see whether goals are being achieved, and (if necessary) resources are redeployed in the interests of efficiency and effectiveness. The idea is that all parts of an organization dovetail into a master plan for goal achievement. The process of management is therefore seen as the activity which makes things more predictable, and directs the energy of people towards that common end. An important implication of this view is that conflict, because it absorbs energy which could be used to other ends, contradicts the fundamental philosophy of unity of purpose, and makes things less predicable, is highly dysfunctional in any form. For this reason it comes to be seen as an aberration, an exception to the norm and associated with imperfect organizational functioning.

A more realistic view is that whilst organizations are created to serve a purpose, they are composed of people who are all different. Individuals are placed into groups and, as noted in Chapter 2, groups develop their own preferences, norms and goals. Moreover, the aims of an individual's group and the group's solutions to problems are usually judged to be superior to those of other groups. As such conflict is an inevitability, and an integral part of the functioning of an organization. For this reason it cannot be outlawed or eradicated, but is more appropriately handled by channelling it into non-destructive forms. As well as negative features, it also has some positive ones. For example, it brings a diversity of opinions to the surface, and from this can flow a more creative range of solutions to problems.

Employee-relations conflicts are perhaps the most deprecated of all, and there are basically three reasons why this is so. First, they are vertical conflicts and thus they challenge the most fundamental building block of an organization: differences in decision-making authority. Conflict of this type becomes a lightly veiled signal to a manager that the people over whom he or she has formal authority no longer accept this authority as legitimate. In a society which (nominally at least) is a meritocracy, and where the assumption is that those who rise to positions of authority are those most fitted to do so, this can be a powerful blow to a manager's self-esteem.

The second reason is the visibility of employee-relations conflict. Interdepartmental conflicts are mostly pursued beneath the surface in a covert political way, and this makes them invisible to those not actually involved. In vertical conflicts those lower down in the hierarchy need to mobilize power to challenge those above. Thus conflict has to be pursued in collective and highly visible ways.

The third reason arises from a general misunderstanding of the aims and purposes of industrial action. There is a widely held view that it is a highly irrational activity made all the worse because all conflicts should be capable of being solved by negotiation and compromise. There is, however, a huge flaw in this view. As was noted in the previous chapter, whilst negotiation is mostly able to resolve the different aims of the parties in employee relations, the whole process is underpinned by a realization that either side can do harm to the other one. Almost inevitably there will be occasions where one side will not modify its position, and so pressures more severe than argument alone will be needed as an inducement for them to do so. Since industrial action is probably the only way that this pressure could be exerted, it is simply a rational extension of the negotiating process.

It cannot be emphasized too strongly that the collective-bargaining relationship is a political one, and so negotiation is a highly political process as well. Therefore, industrial action can be likened to the role that war occupies in the political processes through which nations try to resolve their differences. War is seldom an end itself, but more often a means to an end. It is a recognition that at the present stage in the political process, the argument of force is likely to prove more persuasive than the force of argument. Thus it is politics conducted by other methods (Von Clauswitz, 1986). Like war, industrial action is only ever intended to be a temporary state of affairs to achieve some end, usually to bring the other party back to the negotiating table in a more receptive frame of mind (Hyman, 1984). Just as nations have a range of other sanctions which they will try to use before resorting to war, so too have the parties in employee relations. Despite the popular view to the contrary, the strike is not the only form of industrial action that can be used. As will be described later, both employees and managers have a range of lesser sanctions that they can use to exert pressure on the other party. However, their use is seldom underpinned by a desire to apply pressure for its own sake, but rather to achieve some objective. As with nation states, even when overt conflict breaks out the political processes seldom stop altogether, although they might well take place through an intermediary. Indeed, as will be seen later, overt conflict can be costly to the parties. Thus there can be a great deal of activity behind the scenes to bring the episode to a close.

Industrial conflict in Great Britain

Some misconceptions

Since conflict in employee relations can take many different forms, it is useful to start with a broad definition, and the one adopted here is 'the total range of behaviour and attitudes that express opposition and divergent orientations between owners and managers on one hand, and working people and their organizations on the other' (Kornhauser, 1954, p. 13).

Three important points can be noted from this. First, although the range of possible actions is extremely wide, the most visible form, and the one which most readily springs to mind for most people, is the strike. Indeed, for reasons that will be given presently, the majority of work in the area has focused on strikes. Second, the definition draws attention to the idea that conflict exists because there is a lack of agreement between two parties. It needs to be remembered that this can result in either one of them taking action to put pressure on the other. Whilst it is a common misconception that industrial action is initiated exclusively by employees, management also has its equivalent of the strike: to lock employees out unless they accept what is proposed. It also has its equivalent of lesser actions, for example unilaterally imposing a change and threatening dismissal or suspension to those who do not accept. Indeed, either party can simply use stonewalling tactics at the negotiating table, and if management does this, it virtually forces its employees into taking the next step which is often the use of pressure tactics of some sort. The important point is that if managers do this, they are usually able to convey the impression that it was employees who initiated the action. This leads to the third point, that industrial action is usually only one link in a chain of events. It can often be impossible to discern who is the initiating party unless the whole chain is examined.

Distinctions and definitions

In employee relations it can sometimes be important to distinguish the status of industrial action, as well as the different forms that it can take. The status of action is usually distinguished by whether it is **constitutional** or **unconstitutional**. The former is accepted as a legitimate part of the bargaining relationship and, for example, would normally only be used when all stages of a disputes procedure have been exhausted. Unconstitutional action is that which is used whilst the procedure is still in force, and can often have effects on the bargaining relationship itself. It must be pointed out, however, that whilst the distinction is clear in theory, it is not always so easy to make the distinction in practice. For example, if either party simply uses stonewalling tactics and fails to bargain in good faith, can it truthfully be said that the procedure is still in operation?

Another important distinction is between **official** and **unofficial** action. The former is action which has officially received trade-union support, whilst unofficial action is more commonly initiated by employees direct. Sometimes this occurs as a spontaneous indication of dissatisfaction with the bargaining situation, and sometimes as a revolt against the negotiating stance adopted by the trade union. Here, the distinction can also be a blurred one. As noted above, industrial action is a political activity designed to exert pressure. It is not unknown for a trade union secretly to approve of unofficial action, but for a number of reasons which are connected with the politics of negotiating, it will not want to be seen to give its approval. Thus whilst unofficial action is often unconstitutional as well, the two are not synonymous. Neither is official action necessarily constitutional.

Progress question 11.1
Classifying action

Classify the following types of action:

1. Negotiations have reached a deadlock and as per the disputes procedure both trade union and management have agreed that the matter will be referred to external arbitration. Before this takes place the trade union ballots its members for strike action, and there is an overwhelming yes vote. At this, management calls a special meeting of the negotiating committee and concedes to the trade union's claim.

2. In a factory which uses assembly-line methods shop stewards protest to management about a speeding-up of the line. Management admits that it has increased the speed of the line but states that this is unavoidable owing to a backlog of orders, and refuses to reduce the speed back to its former setting. The matter is reported by the stewards to the convenor who then meets with the Industrial Relations Manager, and formally registers a dispute about the new speed of the line. He claims and obtains an assurance of a return to the *status quo ante* pending the outcome of negotiations on the matter. Some days later the speed of the line has not been reduced, and the workers hold a mass lunchtime meeting. A voice from the body of the meeting proposes that instead of returning to work they all walk out. This is put to the vote, carried, and the factory is idle from then on.

3. At the request of the members affected, the trade union, in protest at the downgrading of jobs in a reorganization, blacklists the posts. It places advertisements in newspapers telling its own members and the public of what has happened. The advertisement advises people that sitting tenants will neither occupy nor apply for the jobs, and that others should do likewise.

4. Clerical workers employed by an airline refuse to do additional work which involves handling cargo. This is work normally done by baggage handlers.

The final distinction is between **organized** and **unorganized** forms of action. Both are manifestations of employee discontent, and the different forms of organized conflict will be discussed presently. For the moment it is sufficient to note that organized action is a conscious attempt to change the situation which is a source of discontent (Hyman, 1984). Unorganized action is usually an individual reaction to being discontented, and can take many forms, varying from absenteeism to sabotage. This, however, is less of an attempt to change the situation than to find some way of psychological escape from having tolerated it to date. Thus it is a reaction of 'flight' rather than 'fight'.

Turning now to the different forms of industrial action, management has a number of ways at its disposal of putting pressure on employees. All employees can be locked out, which is management's direct equivalent of the strike. Seeking to impose a change unilaterally and threatening dismissal if employees do not comply is another pressure tactic that can be used. Indeed, with most actions taken by management the name largely explains the nature of action. With action taken by employees, however, there can sometimes be confusion in the terms. For this reason discussion will be confined to those which can be used by employees in a collective way.

A **strike** is a complete withdrawal of labour. However, strikes can vary between wide limits. A whole workforce can strike indefinitely, as was the case in the 1984 miners' dispute, and at the other extreme quite small groups can withdraw their labour for short periods. This can sometimes happen because their case is unique within an organization. Less frequently it happens because they are key workers whose absence has a serious and immediate impact and they take action on behalf of all employees in the organization. An advantage of this selective striking is clearly that those still in work can voluntarily make up the pay of those on strike. Key workers are usually aware of their strategic importance and can be somewhat wary of being used to fight the battles of others. Moreover, management is seldom blind to the potential for their tactical use in this way, and they are often highly rewarded to try to ensure a lack of militancy (Purcell *et al.*, 1978).

Withdrawing cooperation occurs when employees work strictly to formal operational procedures and refuse any flexibility or cooperation in the myriad of day-to-day adjustments that are usually necessary to keep an organization ticking over. The usefulness of this sanction tends to depend upon the extent to which cooperative relationships have become normal and of value to management. In some situations the loss of cooperation is highly disruptive (Batstone *et al.*, 1979) and, for example, professional groups such as teachers, whose work often involves a great deal of day-to-day adjustment, have successfully used this tactic (Edwards, 1983). Conversely, where the work of employees has little discretionary content, the tactic has far less impact (Armstrong *et al.*, 1981; Edwards and Scullion, 1982).

Working to rule or **working to contract** usually involves a very strict refusal to step outside the duties laid down in job specifications, and often this is accompanied by an insistence that management and supervision give clearly defined instructions on how duties shall be performed. Again, the effect of this varies with the extent to which cooperation and initiative are needed by management. Thus its usefulness to employees is much the same as a withdrawal of cooperation.

Overtime bans are a refusal to work beyond the strict contracted hours. In some situations, usually where basic pay rates are low, employees customarily work well in excess of basic hours, and management can come to rely on this to meet operational requirements. In the public services such as the NHS, for example, this situation is widespread, and things can rapidly grind to a halt when an overtime ban is applied. Since the public as a whole is antagonistic to strike action (Edwards and Bain, 1988), particularly in areas such as the NHS which is financed by public funds, the overtime ban can be used by workers to highlight their plight, but in a way that does not alienate the public. Indeed, it can sometimes actually enlist their sympathy, a case in point being its use by ambulance drivers in 1989 (Kerr and Sachdev, 1992).

A **go-slow** involves working at lower than normal output levels; not, however, to the extent that a breach of contract occurs. In many manufacturing plants pay is made up of a basic element plus a bonus paid for higher levels of output. Manning levels are usually based on the assumption that employees will work at a pace which earns the bonus. Thus a go-slow has an immediate impact on output without depriving the employees of some take-home pay.

Work-ins and **sit-ins** occur when employees occupy the workplace. They are generally used as a form of protest, often when management proposes to close a plant. Interestingly, they are an action which does not alienate the public unduly, and often they attract considerable sympathetic attention to the plight of employees. Moreover, their impact on management is potentially very high. Being 'in control' is very high in the management value system, and there is probably no greater reminder that control has slipped away than when employees occupy a plant but are not under management's direction (Thomas, 1976).

Progress question 11.2
Choice of action

Decide what type of action is likely to have the greatest tactical advantage to the following groups of employees.

1. Semi-skilled workers employed in a firm which sells a mass-produced, highly perishable product in a competitive market. An example here could be bread.

2. Skilled workers in an organization which produces custom-made products for a highly competitive market, but with very long production cycles. Examples here could be shipbuilding or aircraft manufacture.

3. Workers such as street cleaners, refuse collectors or security guards who are normally paid a very low basic rate, and often work additional hours.

4. An organization manufactures a wide range of products and with rather erratic production schedules. To ensure rapid response, maintenance craftsmen and salaried staffs will when necessary do jobs on the production line. In addition, when maintenance workers are fully occupied, production workers will undertake minor maintenance work on their own machines.

The usefulness of different types of action

All the above types of action are a suspension of normality, the impact of which is highly dependent upon the circumstances. A strike, although very visible, can sometimes result in far less pressure on management than other forms. In seasonal industries, for example, where there are periods of stockpiling and over-production, a strike might actually save management unwanted labour costs, whereas a work-to-rule would not. From a trade-union point of view, whilst it is more difficult to obtain membership consent to a strike, strike action, when once obtained, can be far easier to control than other forms. There are few trade-union members who would want to cross a picket line, particularly if there has been a large majority vote for the action. Moreover, picketing is comparatively economical in resources. Action short of a strike, however, is notoriously hard to sustain. Employees are at work, and are susceptible to individual pressure from managers. Nevertheless, sustaining strike action also has its problems. Strikes are not popular with trade-union members, and involve them in significant financial loss. Indeed they may only take part because they assume that the action will be short-lived (Gennard, 1981, 1982). Perhaps for this reason there is an increasing tendency for employees to favour the so-called 'cut price' forms of industrial action (Flanders, 1970; Edwards, 1987b). However, whether the different types of action can be used in this exchangeable way remains a complex question, to which two theoretical answers have been suggested.

The *substitution theory*, which strictly speaking applies to unorganized forms of conflict (Knowles, 1962), reasons that there is a reservoir of protest energy. The form of protest which emerges will therefore vary according to a group's capability to mobilize for collective action. Strongly organized groups will use strikes, those which are less well organized will use action short of strike, and for workers who are not organized at all, individual acts of unorganized conflict such as absenteeism will be more common. The competing *additive* theory (Bean, 1975) is that the different forms of action are complementary. Groups with a tendency to use one type will show a predisposition to use others as well.

Whilst there is no strong evidence to rule out either of these theories, one study has identified a weak correlation between the use of minor stoppages and other forms of action (Kelly and Nicholson, 1980a). In addition, there are studies which show that certain plants tend to use identifiable combinations of the different types of action (Brown, 1981; Edwards, 1983; Daniel and Millward, 1983; Millward and Stevens, 1986), and that over time, the level of action remains fairly constant in many firms (Walsh, 1987). On balance, therefore, the additive theory seems much more likely. Notwithstanding this, there are seldom any hard and fast rules about industrial action. Each incident has its own contextual circumstances and it can be extremely hazardous to predict what will happen. In the author's experience, workgroups that have a long history of timidness sometimes adopt the hardest stance and follow it up with equally hard action. Conversely, and often to the surprise of their trade union, those with a pedigree of militancy can meekly accept a change which has extremely adverse consequences. Therefore, the reasons for deciding to take action and (if so) the type of action taken are probably only understood by those involved. For that matter even they might not fully understand the processes involved, but simply feel that the action is appropriate at the time.

Strike trends in Great Britain

The only consistent statistics kept on industrial action are for strikes, and even these probably underestimate the real level of activity. Only those which involve over 10 employees are recorded, and unless it involves the loss of at least 100 working days, a strike lasting less than one day is not included. Since 60 % of all strikes last less than one day (Brown, 1981), the figures probably only represent a quarter of what occurs. Moreover, there is nothing to compel an employer to report a strike, and it is likely that only two-thirds of those that are eligible to be included are counted (Edwards, 1983). For these reasons statistics do little more than reflect broad trends. However, the trends can be used to point out a number of characteristics of British strikes. To do so, reference is made to Figures 11.1(a)–(c), which give the three main indices of strike activity: numbers of strikes, numbers of workers involved and man-days lost.

As can be seen from Figure 11.1(a), in terms of *numbers of strikes* there was a steady downwards trend from 1960 to 1968, followed by a two-year rise in 1969 and 1970, and after that a steady decline. The patterns for workers involved and days lost, shown in Figures 11.1(b) and (c) respectively, are somewhat different. For *workers involved* the overall trend is fairly flat, but there were three peak years in 1962, 1968 and 1979. With *man-days lost*, there is a slight upwards trend, and again with peak years, but this time in 1972, 1979 and 1984.

In 1962, 1968 and 1970 the number of strikes was about average with a low number of days lost, but relatively large numbers of workers were involved, which means that strikes were of comparatively short duration. The vast majority were in metal manufacturing, and this reflects the nature of strike activity in British manufacturing industry, that is, strikes of short duration, but involving a whole workforce.

In other years the peaks indicate something else. From 1970 onwards the number of strikes shows a steady downwards trend. However, in 1979 a large number of workers were involved, as well as a high number of days lost, and a similar pattern appears in 1982 and 1983. Again this illustrates a major distinguishing feature of British strike patterns. In these years the strikes were in the public sector, the most prominent being the 1984 miners' dispute that lasted almost a year. Because they take in a whole industry and not just a single site, public-sector strikes invariably involve large numbers of workers. Indeed, a general feature of the years shown is that, whilst the annual number of strikes shows a progressive downwards trend, the number of workers involved and the

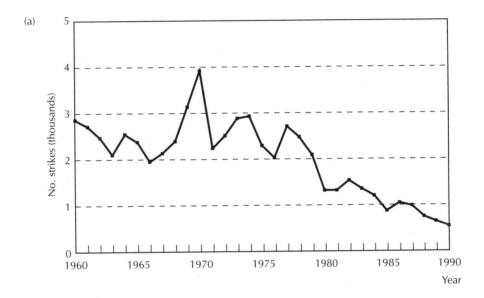

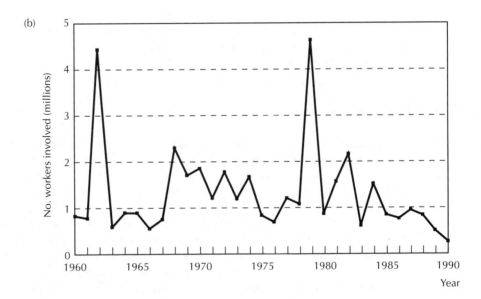

Figure 11.1 Strike trends, 1960–1990. (a) Number of strikes. (b) Number of workers involved. Source: *Employment Gazette*.

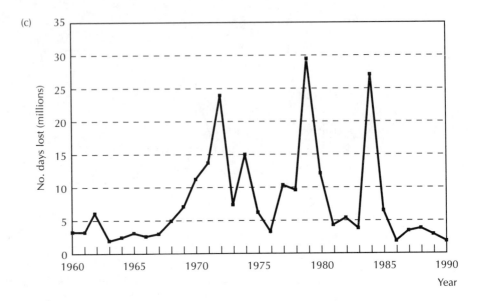

Figure 11.1 *continued.* (c) Number of days lost. Source: *Employment Gazette.*

number of days lost have both moved slightly upwards. This reflects a rising tide of militancy and more effective union organization in the public sector (Terry, 1982; Winchester, 1983).

Explanations of strike activity

Variations in strike activity have long fascinated industrial-relations researchers, and one of the more obvious connections that has been looked for is with the level of *economic activity*. For example, Hansen (1921) reasons that in periods of long-run falling profits, employers will try to reduce real wages and this prompts employees to strike in retaliation. Similarly, in periods of long-run rising prices there will also be higher strike levels as employees try to keep pace with the rising cost of living. More recently and perhaps of more relevance to conditions in the UK, a number of studies have attempted to relate strike activity to the level of unemployment. Creigh and Makeham (1982) show that in periods of high unemployment, employers are less willing to make concessions than in more buoyant times, and strikes tend to be longer. Since analyses of this type also hold up in comparisons across industries (McLean, 1979; McConnel, 1990), they give useful, if somewhat general, indications of why strike patterns can vary.

An approach more directly related to explaining why strike patterns vary between industries is Kerr and Seigal's (1954) attempt to link them with *social values*. Their explanation is that these differences are associated with occupational communities of workers. For example, dockers and coal miners have tough, combative jobs and this is said to engender an independence of spirit and willingness to engage in conflict. Another stream of work has pointed at *institutional factors* as a possible explanation of strike patterns in different industries. For example, high strike levels have been associated with inadequate conflict-handling and bargaining arrangements. This line of thinking has been extremely influential, and has uncovered some remarkably robust conclusions concerning strike activity and bargaining structures (Britt and Galle, 1972, 1974). Indeed, it has been reasoned that mature and stable collective bargaining arrangements promote responsible trade unionism, and that this will lead to an eventual withering away of the strike (Ross and Hartman, 1960).

Useful as these studies are, however, they do not explain why firms within the same industry, or plants within the same firm, can have vastly different strike records. Industry-wide surveys, for example, estimate that 5 % of plants account for 25 % of all strikes (Smith *et al.*. 1978). This suggests that macro-level variables are not capable of giving anything more than a general indication, and this clearly means that attention must be directed to conditions within organizations.

One such explanation is that the type of *technology* used has an effect on industrial conflict. Chinoy (1955) and Walker and Guest (1957) both argue that repetitive, assembly-line work gives conditions ripe for conflict. In a similar vein, Sayles (1958) points out that different types of technology influence the formation and nature of workgroups, which in turn gives them different opportunities to use industrial action.

Whilst all of these explanations have some grain of truth, they only partially explain why workers in one firm could have a stronger tendency to take action than those in another, and why there can be strong differences between groups in the same plant. If there is a satisfactory explanation it is probably unlikely to be found by looking at employees in isolation. When employees act collectively they do so with some aim in mind, and the group concerned will need to perceive that this is likely to be achieved. As such their perceptions of the effects that the action will have on the other party can be a highly important influence on their decision. Since subtle influences of this type can hardly be taken into account in generalist explanations, they are almost bound to be partial and incomplete. Some recognition of this is given in the next section, which considers industrial action as a process which takes place within a context.

The process of industrial action

As noted, each piece of industrial action is unique, and one way to try to understand its complexity is to use a model which lays out all the factors at work. A model of this type is given by Kelly and Nicholson (1980b), which is shown in Figure 11.2. Strictly speaking this applies only to strikes, but with appropriate allowances, it can be used for other forms of collective action as well.

Reading from left to right, assume that an issue has surfaced which could possibly result in industrial action. There are a number of climatic conditions, which in combination have effects on the way those involved will act. *Frames of reference* include the values of employees and managers, and *inter-group perceptions* are a reflection of how they view each. *Perceptions of climate and conflict* influence the willingness of employees to use industrial action. Finally *economic conditions* are one (but only one) source of issues, and can also damp down or amplify the willingness of workers to take action.

Given that the climatic conditions do not preclude action, the existence of the issue on its own is not sufficient to make it happen. It has to be *triggered* by something, such a particular act of management stubbornness at the negotiating table. An example will perhaps illustrate the point about the way the variables interact. Strikes and other forms of industrial action can, of course, be used in pursuit of a pay claim if the bargaining process breaks down. The evidence suggests, however, that where wages and effort are negotiated together, the likelihood of industrial action is much higher (Ingram, 1991). Thus if employees submit a pay claim, and management responds by asking for substantial changes in working practices so that any rise becomes self-financing, this can be perceived by workers as a particularly strong act of intransigence. As such it can shape climates and inter-group perceptions, and in addition be the trigger which sets off a dispute. However, a trigger on its own is seldom sufficient to make action inevitable. For it to occur, there also has to be a degree of *structural facilitation*. That is, employees have to be sufficiently well organized in order to be able to use a particular type of action. A fairly obvious point here is that unless there is a trade union to do the organizing, action is unlikely to occur. Indeed, it is virtually unknown in non-union firms. Here Kelly and Nicholson reason that groups that are well organized and primed for action tend to be those that can use it to most tactical advantage, and are less in need of a management impetus to bring it about. However, action is still not inevitable, and the next stage in the model recognizes that it is an extension of the negotiating process.

The groups have *demand formulations* in which they make comparisons with treatment they receive and the way *reference groups* elsewhere are treated. In essence this means that employees usually compare what they perceive to be their balance of effort and rewards with those of other groups. Similarly, managers probably compare what they see to be the results delivered by their own

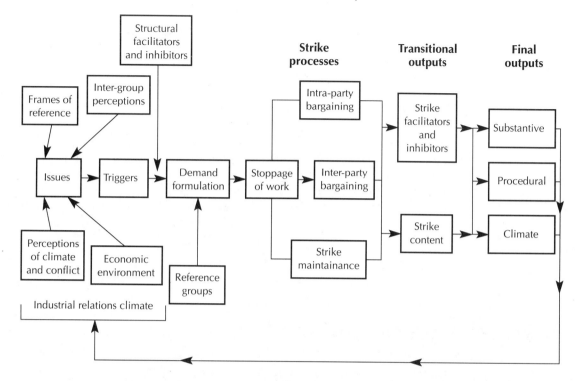

Figure 11.2 Strike causation and processes. (J. Kelly and N. Nicholson, 1980).

workers with perceptions of workers in other firms. The demands which are to be made of the other side are formulated through processes of *intra-party bargaining*. This is the process of intra-organizational bargaining described in the previous chapter, and it occurs between the organizers of the action and rank and file members, to whom it has to be demonstrated that it is worthwhile to carry it out. Activities aimed at *maintaining* the action will also be required; for example, in the case of a strike, picketing and possibly fund raising.

Whilst the action is in progress, and perhaps before it ever commences, there will almost certainly be a degree of inter-party bargaining as well. Either formally or informally, management and union officials will meet occasionally, and as described in the previous chapter the political process of attempting to restructure attitudes will take place. Union officers will try to convince management that employees are holding, or will hold, firm. For their part, managers do whatever they can to undermine the action, probably by trying to convince union officers that the action is having, or will have, little effect. These steps all result in what the authors call 'transitional outputs'. That is, the manoeuvres will either facilitate or inhibit the action. For example, attempts by management to undermine an action sometimes harden the resolve of employees, and violent or acrimonious picketing can often harden management attitudes. Other transitional outputs are the changes that take place in the *demands* by both sides, and their *re-evaluations* of the effects of the action. Therefore at this stage a move towards compromise and an eventual ending of the action is in progress. This leads to the final stage of the model: the outputs or results of the action.

Substantive outputs refer to the terms of the settlement on which the action is called off. *Procedural* outputs can consist of arrangements for resumption of normal working, often an undertaking that the organizers of the action will not be victimized. Perhaps the most important output shown on the model, however, is the *climatic* one. The action is likely to result in an after-taste, and this can affect how things are handled in future. Thus whatever the substantive outcome, and no matter how strong their position at the time of settlement, the winning party needs to let the other one retreat with dignity. Failure to do so can simply mean that the other side goes away and prepares all the harder for the next event. Thus when it comes, it will probably be much more fiercely contested.

Industrial action and the law

There are several ways in which the law has a bearing on industrial action, but to simplify matters attention will be drawn to three areas.

The individual contractual implications

In Great Britain there is no right to strike and, strictly speaking, an employee who does so has (in common law) broken his/her contract of employment. However, a principle established by the Employment Protection (Consolidation) Act 1978 is that if all employees who take action are dismissed for being in breach of contract, this is not discrimination. Thus if there are selective sackings the employer has acted in a discriminatory way, and those dismissed can have some claim for unfair dismissal. Having said this, and as was pointed out in Chapter 5, the Employment Acts of 1980, 1982 and 1988 make it much easier for employers to dismiss individuals selectively, particularly those who have organized strikes.

With action short of strike, the contractual position is always less clear. A great deal depends on what is custom and practice in the particular enterprise, or whether it can be demonstrated that non-strike action is contrary to the spirit of the implied terms of the contract. For example, if a commonly accepted practice is that employees can be asked to work overtime, refusing to 'volunteer' could be deemed a breach of contract. For the same reason in certain circumstances, working to rule can be considered to be a failure to observe the implied contractual terms of 'faithful and efficient service'.

The trade-union implications

Under the Trades Disputes Act (1906) unions have immunity in civil and criminal law from a claim that by instructing their members to take industrial action they have induced them to break their individual contracts of employment. Recent employment legislation, however, has considerably narrowed what can be defined as a bona fide trade dispute. The Employment Act (1982) restricts it to:

(1) *Between employees and their direct employer,* which excludes action in pursuit of general trade-union policies such as opposing privatization or government policy. It also excludes disputes between trade unions.

(2) *Being wholly or mainly connected with employment, non-employment or conditions thereof.* In addition the Employment Act (1980) removes trade-union immunities in the case of most forms of secondary action. This makes it much harder for trade unions to mount supportive action, such as 'blacking' goods from an employer whose workers are on strike.

The 1982 Employment Act enables unions to be held liable for their unlawful actions, and makes it easier for employers to seek a court injunction to halt the action and to sue for damages. Whilst it is probably the case that employers have been encouraged to use the law, and have shown some increased willingness to do so, there seem to be limits to the way it is used. Except in a few notable cases employer action has not been aimed at the punitive destruction of a union, but simply to obtain a court injunction to halt the action. Thus it seems to have been directed less at obtaining damages than at getting the wheels of production rolling again (Evans, 1983, 1985, 1987). Importantly, the Trade Union Act, 1984 makes obtaining an injunction much easier by removing any immunity from a union where industrial action has not been preceded by a properly conducted ballot.

Finally, and perhaps most controversial of all, the 1988 Employment Act introduced what has popularly become known as the 'scab's charter'. Even where a strike has been preceded by a properly conducted ballot, it makes it an offence for a trade union to discipline a member who crosses a picket line. Clearly this makes it much easier for employers to undermine action by putting pressure on employees as individuals.

Implications for the conduct of disputes

This is the one of the few areas where the criminal law becomes operative in employee relations. The main Acts which can be applied are listed in Chapter 5, and will not therefore be repeated here. Since 1906 it has been regarded as intimidation to picket a person's home, and the 1982 Employment Act makes it unlawful for employees to picket anywhere other than their own place of work. It is also important to point out that whilst picketing is a recognized strike activity, the law only recognizes the right of pickets to *peacefully persuade* other employees to join or support the strike. What consists of reasonable and peaceful persuasion is often a matter of judgement, and when tempers get frayed on a picket line, it is not unknown for violence to occur. Perhaps because of the experience of mass picketing in the 1970s, a Code of Practice on picketing was introduced in 1980 (DOE, 1980). Whilst this does not have the force of a law, it could well be taken into account in a court hearing which arises out of a claim for unlawful action. It suggests that a maximum of six pickets is all that is needed for peaceful persuasion at any one entrance. It also recommends that pickets should always be clearly identifiable, perhaps by wearing armbands, and that they should be under the control of an experienced person. This should preferably be a union official who also has a responsibility to maintain close contact with the police.

Progress question 11.3
The law and action

1. During wage negotiations three workers refused to do overtime when asked. Although it was not in their contracts of employment that overtime was required, they were dismissed. Do you feel that they would have a case for unfair dismissal?

2. A strike is in progress on a building site. A union official holding a placard sees a lorry arriving to deliver materials. He walks into the middle of the road and holds up the placard. The lorry driver stops and listens, and then tries to manoeuvre around the official who moves himself in front of the lorry – is this peaceful persuasion?

3. A union official is on picket duty outside a hospital in which management have brought in contract labour in an attempt to break the strike. The police form a cordon around a coach which is bringing in the contract workers and refuse to let the union official speak to its passengers. If he attempted to push through, what would you expect to be the result of this action?

Conclusions and overview

Because it is a way in which one of the parties to the collective-bargaining relationship can exert pressure on the other, industrial action in its various forms should be seen as an extension of the tactics of negotiation. Action can be initiated by either management or employees. Although the strike is the most dramatic form used by employees, and the lock-out the most visible form used by managers, both sides have other methods which can be deployed to put pressure on the other side.

Each piece of industrial action takes place for a purpose, and this is probably only fully understood by those taking part. For this reason, although general explanations of strike patterns say something about conditions that make the use of industrial action more likely, they are not really capable of explaining why a particular incident takes place, nor why it is conducted in the way that it is. These things are only likely to be known if it can be determined what meaning the action has for those who carry it out.

As in almost all areas of employee relations at the current time, there are legal implications of industrial action. For this reason there is a strong connection between the material covered in this chapter and some of that dealt with in Chapter 5. Because taking action requires cohesion and organization of groups of employees there are also connections to what has been said in Chapters 2 and 3. Finally it is stressed again that what has been covered here cannot be divorced from the topics of collective bargaining and negotiation which were covered in the previous two chapters. Thus all three should really be considered as one topic, which for convenience has been divided up to make discussion easier.

Further reading

Edwards P.K. and Scullion M. (1982). *The Social Organization of Industrial Conflict: Control and Resistance in the Workplace*. Oxford: Blackwell

> A very thorough investigation of all forms of conflict action, in a cross-section of organizations. It demonstrates the effects of different contextual circumstances and the way that these are interpreted by management and employees, which give rise to characteristic patterns of action.

Jackson M.P. (1987). *Strikes: Industrial Conflict in Britain, U.S.A. and Australia*. Brighton: Wheatsheaf

> Despite its title the book contains relatively little in terms of international comparisons. However, it gives an excellent overview of the theoretical explanations of industrial conflict.

Hyman R. (1984). *Strikes* 3rd edn. London: Fontana

> A very readable examination of strikes and industrial conflict.

12

Management initiatives

Introduction

Throughout this book reference has been made to human resource management (HRM) as a distinct approach to handling the relationship between an organization and its employees, and Chapter 1 compared it with traditional approaches. This chapter deals with some of the more important features and practices of HRM. However, the chapter should not be taken to be a full explanation of the approach. Rather it describes a number of management-initiated practices that usually receive a strong emphasis in HRM. All of these practices have been in existence for much longer than the term 'human resource management', and in their own ways, all of them are capable of influencing certain aspects of the relationship between an organization and its employees.

Nevertheless, it is important to note that the idea that HRM is a new and distinct approach in its own right is one that currently receives a great deal of emphasis. For example, writers such as Bassett (1986) and Wickens (1987) argue that it is something fundamentally different or a new form of industrial relations. Therefore, without repeating what was said in Chapter 1, but to place what follows in context, it is necessary to highlight some important points about the nature of HRM.

First, it is underpinned by a distinctly different philosophy from the traditional approach. One advocate describes this as:

> 'a strategic approach to acquiring, motivating, developing and managing the organization's human resources ... which is devoted to shaping appropriate corporate cultures, and introducing programmes that reflect and support the core values of the organization and ensure its success'. (Armstrong, 1990, p. 4)

Except for the word 'strategic', this does not look too distant from many of the activities that are traditionally associated with personnel departments. However, other writers emphasize that there could be significant differences. Legge (1989) for example, draws attention to the idea that because HRM involves line managers to a far greater extent, the activities are no longer the exclusive preserve of personnel departments. In addition she points out that HRM strongly focuses on management control of human resources, and emphasizes the use of organizational culture to shape the relationship between an organization and its employees. Another indication of its nature is found in Walton's (1985) statement that it places great emphasis on obtaining a committed workforce. Perhaps the most important idea, however, is that HRM is driven by the overall strategic needs of a business (Miller, 1991). This, according to Hendry and Pettigrew (1990), results in four key characteristics:

- A strong emphasis on planning the use of human resources.
- Coherent employment policies, underpinned by a distinct philosophy.
- The machinery of human resource activities is matched to a clearly stated business strategy.
- A view of people (employees) as a strategic resource for gaining competitive advantage.

Taken together, these features mean that whilst there is some similarity between HRM and more traditional approaches to managing the relationship between an organization and its employees, in their philosophies they are poles apart. The traditional approach is much more pluralist. It contains an assumption that an organization and its employees can have fundamentally different interests, and therefore, there is always some potential for conflict. For this reason it is largely synonymous with the conventional role of the personnel function, where there is a strong emphasis on finding a compromise between the sometimes disparate needs of an organization and its employees. Almost inevitably this means that industrial relations plays a significant (if not the major) role in employee relations.

HRM on the other hand is much more unitarist in its approach, and is almost exclusively orientated to the needs of management. This does not of course mean that the underlying philosophy is genuinely unitarist, that is, that it assumes a complete convergence of interests between an organization and its employees. Indeed, since it has a strong emphasis on gaining the commitment of employees to the goals of management, it could just be a form of pseudo-unitarism where the aim is to persuade the workforce that their interests are the same as those of an organization and its managers, so that they will be more compliant. However, it does mean that there is a barely concealed assumption that an organization which is able to operate in a unitarist way will somehow be better. Thus the concerns of the human resource manager and the traditional personnel specialist are somewhat different. In HRM the primary aim is to meet the needs of the organization. This in turn means that except where meeting the needs of employees results in the employees better serving the organization and its managers, these needs are a secondary consideration.

These, however, are largely theoretical views of what human resource management could (or should) be. Whilst there are those who argue it is something real and new, there are others who deny that it is possible to realize it in practice (Kelly and Kelly, 1991). Whilst it is not the aim to explore these arguments in depth here, it is worth noting that so far the evidence suggests that although it is a theoretical possibility, it is very rare to find that HRM has been adopted in anything other than a piecemeal way (Guest, 1990; Marginson, 1989; Storey and Sisson, 1989). Indeed, in the view of one author, the human resource management approach has been 'talked up' rather than implemented (Guest, 1991). It is for this reason that the chapter steers away from giving a description of HRM and instead covers a number of activities, all of which are management-controlled and have been linked with the human resource management approach. If all were applied together as part of a well-developed strategy, it could probably be asserted that an HRM approach had been adopted. However, because the evidence suggests that this is comparatively rare, they are described simply as management-controlled activities which are used singly or in combination as a way of attempting to influence the relationship between an organization and its employees.

The first activity to be considered is the structural design of the organization, to which some reference has already been made in Chapter 4. Discussion then moves to a topic which has been strongly linked with HRM: cultures and climates, and their control by management to influence employee behaviour. Reward systems and compensation management are discussed next, and the last activities to be considered are employee appraisal, training and development. Finally, since all of these activities can influence each other, the chapter concludes by briefly tracing some of the more important links.

Organizational structure and design

For all practical purposes, the formal structure of an organization is completely decided by its management. The most convenient way to consider structure for the purposes of this chapter is to examine it at two levels: first, the structure of the enterprise as a whole, and second, the structuring of departments or work-groups. Before doing so, however, it can be noted that structure is often viewed in very simplistic terms. Therefore, it is important to give a definition and spell out its implications. Structure is 'the formal, systematic arrangements of the operations and activities that constitute an organization, and the interrelationships of those operations to one another' (Organ and Bateman, 1991, p. 595).

The practical importance of this definition is more precisely identified by Miles (1980) who points out that structure consists of two sets of systematic patterns, **differentiation**, which is the way that the organization is divided up into parts that perform specialized functions, and **integration**, which refers to the processes used to coordinate the actions of the parts. Two highly important points arise from this. First, structure does not just appear of its own accord. It is a design which nominally, at least, has been selected for a purpose, that is, to get done whatever it is the organization does, in a controlled and coordinated way. To facilitate this the overall task of the organization is usually divided up into subtasks, and therefore, the subtasks need to be coordinated in some way. So far as employee relations is concerned, the important point to note is that the overall task of an organization is to produce goods or services. Thus structure is unlikely to be selected primarily for employee-relations reasons; indeed, they may not even be a consideration. Nevertheless, because structure has effects on the behaviour of people, it is likely to have some effect on employee relations.

In some measure the structure of the whole enterprise will almost certainly be designed as a bureaucratic hierarchy. Although the word 'bureaucracy' has become something of a pejorative term, it is nevertheless the most enduring of organizational forms (Ouchi and Price, 1978). Indeed so pervasive is the bureaucratic form it is not really a question of whether or not an organization is a bureaucracy, but how bureaucratic it is. The form has a number of variants, three of which are shown in Figures 12.1(a), (b) and (c).

The *functionally structured organization* is the classical example of the bureaucratic form and is shown in Figure 12.1(a). Here, the differentiation of tasks can be seen by moving from left to right at any level, and integration is achieved by linking them vertically through authority relationships. A variant on this is the *divisionalized organization*. Divisionalization can be based on a number of factors. For example, where a product or product range is placed under a separate management, there are product divisions as shown in Figure 12.1(b). Alternatively, where the same output is produced at a number of sites through-

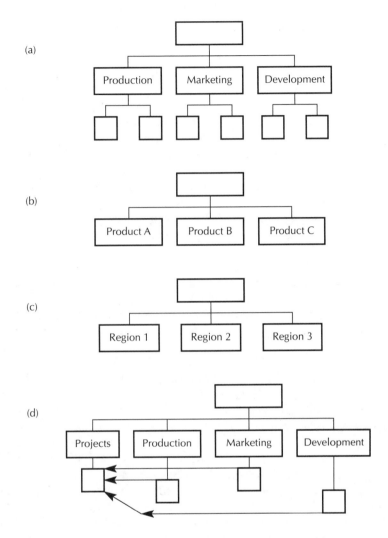

Figure 12.1 Organization structures. (a) Basic functional structure. (b) Product-based structure. (c) Geographic structure. (d) Matrix structure.

out the country, or even the world, there can be geographic divisions, which are shown in Figure 12.1(c).

These structures can often have a strong influence on employee-relations matters. For example, by making the same product at a number of different sites, output is safeguarded if trouble arises at one of them, and this lowers the potential power of employees to disrupt or challenge management's authority. As was pointed out in Chapter 9, if these organizational structures are aligned with bargaining structures, management has a powerful argument which can be used in wage negotiations, that is, it can argue that different plants each have to stand on their own merits in terms of profitability. In addition the alignment of organizational and bargaining structures can exert an almost silent means of control. One of the least appreciated features of bargaining structures is that they have an effect in shaping the aspirations of those within them. Employees are seldom able to assess in absolute terms what is a 'just reward' for the tasks that they perform, so that justice with respect to wages tends to be seen more in terms of comparisons with other groups of workers (Runciman, 1966; Scase, 1974). Therefore, in wage negotiations, if management listens carefully to the comparisons used by employees, there is an implication that they could use the information to select bargaining structures which could lower employee aspirations. For example, in a study of change over a number of years in two very different industries, Brown and Sisson (1975) found that because work structures were changed significantly, prior bases of comparison were lost or weakened to the point where employees had to seek new horizons of comparison.

At lower levels within an organization or one of its divisions, there are other ways in which structure can be used to shape employee behaviour, and thus employee relations. Amongst other things, structure sets out what roles or positions shall exist in the organization. It also lays down the activities that role occupants will undertake, and how they will undertake them. These details are often included in job descriptions, works rules and operational procedures. Thus they become incorporated into the contract of employment, and this gives a large measure of control over employee behaviour. However, it also shapes employee behaviour in other and more subtle ways. Differences in authority not only map out management's power position in a formal way, but also have psychological effects. Management's authority gives it an ability to reward some behaviours and punish others. To some extent it is therefore possible to establish embedded rules of conduct that are taken for granted, and which legitimize management power. For this reason the use of power is less likely to be questioned, and pursuing management's will becomes organizational common sense for employees (Newby, 1977; Weick, 1979).

Another way in which structure affects behaviour is in terms of the patterns of work relationships it can set up. It has long been recognized that a highly bureaucratic structure tends to result in very rigid patterns of behaviour, in which employees can be reluctant to operate outside their defined range of duties. This not only results in inefficiencies in the use of labour in today's fast-moving conditions, it also gives a low degree of organizational flexibility. One model for remedying this was shown in Chapter 1, the so-called flexible firm design. Another way is the *matrix organization* which is shown diagrammatically in Figure 12.1(d). In this an extra leg of project managers is added onto the bureaucratic hierarchy. The general idea is that project managers draw on the specialized resources of functional managers as and when needed, and the project teams are of temporary duration to tackle specific tasks. Both this and core–periphery methods depend on flexibility and team working. Successful team working itself tends to depend acutely on those involved having appropriate patterns of attitudes and values. Importantly, there is some evidence to show that if people can be induced to behave in a certain way for prolonged periods of time, this has a modifying effect on their attitudes (Lieberman, 1956). Thus the structuring of the organization and its roles has some potential to bring about a shift in attitudes.

CASE-STUDY 12.1

Mechanistic and organic structures

Burns and Stalker (1961), in their study of Scottish industries, contrast two structural types: mechanistic and organic. The characteristics of each one are:

Mechanistic

- Tasks facing the concern as a whole are broken down into *specialized functionally differentiated* duties. Individual tasks are *pursued in an abstract way*, and more or less distinct from those of the concern as a whole.

- The *precise definition* of rights, obligations and technical methods is attached to roles, and these are *translated* into the responsibilities of a functional position. The reconciliation, for each level in the hierarchy, of these distinct performance requirements is by the *immediate superiors*. Thus there is a *hierarchic structure* of control, authority and communication.

- A reinforcement of the hierarchic structure by the location of *knowledge* of actualities exclusively at the top of the hierarchy, and a greater importance and prestige attaching to *internal* (local) rather than to general (cosmopolitan) knowledge, experience and skill. A tendency for *vertical interaction* between members of the concern, that is, between superior and subordinate.

- A tendency for operations and working behaviour to be *governed by superiors* and *insistence on loyalty* to the concern and obedience to superiors as a condition of membership.

Organic

- The *contributive nature* of special knowledge and experience to the common task of the concern is emphasized, and the *nature of individual tasks*, seen to be set by the total situation of the concern. *Continual redefinition* of individual tasks through interaction with others, and little *shedding of individual responsibility* upwards, downwards or sideways.

- The *spread of commitment* to the concern beyond any technical definition, and a *network structure* of control authority and communication, with a *lateral* rather than a vertical direction of communication through the organization. Omniscience no longer imputed to the head of the concern; *knowledge* may be located anywhere in the network, this location becoming the centre of authority.

- A content of communication which consists of *information and advice* rather than instructions and decision. *Commitment* to the concern's tasks and to the 'technological ethos' of material progress and expansion is more highly valued than loyalty. Importance and prestige attach to *affiliations and expertise* valid in the industrial, technical and commercial milieux external to the firm.

Questions

i Which of these structures is nearer to the matrix structure, and which is most likely to be suitable for use with the flexible firm model shown in Chapter 1?

ii What are the likely implications of mechanistic and organic structures for the nature of contracts of employment as described in Chapter 2, the nature of the collective bargaining relationship as described in Chapter 9, and the nature of collective agreements as described in Chapter 10?

Organizational cultures and climates

Across the past decade organizational culture, and to a far lesser extent climate, have increasingly become vogue words that have captured the imagination of managers. However, whilst the two concepts are allied, they have different meanings.

Whilst **culture** tends to be defined in slightly different ways by a number of authors, a general definition that encapsulates the essence of what most writers consider it to be is 'the basic values, ideologies and assumptions which guide and fashion individual and business behaviour' (Wilson, 1990, p. 229).

Climate can be defined as 'a general atmosphere or ethos in the workplace, which influences motivation, satisfaction and behaviour of individuals in organizations' (Litwin and Stringer, 1962).

Because both are concerned with mental processes, and reflect how employees experience and feel about an organization, culture and climate clearly have some connection. However, since culture consists of values and ideologies, and these are very deep rooted, its effects tend to be at a subconscious level.

Conversely, people are generally more aware of an organization's climate. Moreover, it is somewhat less permanent than culture, and therefore tends to be more of a short-term feature. Perhaps the strongest connection between the two is that climate can be influenced by culture. For example, if people have absorbed the culture of an organization, and are then asked to do something which contravenes the cultural values, this could have climatic effects.

The management interest in culture can almost certainly be traced to a number of works of popular appeal which appeared in the early 1980s (Peters and Waterman, 1982; Deal and Kennedy, 1982; Goldsmith and Clutterbuck, 1985). All of these contained the central message that successful companies have very strong and distinctive cultures. That is, there is a dominant set of values and ideologies throughout the organization, these guide the actions of people, and this in turn contributes significantly to commercial success. Whilst there seems little doubt that a strong and appropriate culture could give rise to patterns of behaviour which aid organizational success (Seeters, 1986), the cultures described in the popular literature have unfortunately become something of a generalized prescription. To many managers the message was beguilingly simple: obtain these cultural characteristics and *ergo* – the organization will become more successful. Problematically, a quick-fix panacea such as this always seems to generate a surfeit of literature which reinforces the simplicity of the idea. Thus a glut of articles has appeared which not only exhort managers to set about changing cultures, but also give a set of highly simplistic rules for doing so (Sathe, 1983; Smith and Kleiner, 1987; Gorman, 1987). Matters are seldom quite so simple as this, and there are a number of problems, both with the way the word 'culture' has come to be used and with recipes for change.

To start with, the idea that an organization has a single set of cultural values and ideologies throughout receives little, if any, support from serious research work (Megalino *et al.*, 1989; Reynolds, 1986). Different sub-cultures are probably desirable and necessary in most organizations. For example, do we want such diverse groups as accountants and salesmen to have the same ideologies? Is it not the differences in values which gives them their professional perspectives, and makes them valuable in their own distinct ways?

Second, a rather simplistic idea has been extracted from the popular literature, that is, that there is a universal set of cultural criteria to aim for. The evidence here suggests that even if a strong culture can be associated with success, the one required is likely to vary according to the particular industrial context of the organization (Reynolds, 1986).

Finally, even if appropriate characteristics can be identified, there is the question of whether changing the culture of an organization is easily accomplished. A highly important paper by Smircich (1983) draws attention to two distinctly different conceptualizations of culture. The first treats it as something an organization 'has'. Therefore culture is regarded as an organizational characteristic, and like other characteristics such as size, it can be varied at will. In the second, culture is conceptualized as something an organization 'is', which means that it is so deeply ingrained that it becomes part and parcel of the organization itself. Most authoritative writers in the area (Schein, 1990; Pettigrew, 1979) would agree that the second is much more likely, and this means that it is not easily changed. To do so the ideologies and values of employees would need to be modified, and this is a notoriously difficult and expensive task. Indeed, one of the popular books mentioned above freely admits this difficulty, and estimates that culture change is likely to cost between five and ten per cent of what is already spent on the people whose behaviour is to be changed, and at best will then only produce half of the improvement expected (Deal and Kennedy, 1982).

What makes the process so difficult is that a culture which has been absorbed gives employees a sense of security. They know which patterns of behaviour are acceptable, and this makes their environment predictable. Although they are probably unaware that they have absorbed these behavioural norms, any attempt to change culture is likely to draw attention to the fact that the norms exist. Thus the change threatens what is stable and secure. This can set up a climate which is highly resistant to the change itself, and make people highly sceptical about messages from top management (Knights and Collinson, 1987; Oliver and Davis, 1990). Put in the starkest possible terms, there is a strong possibility that for those who have absorbed it, one of the major functions of a culture is to prevent change. Indeed, there is a great deal of evidence to suggest that strong cultures are self-reinforcing, and highly resistant to modification (Thompson and Wildansky, 1986; Ray, 1986). Thus modifying cultures is likely to be at best a long and difficult process, and where it is deeply entrenched, change could involve drastic measures such as replacing large numbers of people. For these reasons, managers need to think carefully about what is in place already. It may be more appropriate to work around the existing culture, and use some of its characteristics to contribute to organizational success (Ackroyd and Crowdy, 1990). This, for example, would seem to be what Japanese firms have done to introduce their production methods into the UK (Reitsperger, 1986). Indeed, the turnaround of the Jaguar car company in the early 1980s was arguably done in this way. Its newly appointed chief executive, Egan, resurrected the craft culture which had lain dormant in the organization for many years, and in so doing was able to graft on other features which were necessary for success in the new situation (Whipp *et al.*, 1989).

CASE-STUDY 12.2

Culture and structure

Look again at the descriptions given of mechanistic and organic structures in Case-study 12.1. In general terms, contrast what you would expect the dominant ideologies and values of employees to be in each one.

Reward systems and reward management

Although most of the practices discussed in this chapter are completely under management's control, the one exception is an organization's reward system. Where trade unions are recognized the collective-bargaining relationship will usually result in employees being able to exert a great deal of influence over pay levels and other types of reward. Nevertheless, certain basic features, such as the types of reward that are available to different categories of employee, are essentially management decisions, and these can have almost as much influence on the relationship between an organization and its employees as the actual levels of rewards.

The totality of rewards obtained by an individual is made up of several different components, and each one can be allocated on a different basis. A fundamental distinction is between **intrinsic rewards** such as status, job satisfaction, and so on, and the **extrinsic** rewards which consist of tangible benefits. Another important distinction is between **deferred payment** and **immediate payment**. Some rewards can be delayed for a considerable time. Pensions and the status that goes with promotion are both prime examples of delayed rewards, the first being an extrinsic one, whilst the other is intrinsic. Finally, it can be important to distinguish the **basis of reward** that is used. Although there is an assumption that employees will expend effort in return for any type of reward that is offered, the link between reward and effort is very much more direct in some cases. The use of any form of reward tends to be underpinned by a set of philosophical assumptions (Duncan, 1989). Usually it is these which give rise to the significant differences in the basis on which rewards are allocated, and the types of reward that are accessible to different groups of employees.

With the basis of reward, many managers have an almost mystical belief that incentive payments place them firmly in control of the effort expended by certain groups of employees. To put it another way, they tend to believe 'that incentives link payment with performance so effectively that the workers can be left on automatic pilot' (Torrington and Hall, 1987, p. 551). The philosophy underpinning this, the so-called theory X, holds that certain groups of workers are naturally idle, and motivated solely by money. This has given rise to a long tradition, particularly with manual workers, of using payment methods which systematically relate their pay to output. To do so, however, a wide variety of different methods have been used. These vary from simple piece-work, where payment is on the basis of so much per item, to measured day work, which is a sort of halfway house between a piece-work system and hourly rates. One problem is that not all work is suited to payment on this basis, for example skilled craft work is not. Another is that even though fairly rigorous methods of work study and time study have been used to design these schemes, most of them decay over time and have a maximum useful life of about five years (Duncan, 1989). When an incentive scheme has decayed sufficiently – that is, employees have discovered the exploitable loopholes or methods have changed significantly – semi-skilled workers can come to receive more pay than the skilled craftsmen. To skilled workers, pay differentials are not usually simply a matter of more money, but probably come to be a mark of status and self-esteem as well. Thus they have an intrinsic component as well as the extrinsic one. For this reason these differentials can also be important to organizations as a way of attracting and retaining a skilled workforce.

In terms of the rewards that are accessible, one of the most significant distinctions in payment has traditionally been between wages and salaries. Salaries have usually had no direct link with output, and for this reason most salary earners have looked upon themselves as distinctly different from those who earn wages. For example, they have perhaps viewed themselves as performing the delegated functions of management (Bain *et al.*, 1973; Batstone *et al.*, 1977). Therefore, any incentives for salaried workers were, and often still are, vague and indeterminate, and consist of merit payments or the prospects of promotion. However, salaries do have other features which are a distinct advantage to those who receive them. They are often incremental, and guarantee some form of automatic increase. In addition, fringe benefits are more common with salaried workers, and their jobs tend to have a higher element of security.

Overall, payment systems have traditionally consisted of different methods applied to groups of workers, often with no relationship between one group and another. Even where an attempt has been made to place jobs in a hierarchy of relative internal worth – for example, by using job-evaluation techniques – this has usually been applied to different groups in different ways. Thus employers have tended to have a pay policy rather than a more comprehensive rewards policy. Moreover, whilst most managers have long realized that pay can be used as an important tool to achieve a variety of different aims, the traditional view has been that wages are a cost that has to be kept under control.

Current trends are somewhat different, and the more recent rewards-management approach takes a wider and arguably more penetrating view. The rapid pace of technological change has rendered some of the prior distinctions between manual and white-collar work obsolete and, in any event, in the increasingly large service sector there is less history of traditional distinctions. In addition, legislation on sexual discrimination and equal pay has created pressures to remove some of the traditional methods of fixing remuneration. Perhaps most significant of all, a more competitive business environment and the need for flexibility has prompted employers to adopt more sophisticated methods. These have been broadly dubbed the rewards-management approach, and their aim is not only to control costs, but also to give competitive, equitable pay schemes that link rewards much more explicitly to the contribution made to organizational performance (Armstrong, 1990). Whilst there are a number of initiatives in this area, two which are currently receiving a great deal of emphasis will be mentioned here.

First, there is an increasing interest in bringing the terms and conditions of manual and non-manual workers closer together, and this can take a number of different forms. At one extreme is the idea of a *single-status* workforce, which gives equal basic conditions to all employees. A somewhat less radical and therefore more common step is *harmonization*, which aims to reduce differences between different categories of employee. However, because this mostly results in staff employees having their conditions lowered, and usually having to be compensated with a lump-sum payment, even this has its associated costs. Nevertheless, firms that have adopted harmonized conditions report enthusiastically of the many advantages they have obtained; for example, simplified salary administration, lowered costs, improved labour productivity, and changed employee motivation and attitudes towards cooperation and flexibility (ACAS, 1982).

A second initiative sounds very similar to harmonization, and is probably much more easily introduced when conditions are harmonized. However, it is something which is conceptually quite distinct, and consists of the selective application to other groups of employees of schemes of reward which have hitherto been used almost exclusively for one group alone; for example, the extension of manual-worker payment systems to salaried staffs, and the use of a payment basis for manual workers similar to that used for non-manuals. Here it can be noted that whilst the use of incentive schemes for manual workers has only risen slightly across the past 10 years, their use for non-manual workers has more than doubled in the same period. In addition, individual merit payments which were hitherto only common for white-collar workers are now in more widespread use with manual employees (Towers, 1987).

CASE-STUDY 12.3

Payments systems and organizational type

Look again at the descriptions of mechanistic and organic structures given in Case-study 12.1. Which of these would you expect to be more likely to adopt a rewards-management perspective, and which a more traditional view?

Recruitment and selection

Selecting people for employment is totally a management prerogative, and the same is true of those promoted within an organization, perhaps the only limitation on management discretion being that the law on sexual or racial discrimination should be observed. In order to try to make the decisions associated with these processes more reliable, management has a range of techniques at its disposal to attract, recruit and select employees. Application forms, references, telephone screening, interviews, psychological testing, and even group role-play exercises can be used singly or in combination to gather information which enables appointment and/or promotion decisions to be made. However, despite the wide range of available methods, selection is not a precise science, and the different methods vary widely in terms of their ability to predict future performance. Their accuracy in this respect is usually expressed as a validity coefficient, in which perfect prediction is given as 1.0 and no predictive ability as zero. Although methods with higher predictive validities have tended to come into greater use, those most commonly used are still references and interviews (Robertson and Makin, 1986; Snape and Bamber, 1989), and these normally have coefficients of only about 0.2 (Reilly and Chao, 1982; Hunter and Hunter, 1984).

The interview in particular has very well-documented weaknesses. Interviewers have a strong tendency to select people who are like themselves (Rand and Wexley, 1975; Dalessio and Imada, 1984). Moreover, they have a tendency to use the process to draw conclusions about a candidate's personality characteristics which are largely invisible (Anderson and Shackleton, 1990). This does not necessarily mean that selection decisions will always be patently incorrect. However, what it does mean is that even where there are a number of people who in other respects are all equally well suited for a vacancy, the selection decision can be strongly influenced by how the interviewer rates (often highly inaccurately) the attitudes and dispositions of candidates. Thus selection is far from a precise art.

Nevertheless, the process enables a line to be drawn between those who shall become organizational members and those who shall not. Therefore, in the long run it can have a very powerful effect on the nature of the relationship between an organization and its employees. For this reason, it is an area where some firms are using an increasingly sophisticated range of techniques to try to obtain a workforce with the characteristics most desired by management. For example, Lowe and Oliver (1991) note the use of psychological testing in firms, not to examine for specific skills, but to try to obtain employees with an appropriate set of attitudes. More significantly, Beaumont and Hunter (1992) describe the screening of 2500 short-listed applicants for 300 manual jobs for a greenfield site in Scotland. All of them were subjected to four interviews and psychological testing, again with the aim of obtaining a workforce which had what management considered to be the right attitudes.

CASE-STUDY 12.4

The implications of selection for employee relations

Without the use of psychological testing it is hard to identify a person's mental attributes, and certain selection decisions can be a chancy business. What are the implications of this for selecting employees in today's fast-moving conditions, where adaptability and flexibility are at a premium, and what are the longer-term implications of this for employee relations in a firm?

Appraisal, training and development

Whilst selection can be likened to a filter that admits only some of those who apply to join an organization, appraisal, training and development are processes which can be used to reinforce the desired characteristics of those people who are admitted. In most appraisal schemes superiors evaluate their subordinates. Moreover, the decision about whether some form of training or development opportunity will be provided for an employee is one that is usually made by the immediate superior. In practice, since the decision about training or development is often made in appraisal, the two processes are strongly linked. As will be seen, they also present an opportunity to try to shape employee characteristics. It is perhaps for this reason that appraisal is usually seen as one of the fundamental building blocks of an effective HRM approach (Formbrun *et al.*, 1984).

In the past, appraisal tended to be applied only to the higher reaches of an organization. Now, however, it is used in a more widespread way for non-managerial employees, and occasionally for manual workers as well (Long, 1986). One reason perhaps is the more widespread use of payment schemes where a proportion of pay is determined on an individual merit basis (Snape and Bamber, 1989). Having said this, appraisal can be used for a wide variety of purposes. In theory at least, all of them can benefit both appraiser and appraisee. However, most of these purposes fall into one or more of three broad categories: *reviewing performance* in the current role, *reviewing potential* to occupy other roles, and reviewing an individual's level of *rewards* (Randell *et al.*, 1984).

CASE-STUDY 12.5

Appraisal roles

What difficulties are likely to arise if an attempt is made to incorporate performance review, potential review and rewards review all in the same appraisal interview?

Most firms, particularly those tending towards an HRM philosophy, usually feel a need to link performance with pay, and if there is only one appraisal process at work, this can quickly lead to problems. To start with, reviewing performance requires the appraiser to be a helper or counsellor. However, the other two purposes require her/him to be a judge. Thus the appraiser is called upon to try to reconcile conflicting roles (Fletcher and Williams, 1985). For example, in order to be able to justify not giving an expected merit increase, or a high rating for future potential, the appraiser can be tempted to criticize current performance without giving a helping hand. For this reason, an appraisee has every incentive to conceal job difficulties for fear of jeopardizing a pay increase. An even worse problem is that because there is an explicit link with rewards (and by implication, sanctions as well), the appraisal process can become little more than a very crude form of psychological conditioning (Salamon, 1978). Employees can be encouraged to shape and mould their behaviour into something which is personally acceptable to their superior. Indeed, because it can force them to accept that the superior's goals must always take precedence over their own, it can wind up stifling a great deal of innovation. Therefore, it is hardly surprising to find that many employees can come to view their organization's appraisal process in a very sceptical way.

As noted above, appraisal often goes hand in hand with training and development. Indeed, one of the major justifications for appraising employees is to identify their training and/or development needs. Training and development are both explicitly concerned with bringing about changes in behaviour. However, there are important differences between the two. Training is usually taken to mean acquiring or improving some skill or other, often a motor skill such as word processing. Development is a much broader concept, and is usually concerned with changing the whole person in some way. For this reason, it is common to hear of 'employee training' and 'management development'.

When people are selected for 'development', it often has implications that they are being groomed for better things, which in turn gives them an incentive to display patterns of behaviour which demonstrate that the decision to single them out in this way was a wise one. Therefore, it is not surprising to find that the whole development process is almost exclusively devoted to bringing about changes in attitudes and values. The techniques used (for example, counselling and monitoring by superiors), although giving the appearance of being focused on broadening an individual's horizons, are perhaps more directed at ensuring that they fit into an acceptable mould. Even training, which is usually more concerned with acquiring skills, frequently has some element of normative reorientation. It is not unusual for it to emphasize that the individual has an obligation to acquire the skills to better serve the organization. Therefore, when taken together, appraisal, training and development are all very powerful tools to shape behaviour. They are processes which can be used to distribute rewards and punishments, both in the present, and in terms of future career opportunities. For this reason they can all have a potentially strong influence on employee relations.

Conclusions and overview

As things have been discussed so far, the management initiatives considered have all been taken separately. In practice, of course, they all have effects on each other. Thus the influence they exert on employee relations rather depends on whether they are all working in the same direction or against each other. Whilst space precludes an extensive examination of this point, it is useful to consider some of the more obvious implications. Since culture management and culture change tend to be seen as the central pillar of human resource management, the most convenient way to do this is to highlight some of the ways in which the other initiatives can affect culture, or alternatively are affected by it. In addition the central plank of HRM (the modification of employee-relations characteristics through cultural change) can be re-examined. As an aid to discussion, an elementary linking of the factors is shown in diagrammatic form in Figure 12.2.

Although culture can be hard to classify, a simple scheme which is useful for the purposes of discussion is one suggested by Harrison (1972), who describes four basic orientations or fundamental sets of values and ideologies prevalent in organizations. As pointed out by Handy (1985), these are really cultural types, namely the *power culture*, the *role culture*, the *task culture*, and the *person culture*. However, since the last is comparatively rare, it will not be discussed here.

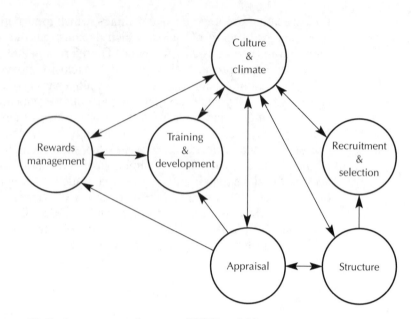

Figure 12.2   Interconnected nature of HRM variables.

The *power culture* is decisive, fast moving, and therefore able to take risks and seize opportunities. It hangs around a source of power and influence, which can be a central figure but is more often a power-holding clique or coalition. In this culture there is little in the way of formal procedures or rules to guide action, and control is exercised by the centre through key individuals. Therefore the organization can be highly political, with decisions taken by the dominant clique on the basis of personal influence rather than according to procedures.

The organization with a *role culture* is one where there is a very strong division of labour into firmly delineated specialized roles. Procedures and standard methods of operation govern the activities of these specialist offices. Therefore, the organization has a firm, stable structure, and action is designed to be uniform. The great strength of these cultures is their capability for rationality, uniformity and high internal efficiency when conditions are stable.

The *task culture* is job- or project-orientated, and based on expert competence. People and resources are brought together with the aim of completing particular tasks, and individual capability rather than age, formal status or position in the hierarchy determines people's standing. Clearly therefore, the culture is highly adaptable.

In most human resource management literature the emphasis is on moving to a task culture. However, the different cultural types consist of different patterns of values and ideologies, and these have practical outcomes in terms of the relationships that people have with each other. It can also be noted that organizational structures can strongly influence the way that people relate. Moreover, structure encourages them to behave in certain ways, and since it sets up criteria

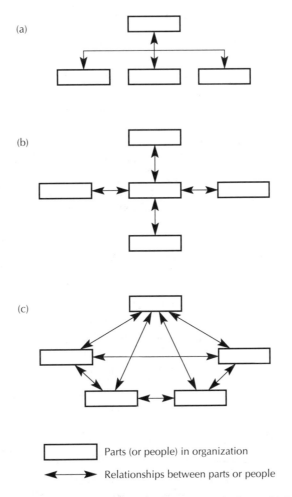

Figure 12.3 Cultures and structures. (a) Role structure/culture. (b) Power structure/culture. (c) Task structure/culture.

against which their behaviour can be evaluated, it also influences the rewards and punishments, and training and development, which they receive. For these reasons there is a relationship between all of the processes which have been discussed in this chapter, and this can be illustrated with the three structure diagrams shown in Figures 12.3(a) to (c).

An organization structured as a bureaucratic hierarchy is likely to have a well-entrenched role culture. Individuals will be selected for entry into the organization on the basis of whether they are likely to be able to perform specialist roles, and it is against this criterion that their performance will subsequently be evaluated. Performance above and beyond the demands of the role is not usually required, and can even be considered disruptive. Training rather than development is therefore normal, and this is directed at role performance. Since a fundamental feature of the structure is that responsibility increases with position in the hierarchy, position is by far the most important basis of reward. In summary therefore, people are selected into the organizational structure, the structure supports and reinforces culture, and rewards, appraisal, training and development all serve to further reinforce features of both culture and structure.

In an organization with a power culture, whilst behaviour is less procedure and role orientated, there is nevertheless a firmly positioned structural hierarchy. Individuals are selected for entry by power holders according to their own personalized criteria of suitability. Duties can vary highly as and when needed, and evaluation and rewards probably follow very closely from power holders' perceptions of an individual's willingness to put the organization or its power holders first. Thus they will be evaluated on loyalty and task performance, and rewards will be allocated or withheld according to these criteria. Again, culture structure, selection, appraisal and any training that is given are all mutually reinforcing.

In the task culture the organization has to be structurally fluid. Unlike the previous situation which uses a very unequal distribution of power to get things done, the task culture works in a different way. It requires that power be shared to some extent, so that people can step outside their normal role when necessary. Indeed, in a strong task culture, roles themselves and hence formal structure can be hard to detect. For this reason people tend to be selected on the basis of their flexibility, and their performance will be evaluated and rewards allocated on the basis of contributions they make to task completion. Again, all the features are mutually compatible.

CASE-STUDY 12.6

Change of cultures

From the way that the different cultures have been described, what steps do you feel would be necessary to effect a complete change from a role culture to a task culture?

Human resource management literature eulogizes about the task culture, and it is held up as the direction in which organizations must move if they are to survive. However, from the descriptions given above, it should be clear that a strong change in this direction would need many other things to be changed as well. Seldom, if ever, do organizations undertake such a revolutionary redesign or rebirth all in one step. Indeed, as noted earlier, the evidence suggests that human resource practices tend to be introduced in a very fragmented and piecemeal way. For this reason, although any of the management-driven initiatives described in this chapter has a potential to change some aspect of the relationship between an organization and its employees, a complete change is unlikely, except perhaps over a very long period. In short therefore, the highly optimistic human resource management picture of a workforce thoroughly committed to an organization's goals is almost certainly no more than wishful thinking. Except in the very rare case where everything is modified together, the characteristics of employee relations are unlikely to be changed significantly.

Further reading

Torrington D. and Hall L. (1987). *Personnel Management: A New Approach.* London: Prentice-Hall

> A comprehensive and very readable description of personnel practices from a specialist approach.

Handy C. (1985). *Understanding Organizations* 3rd edn. Harmondsworth: Penguin

> An easily read description of organizations and their functioning, which contains useful observations on many of the topics in this chapter.

Salamon G. (1979). *Work Organizations: Resistance and Control.* London: Longman

> A highly penetrating analysis of work organizations from a sociological perspective. It describes in an explicit way management practices that are used to obtain compliance and control over employees.

Armstrong M. (1990). *A Handbook of Human Resource Management.* London: Kogan Page

> An easy-to-read book which outlines most of the practices which have collectively come to be known as the HRM approach.

13

Policy and strategy in employee relations

Introduction

In this the final chapter of the book, the important topic of employee-relations policy and strategy is considered. Because it is not always clear in which way the words are used, the first step is to define their meanings. The chapter then examines the argument that firms should develop clear policies and strategies, and reviews some of the evidence about whether this occurs in practice. Discussion then turns to the consideration of factors that are likely to shape an organization's employee-relations policy and strategy. This is done with the aid of a model which explains that a firm's strategy emerges from a complex interaction of external and internal factors. Finally an outline scheme for the development of policy and strategy is given, which is based on the Department of Employment's *Industrial Relations Code of Practice*.

Definitions

Policy and strategy are both words that are in widespread use. However, since they tend to take on different meanings according to the context in which they are used, it is important to define the way in which they will be used here. A widely accepted definition which can be obtained from business literature is that given by Ansoff (1965), who describes 'policies' as guidelines or principles that guide actions, and which can be viewed as rules used to guide future decision making, if and when certain contingencies arise, and 'strategies' as plans or designs to achieve aims, objectives or goals.

Another word which will occasionally be used in the chapter should also be defined. This is 'tactics', which has similar (military) origins to the word 'strategy', and is usually taken to refer to events on a minor scale, that is, manoeuvres or expedients used to achieve strategic aims or objectives. A factor common to all of these is that the activities referred to are all concerned with achieving goals or objectives. Achieving goals usually means that resources must be deployed, in this case an organization's human resources. However, employees are just one of the many resources used by an organization. Therefore, policies, strategies and tactics in employee relations will at best only be a component of policies, strategies and tactics for the organization as a whole. For this reason, the terms are used here in the following way:

> **Policies** are guidelines and rules for decision making. They specify the limits of future actions that can be used to achieve the intended part that employees will play in achieving business aims.
>
> **Strategy** refers to the design or plan which the organization has for its relationship with its employees in terms of the part it is intended that they will play in contributing to the achievement of overall goals or objectives.
>
> **Tactics** are the minor adjustments that have to be made from time to time to achieve the strategic aims within the policy guidelines.

A hypothetical instance will perhaps illustrate the point. Suppose, for example, that a firm has an overall business objective of achieving a high level of profit. One of its employee-relations objectives could be that of keeping labour costs to the minimum feasible level, and from this could flow a policy of keeping manpower down to the level which matches workload. In effect this policy puts a limit on future decisions by specifying that whilst there should always be sufficient manpower to match workloads, surplus labour should not be hoarded in times when output falls.

One strategy for doing this could be to use a flexible core workforce which (when necessary) is supplemented with temporary peripheral workers. Part of this strategy might be the use of remuneration policies to attract and retain flexible core workers. These are designs or planned ways of staying within the policy guidelines. Finally, tactics for monitoring present and projected workloads would be needed, as well as those for the rapid recruitment and termination of temporary workers; for example, by having a pool of local people willing to work on this basis. These are the tactical measures which enable the strategy to be followed. The important point to note from this example is that policy and strategy need to be compatible with each other. Thus if both are to be successful, they need to be derived together from the same set of goals.

Traditional and current trends

Across the years there have been a number of strong advocates of a strategic approach to employee relations. In 1973, for example, the Commission for Industrial Relations argued strongly that an employee-relations plan should be drawn up at corporate level, and that this should be a crucial and integral part of an organization's total strategy to achieve its overall business objectives. In addition it made specific recommendations with respect to the areas on which policies should exist, and a return to these will be made later in the chapter. For the present it is important to note that in the CIR's view, the main purpose of policy is to:

> 'promote consistency in management and to enable all employees and their representatives to know where they stand in relation to the company's intentions and objectives. It further encourages the orderly and equitable conduct of industrial relations to enable management to plan ahead, to anticipate events and to secure and maintain an initiative in changing situations.'
>
> (CIR, 1973, p. 6)

Two important conclusions can be drawn from this. First, if employee-relations policy is part of an overall design to achieve business objectives, then it is clear that the owners and originators of the policy should be the top management of the organization. Second, its primary aim should be to equip those responsible for the day-to-day conduct of employee relations with a set of general principles which are helpful in guiding them in day-to-day decisions (Hawkins, 1978). These ideas are echoed by other writers, who have also argued for a corporate-level approach to employee relations. Writing in 1980, the then Director of Personnel at British Leyland argued that such an approach was essential, and must start at the top (Lowry, 1980). This, however, is not to say that top management must or should construct policy and strategy in splendid isolation. If policies and strategies, and for that matter tactics, are to be workable, they need to be understood and accepted by those lower down. Thus formulation needs to incorporate a great deal of involvement at local levels of management (Hawkins, 1978).

Whether or not most organizations follow these recommendations is still something of an open question. There are firms who have done so for a long time, two notable examples being Marks & Spencer and IBM. However, the approach for many firms seems to have been the use of subjective and informal methods. For example, Marsh (1982), in a survey of manufacturing industries, concluded that top management seldom produced explicit guidelines for the conduct of day-to-day decisions, either for themselves or for managers lower down the organization. Instead, they had a distinct preference for an *ad hoc* reactive approach to industrial-relations issues. Nevertheless, it would be inaccurate to conclude that just because there is no formalized policy statement, policy and strategy do not exist. There is a school of thought which holds that even if they do not recognize it themselves, managers still have policies and strategies (Thurley and Wood, 1983). As an example it will be remembered that in Chapter 4, when dealing with management styles, the short-term opportunist approach adopted by some firms in the recession of the 1980s was contrasted with the approach of other firms which was more orientated to long-term stability. Even though the opportunist 'macho management' style could well have been prompted by a gut feeling that the time was ripe to restore what managers saw as the proper order of things, it could still be classified as a strategy. In any event, conditions in organizations are not always conducive to producing policy and strategy statements for industrial relations. It has been argued, for example, that the entrenched positions and viewpoints of both managers and employees seldom give a climate which is ripe for a highly formalized approach, and that this might only ever be possible in a fresh situation, such as a move of location to a greenfield site (Thurley and Wood, 1983; Whitaker, 1986).

What is more, although Marsh noted top management's reactive approach, he also remarked that a significant number of organizations had become much more formal in setting down rules. This in itself is a strong indication that managers were seeking to maintain a degree of consistency in the way that they dealt with employee-relations matters. Indeed, it can be argued that by using methods such as these, a strategic reconstruction of employee-relations practices has been quietly in progress in British industry for some time. Purcell and

Sisson (1983), for example, draw attention to the idea that the recommendations of the Donovan Commission triggered a whole series of actions which were concerned with the procedural reform of industrial relations at enterprise level. One of the Commission's major recommendations was the need for management to regain the initiative in industrial relations. Moreover, it can be argued that there are distict signs that they may have done so. Since the early 1970s there has been widespread introduction of formalized procedures for collective bargaining, grievance, discipline, disputes and consultation (Brown, 1981; Hawes and Smith, 1981).

Another sign of emerging policies and strategies is the extensive use of technology to restructure work (Martin 1981), and the increased use of sophisticated payment systems to try to link wage levels more directly with output (NBPI, 1968; Daniel, 1976; Brown, 1981; Lloyd, 1976; White, 1981). Yet another sign of policy is the vast amount of procedural reform that has been instituted to separate bargainable and non-bargainable issues. In addition, bargaining structures and units have been carefully selected to reduce pressures for the upwards spiralling of wage costs, and to deny trade unions access to arenas where policy is decided. Thus managements could have been extremely sophisticated in achieving some of their objectives for employee relations. Indeed, it will be recalled from the discussion of collective bargaining in Chapter 9 that whilst top management appears to favour the individual plant as the level for pay determination, local managers could have little autonomy in employee-relations matters, and have to operate under extremely strict policy guidelines set by corporate headquarters (Kinnie, 1985, 1986, 1987; Purcell and Gray, 1986; Purcell and Sisson, 1983).

In summary therefore, it can be argued that whether or not they have been accompanied by written statements of policy, many of the changes of the late 1970s and 1980s could have been strategic ones. For these reasons perhaps the best place to look for evidence of policies and strategies is in what management does rather than in what it writes down. Indeed, there can sometimes be wide discrepancies between the best-drawn-up policies and what goes on in practice. For example, Brewster *et al.* (1983) draw attention to the differences between espoused policy and operational policy. The policies that top management state that they wish to see observed, and the policies which managers lower down the organization feel compelled to observe in practice, are sometimes widely different. Rewards and punishments for junior managers are in the hands of those higher up, and because of this they can feel compelled to respond to the informal signals that they receive from higher managers. These can sometimes indicate that their actions should be quite different from those specified in formal policy documents, and in practical terms, this can have a significant effect on employee relations. Most employees, for example, are probably unfamiliar with formal policies. Therefore, what they experience on a day-to-day basis from their immediate managers tends to be regarded as the reality of organizational policy. If employees respond by observing these policies, clearly it will not be very long before this becomes the *de facto* policy in the organization. Nevertheless, even where this difference between real and espoused policy occurs, there is still a policy and strategy at work. It is therefore relevant to ask what has prompted a more strategic and policy-driven focus, and what is the result in terms of current trends?

With respect to causes, the evidence points largely towards the external factors that were noted in Chapter 1. In the USA for example, there is a strong suggestion that inflationary pressures, coupled with a more competitive business environment, and a trade recession in the early 1980s, forced many managements to radically rethink employee-relations issues. Increasingly they sought to avoid spiralling wage costs, and looked for new ways of managing human resources to try to make organizations more effective and efficient (Cappelli and McKersie, 1987). It has been observed, for example, that American managers are rapidly moving away from their previous reactive approach to labour relations, and instead have adopted a long-term strategic set of initiatives in an attempt to secure a committed, flexible and productive workforce (Kochan and McKersie, 1983). Moreover, de-recognition of trade unions has often been a part of this strategy. Similar market conditions have been prevalent in the UK (Edwards, 1985a, 1985b; Hendry *et al.*, 1988), and thus it is possible that there has been a degree of importation of some US practices. Here it can be noted that UK branches or subsidiaries of foreign-owned firms seem much more likely to have adopted a strategic and policy-driven set of employee-relations practices than their British counterparts (Hamill, 1983; Purcell *et al.*, 1987). In addition, any changes in British firms have probably been more easily brought about by the economic crisis, which has reduced trade-union powers of resistance (Purcell, 1982). So far, however, there is little evidence of the widespread de-unionization that has accompanied the changes in America (Claydon, 1989). Nevertheless, there does appear to be a trend towards a more widespread use of human resource management practices, some of which were discussed in the previous chapter. Since human resource management is essentially a top-level initiative (Guest, 1987) and is strongly linked to overall business strategy (Walton, 1985; Tyson, 1987), it tends to be adopted where an organization has a need to become more competitive; this could well be indicative of a more strategic focus in employee relations.

Factors influencing policy and strategy

If, as the evidence suggests, the impetus for a more strategic approach comes mainly from environmental conditions, it seems likely that the policies and strategies that emerge will be those that are seen as most appropriate to achieve

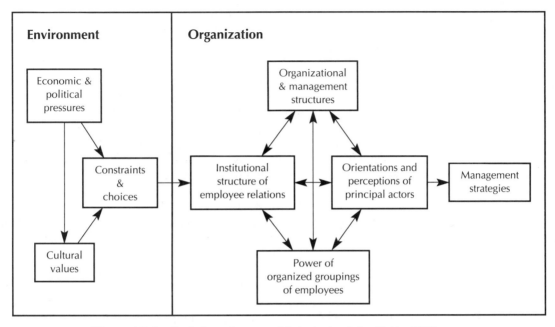

Figure 13.1　Evolution of managerial strategies (after Poole, 1980).

marketing objectives. However, there is a huge diversity in the policies and practices that seem to be followed by different firms, far more than would be expected from simply a need to be flexible in the face of very volatile markets. Thus simply shrugging things off as 'responding to the market' is unlikely to give much in the way of an explanation of all the factors that the management of a firm is likely to take into account to construct what it sees as an appropriate set of policies and strategies. One way of examining these factors, however, is to use a model developed by Poole (1980), a simplified version of which is shown in Figure 13.1.

Whilst the market is influential, Poole's model indicates that a host of other factors play a part in the strategies and policies that emerge. Environment is much more than the market alone, and also consists of political and social pressures, that shape managements' strategic thinking. One of these is the very strong *free market ideology* that managers usually hold. Because of this, and in the interests of being responsive to the market, they have a strong tendency to opt for production-centred policies and strategies that minimize wage costs.

A second powerful influence from environment arises in messages from government. As pointed out in Chapters 5 and 9, for many years British governments of all political persuasion have been concerned about the extent to which industrial disorder makes national economic management more difficult. However, to some extent, the Government's concern stems from the pressures placed upon it by management, for example pressures for State assistance in areas such as investment/development aid, market protection, and restraining trade-union power and influence. In return, management itself becomes the recipient of messages from government which exhort it to play its legitimate part in managing enterprises, and these in turn prompt managers to look for strategies to exercise control.

Even though these pressures can be powerful influences, management still has choice about how it responds to them. Poole suggests that their choices are further shaped by dominant *cultural values*, and these give rise to basic rationalities that shape managers' perceptions about what choices are realistically available. A *material interest rationality*, for example, tends to bring to the forefront strategies and policies that are designed primarily to serve economic, productive and power interests, that is, minimizing wage costs and maximizing productivity. A *moral idealistic rationality* brings principles into play which are keyed to achieving ideological objectives, such as avoiding trade-union incursion into what management sees as its legitimate decision-making areas. Finally, a *technocrat rationality* which roughly equates with a risk avoidance approach can prevail.

All these constraining pressures and choices interact with the specific objectives that managers have for the enterprise and the way in which it will operate. The two which are of most concern here are the objectives of managers with respect to their own role in the enterprise, and objectives for the role of employees; both of these have been covered at length elsewhere in the book, and will not be repeated here. The important point to note about this stage of Poole's model is that it stresses that whilst environment is a source of specific market and budgetary problems, these are not the only things that influence managers. Equally important are the ideas it gives rise to about the role and methods that management should adopt in responding to these pressures.

The second stage in Poole's model deals with factors internal to the organization. Unless the management of a firm has the benefit of starting from scratch on a greenfield site, it has to deal with what already exists. Therefore, current conditions within the enterprise are a further set of constraints, and four factors are of particular importance. First, if it is to be realistic, management's policy and strategy in employee relations must take account of the *relative power position* of the parties within the organization. For this reason, although account must be taken of matters as they are, changing the balance of power can sometimes become an important longer-term policy and strategy objective. Second, *organizational and management structures* are also an important variable. These are invariably hierarchical, with strategic authority located at the very top of the organization, which means that the ideologies and values of those at the top are the ones most likely to be reflected in strategic preferences. Nevertheless, because the policies and strategies chosen by senior management can be influenced by what goes on below, it is often necessary for them to make allowance for this. For example, to reduce uncertainties, managers lower down often foster strong bargaining relationships with employees and their representatives. Therefore, if top management has a policy objective of limiting trade-union power, it needs to take account of the way that this could be constrained by relationships developed lower down. Top management's objectives can also be constrained by the way that line managers and specialist managers sometimes differ significantly in their employee-relations perspectives. Line managers tend to judge employee-relations objectives and strategies in terms of the effect that they have on managerial authority. On the other hand, functional specialists such as personnel managers usually have additional concerns for equity, justice, fairness and satisfaction for employees. Thus the relative status and authority accorded to the two groups within the management structure can clearly affect the balance which is struck on these matters.

A third factor which management has to recognize is the existing *institutional structure of employee relations*. Although largely chosen by management, bargaining structures can be very hard to change, and so what is there already can seriously effect decision-making freedom. Finally, the *orientations and perceptions of principal actors* are another significant factor. Management and employees can perceive each other in distinct ways, and this tends to be reflected in the industrial relations climate. As noted in Chapter 10, climate can have strong effects on patterns of behaviour and this can place a limit on policy and strategy choices.

To summarize, therefore, Poole's model indicates a number of important features about the way that management is likely to derive its policies and strategies in employee relations. Perhaps the most important point to note is that the choice of policy and strategy emerges from an interaction of both internal and external factors. Some of these are likely to come into play through processes of conscious thought, and others in a more subjective way. For this reason policies and strategies are not evolved through a process of considered planning. Nevertheless, it is almost certainly the case that effective and appropriate policies are more likely to be constructed in this way. Thus it is desirable for managers to have a systematic way of tackling the process. This is considered in the next section.

Development of policy and strategy: an outline conceptual approach

In terms of the areas in which policies should desirably be developed, some guidelines are given by the Department of Employment's *Code of Practice on Industrial Relations* (DOE, 1972). Whilst the code is now over 20 years old, it is as timely as ever for this purpose. It recognizes that industrial relations is not just a matter of establishing collective-bargaining arrangements, and that even these should be underpinned by a wider set of employee-relations considerations.

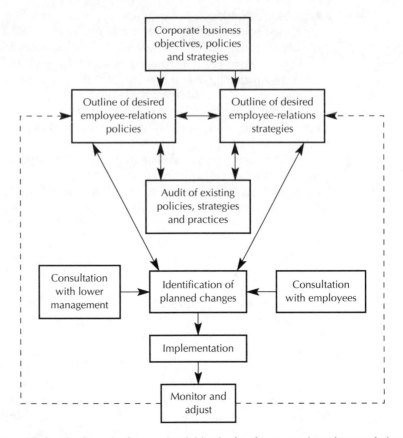

Figure 13.2   Outline of scheme of activities in development of employee-relations policies and strategies.

Indeed, the areas in which it recommends that policies and strategies should be developed are those which currently receive a great deal of emphasis in the human resource management approach.

Since any policies and strategies that are derived are primarily intended for the guidance of managers, the whole process clearly needs to start as a management-led initiative, the aim being that what results is a set of practices that can play a part in supporting business strategy. Having said this, although the exercise is essentially a top-management initiative, it cannot really be formulated by them in isolation. It is lower levels of management that will have to make it work, and thus it is desirable that there should be some opportunity for them to be involved in its formulation (Hawkins, 1978). A somewhat more contentious point is whether trade-union representatives should be involved and, if so, what part they should play. The Code's view on this matter is that whilst employees, trade-union representatives and line managers undoubtedly have a part to play, the initiative for formulating policies must rest with top management, as well as the ultimate responsibility for authorizing them. However, much will depend upon the style of employee relations that top managers wish to foster in the organization. For example, if employee participation or involvement are policy and strategy aims, employees and their representatives probably need to be involved from the outset. Trade unions are not given to underwriting practices about which they have not been consulted, and unless thay are involved at some point, anything that subsequently emerges is likely to be interpreted as little more than pious rhetoric. This can be particularly important if management aims for willing assent to its policies and strategies.

Finally, before giving the outline scheme, it is important to remember that development of policy and strategy should not be thought of as a simple set of steps that occur one after the other. A great deal of working and reworking may be necessary before a thoroughly satisfactory and acceptable set of policies and strategies emerge. Neither should it be thought of as a once-and-for-all exercise. With these cautions in mind, an outline map of the steps involved can be useful as a guide, and one such scheme is given in Figure 13.2.

Stage1: Corporate objectives, policies and strategies

Employee relations is not something discrete from other areas of activity in an organization, but has effects on the whole process of business management. For this reason the policies and strategies which emerge should be an integral part of those for the organization as a whole (DOE, 1972). This is a vital starting point, and from then onwards the steps are designed to evolve ways in which employees will play a part in achieving these business aims.

Stage 2: Desired policies and strategies

The second stage flows from the first, and the aim here is to specify two things: *what* part employees will play in achieving business objectives, and *how* that part should be played. In line with the definitions given at the beginning of the chapter, desired policies will specify the relationships that the enterprise wishes to cultivate with employees and/or their trade unions. Desired strategies would then be the long-term patterns of behaviour it wishes to encourage to bring about these relationships.

Considering both policy and strategy together can be highly important. If policy is to be more than a simple statement of intent, at some point it needs to be translated into action. For this reason, in every area where a policy is developed, a corresponding strategy is needed. This process also needs to start at the top of the organization, and both policy and strategy need to be re-evaluated periodically, probably at least on an annual basis.

Clearly what evolves in terms of desired policies and strategies will be specific to the organization. However, the DOE code stresses the need for policy in a number of areas, and this gives a ready-made agenda for matters which need to be examined. In particular, management is recommended to pay particular attention to the development of policy in the areas which are given below.

Employment issues

Overall the policy aims in this area should be threefold.

(1) To provide the highest degree of employment stability and job security for employees that is consistent with operational efficiency.

(2) That differences in conditions of employment, employee status, and in the facilities available to employees should be based on the requirements of the job, and not on personal grounds, or for non-economic reasons.

(3) A redundancy policy for dealing with any necessary reductions in the workforce, which so far as is possible should be worked out in advance.

Attention is specifically drawn to the need for *the planning and use of manpower*, where it is considered desirable that unnecessary fluctuations in manpower levels should be avoided. In addition, methods which help identify the causes of absenteeism and labour turnover should be developed. *Recruitment and selection* should also be considered, and here it is recommended that management should, wherever possible, fill vacancies by transfer or promotion from within the enterprise. They should also base selection on suitability for the job, and ensure that those who are given the responsibility to make selection decisions are competent to do so. It is also recommended that new employees are given induction training, together with other educational work experience, and job training where necessary.

Payment systems

A policy aim here should be to avoid fluctuations in the level of employee earnings. The Code also argues that payment systems should be kept as simple as possible, and be based on some form of work measurement. Where trade unions are recognized, payment systems should be jointly negotiated, and kept under review to ensure that they suit current circumstances and take account of any substantial changes in the organization of work or job requirements.

Communication and consultation

The Code considers that to promote efficiency, mutual understanding and job involvement (especially in periods of change) communication is essential in all establishments. It argues that the most important method of communication is by word of mouth, which can be supplemented by written information and meetings for special purposes. In particular, management is urged to ensure that information is provided to employees about their jobs, trade-union arrangements, opportunities for promotion, welfare facilities and health and safety. Since good communication is unlikely to happen of its own accord, it is suggested that it should be policy to involve trade unions and their representatives in initiating, setting up and maintaining some form of consultative arrangements that best suit the circumstances of the establishment. It should also be policy that these arrangements should not be used to bypass or discourage trade unions.

Collective bargaining

Because too many small units make it difficult for related groups of employees to be treated consistently, the Code recommends a policy of bargaining units covering as wide a group of employees as is practicable. So long as account is taken of minority interests, it is not considered necessary that the interests of all employees in a bargaining unit be identical. However, there should be a substantial degree of common interest amongst them, and a number of factors should be taken into account in defining bargaining units, for example the nature of the work, common interests, employee wishes, location of the work, the matters to be bargained about, and whether separate bargaining units are needed for particular categories of employees, such as supervisors or employees who represent management in negotiations.

Trade unions

In terms of its policy on trade-union recognition, management is recommended to examine the support that exists amongst employees. It is suggested that where recognition is granted or already exists, relations between management and unions should be based on jointly agreed industrial-relations procedures that provide clear rules and a basis for resolving any differences. It should also be policy to provide for regular contacts between management and unions, not just when trouble arises. Agreements which are concluded should be in writing, and there should be arrangements for regularly checking that procedural provisions have not become out of date. Whilst there is nothing in the Code which inhibits arrangements at enterprise level, it is stressed that there are advantages in agreeing matters which cover an industry as a whole at industry level, for example, terms and conditions which are suitable for general application, guidelines for negotiating at lower levels, and procedures for settling disputes.

At enterprise level it is recommended that management and trade unions should agree the number of shop stewards required in an establishment, and also the workgroup constituency for each steward. To encourage union members to vote in steward elections, it should be policy for management to offer the trade unions facilities to publicize and conduct elections. It is also considered good policy for certain shop-steward facilities to be provided by management, for example union accommodation including telephones and offices, and lists of new employees. Management and unions are also recommended to regularly review the training of shop stewards, and to take all reasonable steps to ensure that stewards receive the training they require.

Conflict-handling methods

The Code states that employees should have a right to seek redress for grievances relating to their employment. As a matter of policy, management and employee representatives are recommended to establish arrangements for raising grievances and having them settled fairly and promptly. Procedures should be in writing, have a number of stages or levels, and include a right of appeal. Where unions are recognized, management is recommended to establish a procedure for settling collective disputes which should be in writing and (i) state the level at which an issue should first be raised; (ii) lay down time limits for each stage of the procedure, with provision for extension by agreement; (iii) preclude a strike, lock-out or other form of industrial action until all stages of the procedure have been completed and a failure-to-agree formally recorded.

Stage 3: Audit of existing practices

After formulating its desired policies and strategies, attention needs to be directed to what currently takes place within the organization. For this reason, the model in Figure 13.2 shows the important step of examining current practices, and the results of this feedback to the development process.

Stage 4: Identification of planned changes

This flows from the previous stage, and strategic plans need to be transformed into tactical or operational plans, which usually cover much shorter time-spans. It can be particularly important to relate operational-level activities back to the organizational policies and, for example, it should be clearly specified what the respective roles and responsibilities of line managers and personnel specialists will be in implementing the objectives.

To make the strategy and policy workable, matters will need to be communicated to those who are affected. This is made much easier if it is set down as a formal written document that can guide management and supervision lower down in the organization. For this reason it is perhaps vital that a coherent statement of what is intended should be produced. If employees or their representatives have not been closely involved in formulation, they will need to be informed eventually, and this is perhaps one of the main reasons why a written statement is desirable. It makes it much more likely that all parties affected receive the same information, and the very act of producing a written document tends to focus the mind, and helps management to be clear about its intentions. If change is involved, the document also sets an agenda for debate.

Policies and strategies will eventually have to be implemented. At this point, particularly if changes are envisaged and the firm is unionized, there is likely to be a need for policies to become a matter of joint discussion. The way that changes in policy are implemented has a strong influence on the way management is judged as an employer. Thus jointly agreed procedures can give employees a feeling that they are protected against arbitrary management action, and can remove a great deal of uncertainty about how any further issues will be resolved.

Stage 5: Implementation

When workable policies and strategies are finally derived, it then remains to put them into practice. However, it is not sufficient simply to give an instruction and leave it at that. Implementation needs to be monitored to ensure that it happens as intended. Because policies and strategies can get out of date, monitoring needs to be a continuous process. Indeed, the code of practice puts heavy emphasis on the notion that policy and strategy need periodic re-evaluation. It is for this reason that Figure 13.2 shows feedback paths from monitoring to the review process at the top of the diagram.

Conclusions and overview

Whilst the idea that firms should develop coherent employee-relations policies and strategies is not new, there is some doubt as to whether the practice of setting them down in a formalized way has been followed by many organizations in the past. However, this does not mean that managers handle employee relations without guidelines of some sort. Rather it seems more likely that policies and strategies are subjectively formulated, and then put into practice. In terms of how these policies are derived, factors external to the firms as well as internal conditions interact to produce the policy and strategy that result.

There are, however, a number of advantages to formalizing the process of policy and strategy formulation. The most important of these is that it gives a greater likelihood of a set of policies which integrates all the different aspects of employee relations. In this sense what has been covered in this chapter relates to almost every other topic in the book. All of the processes covered in Chapters 6 to 12 are areas in which it is recommended that policies and strategies are needed. The exercise of developing them so that they interlock in a coherent way can go a long way towards ensuring that they support an appropriate system of employee relations for the firm. In today's fast-moving conditions this is tremendously important. As was pointed out in Chapter 1 of the book, most organizations have to deal with an increasingly complex and turbulent task environment. Being able to respond to it in an appropriate way can crucially depend on the human resources of a firm, and this is made all the easier if, as a matter of policy, a suitable relationship exists between the organization and its employees.

CASE-STUDY 13.1

Minicost Supermarkets PLC

Minicost Supermarkets PLC is a recently formed organization. It is part of a larger diversified group that has interests in all major areas of retailing. For a number of years the group had owned a small chain of supermarkets, Northern Supermarkets Ltd. After acquiring three more small supermarket chains, a decision was taken to integrate them into a single organization with its own directors, which would operate under the name of Minicost PLC. Group policy for the future is to expand further into supermarkets, either by acquisition of additional small chains or by opening new branches. It is intended that within three years, all existing outlets will operate under the banner of MINICOST SUPERMARKETS, but in the interim period, will continue to trade under their own names.

From an early stage it was recognized that whilst all four chains were equally profitable, they had their own policies and had different methods of operation. Nevertheless, the aim is to merge them into a major integrated group. In recognition of the labour-intensive nature of supermarket operations, an early appointment at senior level had been Ms Elizabeth Thompson as Director of Personnel. She was promoted from elsewhere in the parent group, and although she had no direct experience of supermarkets, she had spent all her working life in various types of retailing activity, mainly in personnel roles.

At an early meeting of Minicost senior executives, Ms Thompson had spoken informally to the heads of the four supermarket chains. She explained that her first task was to advise the board on an employee-relations policy for the new group, but since there were probably some differences in the way that each chain currently operated, the whole matter needed careful thought before one was selected. She stressed that wherever possible, the new policy would consist of appropriate elements drawn from each of the four existing companies. As a first step towards constructing this policy, she arranged to write to the chief executive of each of the four chains to obtain details of the current employee-relations practices. Ms Thompson's letter is shown in Attachment 1 and the four replies in Attachments 2 to 5.

Questions

i What factors do you feel will most influence Ms Thompson and the board of Minicost in choosing an employee-relations policy for the group?

ii Outline the areas in which policy will need to be derived, the major decisions that will need to be made in those areas, and the strategy considerations associated with the decisions.

Attachment 1

MINICOST SUPERMARKETS PLC
Sheffield, South Yorkshire

Dear Mr.............

Employee relations policies

You will no doubt remember that at the recent senior management meeting, we talked about the need to evolve employee-relations policies for the MINICOST group. It is intended that wherever possible, these should consist of the most appropriate practices currently used in the four separate supermarket chains. To enable me to give some preliminary thought to this matter, I am asking your cooperation in supplying me with details of how your particular chain handles employee relations. As a guide to the sort of information I require, perhaps I might suggest the following as a format for your reply.

Staffing levels

How many separate supermarkets do you have, and what are the staffing levels? What are the proportions of male and female workers, part-timers and full-timers, and managerial/supervisory and non-managerial employees?

Employee representation

Do you at present recognize trade unions, if so which ones? Which employees are union members and what facilities are given to the trade unions to operate? What provisions exist for discussing matters of mutual concern or interest?

Recruitment, selection and promotion

What methods do you use for recruiting and selecting new employees? How do you fill any promotional vacancies that occur?

Training and development of employees

What arrangements are made to induct new employees into the organization? What provisions exist to train appropriate employees for positions of greater responsibility? Do you have a system of individual appraisal, performance review, or counselling?

Welfare

Do you have a pension scheme and how is it funded? What are your policies towards sickness, family bereavement and so on?

Yours sincerely

E Thompson
Director of Personnel
To: L. Meers, Chief Executive, Meers Supermarkets
    P. Brown, Chief Executive, Troon Stores
    A. Blunt, Chief Executive, Costwise Ltd
    S. Otter, Chief Executive, Northern Supermarkets

Attachment 2

Chief Executive
Meers Supermarkets
Sheffield
South Yorkshire

Ms Thompson
Director of Personnel

Dear Ms Thompson

Employee relations policies

Thank you for your letter asking for details of the above. You pointed out at the senior management meeting that you might decide to visit us to discuss matters in greater depth. Therefore, I will confine my answer to the questions you specifically ask in your memo.

Staffing levels

We currently have six supermarkets, and as a whole employ approximately 2000 people. Roughly 100 of these are clerical and administrative staffs (50 at our headquarters and the rest in the stores). Since the size of each store varies, the total number of employees at each one ranges from 100 to 400. Although this might appear to be a large number, I should point out that except for a small nucleus of full-time workers at each location (mainly supervision and warehouse personnel), we make a conscious effort to maximize the use of part-time labour. Most of these part-timers are females, or in vacation periods, university and polytechnic students. We try to restrict part-time employees to ten hours or less, per week. This way we can vary our manning requirements according to peak trading hours/days and make continual adjustments to staffing needs. It also has the added advantage of putting the vast majority of our workforce outside of certain employment legislation. In any event, married women only seem to do the work for pin-money and we find they are far less likely to stand on their dignity if we have to dispense with their services. The approximate ratios of male to female, full-time to part-time, and managerial/supervisory to non-supervisory are all 1:10.

Employee representation

Until a few years ago we were a family-run firm and do not recognize or negotiate with trade unions, nor have we ever done so. It is made clear to all new joiners that this is our standard practice and our policy of maximizing the number of part-timers is extremely effective in ensuring that trade unions stand no change of gaining a foothold.

Recruitment selection and promotion

For part-time workers we might occasionally advertise in the local Press, but mainly rely upon word-of-mouth communication between existing employees and their friends and neighbours on local estates. Full-time workers are exclusively recruited from part-timers who wish to transfer to full-time work, as and when we have a vacancy. Because we try to keep the number of full-time employees to a minimum, this seldom occurs. The practice also has the advantage of ensuring that the aspirations of full-time employees are commensurate with the levels of remuneration which we provide.

Training and development

Apart from a short instructional period with an existing experienced member of staff, we do not engage in what could be regarded as an expensive luxury for relatively unskilled work. Supervisory employees can, if they so wish, attend courses at the local technical college in their own time and 50 % of fees will be reimbursed. We have no formal appraisal scheme. It is made clear to all employees on joining that hard work is expected and that there are penalties for not living up to our expectations.

Welfare

We have no pension scheme. With the exception of part-timers, who are only paid for their hours of attendance, standard industry holidays are granted to employees after one year's service.

I hope these details are sufficient for your requirements. If I can be of any assistance in providing more information or making suggestions about appropriate group policies, please do not hesitate to make contact.

Yours sincerely

E Meers

Attachment 3

Personnel and Training Officer
Troon Stores Ltd
Newcastle-upon-Tyne

Ms Thompson
Director of Personnel

Dear Ms Thompson

Our chief executive (Mr. P. Brown) has asked me to reply to your letter which asks for details of our employee-relations policies. The information you request is as follows:

Staffing levels

At present we have 2037 staff spread across 12 retail outlets and headquarters (49 at the latter). The number of people in each retail outlet varies between 98 and 403, approximately 40 % of whom are on full-time contracts. Please note, however, that since we classify a full-time contract as anything above 25 hours per week, this does not mean that all full-timers work either a five-day week or full opening hours.

Approximately 40 % of our employees are male and 60 % of the part-time workers are females. Supervisory and managerial personnel constitute 12 % of the workforce. Because the proportions of male to female, part-time to full-time and so on do vary considerably in each individual outlet, I am not including a complete breakdown of the workforce.

Employee representation

We are not a unionized concern, the decision having been taken many years ago that it was in the best interests of the company not to recognize trade unions. In the past there have been a number of attempts by unions to gain entry, and in order to remain union-free we have always adopted the policy of paying slightly more (+7 %) than local retail pay levels. In addition to these benefits in direct remuneration, our employees enjoy holiday, sickness and pensions benefits above those normally found in retail chains of a comparable size.

Recruitment selection and promotion

We are extremely careful about these practices. All full- and part-time workers are very extensively screened using normal methods of references and interviews. Approximately two years ago, when we were facing a particularly determined attempt by a trade union to gain entry, we took the decision to introduce the additional step of psychological testing in our selection procedures. At that time we were expanding, and very anxious to maintain our non-unionized culture. Therefore, we took this step in order to be able to screen out applicants with undesirable attitudes. I would hasten to add however, that the step was not taken without prior experience of testing. We had, for some years, been using a different type of test to assess managerial and supervisory potential – see below.

Training and development

All new employees receive a two-day induction course to acclimatize them to the organization and its culture. This is followed by on-the-job training under a supervisor for one week. It is also part of our policy to rotate all full-time employees within each retail outlet. The aim here is that each location will have a workforce that is flexible and highly competent.

We are very proud of our annual performance review and appraisal procedures, and every individual below the chief executive takes part in this process. Although all employees are on incremental pay scales, the incremental point is not completely determined by length of service, that is, the merit rating achieved in annual appraisal also plays an important part. Clearly we also rely heavily on this process to identify future supervisors and managerial talent. Indeed, it is our firm belief that we should not just offer employment, but to those individuals that want it, the prospect of a secure and challenging career.

All newly appointed supervisors are enrolled for a course in supervisory management at a local technical college, and we pay their fees and give time-off with pay. In addition, my own department runs a number of in-house courses, for example appraisal and counselling techniques.

Welfare

We have a contributory pension scheme, which all workers may join after a qualifying period; 6 % employee contributions and a like sum by the company. Employees receive a minimum of 20 days paid holiday each year plus statutory days. The usual sickness, maternity benefits and so on are also paid.

If you should require any further details or even wish to observe one of our selection and training programmes, please do not hesitate to say so.

Yours sincerely

A.N. Another
Personnel and Training Officer,
Troon Stores Ltd.

Attachment 4

Personnel Manager,
Costwise Ltd, Manchester

Dear Ms Thompson
Costwise Ltd personnel policies
I have been asked to reply to your letter to our chief executive Mr. Blunt. Given below is the information you request.

Staffing Levels

Costwise Ltd currently operates eight supermarkets. Including those at headquarters, it has a total of 4242 employees. Each retail store is of approximately the same size and the average number of staff at each one is 510.

The statistics you ask for are:

Full Time	Female 61 %	Male 39 %
Part Time	Female 92 %	Male 8 %
Overall %	Part-time 62 %	Full-time 38 %

Supervisory and management: 11 % of employees.

Employee representation

The policy at Costwise is to recognize the Transport and General Workers Union. Although joining is voluntary, all staff below assistant store manager are encouraged to join, and most do. In each store personnel matters are an important formal responsibility of the assistant manager. All stores have some system of workplace representation, and most have recognized senior stewards.

Relationships with the trade union are excellent. This is not, however, to say that they are cosy. The trade union is well organized, and some of its members have considerable bargaining skills. What aids matters is that three years ago, several senior stewards persuaded the union to sanction the formation of a separate branch which covers all of Costwise. When this happened, a number of senior stewards were elected by the rest of the members to become the branch officers and we immediately recognized these people, one of whom (the branch secretary) is granted permanent absence from his work role to perform trade-union duties. We also have a joint negotiating committee which meets bi-monthly to consider matters of mutual interest. The trade-union side of this consists of one representative from each store, plus the branch chairman and secretary. The management side comprises the chief executive, myself and the store managers. Since its formation, and the changes in union organization outlined above, it has never been necessary for a full-time officer of the union to be present at negotiations.

It is our practice to use the committee for consultation and involvement on all developments. Over the last two years we have formalized many of the previous *ad hoc* practices into written agreements, and copies of these can be supplied if you should wish to see them. Prior to the takeover of the company, negotiations were about to commence on a share purchase scheme for employees. For obvious reasons these have been suspended, but it is a matter we would clearly like to see opened up again.

Recruitment selection and promotion

Since there is a manager at each location who is responsible for personnel matters, recruitment of all staff up to first-line supervisor level is handled locally. It is a matter which we take very seriously and currently we are giving consideration to the use of psychological testing.

We place great reliance on development of supervisory and managerial talent internally. To this end, all employees who are considered to show some supervisory potential attend a two-day assessment at headquarters. This is a yearly event and timed to occur after the annual round of performance appraisals. The results of the assessment, together with appraisal notes, are used to select those with the most immediate potential. These persons then attend our own supervisor's course, and after this, appointment to a supervisory position depends upon the existence of a vacancy and whether or not the individual is willing to move work location.

Training and development

All new entrants receive full induction and on-the-job training. In addition we actively promote job rotation, both within and between separate locations. As stated above, we do a certain amount of training internally. All employees, particularly those in supervisory positions, are encouraged to attend appropriate further education courses, and seldom, if ever, would we refuse a request for fees to be paid. Senior managers (assistant manager and above) are all required to study for graduate membership of the Institute of Personnel Management.

Welfare

We are proud to say that we have an excellent contributory pension scheme, and also that a trade-union representative sits on its board of trustees. Together with the union, Costwise is also active in promoting a number of welfare schemes, for example preferential terms for car purchase and discounts with a large furnishing chain.

Yours sincerely

S. Wilkins
Personnel Manager

FROM: Personnel Manager, Northern Supermarkets Ltd
Bradford, Yorkshire.

Dear Ms Thompson

Industrial-relations and personnel practices

I am in possession of your letter to our chief executive, Mr. Otter, who has asked me to reply giving the information you require.

Staffing levels

This company has 2863 employees. Of these, 47 are located at our head-quarters offices, and the remainder in 12 supermarkets where staffing levels vary between 100 and 300 people. Although the proportion varies slightly at each store, the average percentage of full-time employees at each one is 26 % and the male–female split is on average 10 % to 90 % respectively. Supervisory and management personnel constitute about 10 % of employees.

A very strong emphasis is placed on cost control, and for this reason we try to employ the highest number of part-time workers commensurate with the smooth running of the operation. Exact labour requirements vary considerably on a seasonal basis, with additional variation between days of the week and even times of the day. Fine-tuning of labour costs in this situation is always a problem, and is most easily accomplished by having the minimal number of full-time workers. Indeed, some of our part-time employees work only four hours per week; the average being approximately seven hours.

Employee representation

Although union membership is voluntary, we do recognize the Union of Shop Distributive and Allied Workers (USDAW) for negotiating purposes. Union membership hovers around 30 % and is mainly confined to full-time employees. On the whole, relationships with the trade union are smooth. Most of our dealings are with full-time officers who have come to understand our need to achieve labour flexibility in the interests of low costs. There is a semi-formal committee of stewards drawn from the different supermarkets with whom management meets regularly. I would, however, stress that these meetings do not have the status of formal negotiations. The committee is used for consultative purposes, for example as a sounding board and to keep staffs well informed about changes and developments. Nevertheless, employee representatives are invited to comment, voice opinions and make suggestions. This works well, and it would be fair to say that there is a very constructive attitude on the part of staff representatives.

Recruitment selection and promotion

As you can imagine, the high proportion of part-timers that we employ gives a correspondingly high turnover of staff; approximately 50 % per annum. This is no real problem because it is invariably part-timers who leave, usually to obtain longer hours or better paid employment elsewhere. Replacements are normally found by contacting the local job centre, and selection is made by the supermarket manager.

Full-time workers are another matter. Most of these people are in supervisory positions, and it is felt that this core of experienced employees has to be retained. Usually they are selected from part-timers who have expressed a desire to work full-time. This way we are usually able to observe their potential and capabilities for a considerable period before deciding whether or not to offer full-time employment.

Training and development

All workers receive some on-the-job induction training to familiarize them with their duties. Since most new entrants are part-time, we try to arrange that for the first two weeks of their employment, they attend during slack periods of trading. From then on, they are employed during hours when there is most need of their efforts. By the time one of these people is suitable for promotion to a full-time post, they have been thoroughly vetted and there is seldom a need for further training.

If there is a need for specific skills which do not currently exist in the organization, each situation is examined very carefully on a costs–benefits basis. Sometimes this results in retraining of existing employees. A case in point was the recent decision to computerize stock control in all supermarkets, where existing staff were trained to use the new equipment. Conversely, when the decision was taken to upgrade headquarters computing facilities, a new member of staff was employed. This was because there were also longer-term plans for computerization. Here it was cheaper to buy in a single expert who could instruct others.

Welfare

For full-time staffs there is a contributory pension scheme which was introduced after discussions with the trade union. Part-time employees seldom stay long enough to make it worth while joining. The usual nationally agreed minimum holiday provisions and sick pay and so on are granted to all employees.

Should you require any more details please do not hesitate to write or telephone

Yours sincerely.

W. Ericson
Personnel Manager

Further reading

Brewster C.J. and Connock S.L. (1985). *Industrial Relations: Cost Effective Strategies*. London: Hutchinson

> A very readable book which argues for and describes a proactive and strategic approach to employee relations that includes elements of what has now more popularly become known as human resource management.

Thurley K. and Wood S., eds. (1983). *Industrial Relations and Management Strategy*. Cambridge: Cambridge University Press

> A book of readings with a wide diversity of views and evidence on management strategies.

Poole M. and Mansfield R., eds. (1980). *Managerial Roles in Industrial Relations*. Aldershot: Gower

> Another book of readings, that gives a wide variety of perspectives on the role of management in industrial relations.

References

Introduction

Child J. (1984). *Organization: A Guide to Problems and Practice*. London: Harper and Row

Fox A. (1985). *Man Mismanagement* 2nd edn. London: Hutchinson

Homans G.C. (1950). *The Human Group*. New York: Harcourt Brace and World

Hyman R. (1975). *Industrial Relations: A Marxist Introduction*. London: Macmillan

Hyman R. and Brough I. (1975). *Social Values and Industrial Relations*. Oxford: Blackwell

Margerison C. J. (1969). What do we mean by industrial relations: a behavioural science approach. *British Journal of Industrial Relations*, **7**(2), 273–85

Shimmin S. and Singh S. (1972). Industrial relations and organizational behaviour: a critical appraisal. *Industrial Relations Journal*, **4**(3), 37–42

Williams R. and Guest D. (1969). Psychological research and industrial relations: a brief review. *Occupational Psychology*, **43**(2), 201–11

Wood S.J. and Elliot R. (1977). A critique of Fox's radicalisation of industrial relations theory. *Sociology*, **11**, 105–24

Chapter 1

Abegglen J.C. (1958). *The Japanese Factory: Aspects of Its Social Organization*. Glencoe IL: Free Press

ACAS (1985). *Annual Report*. London: Advisory, Conciliation and Arbitration Service

ACAS (1988). *Labour Flexibility in Britain: The 1987 ACAS Survey*. London: Advisory, Conciliation and Arbitration Service

Atkinson J. (1984a). *Manning for Uncertainty: Some Emerging U.K. Work Patterns*. University of Sussex: Institute of Manpower Studies

Atkinson J. (1984b). Manpower strategies for flexible organizations. *Personnel Management*, August, 28–31

Atkinson J. and Meager N. (1986). *Changing Work Practices: How Companies Achieve Flexibility to Meet New Needs*. London: National Economic Development Office

Bain G.S. and Clegg H.A. (1974). A strategy for industrial relations research in Great Britain. *British Journal of Industrial Relations*, **12**(1), 91–113

Banks J.A. (1974). *Trade Unionism*. London: Macmillan

Barbash J. (1988). The new industrial relations in the United States: phase II. *Relations Industrielles*, **43**(1), 32–42

Beynon H. (1973). *Working for Ford*. Harmondsworth: Penguin

Boraston I., Clegg H.A. and Rimmer M. (1975). *Workplace and Union: A Study of Local*

Relationships in Fourteen Trade Unions. Oxford: Heinemann

Brown W. (1986). The changing role of trade unions in the management of labour. *British Journal of Industrial Relations,* **24**(2), 161–8

Clegg H.A. (1976). *Trade Unions Under Collective Bargaining: A Theory Based on Comparisons of Six Countries.* Oxford: Blackwell

Clegg H.A. (1979). *The Changing System of Industrial Relations in Great Britain.* Oxford: Blackwell

Cross M. (1985). Flexibility and integration at the workplace. *Employee Relations.* **7**(1), 11–15

Dill W. (1958). Environment as an influence on managerial autonomy. *Administrative Science Quarterly,* **2**(2), 409–33

Dore R.P. (1973). *British Factory – Japanese Factory: The Origins of National Diversity in Industrial Relations.* London: Allen and Unwin

Dubin R. (1970). Management in Britain: observations of a visiting professor. *Journal of Management Studies,* **7**(2), 183–98

Dunlop J.T. (1958). *Industrial Relations Systems.* New York: Holt

Dworkin J., Feldman S., Brown M. and Hobson C. (1988). Workers' preferences in concession bargaining. *Industrial Relations,* **27**(1), 7–20

Emery F. E. and Trist E. L. (1963). The causal texture of organizational environments. *Human Relations,* **18**(1), 21–32

Feurstenberg F. (1987). Industrial relations in the Federal Republic of Germany. In *International and Comparative Industrial Relations* (Bamber G.J. and Lansbury R.D., eds.), pp. 165–86. London: Allen and Unwin

Fiorito J., Lowman C. and Nelson F. (1987). The impact of human resource policies on union organising. *Industrial Relations,* **26**(2), 113–26

Fox A. (1974). *Beyond Contract: Work Power and Trust Relations.* London: Faber and Faber

Fox A. (1985). *Man Mismanagement* 2nd edn. London: Hutchinson

Glascock S. (1990). In praise of older women. *Management Today,* September, 86–8

Hakim K. (1987). Trends in the flexible workforce. *Employment Gazette,* **95**(1), 549–60

Hakim K. (1990). Core and periphery in employers' workforce strategies: evidence from the 1987 E.L.U.S. survey. *Work, Employment and Society,* **4**(2), 157–88

Hanami T. (1979). *Labour Relations in Japan Today.* Tokyo: Kodansa-International

Hofstede G. (1980). *Cultures Consequences: International Differences in Work Related Values.* London: Sage

IDS (1986). *Flexibility at Work.* Study 360, London: Income Data Services

IMS (1984). *Flexibility, Uncertainty and Manpower Management.* Report No. C.N. 526, University of Sussex: Institute of Manpower Studies

IMS (1985). *New Forms of Work Organization: I.M.S. Manpower Commentary No.30.* University of Sussex: Institute of Manpower Studies

IOD (1985). *Labour Market Changes and Opportunities: New Patterns of Work.* London: Institute of Directors.

IRS (1986). *Flexibility: The Key Concept of the 1980s.* London: Industrial Relations Services

Katz N.C., Kochan T.A. and Gobeille K. (1983). Industrial relations performance, economic performance and quality of working life programs: an inter-plant analysis. *Industrial and Labor relations Review,* **37**(1), 3–17

Katz N.C., Kochan T.A. and Weber M. (1985). Assessing the effects of industrial relations systems and efforts to improve quality of working life on organizational effectiveness. *Academy of Management Journal,* **28**(3), 509–26

Kochan T.A. and McKersie R.B. (1983). Collective bargaining, pressures for change. *Sloan Management Review,* June, 59–65

Kochan T. A., McKersie R. and Cappelli P. (1984). Strategic choice and industrial relations theory. *Industrial Relations,* **23**(1), 16–39

Kuwahara Y. (1987). Japanese industrial relations. In *International and Comparative Industrial Relations* (Bamber G.J. and Lansbury R.D., eds.), pp. 211–31. London: Allen and Unwin

Lawler E.E. (1975). Measuring the psychological

quality of working life. In *The Quality of Working Life* (Davis L. and Cherns A., eds.), pp. 123–33, New York: Free Press

Marchington M. (1990). Analysing the links between product markets and the management of employee relations. *Journal of Management Studies*, **27**(2), 111–32

Marchington M. and Parker P. (1990). *Changing Patterns of Employee Relations*. Hemel Hempstead: Wheatsheaf

Marsden D. and Thompson M. (1990). Flexibility agreements and their significance in productivity in British manufacturing since 1980. *Work, Employment and Society*, **4**(1), 83–104

McClelland D.C. (1961). *The Achieving Society*. New York: Free Press

McKenna S. (1988). Japanization and recent developments in Britain. *Employee Relations*, **10**(4), 6–12

NEDO (1988). *Young People and the Labour Market: A Challenge for the 1990s*. London: National Economic Development Office

NEDO (1989). *Defusing the Demographic Timebomb*. London: National Economic Development Office

OECD (1986). *Employment Outlook*. Paris: Organization for Economic Cooperation and Development

Oliver N. and Wilkinson B. (1989). Japanese manufacturing techniques and personnel and industrial relations practices in Britain: evidence and implications. *British Journal of Industrial Relations*, **27**(1), 73–91

Phelps Brown H. (1990). The counter revolution of our time. *Industrial Relations*, **29**(1), 1–14

Piore M. J. (1986). Perspectives on labour market flexibility. *Industrial Relations*, **25**(2) 331–49

Purcell J. (1987). Mapping management styles in employee relations. *Journal of Management Studies*, **24**(5), 533–48

Purcell J. and Sisson K. (1983). Strategies and practice in industrial relations. In *Industrial Relations in Britain* (Bain G.S., ed.), pp. 95–120. Oxford: Blackwell

Rajan A. and Pearson R. (1986). *U.K. Occupational and Employment Trends to 1990*. Sevenoaks: Butterworth

Robinson O. (1985). The changing labour market: the phenomenon of part-time employment in Britain. *National Westminster Bank Quarterly Review*, November

Sayer A. (1986). New developments in manufacturing: the just-in-time system. *Capital and Class*, Winter, 43–72

Schuler R. S. and Jackson S. E. (1987). Linking competitive strategies with human resource management practices. *Academy of Management Executive*, **1**(3), 207–19

Shipley P. (1991). Personnel management and working women in the 1990s: beyond paternalism. *Personnel Review*, May, 44–7

Steele F. (1977). Is the culture hostile to organizational development? In *Failures in Organizational Development and Change*, (Mirvis P.H. and Berg D.N., eds.), pp. 237-51, New York: Wiley

Tawney R.N. (1961). *Religion and the Rise of Capitalism*. Harmondsworth: Penguin

Taylor R. (1982). *Workers and the New Depression*. London: Macmillan

Thomason G. (1984). *A Textbook of Industrial Relations Management*. London: Institute of Personnel Management

Thurley K.E. (1983). How transferable is the Japanese industrial relations system? Some implications of a study of industrial relations and personnel policies of Japanese firms in western Europe. *Proc. Int. Industrial Relations Association Sixth World Congress*. Geneva: IIRA

Thurley K. and Wood S., eds. (1983). *Industrial Relations and Management Strategy*, pp. 116–31. Cambridge: Cambridge University Press

Towers B. (1987). Trends and developments in industrial relations: managing labour flexibility. *Industrial Relations Journal*, **18**(2), 79–83

Turnbull P. J. (1986). The Japanization of production and industrial relations at Lucas Electrical. *Industrial Relations Journal*, **17**(3), 193–206

Weber M. (1976). *The Protestant Ethic and the Spirit of Capitalism* 2nd edn. London: Allen and Unwin

Wheeler H. (1987). Management–labour relations in the U.S.A. In *International and Comparative Industrial Relations* (Bamber G.J. and Lansbury R.D., eds.), pp. 57–79. London: Allen and Unwin

Chapter 2

Albanese R. and Van Fleet D. (1985). Rational behaviour in groups: the free riding tendency. *Academy of Management Review*, **10**, 244–55

Asch S. (1955). Opinions and social pressure. *Scientific American*, **19**, 31–5

Bain G.S. (1970). *The Growth of White Collar Unionism*. Oxford: Clarendon Press

Beynon H. (1973). *Working for Ford*. Harmondsworth: Penguin.

Blau P. (1964). *Exchange and Power in Social Life*. New York: Wiley

Brown W. (1972). A consideration of custom and practice. *British Journal of Industrial Relations*, **10**(1), 42–61

Brown W. and Sisson K. (1975). The use of comparisons in workplace wage determination. *British Journal of Industrial Relations*, **13**(1), 23–51

Burt C. (1955). The evidence for the concept of intelligence. *British Journal of Educational Psychology*, **25**, 158–88

Dipboye R.L. (1982). Self-fulfilling prophecies in the selection-recruitment interview. *Academy of Management Review*, **7**(3), 579–86

EPCA (1978). *The Employment Protection (Consolidation) Act*. London: HMSO

Epstein S. (1980). The stability of behaviour: implications for psychological research. *American Psychologist*, **35**, 790–806

Feldman J.M. (1981). Beyond attribution theory: cognitive processes in performance appraisal. *Journal of Applied Psychology*, **6**, 194–9

Festinger L. (1957). *A Theory of Cognitive Dissonance*. New York: Harper and Row

Fox A. (1971). *A Sociology of Work in Industry*. London: Macmillan

Fox A. (1974). *Beyond Contract: Work Power and Trust Relations*. London: Faber and Faber

Fox A. (1985). *Man Mismanagement* 2nd edn. London: Hutchinson

Gartrell C. D. (1982). On the visibility of wage referents. *Canadian Journal of Sociology*, **7**(2), 117–43

Harkins S., Latane B. and Williams K. (1980). Social loafing: allocation of effort or taking it easy. *Journal of Experimental Social Psychology*, **16**, 457–65

Hepple B. (1983). Individual labour law. In *Industrial Relations in Britain* (Bain G.S., ed.), pp. 393–418. Oxford: Blackwell

Homans G.C. (1950). *The Human Group*. New York: Harcourt Brace and World

Homans G.C. (1961). *Social Behaviour*. New York: Harcourt Brace and World

Honeyball S. (1989). Employment law and the primacy of contract. *Industrial Law Journal*, **18**(2), 97–108

Hyman R. (1975). *Industrial Relations: A Marxist Introduction*. London: Macmillan

Hyman R. and Brough I. (1975). *Social Values and Industrial Relations*. Oxford: Blackwell

Kahn-Freund O. (1967). A note on status and contract in British labour law. *Modern Law Review*, **30**, 635–44

Kahn-Freund O. (1977a). Blackstone's neglected child: the contract of employment. *Law Quarterly Review*, **113**, 508–28

Kahn-Freund O. (1977b). *Labour and the Law*. London: Stevens

Krech D., Crutchfield R.S. and Ballachey E.L. (1962). *Individual and Society*. New York: McGraw-Hill

Levine M.W. and Shefner J.M. (1981). *Fundamentals of Sensation and Perception*. Reading MA: Addison-Wesley

Mann M. (1977). *Consciousness and Action Among the Western Working Class*. London: Macmillan

McClelland D.C. (1961). *The Achieving Society*. New York: Free Press

Miles T.R. (1957). Contributions to intelligence testing and the theory of intelligence, 1: on defining intelligence. *British Journal of Educational Psychology*, **25**, 158–77

Milgram S. (1974). *Obedience and Authority: An Experimental View*. London: Tavistock

Mischel E. (1968). *Personality and Assessment*. New York: Wiley

Monson T.C., Hesley J.W. and Chernick L. (1982). Specifying when personality traits cannot predict behaviour: an alternative to abandoning the attempt to predict single action criteria. *Journal of Personality and Social Psychology*, **43**, 358–65

Roberts B.C., Loveridge R. and Gennard J. (1972). *Reluctant Militants*. London: Heinemann

Roethlisberger F.J. and Dickson W.J. (1935). *Management and the Worker*. Harvard MA: Harvard University Press

Routh G. (1966). White-collar unions in the United Kingdom. In *White Collar Trade Unions*, (Sturmthal A., ed.), pp. 165–204. Urbana: University of Illinois Press.

Runciman W.G. (1966). *Relative Deprivation and Social Justice*. London: Routledge and Kegan Paul

Scase R. (1974). Relative deprivation: a comparison of English and Swedish manual workers. In *Poverty, Inequality and Class Structure* (Wedderburn D., ed.), pp. 197–216. Cambridge: Cambridge University Press

Simon D. (1954). Master and servant. In *Democracy and the Labour Movement* (Saville J., ed.), pp. 116–32, London: Lawrence and Wishart

Tawney R.H. (1931). *Equality*. London: Allen and Unwin

Terry M. (1977). The inevitable growth of informality. *British Journal of Industrial Relations*, **15**(1), 75–90

Walker C.R. and Guest R.H. (1957). *Man on the Assembly Line*. New Haven: Yale University Press

Wedderburn K.W. (Lord) (1971). *The Worker and the Law* 2nd edn. Harmondsworth: Penguin

Wedderburn K.W. (Lord) (1980). Industrial relations and the courts. *Industrial Law Journal*, **9**, 65–94

Whincup M. (1990). *Modern Employment Law: A Guide to Job Security and Safety*. Oxford: Heinemann

Zand D.E. (1972). Trust and managerial problem solving. *Administrative Science Quarterly*, **17**, 229–39

Zimbardo P.G. (1973). *Proceedings of the American Psychological Associatio Conference*, Montreal, Canada

Chapter 3

Bain G.S. (1970). *The Growth of White Collar Unionism*. Oxford: Clarendon Press

Bain G.S. and Clegg H.A. (1974). A strategy for industrial relations research in Great Britain. *British Journal of Industrial Relations*, **12**(2), 91–113

Bain G.S. and Price R. (1983). Union growth: dimensions, determinants and destiny. In *Industrial Relations in Britain* (Bain G.S., ed), pp. 3–34. Oxford: Blackwell

Bain G.S., Coates D. and Ellis V. (1973). *Social Stratification and Trade Unionism*. Oxford: Heinemann

Batstone E., Boraston I. and Frenkel S. (1977). *Shop Stewards in Action: The Organization of Workplace Conflict and Accommodation*. Oxford: Blackwell

Bemmels B.(1987). How unions affect productivity in manufacturing plants. *Industrial and Labor Relations Review*, **40**(2), 241–53

Blackburn R.M. and Prandy K. (1965). White-collar unionisation: a conceptual framework. *British Journal of Sociology*, **16**, 111–22

Boraston I., Clegg H.A. and Rimmer M. (1975). *Workplace and Union: A Study of Local Relationships in Fourteen Trade Unions*. Oxford: Heinemann

Cameron S. (1987). Trade unions and productivity: theory and evidence. *Industrial Relations Journal*, **18**(3), 170–6

Childs P. (1985). Work and career expectations of insurance company employees and the impact on unionisation. *Sociology*, **19**, 125–35

Clack G. (1966). *Industrial Relations in a British Car Factory*. Cambridge: Cambridge University Press

Clegg H.A. (1976). *Trade Unions Under Collective Bargaining: A Theory Based on Comparisons of Six Countries*. Oxford: Blackwell

Clegg H.A. (1979). *The Changing System of Industrial Relations in Great Britain*. Oxford: Blackwell

Crouch C. (1982). *Trade unions: The Logic of Collective Action*. London: Fontana

Daniel W.W. (1977). *The Next Stage of Incomes Policy*. London: P.E.P. Report No. 568

Daniel W.W. and Millward N. (1983). *Workplace Industrial Relations: The DE/ESRC/PSI/ACAS Surveys*. London: Heinemann

Dickson T., McLachlan H.V., Prior P. and Swale K. (1988). Big Blue and the unions: IBM, individualism and trade union strategy. *Work, Employment and Society*, **2**(4), 506–20

DOE (1971). *The Reform of Collective Bargaining at Plant and Company Level*. London: HMSO Manpower Paper No. 5

Donaldson L. and Warner M. (1974). Bureaucratic and electoral control in occupational interest associations. *Sociology*, **8**, 47–57

Edelstein J.D. and Warner M. (1975). *Comparative Union Democracy: Organization and Opposition in British and American Trade Unions*. London: Allen and Unwin

Edwards C. and Heery E. (1985). The incorporation of workplace trade unionists: some evidence from the mining industry. *Sociology*, **19**, 345–63

Flanders A. (1970). *Management and Unions*. London: Faber and Faber

Goldthorpe J.H., Lockwood D., Bechofer F. and Platt J. (1968). *The Affluent Worker: Industrial Attitudes and Behaviour*. Cambridge: Cambridge University Press.

Guest D. and Dewe P. (1988). Why do workers belong to a trade union: a social psychological study in the U.K. electronics industry. *British Journal of Industrial Relations*, **26**(2), 184–94

Hawkins K. (1981). *Trade Unions*. London: Hutchinson

Hemingway J. (1978). *Conflict and Democracy: Studies in Trade Union Government*. Oxford: Oxford University Press

Howells J.M. and Brosnan A.E. (1970). The ability of managers and trade union officers to predict workers' preferences. *British Journal of Industrial Relations*, **8**(2), 237–51

Howells J.M. and Brosnan P. (1972). The ability to predict workers' preferences: a research note. *Human Relations*, **25**(3), 265–81

Hyman R. (1975). *Industrial Relations: A Marxist Introduction*. London: Macmillan

Hyman R. (1979). The politics of workplace trade unionism: recent tendencies and some problems for theory. *Capital and Class*, Summer, 54–67

Jackson M. (1982). *Trade Unions*. London: Longman

Jones P.R. (1981). Membership of associations and free riders. *Industrial Relations Journal*, **12**(1), 34–44

Kelly J. (1987). Trade unions through the recession 1980–1984. *British Journal of Industrial Relations*, **25**(2), 275–82

Lawler E.E. and Levin E. (1968). Union officers' perceptions of members' pay preferences. *Industrial and Labor Relations Review*, **24**(2), 509–17

Metcalf D. (1988) Trade unions and economic performance: the British evidence. In *Proceedings of Conference of the International Economic Association* (Dell'Aringa C. and Brunetta R., eds.), Venice. London: Macmillan

Michels R. (1915). *Political Parties: A Sociological Study of the Oligarchical Tendencies in Modern Democracy* English edn. London: Free Press

Millerson G. (1964). *The Qualifying Associations*. London: Routledge and Kegan Paul

Millward M. and Stevens M. (1986). *British Workplace Industrial Relations 1980–1984: The DE/ESRC/PSI/ACAS Surveys*. Aldershot: Gower

Moore R.J. (1980). The motivation to become a shop steward. *British Journal of Industrial Relations*, **18**(1), 91–8

Morell K. and Smith J. (1971). The white collar split. *Industrial Society*, August, 7–10

Neill A. (1988). Survival of the fittest. *Personnel Today*, August, 18–19

Nicholson N. (1976). The role of the shop steward: an empirical case study. *Industrial Relations Journal*, **7**(1), 15–26

Nolan P. and Marginson P. (1988). Skating on thin ice?: David Metcalf on trade unions and productivity. *Warwick Papers on Industrial Relations*, No. 22

Ogden S.G. (1981). The reform of collective bargaining: a managerial revolution?. *Industrial Relations Journal*, **12**(5), 30–42

Olson M. (1965). *The Logic of Collective Action: Public Goods and the Theory of Groups*. Harvard MA: Harvard University Press

Pedler M.J. (1973). Shop stewards as leaders. *Industrial Relations Journal*, **3**(1), 43–60

Pelling H. (1987). *A History of British Trade Unionism* 4th edn. Harmondsworth: Pelican.

Prandy K., Stewart A. and Blackburn R.M. (1983). *White-Collar Unionism*. London: Macmillan

Roberts B.C. (1987). Mr. Hammond's cherry tree: the morphology of union survival. *Institute of Economic Affairs*, Occasional Paper No.76

Roberts B.C. (1988). A new era in industrial relations. In *New Departures in Industrial Relations: Developments in the U.S., U.K., and Canada*. British-North American Committee, Occasional Paper, 11–30

Rollinson D. (1991). Attitudes of trade union activists: some evidence on the theory of workplace incorporation. *Work, Employment and Society*, **5**(1), 81–100

Routh G. (1966). White collar unions in the United Kingdom. In *White Collar Trade Unions* (Sturmthal A., ed.), pp. 165–204. Urbana: University of Illinois Press.

Schuller T. and Robertson D. (1983). How representatives spend their time: shop steward activity and membership contact. *British Journal of Industrial Relations*, **21**(3), 330–42

Shafto T. (1983). The growth of shop steward management functions. In *Industrial Relations and Management Strategy* (Thurley K. and Wood S., eds.), pp. 45–52. Cambridge: Cambridge University Press

Spencer B. (1981). Shop steward resistance in the recession. *Employee Relations*. **7**(5), 12–16

Terry M. (1983). Shop steward development and managerial strategies. In *Industrial Relations in Britain* (Bain G.S., ed.), pp. 67–94. Oxford: Blackwell

Terry M. (1986). How do we know if shop stewards are getting weaker? *British Journal of Industrial Relations*, **24**(2), 169-79.

TULRA (1974). *Trade Union and Labour Relations Act (1974)*. London: HMSO.

Turner H.A. (1962). *Trade Union Growth, Structure and Policy*. London: Allen and Unwin

Turner H.A., Roberts G. and Roberts D. (1977). *Management Characteristics and Labour Conflict: A Study of Managerial Organization, Attitudes and Industrial Relations*. Cambridge: Cambridge University Press

Willman P. (1980). Leadership and trade union principles: some problems of management sponsorship and independence. *Industrial Relations Journal*, **11**(1), 39–49

Chapter 4

Adams J.S. (1963). Towards an understanding of inequity. *Journal of Abnormal and Social Psychology*, **67**, 425–31

Bamber G. (1976). Trade unions for managers. *Personnel Review*, **5**(4), 36–41

Bradley K. and Hill S. (1987). Quality circles and managerial interests. *Industrial Relations*, **26**(1), 68–82

Brown W. (1972). A consideration of custom and practice. *British Journal of Industrial Relations*, **10**(1), 42–61

Brown W. (1986). The changing role of trade unions in the management of labour. *British Journal of Industrial Relations*, **24**(2), 161–8

Cappelli P. and McKersie R. (1987). Management strategy and the redesign of workrules. *Journal of Management Studies*, **24**(5), 441–62

Child J. (1972). Organizational structure, environment and performance. *Sociology*, **6**, 1–22

Child J. (1986). *Organization: A Guide to Problems and Practice*. London: Harper and Row

Dickson T., McLachlan H.V., Prior P. and Swales K. (1988). Big Blue and the unions: IBM, individualism and trade union strategy. *Work, Employment and Society*, **2**(4), 506–20

Dill W.R., Hilton T.L. and Rietman W.R. (1962). *The New Managers*. New York: Prentice-Hall

Fox A. (1974). *Beyond Contract: Work Power and Trust Relations*. London: Faber and Faber

Gospel H.F. (1973). An approach to a theory of the firm in industrial relations. *British Journal of Industrial Relation*, **11**(2), 211–28

Gowler D. and Legge K. (1986). Personnel and paradigms: four perspectives on the future. *Industrial Relations Journal*, **17**(3), 225–35

Guest D. (1987). Human resource management and industrial relations. *Journal of Management Studies*, **24** (5), 503–21

Hamill J. (1983). The labour relations practices of foreign-owned and indigenous firms. *Employee Relations*, **5**(1), 14–15

Herzberg F. (1966). *Work and the Nature of Man*. New York: World Publishing Company

Lawrence P. R. and Lorsch J.W. (1967). *Organization and Environment*. Harvard MA: Harvard University Press

Mansfield R., Poole M., Blyton P. and Frost P. (1981). *The British Manager in Profile*. London: British Institute of Management

Marchington M. (1982). *Managing in Industrial Relations*. Maidenhead: McGraw-Hill

Maslow A. (1970). *Motivation and Personality* 3rd edn. New York: Harper and Row

McGregor D. (1960). *The Human Side of Enterprise*. New York: McGraw-Hill

Paul W.J. and Robertson K.B. (1970). *Job Enrichment and Employee Motivation*. Aldershot: Gower

Poole M., Mansfield R., Frost P. and Blyton P. (1982). Managerial attitudes and behaviour in industrial relations: evidence from a national survey. *British Journal of Industrial Relations*, **20**(3), 285-307

Purcell J. (1987). Mapping management styles in industrial relations. *Journal of Management Studies*, **24**(5), 535–48

Purcell J. and Sisson K. (1983). Strategies and practice in industrial relations. In *Industrial Relations in Britain* (Bain G.S., ed.), pp. 95–120. Oxford: Blackwell

Purcell J., Marginson P., Edwards P. and Sisson K., (1987). The industrial relations practices of multiplant foreign owned firms. *Industrial Relations Journal*, **18**(3), 130–7

Reddish H. (1967). From *Memoranda of Evidence submitted by Sir Halford Reddish, F.C.A., Chairman and Managing Director, The Rugby Portland Cement Co. Ltd., in advance of the Oral Hearing*. Royal Commision on Trade Unions and Employers Associations, Commission/s Reference WE/383

Roethlisberger F.J. and Dixon W.J. (1939).

Management and the Worker. Harvard MA: Harvard University Press

Salamon M. (1987). *Industrial Relations: Theory and Practice*. London: Prentice-Hall

Storey J. (1976). Workplace collective bargaining and managerial prerogatives. *Industrial Relations Journal*, **7**(3), 40–5

Storey J. (1983). *Managerial Prerogative and the Question of Control*. London: Routledge and Kegan Paul

Taylor F.W. (1947). *Scientific Management*. New York: Harper and Row

Terry M. (1977). The inevitable growth of informality. *British Journal of Industrial Relations*, **15**(1), 75–90

Torrington D. and Hall L. (1987). *Personnel Management: A New Approach*. London: Prentice-Hall

Tyson S. (1987). The management of the personnel function. *Journal of Management Studies*, **24**(5), 523–32

Vroom V.H. (1964). *Work and Motivation*. New York: Wiley

Walton R.E. (1985). From control to commitment in the workplace. *Harvard Business Review*, March/April, 77–84

Wilson J.G. (1966). Innovation in organizations: notes towards a theory. In *Approaches to Organizational Design* (Thompson J.D., ed.), pp. 193–218. Pittsburg PA: University of Pittsburg Press

Chapter 5

Armstrong E.A.G. (1969). *Industrial Relations*. London: Harrap

Armstrong E.A.G. (1985) Evaluating the advisory work of ACAS. *Employment Gazette,* April, 143–7

Ball A. (1981). *British Political Parties*. London: Macmillan

Bridgford J. and Stirling J. (1991). Britain in social Europe: industrial relations and 1992. *Industrial Relations Journal*, **22**(4), 263–72

Clegg H.A. (1979). *The Changing System of Industrial Relations in Great Britain*. Oxford: Blackwell

Crouch C. (1982). *The Politics of Industrial Relations* 2nd edn. London: Fontana

Denham D.J. (1990). Unfair dismissal law and the legitimation of managerial control. *Capital and Class*, **41**(Summer), 83–101

EEC (1974). The social action programme. *Bulletin of the European Community*, **10**, 370–80

EEC (1983a). Amended proposal for a Council directive on procedures for informing and consulting employees. *European Economic Commission*. Brussels: CEC

EEC (1983b). Amended proposals for a Council directive on voluntary part-time work. *Official Journal of the European Communities*, **22**

Evans S. (1987). The use of injunctions in industrial disputes May 1984–April 1987. *British Journal of Industrial Relations*, **25**(3), 419-35

Hendy J. and Eady J. (1991). Creeping assault on worker's rights. *The Guardian*, 9th August

Jones M. and Dickins L. (1983). Resolving industrial disputes: the role of ACAS conciliation. *Industrial Relations Journal*, **14**(1), 14–25

Kahn-Freund O. (1960). The legal framework. In *The System of Industrial Relations in Great Britain* (Flanders A. and Clegg H.A., eds.), pp. 44–58. Oxford: Blackwell

Keegan V. (1991) Europe and the decade of disillusionment. *The Observer*, 8th December

Lewis R. (1983). Collective labour law. In *Industrial Relations in Britain* (Bain G.S., ed.), pp. 361–92, Oxford: Blackwell

LRD (1985a). *Fall in Company Funds to the Tories*. London: Labour Research Department, August

LRD (1985b). *Company Cash for the Liberals*. London: Labour Research Department, May

Mackie K.J. (1989). Changes in the law since 1979: an overview. In *A Handbook of Industrial Relations Practice* (Towers B., ed.), pp. 265–99. London: Kogan Page

Mazey S. (1988). European Community action on behalf of women: the limits of legislation. *Journal of Common Market Studies*, **27**(1), 63–84

Mill C. (1992). Was Maastrict the end of the chapter? *Personnel Management*, February, 14–15

Porket J.L. (1978). Industrial relations and participation in management in the Soviet-type communist system. *British Journal of Industrial Relations*, **16**(1), 70–81

Roberts I. (1992). Industrial relations and the European Community. *Industrial Relations Journal*, **23**(1), 3–13

Thomson A.W.J. and Beaumont P.B. (1978). *Public Sector Bargaining: A Study of Relative Gain*. Farnborough: Saxon House

Towers B. (1992). Two speed ahead: social Europe and the UK after Maastrict. *Industrial Relations Journal*, **23**(2), 83–9

Weeks B., Mellish M., Dickens L. and Lloyd J. (1971). *Industrial Relations and the Limits of the Law: The Industrial Effects of the Industrial Relations Act 1971*. Oxford: Blackwell

Winchester D. (1983). Industrial relations in the public sector. In *Industrial Relations in Britain* (Bain G.S., ed.), pp. 155–78. Oxford: Blackwell

Wolf J. (1991). Britain warned of dangers of isolation in Europe. *The Guardian*, 14th December

Chapter 6

ACAS (1977). *Disciplinary Practice and Procedures in Employment*. London: Advisory, Conciliation and Arbitration Service

ACAS (1987). *Discipline at Work: The ACAS Advisory Handbook*. London: Advisory, Conciliation and Arbitration Service

ACAS (1989). *Annual Report*. London: Advisory, Conciliation and Arbitration Service

Aikin O. (1984). Law at work: a need to reorganise. *Personnel Management*, February, 37–41

Ashdown R.T. and Baker K.H. (1973). *In Working Order*. Department of Employment Manpower Paper No. 6. London: H.M.S.O.

Barrett-Howard E. and Tyler T.R. (1986). Procedural justice as a criterion in allocation decisions. *Journal of Personality and Social Psychology*, **50**(2), 296–304

Beck C.E. and Beck E.A. (1986). The managers open door and communications climate. *Business Horizons*, January/February, 15–19

Bemmels B. (1991). Attribution theory and discipline arbitration. *Industrial and Labor Relations Review*, **44**(3), 548–61

Bemmels B., Reshef Y. and Stratton-Devine K. (1991). The roles of supervisors, employees and stewards in grievance initiation. *Industrial and Labor Relations Review*, **45**(1), 15–30

Beyer J.M. and Trice H.M. (1981). Managerial ideologies and the use of discipline. *Academy of Management Proceedings*, 259–63

Briggs S. (1981). The grievance procedure and organizational health. *Personnel Journal*, June, 471–4

Dalton D.R. and Todor W.D. (1981). Grievances filed and the role of the union stewards vs the rank and file member: an empirical test. *International Review of Applied Psychology*, **30**, 199–207

Dickens L. (1982). Unfair dismissal law: a decade of disillusion?. *Personnel Management*, February, 25–8

Edwards P.K. and Whitston C. (1989). Industrial discipline, the control of attendance and the subordination of labour: towards an integrated perspective. *Work, Employment and Society*, **3**(1), 1–28

Fleishman E.A. and Harris E.F. (1962). Patterns of leadership behaviour related to employee grievances and turnover. *Personnel Psychology*, **15**, 43–56

Fogler R., Rosenfield D. and Robinson T. (1983). Relative deprivation and procedural justifications. *Journal of Personality and Social Psychology*, **45**(2), 268–73

Fox A. (1974). *Beyond Contract: Work Power and Trust Relations*. London: Faber and Faber

Goodstat B. and Kipniss D. (1970). Situational effects on the use of power. *Journal of Applied Psychology*, **54**(3), 201–7

Gordon M.E. and Bowlby R.L. (1985). Propositions about grievance settlements: finally, consultation with grievants. *Personnel Psychology*, **41**, 107–23

Gough H.G. (1948). A sociological theory of psychopathy. *American Journal of Sociology*, **153**, 359–66

Greer C.R. and Labig C.E. (1987). Employee reactions to disciplinary action. *Human Relations*, **40**(8), 507–42

Guest D. (1987). Human resource management and industrial relations. *Journal of Management Studies*, **24**(2), 503–21

Henry S. (1987). Disciplinary pluralism: four models of private justice in the workplace. *Sociological Review*, **35**(2), 279–319

Hogan J. and Hogan R. (1989). How to measure employee reliability. *Journal of Applied Psychology*, **74**(2), 273–9

Huberman J. (1975). Discipline without punishment lives. *Harvard Business Review*, July/August, 6–8

ILO (1965). Examination of grievances and communications within the undertaking. In *International Labour Conference Report No. 7*, pp. 7–9. Geneva: International Labour Office

Kadzin A.E. (1986). *Behaviour Modification in Applied Settings*. New York: Dorsey

Klass B.S. and De Nisi A.S. (1989). Managerial reactions to employee dissent: the impact of grievance activity on performance ratings. *Academy of Management Journal*, **32**(4), 705–17

Kulick J.A. and Brown R. (1979). Frustration, attribution of blame aggression. *Journal of Experimental Social Psychology*, **15**, 183–94

Larwood L., Rand P. and Der Hovanessian A. (1979). Sex differences in response to simulated disciplinary cases. *Personnel Psychology*, **32**, 539–50

Maier N. and Danielson L. (1956). An evaluation of two approaches to discipline in industry. *Journal of Applied Psychology*, **40**(5), 319–23

Marsh A.I. and Evans E.O. (1973). *The Dictionary of Industrial Relations*. Cheltenham: Hutchison

McKersie R.B. (1964). Avoiding written grievances by problem solving: an outside view. *Personnel Psychology*, **17**, 367–79

Millward N. and Stevens M. (1986). *British Workplace Industrial Relations 1980–1984: The DE/ESRC/PSI/ACAS Surveys*. Aldershot: Gower

Mitchell T.R. and Wood R.E. (1980). Subordinate poor performance: a test of an attributional model. *Organizational Behaviour and Human Performance*, **25**, 123–38

Mulder F. (1971). Characteristics of violators of formal company rules. *Journal of Applied Psychology*, **55**(5), 500–602

Norsworthy J.R. and Zabala C.A. (1985). Worker attitudes, worker behavior, and productivity in the U.S. automobile industry, 1959–76. *Industrial and Labor Relations Review*, **38**(4), 544–7

O'Reilly C.A. and Weitz B.A. (1980). Managing marginal employees: the use of warnings and dismissals. *Administrative Science Quarterly*, **25**(4), 467–84

Ronan W.W. (1963). Work group attributes and grievance activity. *Journal of Applied Psychology*, **47**(1), 38–41

Salamon M. (1987). *Industrial Relations: Theory and Practice*. London: Prentice-Hall

Sayles L.R. (1958). *The Behaviour of Industrial Work Groups*. New York: Wiley

Singleton N. (1975). *Industrial Relations Procedures*. Department of Employment Manpower Paper No. 14. London: HMSO.

Swann J.P. (1981). Formal grievance procedures and non-union plants: do they really work? *Personnel Administrator*, August, 66–70

Terry M. (1977). The inevitable growth of informality. *British Journal of Industrial Relations*, **15**(1), 76–90

Thomson A.W.J. and Murray V.V. (1976). *Grievance Procedures*. Farnborough: Saxon House

Torrington D. and Hall L. (1987). *Personnel Management: A New Approach*. London: Prentice-Hall

Turner J.T. and Robinson J.W. (1972). A pilot study of the validity of grievance settlement as a predictor of union management relationships. *Journal of Industrial Relations*, **14**, 314–22

Walton R.E. (1985). From control to commitment in the workplace. *Harvard Business Review*, March/April, 77–84

Wheeler H.M. (1976). Punishment theory and industrial discipline. *Industrial Relations*, **15**(2), 235–43

Zipf S.G. (1960). Resistance and conformity under reward and punishment. *Journal of Abnormal and Social Psychology*, **6**(1), 102–09

Chapter 7

ACAS (1972). *Disclosure of Information to Trade Unions for the Purposes of Collective Bargaining*. London: Advisory, Conciliation and Arbitration Service

ACAS (1990). *Workplace Communications*. Advisory Booklet No. 8. London: Advisory, Conciliation and Arbitration Service

Argyle M. (1973). *Social Interaction*. London: Tavistock

Argyle M. (1975). *Bodily Communication*. London: Methuen

CIR (1973a). *Small Firms and the Code of Industrial Relations Practice*. Commission on Industrial Relations, Report No. 69. London: HMSO

CIR (1973b). *Communications and Collective Bargaining*. Commission on Industrial Relations, Report No. 39. London: HMSO

Cook M. (1979). *Perceiving Others*. London: Methuen

DOE (1972). *Industrial Relations Code of Practice*. Department of Employment. London: HMSO

Ekman P. and Friesen W.V. (1975). *Unmasking the Face*. New York: Prentice-Hall

EPA (1975). *Employment Protection Act* (1975). London: HMSO

Foy N. (1983). Networkers of the world unite. *Personnel Management*, March, 16–19

Goss D.M. (1988). Social harmony and the small firm: a reappraisal. *Sociological Review*, **36**(1), 114–32

Grummit J. (1983). *Team Briefing*. London: The Industrial Society

Hussey R. and Marsh A. (1983). *Disclosure of Information and Employee Reporting*. Aldershot: Gower

Keltner J. (1970). *Interpersonal Speech Communication*. Belmont CA: Wadsworth

Lengel R.H. and Draft R.L. (1988). The selection of communication media as an executive skill. *Academy of Management Executive*, August, 225–32

Marchington M., Parker P., Prestwich A. (1989). Problems with team briefing in practice. *Employee Relations*, **11**(4), 21–30

Middleton R. (1983). *A Briefer's Guide to Team Briefing*. London: The Industrial Society

Mitchell F., Sams K. and White P.J. (1987). Research note: employee involvement and the law: section 1 of the 1982 Employment Act. *Industrial Relations Journal*, **18**(3), 362–7

Moore R. (1980). Information to unions: use or abuse?. *Personnel Management*, May, 33–7

Ostell A., MacFarlane I. and Jackson A. (1980). Evaluating the impact of a communication exercise in an industrial works. *Industrial Relations Journal*, **11**(2), 37–48

Pincus J.D. (1986). Communication, job satisfaction and job performance. *Human Communications Research*, Spring, 395–419

Rainnie A. and Scott M.G. (1986). Industrial relations in the small firm. In *The Survival of the Small Firm* (Curran J., ed.), pp. 98–117. Aldershot: Gower

Rostnow R.L. (1980). Psychology in rumour reconsidered. *Psychological Bulletin*, May, 578–91

Secord P.F. and Blackman C.W. (1964). *Social Psychology*. New York: McGraw-Hill

Schramm W. (1953). How communication works. In *The Process and Effects of Mass Communication* (Schramm W., ed.), pp. 2–22, Urbana: University of Illinois Press

TUC (1971) *Good Industrial Relations*. London: Trades Union Congress

Chapter 8

Alutto J.A. and Acito F. (1974). Decisional participation and sources of job satisfaction: a study of manufacturing personnel. *Academy of Management Journal*, **17**(1), 160–7

Alutto J.A. and Belassco, J.A (1972). A typology for participation in organizational decision making. *Administrative Science Quarterly*, **17**, 117–25

Barrick M.R. and Alexander R.A. (1987). A review of quality circle efficacy and the existence of positive findings bias. *Personnel Psychology*, **40**, 579–92

Bassett P. (1987). Consultation and the right to manage. *British Journal of Industrial Relations*, **25**(2), 283–6

Bate S.P. and Murphy A.K. (1981). Can joint consultation become employee participation? *Journal of Management Studies*, **18**(4), 389–409

Bennis W. (1966). *Changing Organizations*. New York: McGraw-Hill

Board of Trade (1977). *Report of the Committee of Enquiry on Industrial Democracy (Bullock Committee)*. London: HMSO

Bradley K. and Hill S. (1983). After Japan: the quality circle transplant and productive efficiency. *British Journal of Industrial Relations*, **21**(4), 291–311.

Bradley K. and Hill S. (1987). Quality circles and managerial interests. *Industrial Relations*, **21**(1), 68–82

Brannen P. (1983). *Authority and Participation in Industry*. London: Batsford.

Brannen P., Batstone E., Fatchett D. and White P. (1976). *The Worker Directors*. London: Hutchinson.

Burpa-Di Gregoria M.Y. and Dickson J. (1983). Experience with quality circles in the south west United States. *Employee Relations*, **5**(2), 12–16

Chadwick M. (1983). The recession and industrial relations: a factory approach. *Employee Relations*, **5**(5), 5–12

Chamberlain N.W. and Kuhn J.W. (1966). *Collective Bargaining*. New York: McGraw-Hill.

Chell E. and Cox D. (1979). Worker directors and collective bargaining. *Industrial Relations Journal*, **10**(3), 25–31

Clegg H.A. (1974). Trade unions as an opposition which can never become a government. In *Trade Unions* (McCarthy W.E.J., ed.), pp. 74–86. Harmondsworth: Penguin

Daniel W.W. and Millward N. (1983). *Workplace Industrial Relations: The DE/ESRC/PSI/ACAS Surveys*. Oxford: Heinemann

Dickson J.W. (1980). Perceptions of direct and indirect participation. *Journal of Applied Psychology*, **66**(2), 226–32

Dickson J.W. (1981a). Participation as a means of organizational control. *Journal of Management Studies*, **18**(1), 159–76

Dickson J.W. (1981b). The relation of direct and indirect participation. *Industrial Relations Journal*, **12**(4), 27–35

Dewe P., Dunn S. and Richardson R. (1988). Employee share option schemes: why workers are attracted to them. *British Journal of Industrial Relations*, **26**(1), 1–20

DOE (1987). *Worker Directors in Private Manufacturing Industry in Great Britain*. Department of Employment, Research Paper No. 29. London: HMSO

Drago R. (1988). Quality circle survival: an exploratory analysis. *Industrial Relations*, **27**(3), 336–51

Drago R. and Wooden M. (1991). The determinants of participatory management. *British Journal of Industrial Relations*, **29**(2), 177–204

Driscoll J.W. (1978). Trust and participation in organizational decision making as predictors of satisfaction. *Academy of Management Journal*, **21**(1), 44–56

Duncan C. (1988). Why profit related pay will fail. *Industrial Relations Journal*, **19**(3), 186–200

Farnham D. and Pimlott J. (1987). *Understanding Industrial Relations*. London: Cassell

Griffin R.W. (1988). Consequences of quality circles in an industrial setting: a longitudinal assessment. *Academy of Management Journal*, **31**(2), 338–58

Guest D. (1987). Human resource management and industrial relations. *Journal of Management Studies*, **24**(5), 502-21

Hackman J.R. and Oldham G. (1980). *Motivation Through the Design of Work*. Reading MA: Addison-Wesley

Hanson C. and Rathkey P. (1984). Industrial democracy: a post-Bullock shopfloor view. *British Journal of Industrial Relations*, **22**(2), 154–68

Herzberg F. (1966). *Work and the Nature of Man*. New York: World Publishing Company

IPA/IPM (1983a). *Employee Involvement and Participation: Principles and Standard of Practice*. London: Industrial Participation Association/Institute of Personnel Management

IPA/IPM (1983b). *Employee Involvement and Participation: Action Guide*. London: Industrial Participation Association/Institute of Personnel Management

IPM (1981). *Practical Participation and Involvement, 2 Representative Structures*. London: Institute of

Personnel Management

Ivancevich J.M. (1977). Different goal setting treatments and their effects on performance and job satisfaction. *Academy of Management Journal*, **20**(3), 406–19

Joyce P. and Woods A. (1984). Joint consultation in Britain: results of a recent survey during the recession. *Employee Relations*, **6**(3), 2–7

Kelly J. and Kelly C. (1991). Them and us: the social psychology of the new industrial relations. *British Journal of Industrial Relations*, **29**(1), 25–48

Lawler E.E. and Mohrman S.A. (1987). Quality circles: after the honeymoon. *Organizational Dynamics*, **15**(4), 42–54

Levitan S.A. and Johnson, C.N. (1983). Labor and management: the illusion of cooperation. *Harvard Business Review*, September/October, 8–16

Lewin K. (1951). *Field Theory in Social Science*. New York: Harper and Row

Likert R. (1967). *The Human Organization*. New York: McGraw-Hill

Lischeron J.A. and Wall T.D. (1975). Employee participation: an experimental field study. *Human Relations*, **28**(9), 863–84

Long R.J. and Warner M. (1987). Organizations, participation and recession: an analysis of recent evidence. *Relations Industrielles*, **44**(4), 65–91

Marchington M. and Armstrong R. (1981). A case for consultation. *Employee Relations*, **3**(1), 10–16

Marchington M. and Armstrong R. (1983). Shop steward organization and joint consultation. *Personnel Review*, **12**(1), 24–31

Marchington M. and Armstrong R. (1986). The nature of the new joint consultation. *Industrial Relations Journal*, **17**(2), 158–70

Marks M.L., Hackett E.J., Mirvis P.H. and Grady, J.F. (1982). Employee participation in a quality circle program: impact on quality of work life, productivity and absenteeism. *Journal of Applied Psychology*, **71**(1), 61–9

Maslow A. (1970). *Motivation and Personality*, 3rd edn. New York: Harper and Row

McGregor D. (1960). *The Human Side of Enterprise*. New York: McGraw-Hill

McKersie R.B. (1987). The transformation of American industrial relations: the abridged story. *Journal of Management Studies,* **24**(5), 433–40

Millward N. and Stevens M. (1986). *British Workplace Industrial Relations 1980–1984: The DE/ESRC/PSI/ACAS Surveys.* Aldershot: Gower

Mitchell D.J.B. (1987). The share economy and industrial relations. *Industrial Relations,* **26**(1), 1–17

Mitchell T.R. (1979). Organizational behaviour. *Annual Review of Psychology,* **30**, 243–81

Mohrman S.A. and Lawler E.E. (1988). Parallel participation structures. *Public Administration Quarterly,* **13**(2), 255–72

Nuti D. M. (1987). Profit sharing and employment: claims and overclaims. *Industrial Relations,* **26**(1), 18–29

Pateman C. (1970). *Participation and Democratic Theory.* Cambridge: Cambridge University Press

Poole M. (1988). Factors affecting the development of employee financial participation in contemporary Britain: evidence from a national survey. *British Journal of Industrial Relations,* **26**(1), 21–36

Ramsay H. (1977). Cycles of control: worker participation in sociological and historical perspective. *Sociology,* ll, 481–506

Ramsay H. (1991). Reinventing the wheel? A review of the development and performance of employee involvement. *Human Resource Management Journal,* **1**(4), 1–22

Rosen C. and Quarrey M. (1987). How well is employee ownership working? *Harvard Business Review,* September/October, 126–32

Rosenberg R.D. and Rosenstein E. (1980). Participation and productivity: an empirical study. *Industrial and Labor Relations Review,* **33**(3), 355–67

Russell S. and Dale S. (1989). Quality circles – a broader perspective. *ACAS Work Research Unit Occasional Paper No. 43.* London: Advisory, Conciliation and Arbitration Service

Steele R.P. and Lloyd R.F. (1988). Cognitive, affective and behavioural outcomes of participation in quality circles: conceptual and empirical findings. *Journal of Applied Behavioural Science,* **24**(1), 1–17

Steele R.P. and Shane G.S. (1986). Evaluation research on quality circles: technical and analytical implications. *Human Relations,* **39**(5), 449–68

Steele R.P., Mento A.J., Dilla B.L., Ovalle N.K. and Lloyd R.F. (1985). Factors influencing the success and failure of two quality circle programs. *Journal of Management,* **11**(1), 99–119

Vanek J. (1970). *The General Theory of Labour-Managed Market Economies.* Cornell: Cornell University Press

Vroom V. H. (1964). *Work and Motivation.* New York: Wiley

Wagner J.A. and Gooding R.Z. (1987). Shared influence and organizational behaviour: a meta analysis of situational variables expected to moderate participation–outcome relationships. *Academy of Management Journal,* **30**(3), 524–41

Walton R.E. (1985). From control to commitment in the workplace. *Harvard Business Review,* March/April, 77–85

Warner M. (1983). Different sides of the fence?: a study of managerial and shop steward perceptions of employee influence. *Personnel Review,* **12**(1), 33–7

Weitzman M.L. (1984). *The Share Economy.* Harvard: Harvard University Press

Wilson F. (1989). Productive efficiency and the employment relationship – the case of quality circles. *Employee Relations,* **11**(1), 27–32

Wilson N., Cable J.R. and Peel M.J. (1990). Quit rates and the impact of participation, profit sharing and unionisation: empirical evidence from U.K. engineering firms. *British Journal of Industrial Relations,* **28**(2), 197–213

Chapter 9

ACAS (1982), *Developments in Harmonisation, Discussion Paper No. 1.* London: Advisory, Conciliation and Arbitration Service

Bassett P. (1986). *Strike Free: New Industrial Relations in Britain.* London: Macmillan

Brewster C. (1989). Collective agreements. In *A Handbook of Industrial Relations Practice* (Towers B., ed.), pp. 112–31. London: Kogan Page

Brown W. (1972). A consideration of custom and practice. *British Journal of Industrial Relations*, **10**(1), 42–61

Brown W. (1987). Pay determination: British workplace industrial relations 1980–84. *British Journal of Industrial Relations*, **25**(2), 291–4

Chamberlain N.W. and Kuhn J.W. (1965). *Collective Bargaining*. New York: McGraw-Hill

Claydon T. (1989). Union derecognition in Britain in the 1980s. *British Journal of Industrial Relations*, **27**(2), 214–24

Clegg H.A. (1951). *Industrial Democracy and Nationalisation*. Oxford: Blackwell

Clegg H.A. (1976). *Trade Unionism under Collective Bargaining: A Theory Based on Comparisons of Six Countries*. Oxford: Blackwell

Clegg H.A. (1979). *The Changing System of Industrial Relations in Great Britain*. Oxford: Blackwell

Cooke W.N. (1989). Improving productivity and quality through collaboration. *Industrial Relations*, **28**(2), 299–319

Creigh S.W. and Makeham P. (1982). Strike incidence in industrial countries: an analysis. *Australian Bulletin of Labour*, **8**(3), 139–55

Daniel W.W. and Millward N. (1983). *Workplace Industrial Relations: the DE/ESRC/PSI/ACAS Surveys*. Oxford: Heinemann

Dastmalchian A., Blyton P. and Abdollahyan R. (1982). Industrial relations climate and company effectiveness. *Personnel Review*, **11**(1), 35–9

Deaton D.R. and Beaumont P.B. (1980). The determinants of bargaining structure: some large scale survey evidence. *British Journal of Industrial Relations*, **18**(2), 206–16

Dubin R. (1954). Constructive aspects of conflict. In *Industrial Conflict* (Kornhauser A., Dubin R. and Ross A, eds.), pp. 37-47. New York: McGraw-Hill

Dubin R. (1957). Power and union management relations. *Administrative Science Quarterly*, **12**, 60–81

Dubin R. (1973). Attachment to work and union militancy. *Industrial Relations*, **12**, 51–64

Dyer L., Lipsky D.B. and Kochan T.A. (1977). Union attitudes towards management cooperation. *Industrial Relations*, **16**(2), 163–72

EPA (1975). *Employment Protection Act (1975)*. London: HMSO

Farnham D. and Pimlott J. (1987). *Understanding Industrial Relations* 3rd edn. London: Cassell

Flanders A. (1964). *The Fawley Productivity Agreements*. London: Faber and Faber

Flanders A. (1968). Collective bargaining: a theoretical analysis. *British Journal of Industrial Relations*, **6**(1), 1–26

Fox A. (1975). Collective bargaining: Flanders and the Webbs. *British Journal of Industrial Relations*, **13**(2), 151–74

Goodrich C.L. (1975). *The Frontier of Control*. London: Pluto Press

Gregory M. (1986). The no strike deal in action. *Personnel Management*, December, 21–7

Harbison F. and Coleman J. (1951) *Goals and Strategy in Collective Bargaining*. New York: Harper

Hawkins K. (1979). The institution of collective bargaining. In *Industrial Relations: A Social Psychological Approach* (Stephenson G.M. and Brotherton C.J., eds.), pp. 157–80. Chichester: Wiley

Jenkins C. and Sherman B. (1977). *Collective Bargaining*. London: Routledge and Kegan Paul

Kinnie N. (1985). Changing management strategies in industrial relations. *Industrial Relations Journal*, **16**(4), 17–24

Kinnie N. (1986). Patterns of industrial relations management. *Employee Relations*, **8**(2), 17–21

Kinnie N. (1987). Bargaining within the enterprise: centralised or decentralised. *Journal of Management Studies*, **24**(5), 463–77

Lansbury R. and Davis E. (1987). Australian industrial relations. In *International Comparative Industrial Relations* (Bamber G. and Lansbury R., eds.), pp. 97–117. London: Allen and Unwin

Lewis R. (1990). Strike free deals and pendulum arbitration. *British Journal of Industrial Relations*, **28**(1), 32–56

Marsh A. (1966). Disputes procedures in British industry. *Royal Commission on Trade Unions and Employers Associations, Research Papers 2*. London: HMSO

Martin J. (1980). Federal union management

relations: a longitudinal study. *Public Administration Review*, September/October, 434–42

Martin J.E. and Biasatti L.L. (1979). A hierarchy of important elements in union management relations. *Journal of Management*, **5**(2), 229–40

McKersie R.B. and Hunter L.C. (1973). *Pay, Productivity and Collective Bargaining*. London: Macmillan

Millward N. and Stevens S. (1986). *British Workplace Industrial Relations 1980–84: the DE/ESRC/PSI/ACAS Surveys*. Aldershot: Gower

Ogden S.G. (1981). The reform of collective bargaining: a managerial revolution? *Industrial Relations Journal*, **12**(5), 30–42

Purcell J. (1979). The lessons of the commission on industrial relations: attempts to reform British workplace industrial relations. *Industrial Relations Journal*, **10**(2), 9–22

Purcell J. and Gray A. (1986). Corporate personnel departments and the management of industrial relations: two case studies in ambiguity. *Journal of Management Studies*, **23**(2), 205–23

Purcell J. and Sisson K. (1983). Strategies and practice in the management of industrial relations. In *Industrial Relations in Britain* (Bain G.S., ed.), pp. 95–120. Oxford: Blackwell

Roberts C. (ed). (1985). *Harmonisation: Whys and Wherefores*. London: IPM

Rollinson D.J. (1987). *Approaches to issues of job regulation*. Ph.D Thesis, University of Aston

Schuster M. (1983). The impact of union–management cooperation on productivity and employment. *Industrial and Labour Relations Review*, **36**(3), 415–30

Storey J. (1976). Workplace collective bargaining and managerial prerogatives. *Industrial Relations Journal*, **7**(3), 40–55

Terry M. (1977). The inevitable growth of informality. *British Journal of Industrial Relations*, **15**(1), 76–90

Thompson M. (1987). Canadian industrial relations. In *International Comparative Industrial Relations* (Bamber G. and Lansbury R., eds.), pp. 80–96. London: Allen and Unwin

Tracy L. and Peterson R.B. (1977). Differences in reactions of union and management negotiators to the problem solving process. *Industrial Relations Journal*, **8**(4), 43–53

Treble J.G. (1986). How new is final offer arbitration? *Industrial Relations*, **25**(1), 92–4

Walton R.E. and McKersie R.B. (1965). *A Behavioural Theory of Labour Negotiations*. New York: McGraw-Hill

Webb S. and Webb B. (1902). *Industrial Democracy*. London: Longman

Chapter 10

Anthony P. (1977). *The Conduct of Industrial Relations*. London: Institute of Personnel Management

Anthony P. and Crichton A. (1969). *Industrial Relations and the Personnel Specialist*. London: Batsford

Balke W.M., Hammond K.R. and Meyer G.D. (1973). An alternative approach to labour-management relations. *Administrative Science Quarterly*, **18**, 311–27

Biasatti L.L. and Martin J.E. (1979). A measure of the quality of union management relationships. *Journal of Applied Psychology*, **64**(4), 387–90

Bonham M.G. (1971). Simulating international disarmament negotiations. *Journal of Conflict Resolution*, **15**, 299–315

Douglas A. (1962). *Industrial Peacemaking*. New York: Columbia University Press

Fisher R. (1969). *International Conflict for Beginners*. New York: Harper and Row

Fisher R. and Ury W. (1987). *Getting to Yes*. London: Arrow Books

Gottshalk A.W. and Mee L.G. (1972). The process of plant productivity bargaining. In *Bargaining for Change* (Towers B., Whittingham T.G. and Gottshalk A.W., eds.), pp. 152–76. London: Allen and Unwin

Harbison F. and Coleman J. (1951). *Goals and Strategy in Collective Bargaining*. New York: Harper

Hawkins K. (1979). *A Handbook of Industrial Relations Practice*. London: Kogan Page

Kennedy G., Benson J. and McMillan J. (1980). *Managing Negotiations*. London: Business Books

Kniveton B.H. (1974). Industrial negotiating: some training implications. *Industrial Relations Journal*, **5**(3), 27–37

Magenau J.M. and Pruitt D.G. (1979). The social psychology of bargaining. In *Industrial Relations: A Social Psychological Approach* (Stephenson G.M. and Brotherton C.J., eds.), pp. 197–222. Chichester: Wiley

Marsh A. (1974). *Contract Negotiation Handbook*. Aldershot: Gower

Morley I.E. (1979). Behavioural studies of industrial bargaining. In *Industrial Relations: A Social Psychological Approach* (Stephenson G.M. and Brotherton C.J., eds), pp. 211–36. Chichester: Wiley

Morley I.E. (1981). Negotiating and bargaining. In *Social Skills At Work* (Argyle M., ed), pp. 84–115. London: Methuen

Morley I.E. (1984). Bargaining and negotiating. In *Psychology for Managers* (Cooper C. and Makin P., eds.), pp. 214–34. London: Macmillan

Morley I.E. and Stephenson G.M. (1977). *The Social Psychology of Bargaining*. London: Allen and Unwin

Nicholson N. (1979). Industrial relations climate: a case study approach. *Personnel Review*, **8**(3), 20–5

Rackham N. and Carlisle J. (1978). The effective negotiator – part 2: planning for negotiations. *Journal of European Industrial Training*, **2**, 2–5

Rim Y. and Mannheim B.F. (1979). Factors related to attitudes of management and union representatives. *Personnel Psychology*, **64**(4), 387–90

Torrington D. (1972). *Face-to-Face*. Aldershot: Gower

Walton R.E. (1969). *Interpersonal Peacemaking: Consultations and Third Party Consultation*. Reading, MA: Addison-Wesley

Walton R.E. and McKersie R.B. (1965). *A Behavioural Theory of Labour Negotiations*. New York: McGraw-Hill

Chapter 11

Alderfer C. and Smith K.J. (1982). Studying intergroup relations embedded in organizations. *Administrative Science Quarterly*, **27**, 35–64

Armstrong J.F.B., Goodman J.D. and Hyman R. (1981). *Ideology and Shop Floor Industrial Relations*. London: Croon Helm

Batstone E., Boraston I. and Frenkel S. (1979). *Shop Stewards in Action: The Organization of Workplace Conflict and Accommodation*. Oxford: Blackwell

Bean R. (1975). Research note: the relationship between strikes and unorganised conflict in manufacturing industry. *British Journal of Industrial Relations*, **13**(1), 98–101

Britt D. and Galle O.R. (1972). Industrial conflict and unionisation. *American Sociological Review*, **37**, 46–57

Britt D. and Galle O.R. (1974). Antecedents of the shape of strikes: a comparative analysis. *American Sociological Review*, **39**, 642–51

Brown W. A. (1981). *The Changing Contours of British Industrial Relations: A Survey of Manufacturing Industry*. Oxford: Blackwell

Chinoy E. (1955). *Automobile Workers and the American Dream*. New York: Doubleday

Creigh S.W. and Makeham D. (1982). Strike in industrial countries: an analysis. *Australian Bulletin of Labour*, **8**(3), 139–49

Daniel W.W. and Millward N. (1983). *Workplace Industrial Relations: The DE/ESRC/PSI/ACAS Surveys*. Aldershot: Gower

DOE (1980). *Code of Practice, Picketing*. London: HMSO

Edwards P.K. (1983). The pattern of collective action. In *Industrial Relations in Britain* (Bain G.S., ed.), pp. 209–36. Oxford: Blackwell

Edwards P.K. (1987a). *Conflict at Work*. Oxford: Blackwell

Edwards P.K. (1987b). Industrial action 1980–84. *British Journal of Industrial Relations*, **13**(1), 98–101

Edwards P.K. and Bain G.S. (1988). Why are trade unions becoming more popular? Unions and public opinion in Britain. *British Journal of Industrial Relations*, **2**(3), 311–26

Edwards P.K. and Scullion H. (1982). *The Social Organization of Industrial Conflict: Control and Resistance in the Workplace*. Oxford: Blackwell

Evans S. (1983). The labour injunction revisited: picketing employees and the Employment Act 1980. *Industrial Law Journal*, **14**, 129–47

Evans S. (1985). Research note: the use of injunctions in industrial disputes. *British Journal of Industrial Relations*, **23**(2), 133–7

Evans S. (1987). The use of injunctions in industrial disputes, May 1984–April 1987. *British Journal of Industrial Relations*, **25**(3), 419–35

Fayol H. (1949). *General and Industrial Management*. London: Pitman

Flanders A. (1970). *Management and Unions*. London: Faber and Faber

Gennard J. (1981). The effects of strike activity on households. *British Journal of Industrial Relations*, **19**(3), 327–44

Gennard J. (1982). The financial costs and returns of strikes. *British Journal of Industrial Relations*, **20**(2), 247–56

Hansen A.H. (1921). Cycles of strikes. *American Economic Review*, **11**(4), 618–30

Hutt W.N. (1973). *The Strike Threat System*. London: Arlington House

Hyman R. (1984). *Strikes* 3rd edn. London: Fontana

Ingram P.N (1991). Changes in working practices in British manufacturing in the 1980s: a study of employee concessions made during wage negotiations. *British Journal of Industrial Relations*, **29**(1), 1–13

Katz D. and Kahn R.L. (1978). *The Social Psychology of Organizations* 2nd edn. New York: Wiley

Kelly J. and Nicholson N. (1980a). Strikes and other forms of industrial action. *Industrial Relations Journal*, **11**(5), 20–31

Kelly J. and Nicholson N. (1980b). The causation of strikes: a review of theoretical approaches and the potential contribution of social psychology. *Human Relations*, **33**(12), 853–83

Kerr A. and Sachdev S. (1992). Third among equals: an analysis of the 1989 ambulance dispute. *British Journal of Industrial Relations*, **30**(1), 127–43

Kerr C. and Seigal A. (1954). The inter-industry propensity to strike. In *Industrial Conflict*, (Kornhauser A., Dubin R. and Ross A., eds.), pp. 189–212. New York: McGraw-Hill

Knowles K.G.K. (1962). *Strikes*. Oxford: Oxford University Press

Kornhauser A. (1954). Human motivations underlying industrial conflict. In *Industrial Conflict*. (Kornhauser A., Dubin R. and Ross A., eds.), pp. 62–85. New York: McGraw-Hill

McConnel S. (1990). Cyclical fluctuations in strike activity. *Industrial and Labor Relations Review*, **44**(1), 130–43

McLean R.A. (1979). Inter-industry differences in strike activity. *Industrial Relations*, **18**(1), 103–9

Millward N. and Stevens S. (1986). *British Workplace Industrial Relations 1980-1984: The DE/ESRC/PSI/ACAS Surveys*. Oxford: Heinemann

Pfeffer J. (1981). *Power in Organizations*. Marshfield MA: Pitman

Purcell J., Dalgleish L., Harrison J., Lonsdale I., McConaghy I. and Robertson A. (1978). Power from technology: computer staff and industrial relations. *Personnel Review*, **7**(1), 31–9

Robbins S. (1979). *Organizational Behaviour*. London: Prentice-Hall

Ross A.M. and Hartman P.T. (1960). *Changing Patterns of Industrial Conflict*. New York: Wiley

Sayles L.R. (1958). *Behaviour of Work Groups*. New York: Wiley

Smith C.T.B., Clifton R., Makeham P., Creigh S.W. and Burn R.V. (1978). *Strikes in Britain*. Department of Employment, Manpower Paper No. 15, London: HMSO

Terry M. (1982). Organising a fragmented workforce: shop stewards in local government. *British Journal of Industrial Relations*, **20**(1), 1–19

Thomas C. (1976). Strategy for a sit-in. *Personnel Management*, January, 32–5

Urwick L. (1943). *The Elements of Administration*. New York: Harper

Von Clauswitz C. (1986). *On War*. English translation, Harmondsworth: Penguin

Walker C.R. and Guest R.H. (1957). *Man on the Assembly Line*. New Haven: Yale University Press

Walsh K. (1987). Are disputes in decline: evidence from UK industry. *Industrial Relations Journal*, **18**(1), 7–13

Winchester D. (1983). Industrial relations in the public sector. In *Industrial Relations in Britain* (Bain G.S., ed.), pp. 155–78. Oxford: Blackwell

Chapter 12

ACAS (1982). *Developments in Harmonisation: Discussion Paper No. 1*. London: Advisory, Conciliation and Arbitration Service

Ackroyd S. and Crowdy P.A. (1990). Can culture be managed? Working with raw material: the case of English slaughtermen. *Personnel Review*, **19**(5), 3–13

Anderson H. and Shackleton V. (1990). Decision making in the graduate selection interview: a field study. *Journal of Occupational Psychology*, **63**(1), 63–76

Armstrong M. (1990). *A Handbook of Human Resource Management*. London: Kogan Page.

Bain G.S., Coates D. and Ellis V. (1973). *Social Stratification and Trade Unionism: A Critique*. London: Heinemann

Bassett P. (1986). *Strike Free*. London: Macmillan

Batstone E., Boraston I. and Frenkel S. (1977). *Shop Stewards in Action: The Organization of Workplace Conflict and Accommodation*. Oxford: Blackwell

Beaumont P.B. and Hunter L.C. (1992). Competitive strategy, flexibility and selection: the case of Caledonian Paper. *Industrial Relations Journal*, **23**(2), 222–8

Brown W. and Sisson K. (1975). The use of comparisons in workplace wage determination. *British Journal of Industrial Relations*, **13**(1), 23–51

Burns T. and Stalker G.M. (1961). *The Management of Innovation*. London: Tavistock

Dalessio A. and Imada A.S. (1984). Relationships between interview selection decisions and perceptions of applicant similarity to an ideal employee and self: a field study. *Human Relations*, **37**, 67–80

Deal T. and Kennedy A. (1982). *Corporate Cultures*. Harmondsworth: Penguin

Duncan C. (1989). Pay and payment systems. In *A Handbook of Industrial Relations Practice* (Towers B., ed.), pp. 217–47. London: Kogan Page

Fletcher C. and Williams R. (1985). *Performance Appraisal and Career Development*. London: Hutchinson

Formbrun C., Tichy N.A. and Evan M.A. (1984). *Strategic Human Resource Management*. New York: Wiley

Goldsmith W. and Clutterbuck D. (1985). *The Winning Streak*. Harmondsworth: Penguin

Gorman I. (1987). Corporate culture – why managers should be interested. *Leadership and Organizational Development Journal*, **8**(5), 3–9

Guest D. (1990). Human resource management and the American dream. *Journal of Management Studies*, **27**(4), 377–97

Guest D. (1991). Personnel management: the end of orthodoxy? *British Journal of Industrial Relations*, **29**(2), 149–75

Handy C. (1985). *Understanding Organizations* 3rd edn. Harmondsworth: Penguin

Harrison R. (1972). Understanding your organization's character. *Harvard Business Review*, May/June, 119–28

Hendry C. and Pettigrew A. (1990). Human resource management: an agenda for research. *International Journal of Human Resource Management*, **1**, 17–43

Hunter J.E. and Hunter R.F. (1984). Validity and utility of alternative predictors of job performance. *Psychological Bulletin*, **96**, 72–98

Kelly C. and Kelly J. (1991). Them and us: a social psychological analysis of the new industrial relations. *British Journal of Industrial Relations*, **29**(1), 25–48

Knights D. and Collinson D. (1987). Disciplining the shopfloor: a comparison of the disciplinary effects of managerial psychology and financial accounts. *Accounting, Organizations and Society*, **12**(5), 457–77

Legge K. (1989). Human resource management: a critical analysis. In *New Perspectives on Human Resource Management* (Storey J., ed.), pp. 19–40. London: Routledge

Lieberman S. (1956). The effects of changes in roles on the attitudes of role occupants. *Human Relations*, **9**(4), 385–402

Litwin G.H. and Stringer R.A. (1962). *Motivation and Organisational Climate*. Harvard MA: Harvard University Press

Long P. (1986). *Performance Appraisal Revisited*. London: Institute of Personnel Management

Lowe J. and Oliver N. (1991). Notes and issues – the high commitment workplace: two cases from a high-tech industry. *Work, Employment and Society*, **5**(3), 437–50

Marginson P. (1989). Employment flexibility in large companies: change and continuity. *Industrial Relations Journal*, **20**(2), 101–09

Megalino B.M., Ravlin E.C. and Adkins C.L. (1989). A work values approach to corporate culture: a field test of the value, congruence process and its relationship to individual outcomes. *Journal of Applied Psychology*, **74**(3), 424–32

Miles R.H. (1980). *Macro Organizational Behaviour*. Santa Monica CA: Goodyear

Miller P. (1991). Strategic human resource management: an assessment of progress. *Human Resource Management Journal*, **1**(4), 23–39

Newby H. (1977). *The Deferential Worker*. Harmondsworth: Penguin

Oliver N. and Davies A. (1990). Adopting Japanese-style manufacturing methods: a tale of two (U.K.) factories. *Journal of Management Studies*, **27**(5), 555–70

Organ D.W. and Bateman T.S. (1991). *Organizational Behaviour*. Homewood IL: Irwin

Ouchi W.G. and Price R.L. (1978). Hierarchies, clans and theory 'Z'. *Organizational Dynamics*, Autumn, 24–44

Peters T. and Waterman R. (1982). *In Search of Excellence: Lessons from America's Best Companies*. New York: Harper and Row

Pettigrew A. (1979). On studying organizational culture. *Administrative Science Quarterly*, **24**, 570–81

Rand T.M. and Wexley K.N. (1975). Demonstration of the effect of similar-to-me, in simulated employment interviews. *Psychological Reports*, **36**, 535–44

Randell G., Packard P. and Slater J. (1984). *Staff Appraisal*. London: Institute of Personnel Management

Ray C.A. (1986). Corporate culture: the last frontier of control. *Journal of Management Studies*, **23**(3), 287–97

Reilly R.R. and Chao G.T. (1982). Validity and fairness of some alternative employee selection procedures. *Personnel Psychology*, **35**, 1–62

Reitsperger W.D. (1986). Japanese management: coping with British industrial relations. *Journal of Management Studies*, **23**(1), 72–87

Reynolds P.D. (1986). Organizational culture as related to industry, position and performance. *Journal of Management Studies*, **23**(3), 335–45

Robertson I. and Makin P. (1986). Management selection in Britain: a survey and critique. *Journal of Occupational Psychology*, **59**(1), 45–57

Runciman W.G. (1966). *Relative Deprivation and Social Justice*. London: Routledge and Kegan Paul

Salamon G. (1978). Management development and organization theory. *Journal of European Industrial Training*, **2**(7), 7–11

Sathe V. (1983). Implications of corporate culture: a manager's guide to action. *Organizational Dynamics*, Autumn, 5–23

Scase R (1974). Relative deprivation: a comparison of English and Swedish manual workers. In *Poverty, Inequality and Class Structure* (Wedderburn D., ed.), pp. 197–216. Cambridge: Cambridge University Press

Schein E.H. (1990). Organizational culture. *American Psychologist*, **45**, 109–19

Seeters J.L. (1986). Excellent companies as social movements. *Journal of Management Studies*, **23**(3), 299–312

Smircich L. (1983). Concepts of corporate culture and organizational analysis. *Administrative Science Quarterly*, **28**, 339–58

Smith G.I. and Kleiner B.H. (1987). Differences in corporate cultures and their relationship to organizational effectiveness. *Leadership and Organizational Development Journal*, **8**(5), 10–12

Snape E. and Bamber G. (1989). Managing professional and managerial staff. In *A Handbook of Industrial Relations Practices* (Towers B., ed.), pp. 181–96. London: Kogan Page

Storey J. and Sisson K. (1989). Limits to transformation: human resource management in the British context. *Industrial Relations Journal*, **20**(1), 60–5

Thompson M. and Wildansky A. (1986). A cultural theory of information bias in organizations. *Journal of Management Studies*, **23**(3), 273–86

Torrington D. and Hall L. (1987). *Personnel Management: A New Approach*. London: Prentice-Hall

Towers B. (1987). Trends and developments in industrial relations: managing labour flexibility. *Industrial Relations Journal*, **18**(2), 79–83

Walton R.E. (1985). From control to commitment in the workplace. *Harvard Business Review*, **63**, 76–84

Weick K. (1979). *The Social Psychology of Organizing* 2nd edn. Reading MA: Addison-Wesley

Whipp R., Rosenfield R. and Pettigrew A. (1989). Culture and competitiveness: evidence from two mature U.K. industries. *Journal of Management Studies*, **26**(2), 561–85

Wickens P. (1987). *The Road to Nissan*. London: Macmillan

Wilson D.C. (1990). *Managing Organizations*. Maidenhead: McGraw-Hill

Chapter 13

Ansoff H.I. (1965). *Corporate Strategy*. Harmondsworth: Penguin

Brewster C.J., Gill C.S. and Richbell S. (1983). Industrial relations and policy: a framework for analysis. In *Industrial Relations and Management Strategy* (Thurley K. and Wood S., eds.), pp. 67–72. Cambridge: Cambridge University Press

Brown W., ed. (1981). *The Changing Contours of British Industrial Relations*. Oxford: Blackwell

Cappelli P. and McKersie R.B. (1987). Management strategy and the redesign of workrules. *Journal of Management Studies*, **24**(5), 441–62

CIR (1973). *The Role of Management in Industrial Relations*. Commision on Industrial Relations. London: HMSO

Claydon T. (1989). Union derecognition in Britain in the 1980s. *British Journal of Industrial Relations*. **27**(2), 214–24

Daniel W.W. (1976). *Wage Determination in Industry*. Report No. 83. London: Political and Economic Planning

DOE (1972). *Industrial Relations Code of Practice*. Department of Employment, London: HMSO

Edwards P.K. (1985a). Managing labour relations through the recession. *Employee Relations*, **7**(2), 3–7

Edwards P.K. (1985b). Managing labour relations through the recession: the plant and company. *Employee Relations*, **7**(3), 4–8

Guest D.E. (1987). Human resource management and industrial relations. *Journal of Management Studies*, **24**(5), 503–21

Hamill J. (1983). The labour relations practices of foreign-owned and indigenous firms. *Employee Relations*, **5**(1), 14–16

Hawes W.R. and Smith G. (1981). *Patterns of Representation of the Parties in Unfair Dismissal Cases: A Review of the Evidence*. Research paper No. 22. London: Department of Employment

Hawkins K. (1978). *The Management of Industrial Relations Practice*. Harmondsworth: Penguin

Hendry C., Pettigrew A. and Sparrow P. (1988). Changing patterns of human resource management. *Personnel Management*, November, 37–41

Kinnie N. (1985). Changing management strategies in industrial relations. *Industrial Relations Journal*, **16**(4), 17–24

Kinnie N. (1986). Patterns of industrial relations management. *Employee Relations*, **8**(2), 17–21

Kinnie N. (1987). Bargaining within the enterprise: centralised or decentralised. *Journal of Management Studies*, **24**(5), 463–77

Kochan T.A. and McKersie R.B. (1983). Collective bargaining pressures for change. *Sloan Management Review*, Summer, 59–65

Lloyd P.A. (1976). *Incentive Payment Systems: Management Survey Report. No. 34*. London: British Institute of Management

Lowry P. (1980). Quoted in 'The Union Gap that Leyland will try to Ban' (Terrode J.). *The Guardian*, 10th July

Marsh A. (1982). *Employee Relations Policy and Decision Making: A Survey of Manufacturing Companies carried out for the CBI*. Aldershot: Gower

Martin R. (1981). *New Technology and Industrial Relations in Fleet Street*. Oxford: Clarendon Press

NBPI (1968). *Job Evaluation*. National Board for Prices and Incomes. Report No. 83, London: HMSO

Poole M. (1980). Managerial strategies in industrial relations. In *Managerial Roles in Industrial Relations* (Poole M. and Mansfield R. eds.), pp. 38–49. Aldershot: Gower

Purcell J. (1982). Macho managers and the new industrial relations. *Employee Relations*, **4**(1), 3–5

Purcell J. and Gray A. (1986). Corporate personnel departments and the management of industrial relations: two case studies in ambiguity. *Journal of Management Studies*, **23**(2), 205–23

Purcell J. and Sisson K. (1983). Strategies and practice in the management of industrial relations. In *Industrial Relations in Britain* (Bain G.S., ed.), pp. 95–120. Oxford: Blackwell

Purcell J., Marginson P., Edwards P.K. and Sisson K. (1987). The industrial relations practices of multi-plant, foreign owned firms. *Industrial Relations Journal*, **18**(3), 130–7

Thurley K. and Wood S. (1983). Introduction. In *Industrial Relations and Management Strategy* (Thurley K. and Wood S., eds.), pp. 1–6. Cambridge: Cambridge University Press

Tyson S. (1987). The management of the personnel function. *Journal of Management Studies*, **24**(5), 523–32

Walton R.E. (1985). From control to commitment in the workplace. *Harvard Business Review*, March/April, 77–84

Whitaker A. (1986). Managerial strategy and industrial relations: a case study in plant relocation. *Journal of Management Studies*, **36**(6), 657–78

White M. (1981). *Payment Systems in Britain*. Aldershot: Gower

Author Index

Subject Index